CRIMINAL JUSTICE AND THE IDEAL DEFENDANT IN THE MAKING OF REMORSE AND RESPONSIBILITY

This book investigates how defendants are assessed by criminal justice decision-makers, such as judges, lawyers, probation officers, parole board members and those involved in restorative justice. What attitudes and emotions are defendants expected to show? How are these expectations communicated?

With contributors from across the world, the book opens new comparative possibilities and research agendas.

The book argues that defendants, at various stages of the criminal justice process, are expected to show a (more or less) free acceptance of guilt and individual responsibility along with a display of 'appropriate' emotions, ideally including 'genuine' remorse. It examines why such expressions of individual responsibility and remorse are so important to decision-makers and the state.

'*Criminal Justice and The Ideal Defendant* is a dazzling contribution. It takes the debate in important new directions, and poses a powerful challenge to conventional wisdom.'

Susan A. Bandes, Centennial Professor of Law Emeritus, DePaul University College of Law, USA

'*Criminal Justice and The Ideal Defendant* originates new research agendas and fresh perspectives on the key problem of remorse and responsibility.'

Julian Roberts, Emeritus Professor of Criminology, Oxford University, UK

'This fascinating volume reveals the complex role of emotions in criminal justice; a topic that requires and deserves our urgent attention, if we are to find our way towards more honest and more just systems and practices.'

Fergus McNeill, Professor of Criminology & Social Work, Glasgow University, Scotland

'Stewart Field and Cyrus Tata have brought together leading scholars from a range of disciplines to explore the crucial puzzle that is "the ideal defendant." This is the ideal collection on the ideal defendant."'

Steven Tudor, Senior Lecturer, La Trobe University, Australia

'Criminal Justice and The Ideal Defendant is a ground-breaking international, interdisciplinary volume'.

Rob Canton, Professor in Community and Criminal Justice, De Montfort University, England

Oñati International Series in Law and Society

A SERIES PUBLISHED FOR THE OÑATI INSTITUTE FOR THE SOCIOLOGY OF LAW

Recent titles in this series

Digital Family Justice: From Alternative Dispute Resolution to Online Dispute Resolution?
Edited by Mavis Maclean and Bregje Dijksterhuis

The Legacies of Institutionalisation: Disability, Law and Policy in the 'Deinstitutionalised' Community
Edited by Claire Spivakovsky, Linda Steele and Penelope Weller

Gender and Careers in the Legal Academy
Edited by Ulrike Schultz, Gisela Shaw, Margaret Thornton and Rosemary Auchmuty

Contesting Austerity: A Socio-Legal Inquiry
Edited by Anuscheh Farahat and Xabier Arzoz

The Right to the Continuous Improvement of Living Conditions: Responding to Complex Global Challenges
Edited by Jessie Hohmann and Beth Goldblatt

Supporting Legal Capacity in Socio-Legal Context
Edited by Mary Donnelly, Rosie Harding and Ezgi Tascioglu

What Is a Family Justice System For?
Edited by Mavis Maclean, Rachel Treloar and Bregje Dijksterhuis

Combining the Legal and the Social in Sociology of Law: An Homage to Reza Banakar
Edited by Håkan Hydén, Roger Cotterrell, David Nelken and Ulrike Schultz

Criminal Justice and The Ideal Defendant in the Making of Remorse and Responsibility
Edited by Stewart Field and Cyrus Tata

For the complete list of titles in this series
see www.bloomsbury.com/uk/series/oñati-international-series-in-law-and-society

Criminal Justice and The Ideal Defendant in the Making of Remorse and Responsibility

Edited by
Stewart Field
and
Cyrus Tata

Oñati International Series in Law and Society

A SERIES PUBLISHED FOR THE OÑATI INSTITUTE FOR THE SOCIOLOGY OF LAW

•HART•
OXFORD • LONDON • NEW YORK • NEW DELHI • SYDNEY

HART PUBLISHING

Bloomsbury Publishing Plc

Kemp House, Chawley Park, Cumnor Hill, Oxford, OX2 9PH, UK

1385 Broadway, New York, NY 10018, USA

29 Earlsfort Terrace, Dublin 2, Ireland

First published in Great Britain 2023

A catalogue record for this book is available from the British Library.

A catalogue record for this book is available from the Library of Congress.

Library of Congress Control Number: 2023930401

ISBN: HB: 978-1-50993-991-6
ePDF: 978-1-50993-993-0
ePub: 978-1-50993-992-3

Typeset by Compuscript Ltd, Shannon
Printed and bound in Great Britain

Acknowledgements

THE EDITORS WOULD like to acknowledge the generous funding of the Centre of Law and Society (School of Law and Politics, Cardiff University), which made possible the workshop in September 2018 that started the discussions which led to this volume. Cyrus Tata wishes to express his deep gratitude to the incomparable Ashley Lennon, as well as Sylvie Tata and Elodie Tata. Stewart Field wishes to thank Pauline Roberts and Adam and Sam Field: they have lived with this book project for a long time.

Contents

PART 3
THE POLITICAL AND CULTURAL SIGNIFICANCE OF REMORSE AND RESPONSIBILITY

List of Contributors

Author Editors

Stewart Field is Professor of Law at the School of Law and Politics at Cardiff University. His research interests are in comparative criminal justice and in particular the influence of legal cultures and procedural traditions on criminal justice practices. He has published a number of bilateral comparative studies comparing England and Wales to the Netherlands, France and Italy. Professor Field has been a member of the Editorial Board of the *Journal of Law and Society* since 1989. He has recently co-edited with Dr Renaud Colson (University of Nantes) a Special Issue of the Journal entitled *Learning from Elsewhere: from cross-cultural explanations to transnational prescription?* (2019).

Cyrus Tata is Professor of Law and Criminal Justice at Strathclyde University Law School, where he is director of the Centre for Law, Crime & Justice. He has conducted and published research into: pre-trial decision-making, and plea negotiation; the effects of changes to lawyer legal aid remuneration in criminal cases; sentencing decision-making; mitigation and pre-sentence reports; the use and quality of data and information technology in judicial decision-making; and executive release from prison. He is currently undertaking three areas of empirical research: the perceptions of sentenced people, judicial sentencers and defence lawyers of the process of sentencing communications; the experiences of victims and bereaved families; and thirdly, public attitudes to and knowledge of sentencing. He is Chair of the ESC European Group on Sentencing & Penal Decision-Making. His most recent book is *Sentencing: a Social Process – Rethinking Research and Policy* (Palgrave Socio-Legal Series, 2020).

Author Contributors

Virginie Gautron is Associate Professor of criminal law at the University of Nantes. She has conducted and published research into public crime-prevention policies; partnerships in the area of prevention and security; exchanges of confidential information between operators in the criminal justice system; police databases; sentencing decision-making; risk assessment; public perceptions about criminal justice and sentencing. She is currently conducting research about the intersection between crime-prevention and medical approaches in the provision of care to offenders. She has been a member of the Editorial Boards of the scientific journals *Déviance & Société* since 2013 and *Champ Pénal/Penal Field* since 2009.

Jacqueline Hodgson is Professor of Law at the School of Law in the University of Warwick, where she is also Deputy Pro Vice Chancellor for Research. Her research interests are in European and comparative criminal justice, focusing on France and England and Wales in particular. She has conducted a variety of empirical projects over the last 30 years looking at the role and culture of defence lawyers in England and Wales and across Europe; the investigation and prosecution of crime, including counter-terrorism, in France; the effectiveness of safeguards for adult and juvenile suspects across several European jurisdictions; and the work of the Criminal Cases Review Commission (CCRC). Her most recent monograph is *The Metamorphosis of Criminal Justice* (2020, OUP) She co-directs the Centre for Operational Police Research and is currently investigating the role of arts and culture in policing. She has worked on policy reform; provided expert evidence in European Arrest warrant and other extradition cases; is an elected member of the Council of JUSTICE; and in 2014 was elected as a Fellow of the Academy of Social Sciences.

Louise Victoria Johansen is Associate Professor within the area of law and anthropology at the Faculty of Law, University of Copenhagen, where she is Head of the Centre for Interdisciplinary Studies of Law. She is theoretically inspired by the field of sociology of knowledge, intersectionality, and the role of emotion in law. Her research has focused on knowledge processes across different criminal justice institutions such as the police, the judiciary, the prosecutor's office, and the prison and probation service. Using ethnographic methods in these settings, she has studied the production and use of pre-sentence reports; lay adjudication; victims' perceptions of the criminal justice process; and remand prisoners' expectations of 'a fair trial'. Her current research concerns the judiciary's moral communication of punishment to defendants in different kinds of criminal cases.

Kathy Mack is Emerita Professor, Flinders University. Before coming to Australia, Kathy practiced law in California, mainly criminal law. She is the author of a monograph, book chapters and articles on alternative dispute resolution (ADR) and articles on legal education and evidence. Since 1994, in collaboration with Matthew Flinders Distinguished Professor Sharyn Roach Anleu, she has been engaged in socio-legal research into the Australian courts and judiciary, beginning with an investigation of the production of guilty pleas, and continuing with research into the everyday work of the judiciary, through the Judicial Research Project at Flinders University. Their latest book is *Judging and Emotion: A Socio-Legal Analysis* (Routledge, 2021) and in 2017 they published *Performing Judicial Authority in the Lower Courts* (Palgrave).

Giuseppe Maglione is a Lecturer in Criminology in the School of Social Policy, Sociology and Social Research at the University of Kent, where he is also the Director of the Restorative Justice Clinical Program. He has conducted research on the historical development, philosophical underpinnings and local delivery of restorative justice at the universities of Durham, Cambridge, Oslo and at the Max Planck Institute in Freiburg. His recent works have been published in *The International Handbook of Restorative Justice, Theoretical Criminology, Criminology & Criminal Justice, Critical Criminology and Social & Legal Studies*. Additionally, he has worked extensively as a victim-offender mediator and trainer in restorative justice in Italy, Scotland and Norway.

Nicola Padfield is Emeritus Professor of Criminal and Penal Justice at the Law Faculty, University of Cambridge, where she worked for more than 30 years, and Life Fellow of Fitzwilliam College, Cambridge. She has a broad research lens, engaged in both 'hard' law and in socio-legal-criminological research. She is a leading European expert on sentencing law, including the law and practice of release from (and recall to) prison. She has carried out a number of empirical studies of the Parole Board. A barrister by training, she has published widely on criminal law, sentencing and criminal justice. Her books include *The Criminal Justice Process: Text and Materials* (5th edn, 2016); *Criminal Law* (10th edn, 2016); *Beyond the Tariff: Human rights and the release of life sentence prisoners* (2002). She has edited collections of essays, and for nearly 20 years was the editor of the influential monthly *Archbold Review*. She sat as a Recorder (part-time judge) in the Crown Court from 2002-2014, and is a Bencher of the Middle Temple.

Sharyn Roach Anleu is Matthew Flinders Distinguished Professor of Sociology in the College of Humanities, Arts and Social Sciences at Flinders University, Adelaide, and Fellow of the Australian Academy of the Social Sciences. She is a past president of The Australian Sociological Association and recently received the 2023 TASA Distinguished Service to Australian Sociology Award. Sharyn is the author of *Law and Social Change* and four editions of *Deviance, Conformity and Control*. She has contributed to the Masters Program at the International Institute for the Sociology of Law, Oñati, Spain and is currently co-Chair of the Law and Society Association's Collaborative Research Network: Law and Emotion (CRN 42). With Emerita Professor Kathy Mack she leads the Judicial Research Project at Flinders University which undertakes socio-legal research into the Australian judiciary and its courts. Their latest book is *Judging and Emotion: A Socio-Legal Analysis* (Routledge 2021) and in 2018 Sharyn and Jessica Milner Davis co-edited *Judges, Judging and Humour* (Palgrave).

Kate Rossmanith is an ethnographer, a nonfiction writer, and an Associate Professor at Macquarie University, Australia. She researches emotion, enactment, and narrative in legal processes, as well as forms of nonfiction writing (essay, memoir, ethnography, reportage). She has a background in Performance Studies that combines theatre, sociology, and anthropology to study how we perform ourselves in everyday life. In 2021 Kate was awarded a four-year Australian Research Council Future Fellowship for her project on 'closure' in the justice system and in our lives. She has written extensively on the subject of 'remorse'.

She is the author of *Small Wrongs: How we really say sorry in love, life and law* (nominated for national and international literary awards), and co-editor of *Remorse and Criminal Justice: Multi-disciplinary perspectives* (Routledge, 2022). Kate is co-founder and Deputy Director of the Creative Documentary Research Centre, leading the portfolio 'Writing, Language, Narrative'.

Irene van Oorschot is Assistant Professor at the Department of Social and Behavioral Sciences (ESSB), Erasmus University Rotterdam (EUR), the Netherlands. Throughout her work she has ethnographically explored the production and circulation of knowledges and the making of practical judgments. Published in 2021, her recent monograph *The Law Multiple: Judgment and Knowledge in Practice* investigates and analyses practices of everyday adjudication and sentencing in a Dutch context, focusing on everyday work practices, common-sense judgments on remorse, and the role of objects and artifacts – especially case files – in these practices. Having received a Marie Curie Skłodowska Individual Fellowship (2020) and a Veni grant (Dutch Scientific Council, 2021), she is currently conducting research into environmental managers' practical knowledges and modes of judgment, and the ways these are reshaped in anticipation of climate change.

Richard Weisman is Professor Emeritus in the Law and Society Program in the Department of Social Science at York University in Toronto, Canada. He has written extensively on the role of remorse in law and its impact on sentencing, wrongful conviction, capital punishment, and restorative justice among other topics. His work has been published in major interdisciplinary journals in law and social science as well as in chapters in anthologies on the role of emotion in law. He is the author of *Showing Remorse: Law and the Social Control of Emotion*, Routledge, 2014 and a co-editor of *Remorse and Criminal Justice: Multi-Disciplinary Perspectives*, Routledge, 2022.

Part 1

The Making of Remorse and Responsibility

1

Locating the Ideal Defendant: Punishment, Violence and Legitimacy

STEWART FIELD* AND CYRUS TATA†

This chapter outlines the central propositions of this book as a whole by drawing on its component chapters. In a nutshell, the book demonstrates that, within a variety of criminal justice systems, an implicit model of the 'ideal defendant' is at work. There is an expectation that defendants (by which we mean anyone proceeded against by the state) should display certain characteristics. This model of the ideal defendant is based on individual character, and on attitudes towards the state, the alleged offence and likely future offending. A key component of these norms is that defendants are expected to demonstrate a free and sincere acceptance of their personal responsibility for the offending. Ideally, this admission of responsibility should be so wholehearted that defendants can be seen as expressing 'genuine' remorse. While this is the ultimate ideal and defendants' representations typically fall short of this, they are nonetheless encouraged to align themselves as closely as possible to that ideal. These expectations of defendants are brought home to them at all stages of their journey through the system not just by judges and prosecutors, but also by lawyers, probation officers and therapeutic professionals (eg psychologists, psychiatrists, social workers). Defendants are evaluated on the extent to which they perform in accordance with the ideal. This 'grading' of defendant emotion and its expression has consequences – whether negative or positive – for the subsequent state penal response to the defendant. In practice, encouragement and evaluation mesh so that expressions of remorse-like feelings and responsibility are constructed through interactions between defendant and criminal justice practitioners. This 'making' of remorse and responsibility is fraught with cultural misinterpretations and unrealistic expectations of particular defendants. Yet, the public acknowledgement by defendants of the legitimacy of their own punishment serves a latent function: it reassures practitioners that the routine coercion of their systemic practices does not represent injustice. It also enables

* Professor, School of Law and Politics, Cardiff University, Wales.
† Professor of Law & Criminal Justice, Law School, University of Strathclyde, Scotland.

the enactment of an apparent mutuality between state and citizen at a moment of rupture in that relationship.

I. THE IDEAL DEFENDANT IN THE MAKING OF REMORSE AND RESPONSIBILITY

THIS BOOK SHOWS that, within a variety of criminal justice systems, an implicit model of the 'ideal defendant'[1] is at work: there is an expectation that defendants should display certain characteristics, and they are judged on the basis of those expectations and treated accordingly.[2] This model of the ideal defendant is based on assessment of individual character, the defendant's attitudes towards the state, the alleged offence and likely future offending. Central to the state's evaluation of defendants' performances of expectations is a judgement as to whether they are compliant and accepting, or, uncooperative and defiant. The ideal defendant admits guilt, accepts individual responsibility for the alleged crime and, in the process, shows particular kinds of emotions, especially the authentic demonstration of remorse, or at least 'retractive'[3] feelings (eg regret, guilt, shame, embarrassment) which appear to approximate to remorse. In so doing, defendants are seen – implicitly or explicitly – to be acknowledging the legitimacy of state coercion and its claims to administer fair and humane punishment.

How well the defendant appears to align with these expectations shapes the state's assessment of the individual's character and personality, and this informs the state's penal response both to the act it defines as criminal and to the offender. For instance, the state may offer humane treatment that is responsive to the needs of the individual, but this penal response depends upon the defendant showing alignment to expectations. Thus, constructions of the 'ideal defendant' involve a process of classification and 'normalisation' of defendants.[4] Therefore, this book examines the interplay – in different procedural fora and jurisdictions – between the normative construction of defendants, their acceptance of responsibility and demonstrations of remorse, and their management through the criminal justice system.

[1] C Tata, 'Ritual Individualization: Creative Genius at Sentencing, Mitigation and Conviction' (2019) 46 *Journal of Law and Society* 112.

[2] We use the generic term 'defendant' to refer to any person proceeded against by the state. This includes different statuses, which may vary between different national jurisdictions: suspect, accused, convicted offender awaiting sentence, sentenced offender, supervisee and parole applicant.

[3] M Proeve and S Tudor, *Remorse: Psychological and Jurisprudential Approaches* (London, Taylor & Francis, 2010).

[4] By 'normalisation' we mean a process by which defendants are required to conform to certain norms or standards. This process of normalisation means that unique features of individual cases tend to be diminished and there is greater standardisation: cases become quickly recognisable as one of a kind to practitioners. This process is common to professional work in other fields beyond criminal justice.

II. CONTEXTUALISING THE BOOK

This book focuses on the role of the presentation of the self in the categorisation and management of defendants. In doing so, it bridges two apparently distinct strands in recent criminal justice scholarship. First, there is work on the role of categorisation and sorting: for example, focusing on the impact of social categories (such as gender, race and social class) on the assessments and decisions of officials.[5] A second strand examines the influence of categorisation using state managerial tools or performance indicators (based on, for example, speed, targets, risk and efficiency).[6] This scholarship provides important insights into the operation of categorisation and sorting within the criminal justice system. But there is a need to integrate into that analysis an empirically informed conceptualisation of the role of defendants' displayed emotions and presentations of self (as constructed in interactions with criminal justice practitioners).

The focus of this book on the significance of defendants' presentation of self to the functioning of criminal process adds a new dimension to a broader, emerging, multidisciplinary and international interest in the role of emotions in legal decision-making and their implications for the legitimacy of state processes.[7] Part of this attention to emotion has been aimed at remorse. Existing criminal justice scholarship on remorse and its relationship with criminal responsibility addresses many important questions: whether remorse affects the tendency to reoffend; its relationship with risk; the feelings of victims; and public attitudes to the role of remorse in sentencing.[8] Normative work examines whether remorse ought to be a factor in decision-making (particularly in sentencing and parole) and considers how this relates to philosophical theories justifying punishment.[9] The book adds to this scholarship by focusing on perceived remorse and the acceptance of responsibility as key means of classifying and managing defendants.

This book, therefore, brings together insights into emotion and concerns about classification. It argues that emotions are themselves a key consideration

[5] S Walker, C Spohn and M Delone, *The Color of Justice: Race, Ethnicity, and Crime in America*, 5th edn (Belmont, Wadsworth Thomson Learning, 2012). See generally the work of Darrell Steffensmeier: https://sociology.la.psu.edu/people/d4s.

[6] K Hannah-Moffat, 'Criminogenic Needs and the Transformative Risk Subject: Hybridizations of Risk/Need in Penality' (2005) 7 *Punishment and Society* 29; P Maurutto and K Hannah-Moffat, 'Assembling Risk and the Restructuring of Penal Control' (2006) 46 *British Journal of Criminology* 438; M Tonry, 'Sentencing in America, 1975–2025' in M Tonry (ed), *Crime and Justice in America, 1975–2025* (Chicago, University of Chicago Press, 2013); M Tonry, 'Punishment and Human Dignity: Sentencing Principles for Twenty-First Century America' (2018) 47 *Crime and Justice* 119.

[7] S Bandes, 'Remorse and Criminal Justice' (2015) 8 *Emotion Review* 14; S Roach Anleu and K Mack, *Judging and Emotion: A Socio-legal Analysis* (London, Routledge, 2021).

[8] Proeve and Tudor (n 3); A Hough and J Roberts, 'Public Opinion, Crime, and Criminal Justice' in S Maruna, A Liebling and L McAra (eds), *The Oxford Handbook of Criminology*, 6th edn (Oxford, Oxford University Press, 2018).

[9] Bandes (n 7); R Duff, *Trials and Punishment* (Cambridge, Cambridge University Press, 1986); H Maslen *Remorse, Penal Theory and Sentencing* (Oxford, Hart Publishing, 2015); Proeve and Tudor

in the classification of defendants and central to the managerial efficiency of the criminal justice system. Framing the criminal process around the expression of emotions like remorse, and the broader acceptance of responsibility, has implications for individual defendants and their relations with the state. The result may not always be catharsis, healing or therapy or even genuine recognition of the unique individual. The price of continued recognition as an individual, as a citizen and as a member of the community may be conformity to certain expectations about appropriate displays of emotion, such as remorse and the acceptance of responsibility. The book investigates the challenges and paradoxes that emerge when an emotion such as remorse (and emotions perceived to be broadly similar) is made part of a system of normalised expectations and even statutory requirement. It goes beyond the conceptual and empirical research on classification and emotion by examining what happens when the perceived emotion itself becomes classified.

III. UNDERPINNING THEMES, CONCERNS AND CONCEPTS

A. From Case Factors to Case Process: Relationships in the Making of Remorse

There is a long and valuable analytical scholarly tradition of studying case characteristics to see what effect they may have on criminal justice decision-making. Without any explicit intention to do so, this analytical tradition conceptualises decision-making through the implicit lens of autonomous individualism.[10] The holy grail has been to isolate (seemingly) autonomous case 'factors' as individual stimuli, which are thought more or less to determine decision outcomes. While this is one valuable way of explaining decision-making, its weakness is that it ignores *relationships* in two ways.

First, at best, this tradition marginalises the relationships within cases by seeking to abstract and isolate supposedly independent, autonomous individual 'factors', rather than seeking to understand the ways in which decision-makers intuitively grasp the meaning of cases as 'typified whole case stories'.[11] Second, it cannot attend to the social relationships between and among those inflicting and receiving punishment. While a sufficiently complex model of

(n 3); J Roberts (ed), *Mitigation and Aggravation at Sentencing* (Cambridge, Cambridge University Press, 2011); J Roberts (ed), *Exploring Sentencing Practice in England and Wales* (London, Palgrave Macmillan, 2015); A von Hirsch, AJ Ashworth and JV Roberts (eds), *Principled Sentencing: Readings on Theory and Policy* (Oxford, Hart Publishing, 2009); A von Hirsch, *Deserved Criminal Sentences* (Oxford, Hart Publishing, 2017).

[10] C Tata, *Sentencing: A Social Process – Rethinking Research and Policy* (Cham, Springer, 2020).

[11] ibid; C Tata, 'Sentencing as Craftwork and the Binary Epistemologies of the Discretionary Decision Process' (2007) 16 *Social & Legal Studies* 425.

independent and dependent variables can strive to re-aggregate these relationships, it cannot understand them as a dynamic social process in situ. For example, how do those inflicting harm, pain, control, etc on those receiving it make sense of what they do as legitimate punishment? How do they understand the way(s) that punishment is understood and interpreted by those receiving it? How can, and should, empirical research and theoretical scholarship confront these questions?

B. The Legitimacy Problem Confronting Professionals and the Urgent Demand to Justify State Violence

As philosophers have repeatedly noted, if criminal justice and its power to control, hurt or harm is to be more than sheer coercion, its practices must be legitimate. How, if at all, can and does the state and its officials morally distinguish between actions such as: abduction/kidnapping and arrest; extortion and the payment of a fine; community service and slavery; entrapment and imprisonment? This book takes as its starting point that those charged with determining this coercion cannot ignore the demand to make these moral distinctions: to show to themselves that their work is just, or at least not unjust.

Take, for example, the work of judges. Like other penal decision-making professionals, it would be unthinkable for a judge to declare that she or he does not care about and has no interest in 'justice'. Would a judge, lawyer, psychiatrist, probation officer, etc declare that their work is simply the equivalent of a violent mafia exercising naked coercion? After all, mafia/gangsters control a certain territory and enjoy the habit of obedience from their population, but need not be concerned about this obedience having any morally justifiable basis. No criminal justice professional would, or could, ever suggest that the obedience and compliance they require is morally indistinguishable from that of gangsters. To do so would negate their social, moral and financial capital.

How, then, does the state and its officials seek to draw this moral distinction between their actions and those of gangsters? One answer to this question is provided by normative penal philosophy.

Normative penal philosophy endeavours to guide decision-makers on what they *ought* to do. For example, ought the existence or lack of remorse make a difference to sentencing and, if so, how? How ought sentencing, parole and probation decision-making take account of the deprivation and poverty of the person to be punished? All of this is important and valuable in determining laws, policy and decision-making practices.

However, the focus of this book is different. Its purpose is not to determine what penal decision-makers ought to do, or how laws and policies ought to be written. Instead, it is preoccupied with the reality of what *is* happening. It seeks to develop an empirically grounded conceptualisation of the everyday reality of the relationships and roles of those inflicting and receiving punishment. How do decision-makers make their decisions? How do they interpret and justify them? How do they understand the ways in which defendants, as direct recipients of these decisions (and, indeed, additional audiences, like other professionals, victims, the public, etc), perceive and interpret those decisions and the wider legitimacy of criminal justice?

This is not to say that we eschew interest in the normative (or moral) philosophy of punishment. Indeed, the book draws on categories and debates in the philosophy of punishment. Likewise, empirical research can shed valuable light on how those normative ideas are interpreted and operationalised, often in unexpected ways. An empirically led analysis can contribute to the development of normative penal philosophy: by knowing what is happening, we have more of a chance of thinking about what ought to be and how to get there. But here, our primary interest is in thinking about what happens on the ground. In particular, we are interested in the everyday anxieties and dilemmas faced by those inflicting punishment.

While normative penal philosophy must (rightly) stand back from the fray of everyday criminal justice work to think logically and imaginatively about a truly just penal order, penal decision-makers (as they rightly remind academic scholars) do not have that luxury. They are faced every day with decisions which must be made, the palpable distress of those entangled in criminal justice and the risks and dangers to individuals and society of different courses of action. They cannot meditate for long on demands to justify their violence as legitimate punishment. The obligation to decide and act is an immediate demand of the here and now.

It is for this reason that this book shows that the search by criminal justice decision-makers to confirm the legitimacy of the punishment they inflict is found in the immediacy of social interactions and relationships, as much as it is in abstract intellectual ideas and formal legal requirements. Criminal justice practitioners are acutely conscious that, in general, decisions must be made rapidly. Decisions must be seen to be made fairly, but also expeditiously. Practitioners depend on each other to 'get through the list'[12] and 'dispose' of cases quickly. To manage to achieve a sense of both fairness *and* efficiency, uncertainty and doubt about the legitimacy of such decisions has to be minimised. To square this circle, decision-makers must see themselves acting in ways which they can regard as legitimate *because* others appear also to see those actions as legitimate. It is not enough, this book argues, for decisions to be considered legitimate in purely abstract, intellectual terms. Rather, how decisions are or appear to be perceived by their audience (other practitioners and, crucially, those directly affected, like defendants) is critical.

[12] S Roach Anleu and K Mack, '"Getting Through the List": Judgecraft and Legitimacy in the Lower Courts' (2007) 16 *Social & Legal Studies* 341.

As previous empirical research has found, decision-making operates not as an individual intellectual or cognitive exercise, but as a social practice, communicating ideas and relationships typically within and between professional communities. Courts, for example, are able to get through the list of their cases quickly and efficiently because professionals (eg judges, defence and prosecuting lawyers, probation officers) work together in largely cooperative and convivial ways, in more or less shared cultures.[13] They work in ways which follow taken for granted habits of seeing, interpreting and acting, which themselves are established by conventions and familiar scripts. Rather than each individual case being seen as completely unique, they can recognise the familiar 'typical' case plot.[14] In this way, professionals can dispose of the case 'efficiently' because they know each other's expectations and what is being implicitly communicated. They know what they need to do so that other professionals can agree the case has been dealt with adequately. This is a recursive practice of checking and adjusting behaviour and decisions so that in general there are not too many unpleasant surprises.[15]

In the same way, this book argues that the search for legitimacy is partly answered by the responses of professionals to each other: checking, adjusting, reassuring each other of what they are doing. Thus, the twin potential problems of uncertainty as to what to do and doubt about its fairness – which could easily paralyse decision-making – are largely avoided.

As important as the affirmation of other professionals is, the need to justify the infliction of violence can most immediately and powerfully be answered by the perceived reaction of the person thought least likely to accept it: the person upon whom that violence is inflicted (ie the defendant). Nothing is more potent in showing to officials that their actions are morally justified than the person who is to be harmed appearing willingly to accept it as justified and deserved punishment. Rightly or wrongly, the perceived reaction of those with an immediate stake in the case tends to trump abstract, logical intellectual arguments about what ought to be done. It is the immediacy of this human and social interaction which vividly defeats potentially debilitating doubt and uncertainty. So it is that practitioners can move forward with confidence in what they do to get the case 'done'.

[13] For an empirical analysis of the way defence lawyers in France largely accommodate to assumptions about the functioning of the inquisitorial tradition shared with judges and prosecutors, see S Field and A West, 'Dialogue and the Inquisitorial Tradition: French Defence Lawyers in the Pre-trial Criminal Process' (2003) 14 *Criminal Law Forum* 261. For an empirical analysis of how Italian and Welsh youth justice practice is built on contrasting assumptions shared between practitioners within each system about the trust to be invested in families, see S Field and D Nelken, 'Reading and Writing Youth Justice in Italy and (England and) Wales' (2010) 12 *Punishment and Society* 287.

[14] Tata, *Sentencing: A Social Process* (n 10).

[15] M Heumann, *Plea Bargaining* (Chicago, Chicago University Press, 1978).

This is why perceived 'retractive' feelings more or less approximating to remorse and the full and sincere acceptance of responsibility are so coveted by those inflicting punishment. Nothing can feel so potently affirming of one's actions in inflicting this harm and violence than the reaction of the person who is shown freely and sincerely to accept it. By appearing to show full and sincere acceptance of individual responsibility, even remorse, the tendency of criminal justice to view its clientele as consisting of presumed 'offenders', even before they have been convicted, seems justified. The image and demonstration of the person who exhibits (or appears to exhibit) full and sincere acceptance is taken to legitimate that violence as justified and deserved punishment.

Remorse is the ultimate indicator of the ideal defendant who completely and wholeheartedly accepts the legitimacy of her impending punishment. It shows to the state, its officials and all those involved in making decisions that they not only have the right, but *are* right, to punish this specific individual. So much so that she herself is seeking to punish herself. Nothing could be more legitimating to the authority of the state and its officials than the appearance of the genuinely remorseful defendant.

C. What Do We Mean by 'the Defendant'?

Eagle-eyed readers will note that this book uses the term 'defendant' in an expansive way. Officially, the term 'defendant' typically refers to someone who has been charged by the prosecution but not convicted of those criminal charges. In this book, we use the term 'defendant' to refer, for example, to: those proceeded against by the state but not (yet) prosecuted through court; those prosecuted but who have not (yet) been convicted; those who have been convicted; those who are about to be or have been sentenced; and those serving a sentence, such as those being considered for parole. Why do we use the term to refer to such a wide range of people? The reason is that in this book we are focused on how the person proceeded against by the state is *expected* to admit, freely acknowledge, and indeed often explain, their guilt and individual responsibility for the alleged offence. This book shows how the person has to imagine and anticipate the future consequences of her posture towards state authority and its officials. So it is that the unconvicted person has to imagine the negative consequences (eg in terms of sentencing, the reality of any sentence) of denying guilt if she is then convicted at trial. The subjective experience of the person blurs the formal, temporal segmentation of official identities (eg police suspect, accused person at court, unsentenced convicted person, sentenced person). The person cannot simply imagine herself in only a single official identity, but has mentally to traverse these supposedly discrete identities.

The most technically accurate term to cover all of these different official statuses would have been 'the person proceeded against by the state', but that would have been quite a mouthful; 'defendant' seems the most intuitive alternative.

IV. OVERALL STRUCTURE AND INDIVIDUAL CHAPTERS

The book is divided into three parts. Part 1 is about the 'Making of Remorse and Responsibility': the 'how' of it, the process of constructing and evaluating remorse and acceptance of responsibility as a characteristic of the ideal defendant. Part 2 is titled 'Beyond Remorse', and explores variations to the initial themes around remorse. We note that decision-makers may look for remorse but actually demand more of the defendant. Remorse may not be enough. But sometimes courts will 'make do' with much less by elaborately and publicly treating the mere fact of a guilty plea (however qualified, grudging and reluctant) as if it were an open, full and voluntary acceptance of responsibility. Finally, sometimes the political and institutional contexts may lead penal agencies to move away from close examination of remorse to focus on risk. The final part (Part 3) examines the political and cultural significance of remorse. It asks what the public performance of acceptance of responsibility and remorse does for the criminal process, the state and the relations between state and citizen.

A. The Making of Remorse and Responsibility

(i) Tracing the Subterranean Influence of Remorse in the Dossier

Virginie Gautron's chapter explores a paradox. French criminal justice is shaped by a scientific, rationalist tradition that sees laws as detached from morality and religion. As a result, statutes and regulations avoid all reference to defendants' feelings and remorse. Yet Gautron, as one of the leading empirical criminal justice researchers in France, examines large case-file samples and extensive semi-structured interviews with practitioners drawn from two of her recent empirical studies to show that realities on the ground are different. She provides ample empirical evidence that all the key professional actors (judges, lawyers, police officers, probation officers, and psychiatric and psychological experts) refer regularly to feelings of remorse across the various phases of criminal justice, from police interrogation to judicial implementation of sentences. Yet Gautron characterises the influence of remorse as 'subterranean'. This is not only because it is not explicitly referenced in legislation, but also because its relevance in published case law is obscured by limited reporting, terse reasoning and difficulties in distinguishing its influence from those of related criteria, like regret, shame and guilt.

This brings out the importance of Gautron's close empirical study of the world of practice across all phases of French criminal justice. The official dossier is central to the French interpretation of the inquisitorial tradition. Gautron is able to trace this subterranean influence in the dossier to show the way defendants are penalised for what she describes as 'emotional deviance': the expression of feelings that are socially inappropriate. Not only are defendants expected to show remorse, but practitioners will look for evidence that may confirm or deny the authenticity of that remorse. Gautron describes this as a process of 'objectifying emotional states'. The evidence sought is related to three modes for the expression of remorse identified by Proeve and Tudor: first, the language; secondly, the behaviour and attitudes associated with that language; and finally, the actions that express or are motivated by remorse.[16] Practitioners are looking for spontaneity, consistency and detail in what is said and corroborating evidence from elsewhere in the case file. They are looking for evidence of self-reflection that brings out, rather than minimises, their responsibility and looks primarily to the consequences for the victim rather than the offender. And what is said should be matched by appropriate gestures and other non-verbal signs that the words express real emotions. Even beyond that, practitioners are looking for practical action such as compensation or apology and, more broadly, signs of moral transformation: this is evidenced by acceptance of punishment and commitment to personal change.

Gautron concludes that what is going on is the 'punishment of emotional deviance'. The less experts see what they consider to be genuine expressions of remorse, the less positive their prognosis for the future. Where such 'feeling rules' are followed, the empirical evidence from Gautron's studies suggests they are rewarded not only by greater use of alternatives to punishment and less severe sentences, but also by sentence adjustments during the course of a punishment. On the other hand, emotional deviance is punished by longer custodial sentences.

(ii) Relations on the Ground: Appropriately Performing Remorse-Like Feelings is Produced through in Situ Relations

For over two decades, Sharyn Roach Anleu and Kathy Mack have conducted a major programme of research into the everyday practices of judicial officers in Australia. This includes how judicial officers manage the emotions of those coming before the court as well as their own emotions. Through their rich empirical data (including interviews with judicial officers, court observations and transcripts of observed court sessions), they argue that the emotions of defendants (such as remorse or other more or less 'ideal attitudes') do not simply exist as things in themselves. Roach Anleu and Mack show how remorse must be appropriately *displayed*. For instance, defendants should comport themselves in ways that the court finds sincere and credible. They should sit,[17] stand,[18]

[16] Proeve and Tudor (n 3). This suggests significant similarities with the way remorse is evaluated in common law jurisdictions from the adversarial tradition and those from the inquisitiorial tradition.

[17] I van Oorschot, P Mascini and D Weenink, 'Remorse in Context(s): A Qualitative Exploration of Remorse and its Consequences' (2017) 26 *Social & Legal Studies* 359.

[18] K Rossmanith, 'Affect and the Judicial Assessment of Offenders: Feeling and Judging Remorse' (2015) 21 *Body & Society* 167.

speak,[19] cry 'appropriately'.[20] In doing so, the defendant is seen to acknowledge the authority of the court. By contrast:

> [A] person who does not comply with the feeling rules and appears to be without emotion or as expressing the wrong emotions may be viewed as rejecting the authority of the court … [it can be interpreted as] disengagement from the court proceedings, lack of respect for the sentencing process …

Moreover, this appropriate display is not something that defendants can simply 'switch on' by themselves. It is the result of their relational interactions: the defendant is encouraged, coaxed, cajoled towards the appropriate display of feelings.

> To focus on 'true' remorse – as a discoverable 'thing', which just needs precise indicators to enable accurate identification – diverts attention from the social, relational and interactive nature of emotion experience and display. Judicial officers are active in the process of constituting remorse … [Judicial officers] use emotion language in interaction that elicits in the defendant feelings of shame, embarrassment, guilt or remorse.

Roach Anleu and Mack's point is highly significant for research and scholarship. That the production of the appropriate display of emotions (eg remorse) is collaboratively produced through in situ relations means that scholars should re-examine attempts to abstract and reify 'remorse' as a case 'factor' that somehow exists autonomously in itself regardless of social relations:

> Approaching emotion as a relational process means that finding remorse is much more than registering or correctly labelling an emotion as present, absent or sufficient. It entails a process of construction that is embedded in the courtroom context shaped by the structural relations and inter-personal interaction between judicial officers and other courtroom participants.

(iii) Temporal Shuttling – Reimagining Oneself 'as if' the Ideal Culpable Offender

Louise V Johansen's chapter examines the practice in the Danish courts of encouraging defendants who deny the charges against them nonetheless to imagine themselves 'as if' they have been found guilty and are culpable offenders. As a leading legal anthropologist, Johansen has studied and thought deeply about social relations in criminal justice and the ways in which appropriate emotions are encouraged and displayed.

Denmark's criminal courts practise a 'hybrid' system combining ideals from both adversarial and inquisitorial traditions. On the one hand, and in common

[19] S Roach Anleu and K Mack, *Performing Judicial Authority in the Lower Courts* (London, Palgrave, 2017).

[20] T Hawker-Dawson, 'Defendants in the Crown Court' (PhD Thesis, University of Cambridge, 2022).

with adversarial systems, defendants enter a formal plea of 'guilty' or 'not guilty'. On the other hand, in common with inquisitorial ideals, examination of the defendant's character and attitude to the alleged offending is conducted even when the defendant pleads not guilty. Here, personal investigation reports are conducted by the probation service *not* after conviction and before sentencing (as in pre-sentence reports in adversarial countries), but prior to and regardless of any conviction.[21]

So, a person who formally denies guilt is expected to engage with this examination of character (a practice noted by Field in his chapter on French criminal courts). Denmark's strong emphasis on the value of rehabilitation makes defendant engagement with this examination particularly significant. Defendants need to defer to this examination and express appropriate emotions. It is in the nature of rehabilitative work that defendants have to examine, and be seen to examine, their 'inner core'. In doing so, defendants who have not admitted guilt are asked to imagine their attitude 'as if' they are guilty. Ostensibly, the collection of this 'knowledge' (through the personal investigation interview) about the inner character of the person (eg what might motivate the offending *if* the person is found guilty: anger issues, etc) is collected and presented 'just in case' it is later needed by the court. However, the reality and effect are less innocuous. Although Denmark's enduring attachment to rehabilitative ideals may have benign effects in humanising defendants, in the context of personal investigation reports it also means that the defendant has to imagine herself as the ideal culpable offender:

> The Danish penal system emphasises rehabilitation and treatment. To be able to offer treatment, however, one needs an offender who openly reflects on and copes with personal problems and accepts treatment. This necessity is met by interweaving emotions in the 'time–space'[22] surrounding the defendant and the criminal act as presented in the pre-sentence report. Probation work is structured so as to enable workers to move back and forth between past, present and future events.

While ostensibly respecting the formal principle of the presumption of innocence, the defendant is in fact more or less expected to reimagine herself as a culpable offender (again moving her self-presentation closer to the ideal of someone willingly participating in her own punishment). In this subtle way, rehabilitative and therapeutic work tends to encourage the appearance of admissions of guilt and self-incrimination.

(iv) Using 'Culture' as a Lens to 'Read' Defendants

The problem posed by the defendant who fails (or is believed to fail) to open her soul to state officials is that the state's violence cannot be justified by the

[21] See also R Wandall, *Decisions to Imprison* (London, Routledge, 2008).

[22] T Scheffer, *Adversarial Case-making: An Ethnography of the English Crown Court* (Amsterdam, Brill, 2010).

defendant's reaction. While there are occasional examples of defendants who overtly challenge state authority, this challenge more commonly arises by implication from silence, non-engagement and state officials being unable to 'read' defendants. Here, the problem of the demographic chasm between those judging and those being judged is immense. Bandes has noted, for instance, how difficult it can be for judges to know whether or not a defendant is truly remorseful and how that is complicated by, say, issues of class.[23] In general, middle-class defendants are more likely than working-class defendants to be able to pick up cues and clues about how they are expected to perform in the courtroom. This issue of judges knowing whether or not the defendant accepts the authority of the court is brought into sharp relief for judges in cases in which they perceive the defendant to be from an 'other' culture. They cannot dispose of cases (and certainly not with professional pride) unless they feel they are able to 'read' the defendant's communication.

Irene van Oorschot has been conducting penetrating and imaginative research into the use of 'race' and 'culture' and the relationship between them in the work of the criminal courts in the Netherlands, especially during sentencing. In her chapter, she draws on her own empirical research to show how vernacular or everyday ideas about 'other cultures' are used as a 'sense-making resource' to understand what particular cases are about. In this way, van Oorschot explains, the idea of defendants being from a different 'culture' is paradoxical. On the one hand, it is seen as an obstacle to understanding defendants' attitudes (or a veil). On the other, 'culture' is used as a lens through which to see defendants. As amateur or casual anthropologists, judges use ideas of culture (and sometimes stereotypes) to explain the attitudes of defendants towards the authority of the court. This enables judges to reassess as acceptable communications those which would otherwise seem less than ideal: 'Culture, in other words, can be mobilised to account for and at times excuse certain words and actions that do not fit judges' preferred mode of communication.'

Focusing empirically on judges' different uses of culture in relation to three received distinct ethnic minority groups, van Oorschot observes that judges know that culture is an imperfect way to understand and apprehend individual differences. Culture is understood as:

> A screen behind which hides the 'real' defendant. In precisely this double sense, [judges] *see through culture*: on the one hand, they can use it as a lens to see the individual defendant more clearly; on the other, it operates as a veil that the judge needs to strive to see through or beyond …

As a scholar of anthropology and performance, Kate Rossmanith has conducted studies examining judicial experiences of defendant emotions (most notably remorse) not only in their perceived verbal but also bodily expression.

[23] S Bandes, 'Remorse and Judging' in S Tudor et al, *Remorse and Criminal Justice: Multidisciplinary Perspectives* (London, Routlege, 2022).

Her chapter reflects on attempts to inform judicial assessment of defendants from 'other' cultures through cultural sensitivity training. What effects do these programmes have in practice? They are intended to promote cultural awareness and sensitivity, but how do they play out in everyday judicial working practice and specifically in the practice of remorse assessment? The overwhelming view among policy-makers, practitioners and scholars is that such programmes can only be a 'good thing' in making judges more aware of other cultures. Rossmanith scrutinises this assumption by thinking about some points that arose from her research into the study of how judges identify remorse. While cultural sensitivity programmes can be useful, we should, she cautions, be mindful that how they play out in practice is mediated by a much more complex world than can ever be replicated in the judicial classroom. In particular, judges (like any other professionals) have to read the attitude of those coming before them. Carrying the heavy duty of trying to do justice in individual cases in an unjust society, judges (rightly) take pride in performing their role fairly and impartially.

Rossmanith argues that in order to assess whether training is *effective*, we need to understand how it works *affectively*. As conscientious professionals who feel the weight of responsibility to be fair (almost heroically so), Rossmanith explains that judges may become anxious when they find that the tools that were given in training do not seem to work in making the defendant 'legible'. Such frustration can lead to irritation with the defendant for failing to make themselves more transparent. This is a paradox and a potentially counter-productive effect of such training. On the one hand, training programmes are attractive because they enable professionals to move ahead with greater certainty and to dispose of high caseloads more efficiently. Yet, on the other hand, when that training does not seem to solve the problem, professionals (especially those responsible for 'justice') may experience frustration, shame, even anger with themselves or those who appear to have made themselves 'illegible'.

Like van Oorschot, Rossmanith observes how judges sometimes use 'culture' to reinterpret what appear to be resistant or hostile defendant attitudes as, in fact, indicative of qualities closer to the ideal defendant. For example, judges talked about the 'posturing' of 'young Lebanese men' as something that they initially saw as a challenge to the court's authority, but later came to see it as manifesting their discomfort, their sense of not fitting into society. In her chapter, Rossmanith sketches conceptual outcomes of cultural sensitivity training, for example how such training can result in judges attempting to balance confidence and varying degrees of doubt in their decision-making and how the training might also propagate judicial expectations regarding offender legibility: the idea that offenders produce non-verbal signs that judges then read and make sense of. Rossmanith considers a training outcome whereby judges expect to understand people's comportments. On the one hand, this lends judges a sense of pride that their skill and knowledge enables them correctly to read defendants, especially where defendant attitudes can appear more or less consistent with qualities of the ideal defendant. The corollary is, however, that where defendants do not seem to present themselves in a legible way, judges might respond more negatively with confusion, anxiety, shame and frustration. In such circumstances, judges may sometimes grow frustrated with the offender, blaming offenders for their illegibility. Instead of judges framing the situation as not understanding offenders, judges may describe instances of offenders 'not making themselves understood'.

B. Beyond Remorse

The opening part of the book sets out various ways in which expressions of remorse and the acceptance of responsibility are cultural expectations in diverse stages of many different criminal justice systems. Our second part acknowledges that sometimes decision-makers may look for remorse but actually demand more of the defendant. On the other hand, it shows that sometimes courts 'make do' with much less than an open, full and voluntary acceptance of responsibility, and that the political and institutional contexts may lead penal agencies to move away from close examination of remorse.

(i) Remorse May Not Be Enough

Richard Weisman's chapter analyses the relationship between remorse and 'insight' and the parallel but distinguishable roles they play in the treatment of offenders in Canada and the US. Analysing the discourses in 66 Canadian criminal cases decided between 2010 and 2020 that applied both concepts to the same offenders, Weisman points out overlaps, differences and conflicts in the way these distinct but related concepts express the characteristics the ideal defendant is expected to demonstrate. Both concepts express qualities that defendants must show to make clear the moral separation between the person that committed the past wrong and the person they are now. Weisman describes this as a 'moral performance': a presentation of the self before an audience that feeds into a moral judgement of the status of the defendant based on an assessment of that performance. Weisman concludes that remorse is still the paramount consideration in Canadian sentencing courtrooms whereas 'insight' prevails on the Parole Boards. Yet he identifies a temporal shift: insight was already discernible as a key concept in parole decisions in North America two decades ago, but its influence is now becoming more evident in sentencing decisions as well.

But what are the differences between these concepts as revealed by their discursive use in criminal cases in Canada? Weisman concludes that remorse is about how offenders feel about their crime: it requires a genuine and fully expressed acceptance of personal moral responsibility. But to demonstrate insight, it is not enough to feel and express a profound sense of regret about one's act and acknowledge fully its moral wrongness: the necessary transformation requires the defendant to have identified and addressed the underlying causes of the offending. This insight must be developed or gained over time through a learning process that requires certain cognitive and verbal capacities. Remorse, on the other hand, can be demonstrated by spontaneous emotional display. These differences are evident in the contrasting meanings attributed to incoherence in a defendant's discourse. Incoherence may suggest authenticity in conveying the emotional weight of remorse. But incoherence may suggest limitations of cognitive capacity, which may prevent effective self-analysis of the cause of the offence or expression of that understanding. Noticeably, Weisman found several instances where offenders were attributed with remorse, but no offender was believed to have acquired insight without also being attributed with remorse. Hence, expressing feelings of remorse is necessary to the moral performance of ideal defendants in Canada but increasingly is not enough.

Weisman reflects on the significance of the increasing salience of insight as a criterion for evaluation. He sees this not just as a change of emphasis, but as a change in discourse that elevates the findings of the court to an apparently more objective plane. An 'actuarial standard of risk and the likelihood of reoffending' is presented as bringing the capacity for greater predictive power. Although lack of awareness or insight is a moral standard in that it is founded on expectations of what an ordinary member of the community should understand, its adoption represents a shift from the overtly moral discourse of remorse to the more specialised language of risk and dangerousness. Yet it is not clear whether insight is in fact a more effective test than remorse of defendants' readiness to return to the community.

For the individual defendant, demonstrating insight carries a number of challenges. The elevation of cognitive and verbal competence to a necessary requirement has adverse consequences for those who are socially disadvantaged or suffering from cognitive disability. Furthermore, the individual's causal analysis of the crime is expected to focus on those factors found within the individual rather than external situational factors. Evoking the latter risks a judicial critique of the defendants' minimising of their responsibilities. And simultaneously demonstrating both remorse (with its requirements of authenticity and genuine emotion) *and* insight (with its requirements of verbal dexterity) may be particularly challenging. The smooth verbal performance necessary to demonstrate insight may arouse suspicions as to the genuineness of expressed emotion. Ultimately, this tight control of what Weisman describes as the 'scripting of redemption' meant that only a small number of the offenders within his database were able to demonstrate both.

(ii) Taking What You Can Get

There is evidence that in some contexts the courts are looking for the fullest and most sincere expressions of remorse (closely examining signs of this in words, gestures and practical action). But very often courts seem to be happy to accept representations of the acceptance of responsibility that are much 'thinner' and more formal, such as a guilty plea or confession. These are often more like acquiescence than acceptance.[24] But even then, it is necessary to keep up appearances, to maintain certain representations around the acceptance of responsibility.

Key to this is a public acting out of voluntariness that ignores and obscures the range of incentives and pressures exerted to encourage confessions and guilty pleas. This is the core to Jackie Hodgson's chapter, where she argues that the ideal defendant is one who pleads guilty. But the legitimacy of these pleas depends on the idea that they represent a voluntary and informed decision not to contest guilt but to acknowledge responsibility. In England and Wales, this legitimacy is rooted in an idea central to notions of procedural fairness within the adversarial tradition, namely a party's autonomy to pursue self-interest in a legal dispute. The role of the defence lawyer is seen as a key guarantee that this party autonomy is 'real' in that decision-making is not only voluntary, but also informed (something itself critical to the equality of arms underpinning adversarial due process). Thus, the defence lawyer's role is central to the legitimacy of guilty pleas and the broader criminal process exactly because it suggests that defendants are making a free and informed choice. Once made with the support of a defence lawyer, it is very hard to challenge the legal validity of a guilty plea even where there is ambivalence in the plea or ambiguity in the evidence. The smooth processing of cases is thus assured.

Yet Hodgson points to widespread evidence that incentives are routinely offered and pressures applied to encourage guilty pleas. This is done not only by prosecutors, judges, magistrates and their advisers, but also by defence lawyers. In general, these incentives and pressures cannot be acknowledged as such: in the case of the defence lawyer, this is presented as the giving of advice necessary to an informed choice. But defence practice is itself materially and professionally encouraged by the time and resource constraints involved in running a profitable practice and the peer pressures from practitioner groups working a system whose collective functioning is seen as dependent on guilty pleas. This means that processing guilty pleas may often be the preferable option for defence lawyers. Yet all these pressures (on both defendants and defence lawyers) must remain hidden in the public court discourse. Attempts are made to limit defendants' public participation to a defined role consistent with the plea. Case law emphasises not just the legitimacy, but also the professional imperative of strong advice about the advantages of a guilty plea while ignoring the ambivalence and contradiction in many such pleas. What we have here is a remarkably flexible concept of 'voluntariness' that enables the courts to accept as meaningful almost any public acceptance of responsibility however grudging or confused. On this depends the state's capacity to process efficiently high volumes of cases while maintaining its public authority to punish.

Hodgson draws comparisons with France. There, too, admissions of responsibility are systematically encouraged and then largely rendered immune from

[24] J Gormley and C Tata, 'Remorse and Sentencing in a World of Plea Bargaining' in Tudor et al (n 23).

scrutiny at trial. But the institutional framework that lends legitimacy and credibility to those admissions is differently constructed. Rather than the procedural fairness of party autonomy and equality of arms, it is pre-trial judicial supervision of police investigations (by judges or prosecutors) that is presumed to give integrity and thus credibility to that which is recorded in the official dossier (including admissions to the police). Yet Hodgson suggests that judicial supervision in most cases does not provide a rigorous examination of the conditions under which confessions have been produced but rather provides retrospective bureaucratic scrutiny limited to the documentation within the dossier. Nevertheless, the inquisitorial procedural tradition invests legitimacy and credibility to everything within the dossier (including confessions) for all professionals (including defence lawyers).

Thus, again – though by a different mechanism – systematic incentives are produced to encourage the ideal defendant to accept responsibility. In France, much of this 'incentivising' work is still done in the police station, where defence lawyer participation remains marginalised and interrogation recordings are rare. As a result, the realities underpinning the 'voluntary' assumptions of responsibility that determine the outcome of most cases are largely obscured. The dominant assumption at public trial is that what is in the official dossier gains credibility from the fact that it is the outcome of a judicially supervised pre-trial process. And admissions of responsibility will often lead to prosecutors processing cases through abbreviated procedures that limit scrutiny of pre-trial evidence while maintaining the public image of judicial verification of the truth of the dossier. Such procedures, including a relatively new form of formal plea procedure, are formally subject to the consent of the defendant. Yet that consent is itself encouraged by the incentive of reduced sentences. Thus, in both France and England and Wales, there are routine backstage pressures to admit responsibility, the extent and significance of which is obscured. In England and Wales, this is done by the public courtroom portrayal of guilty pleas as voluntary and informed acts of an autonomous party. In France, a similar role is performed by the courtroom presumption of credibility that is invested in the official dossier and by pre-trial judicial supervision.

(iii) Marginalising Remorse

Nicola Padfield examines the role of remorse in Parole Board decision-making in England and Wales as opposed to initial sentencing decisions. She reviews case law and the evidence from two empirical studies that she conducted in 1999 and 2016–17 (based on observation of Parole Board hearings and formal interviews with participants). In the earlier study, the researchers concluded that panels considered remorse relevant as part of the 'making progress' in prison that they were looking for in their assessment of risk (though this was often discussed in other terms, such as victim empathy or appreciating the impact of the offence on victims). But by 2016–17, remorse had become a much less salient feature of discussion. Future risk assessment still depended on assessment of behavioural change and victim empathy might still be relevant, but remorse itself was seldom mentioned.

Padfield concludes that there has been a shift in England and Wales to a narrower focus in Parole Board decision-making on evaluation of future risk and its management. This has been accompanied by the marginalisation of remorse. Padfield also considers recent case law. In reviews of Parole Board decisions – whether by judicial review or the relatively new 'reconsideration' mechanisms – there is evidence of arguments made around remorse by applicants and in reports on them, but they do not seem to be decisive to the decisions. In contrast, in cases involving review of minimum terms or tariffs in relation to indeterminate life sentences, remorse remains relevant and, in relation to young people detained at His Majesty's pleasure, remorse is an explicit criterion under the relevant guidance. Padfield points out that these latter categories of decision are much more akin to re-sentencing exercises than the narrower risk assessment exercise for post-tariff release decisions.

Padfield is reluctant to offer clear-cut conclusions as to precise mechanisms by which remorse has been marginalised in the period between 1999 and 2007. She does, however, point out that over the relevant period there has been a shift in the nature and role of the Parole Board and the political context within which it operates. Criminal Justice Acts in 1991 and 2003 shifted the focus of Parole Board decision-making from decisions about discretionary early release from determinate sentences towards decisions about either late release or recall of 'dangerous' offenders with indeterminate sentences who had already served their tariff period for retributive purposes. The political context in which these changing functions are performed has also shifted. The Parole Board has moved from a small body of experts working at least in part for rehabilitative purposes to one rooted less in practitioner experience and shaped more by a prevailing penal populism. This has been reflected in the prioritisation of protection of the public over broader notions of promoting law-abiding lifestyles. Initial sentencing embraces a range of purposes to which remorse might be thought relevant. But these changes mean that post-tariff release decisions have a much narrower focus on predicting and managing risks of recidivism. Given that there is no evidence that remorse correlates with such risks, Padfield is not surprised by the lack of significance accorded now to remorse: it reflects the task now assigned to the Parole Board in England and Wales. But if one were looking to help offenders take responsibility for their offending then the Board might regard remorse as more relevant. She points to contrasts with France and the role of the *juge d'application des peines* (JAP; a judge with broad responsibility for enforcing and in some cases varying sentences), where reintegration remains a key function. Crucially, perhaps, Gautron provides evidence that remorse matters to the JAP.[25]

[25] Note also that remorse remains an explicit criterion for parole decisions in California. For a recent discussion of how that is interpreted, see K Young and H Chimowitz, 'How Parole Boards Judge Remorse: Relational Legal Consciousness and the Reproduction of Carceral Logic' (2022) 56 *Law and Society Review* 237.

Padfield also makes a strong case for the view that it would be inappropriate to seek to identify and evaluate remorse in a parole hearing. She points out the acute cultural difficulties of expressing remorse as a prisoner in such a formal public penal context. Yet many prisoners did express to the researchers their remorse and desire to make amends. Padfield concludes that, even for those with the capacity to express themselves in a formal parole hearing, the injustices and the degradations of prison life generate anger, resentment and personal survival strategies that render unthinkable public expressions of remorse to the system that has done this to them. Padfield does not say this explicitly, but in the light of other chapters, we might speculate that, for prisoners, expressing remorse to the state would feel like acknowledging publicly the legitimacy of what that state is doing to them. And this they will not do.

C. Cultural Meanings of Remorse: What Does Performance of Acceptance of Responsibility and Remorse Do for the Criminal Process, the State and Relations between State and Citizen?

(i) The Ideal Defendant as Citizen: Criminal Process and Political Cultures

The public performance of remorse and acceptance of responsibility as expectations of the ideal defendant represents a recognition of the legitimacy of state punishment. It symbolically (re)affirms – despite the offence – a certain continuing apparent mutuality in the relationship between state and citizen. As such, Stewart Field's chapter argues, it should be seen as a resonant moment in the enactment of political cultures. Field is a comparative lawyer originally brought up in the adversarial tradition of criminal procedure and the liberal political culture of Anglo-American liberalism. He uses practitioner interviews and courtroom observations of the French *cours d'assises* (CA; the highest first instance criminal courts) to explain how different court practices are shaped by, and enact, particular normative conceptions of the political relations between state and citizen. In so doing, Field explicitly puts into concrete practice David Garland's injunction to see penal practice as positively constructing cultural relations.[26] This is not just a matter of representing and reproducing images of individual subjects ('normal persons and normal attributes'), but also one of social authority and social relations. By representing a certain style of state authority to victims, defendants, court professionals and the public, the court acts out a distinct sense of how social relations are (and should be) constituted in that society, for example by reproducing a particular way of understanding the breakdown of social relations. The appropriate role of both citizen and state in this process is publicly acted out.

Field argues that the way in which defendant remorse and acceptance of responsibility is constructed and performed before the CA reflects a concept

[26] D Garland, *Punishment and Modern Society* (Oxford, Clarendon Press, 1990) ch 11.

of state and citizens rooted in a French republican tradition that is significantly different to that of Anglo-American liberalism. The French state expects a broader commitment from the French citizen defendant than would be the case in equivalent Anglo-American courts. True, the 'good accused' accepts responsibility, expresses remorse and shows commitment to personal change in the Anglo-American criminal process as well as the French. But this is only part of the established expectations before the CA: the ideal defendant must also actively participate in a detailed examination of how and why the offence was committed that is set within the context of the defendant's character and journey in life. And participation in this broad ranging discussion is expected to come from the defendant herself. In Anglo-American systems, the norm of a guilty plea means that the defendant is not directly questioned by the court (rather, her voice is mediated through her defence lawyer's plea in mitigation and/or in the pre-sentence report).

In contrast, the defendant in the CA is expected to respond directly to the judge. And, rather than formally segmenting the question of criminal conduct (guilt-determination, or what Anglo-Americans call a 'trial) from that of the character of the person (sentencing), the CA (like other continental European courts) operates a unitary model in which character and alleged conduct are examined together. So it is that the judge may begin court proceedings with an examination of the defendant's life and character – something largely excluded by the evidential rules adopted within the liberal Anglo-American tradition.

In this way, rather than delegating the examination of the defendant's character and attitude to the offence to pre-sentence report writers and the defence lawyer's plea in mitigation prior to sentence (as is the case in Anglo-American countries, where guilty pleas are the norm), the defendant is expected to explain herself directly to the court in response to direct judicial questioning not just about the offence and her attitude to it, but also about her character, prior to any guilt having been established. Thus, the defendant is expected to participate more actively, to a greater depth and for a greater duration than in Anglo-American court practices. And all of this is done through the public 'front-stage' work of the court rather than through the 'backstage' case-cleansing work of pre-sentence reports in other jurisdictions (see Tata on Scotland), or even the rapid public lawyer-led mitigatory work of a sentencing hearing.

In return, the French state is publicly making two offers that go further than either the negotiated settlement of the Anglo-American guilty plea or the narrowly constructed party conflict of adversarial trial: first, to engage in a careful and meaningful dialogue with defendants about their responsibilities in the light of the reciprocal responsibilities of the French state and other citizens; and secondly, to offer a viable route back to full citizenship and reintegration into the polity.[27] Field argues that what is being acted out in the CA is a symbolic

[27] Field expresses significant doubts as to whether the French state is actually delivering on these promises.

exchange between citizen and state based on certain background assumptions about normal underlying relationships between state and citizen. These evoke a positive concept of the French citizen and the place of the state in defining the identity of the nation and its citizens that reflects a polity that is significantly at odds with dominant notions of liberal pluralism as understood in Anglo-American society.

(ii) Legitimising Violence: Working Separately yet Together

Tata's chapter argues that the practices of distinct professional groups (particularly judges, lawyers and probation officers[28]) in reality work together to manage two related tensions in their working lives: first, that between justice and efficiency; and secondly, that between legitimate punishment and unjustified violence.

Professionals who operate a system that ultimately involves the routine application of violence and coercion need to see that system, and especially their work in it, as more or less just and legitimate. Yet the everyday reality is of a criminal justice system seeking the 'efficiency' of the cheap and rapid mass processing of cases. How do practitioners maintain their distinct professional ideals about what they do in the face of these pressures? For probation officers, it is by seeing their therapeutic support as enabling positive defendant self-change; for defence lawyers, it is providing legal advice and support for the free choices of autonomous clients; for judges, it is the appropriate penal response to a particular offence and offender. Yet the system, in order to promote the 'efficient' processing of convictions, relies on the defendant realigning her posture closer to that of the ideal defendant, who sincerely accepts both responsibility for the alleged crimes and the legitimacy of the state's punishment. And practitioners of all types play key roles in encouraging defendants to make this adjustment.

Drawing on an empirical study of the Scottish sentencing processes, Tata argues that these apparent tensions are managed through an implicit 'symbiotic' cooperation between legal and therapeutic professionals. By this, he means that autonomous professional groups, despite their different occupational ideologies and functions, depend on and sustain each other's work in ways that encourage and oblige people to behave more or less as 'ideal defendants' who are seen to accept sincerely their culpability and impending punishment.

The symbiosis of this work by the two professional groups is 'blind'. By this, Tata means that it operates without any acknowledgement that the work of legal and therapeutic professionals is mutually sustaining. This symbiotic professional co-working is obscured by official, academic and professional portrayals of criminal justice as a linear, step-by-step system in which individuals proceed from one distinct, autonomous decision moment to the next. According to this prevailing image, each of these autonomous steps is dominated by distinct

[28] Known in Scotland as criminal justice social workers.

professional groups performing separate functions. For example, therapeutic professionals' character assessments are formally seen as relevant only after guilt has been determined or accepted following defendants' interactions with judges and lawyers. Yet, pleading guilty but then providing to pre-sentence report writers an account of the event and of oneself that does not fully and coherently accept responsibility attracts negative consequences. That is not what the ideal defendant is expected to do; it challenges the legitimacy of the process. Thus, Tata argues, defendants cannot afford to treat decisions about guilt and presentations of their moral character as separate.

Rather than being in any sense a planned or deliberate conspiracy, practitioners work separately but in mutually supporting ways to bring home these realities to defendants. So, Tata suggests, defence lawyers are concerned that probation officers' pre-sentence reports set out a defendant account that aligns with the formal plea. This encourages clients to take the opportunity of the interview with the probation officer for their pre-sentence report to emphasise clear and unambiguous acceptance of responsibility and show remorse. In turn, probation officers themselves in those pre-sentence reports reformulate representations of events and contexts made to them by defendants in interview so that they align more closely to these same expectations of the ideal defendant. Yet judges reading these reports do not appear to be aware that this double re-modulation of defendants' voices is taking place: they appear to assume that the reports express defendants' unfiltered views and attitudes. That, in turn, maximises the opportunity for judges to treat those representations as a free and voluntary acceptance of responsibility. This is the unacknowledged symbiotic relationship that exists between the work of lawyers and judges and that of probation officers. It enables – but at the same time obscures – the sustained obligation that is exerted on defendants to conform to the model of the ideal penal subject.

In what way are the inconsistencies between the reality of those sustained pressures and the ideal of voluntary defendant participation and the presumption of innocence obscured from view? Tata argues that official temporal and professional separations between practitioners and their roles are key. Judges do not appear to know the detailed work that defence lawyers and probation officers do to persuade defendants to act as the ideal penal subject (or to reframe their words so that they appear to be so acting). And the clear separation between the formal roles of defence lawyers and therapeutic professionals obscures the mutually assisting work they each do (and thus also the appearance of pressure being exerted on the defendant). The integrity of cherished ideas around free participation is thus preserved by obscuring from view this 'cross-contamination' of legal and therapeutic casework. The 'blindness' of each professional group to the detailed work of the other enables each to remain (or at least appear to be) more or less unaware of the full reality of the process for defendants. Yet, the two key decisions made by defendants, which are formally separate and involve interaction with different practitioners – do I plead guilty and what kind of account do I give of myself, my motives and my circumstances – need to be carefully aligned in order to get the benefits of being considered an 'ideal defendant' and avoid the sanctions attached to being considered less than ideal. Thus, the 'blindness' of practitioners to the detail of each other's work enables them together, without bad faith, to create a reality for defendants that is one of sustained pressure while maintaining professional ideologies built on the idea of defendant autonomy. Tata concludes by calling for research to address more directly, comparatively and longitudinally the way that defendants (and in comparison with practitioners) experience the criminal justice system, the decisions that they have to make in it and the pressures to which they are subject.

(iii) Individualising Responsibility: Remorse and Restorative Justice

Giuseppe Maglione looks at the significance of remorse within the context of restorative justice (RJ). RJ is seen as a global reform movement advocating a non-punitive and participatory approach to wrongdoing. It is mainly pursued through facilitated, voluntary, face-to-face meetings between the offender and the victim in the presence of mediators and/or facilitators and one or more supporters of the offender and victim. Analysing the official policy documentation on RJ, Maglione examines its concept of the 'ideal offender' and shows the importance to that ideal of defendants showing remorse and taking individual responsibility. He traces its emergence to political shifts under 'New Labour' in the late 1990s and 2000s: RJ was a 'third way' justice that did not supplant rehabilitation or retribution. RJ presents itself as 'non-punitive, inclusive, stakeholder-led, emotionally intelligent and community based intervention on minor crimes'. But such crimes are seen as matters of interpersonal conflict to be dealt with by the conflicting parties: 'the role of social structural determinants or macro-relations of power, is neglected if not denied'. As RJ has been constructed as an 'institutionally-organised self-allocation of blame', remorse has become a crucial and recurrent component in normative representations of the offender involved in it. Maglione calls RJ a 'etho-political' ritual in that it bridges the realms of the individual/moral and the political. The expression of remorse is critical to this in that it is an essential step in the 'responsibilising journey' that frees the victim and offender of the burden of the crime while 'commit[ting] visibly and morally to the norms that govern group affiliation and determine group membership'. Maglione argues that if the state is to use RJ to respond to these social harms through punishment and the individualising of responsibility, then this requires remorse. But a 'remorseless' RJ would open up the possibility not of a 'better criminal justice, but something *better* than criminal justice': this critical RJ might be a space to think about harms and conflicts by looking more broadly at the wider social, cultural and economic conditions of social harms and issues around criminalisation. Thus, the expectation that defendents show remorse and accept individual responsibility for the harm as part of the RJ discourse plays a key part in narrowing down the scope of these encounters. For Maglione, remorse renders RJ 'a distinctive justice ritual with a specific political import'. While remorse may appear benign, it shifts the burden of judgment from the court onto the offender and onto the victim:

> Such a shift does not empower stakeholders within RJ processes; it actually binds them to an individualising process, however disguised. If RJ aims to be a progressive challenge to the very idea of punishment, the role of remorse needs to be critically re-assessed, possibly leading to a demotion of its centrality as a defining aim of the ideal offender's moral performance toward the victim.

This book, based on contributions from different jurisdictions and in different institutional settings, examines the diverse ways that manifesting the sincere acceptance of responsibility and expressing remorse are part of the normative expectations of the 'ideal defendant'.[29] It shows how practitioners evaluate defendant performance of these expectations and the structural inequalities that any such evaluation obscures. But above all, it shows how this system of normative classification of emotions helps practitioners to resolve underlying tensions within their criminal justice systems. State violence needs to be legitimatised by the promise of close attention to the particular unique circumstances of individuals and their alleged offences. Yet the sheer volume of interventions is *also* seen as calling for rapid and cheap processing of convictions in order to 'get through the list' and dispose of cases 'efficiently'. Performance of remorse (or at least some public acceptance of responsibility) can be seen to square the circle by an acknowledgement – by those who will ultimately suffer the coercion and violence – of the legitimacy of their punishment by the state. As such, it is a key part of a public performance that emphasises mutuality at a moment of acute conflict between state and citizen.

The paradox, however, is that this apparent mutuality is in part procured by state inducements. The rewards for the 'ideal defendant' are inevitably mirrored by penalties for those who do not (and perhaps cannot) conform. In turn, that public performance is organised in a way that obscures the significance of both inducement and penalty.

[29] And related feelings such as regret, guilt and shame that might be thought as less than 'ideal'.

2

Remorse in the French Criminal Justice System: A Subterranean Influence

VIRGINIE GAUTRON*

A comparison of the theory of French criminal law and its practical implementation reveals a strange paradox. Aiming to maintain the positivist tradition of scientific, rational laws detached from morality and the religious roots of penal philosophy, legislators are writing texts devoid of the slightest reference to how offenders feel about what they have done and the extent to which they feel remorse. Judges, however, regularly refer to those feelings at every stage of the criminal process. Providing objective evidence of the influence of those feelings on judicial decision making is nonetheless a hazardous undertaking, not only because French judges are not required to fully explain their reasoning, but also because those feelings are diluted in a broad spectrum of overlapping criteria. Based on the results of empirical research using both qualitative and quantitative methods, this contribution aims to highlight and explain the subterranean role remorse and broader attitudes around responsibility for the offence play in criminal judgments. This role is strengthened as multiple professionals charged with providing information to judges, from arrest to the carrying out of the sentence, focus on suspects' and offenders' feelings about the offence. Police officers, social background investigators, psychiatric experts and probation officers use similar methods to typify and interpret those feelings, and most draw on them to categorize the situations they assess, then use them to support their arguments in the documents they submit to judges. Influenced by all these medical, criminological and moral inferences, judges then tend to penalize emotional deviance.

As EVIDENCED BY this book, international research is beginning to unearth the influence of remorse as a judicial decision-making criterion. French researchers, however, have focused primarily on the role admissions of guilt play in establishing the truth, and have rarely addressed their 'effect on the moral identity of those who make or concede to them'.[1] In French

* Associate Professor at University of Nantes, France. English translation by Naomi Norberg.

[1] R Dulong, *L'aveu comme fait juridique et comme phénomène moral* (Paris, EHESS, 1999) 22.

criminal justice, statutes, regulations and ministerial circulars make no mention of the concept of remorse or the various related emotions (regret, shame, guilt, etc). They thus seem to relegate the religious sources of penal philosophy, which gave pride of place to penitence, moral regeneration and pardon, to the past.[2] After World War II, lawmakers and most criminal law scholars progressively set aside the concept of 'moral improvement' (*amendement moral*) in favour of 'social readjustment' or 'resocialisation'. Marc Ancel, founder of the New Social Defence movement, which influenced lawmakers for several decades, decried the 'somewhat simplistic view of a *homo delinquens* who, thanks to solitary confinement, would recover his senses, become aware of his wrongdoing and, riddled with remorse, resolve not to slide back into delinquency'.[3] Ancel emphasised the 'deep, natural, psychological feeling of responsibility', but tended to 'distrust both a certain masochism of requested or accepted punishment and, conversely, a certain ease with which one redeems the wrongdoing cheaply through later penitence ... The New Social Defence ... rejects obsessive remorse as sentimental expiation'.[4] Yet the concept of improvement has certainly not disappeared entirely: in recent years, the French Constitutional Council[5] has held that the need to 'promote the improvement' of offenders[6] and 'the moral recovery of delinquent children'[7] are fundamental principles recognised by the laws of France. Furthermore, an Act of 15 August 2014 paved the way for a troubling regression by reintroducing 'improvement' as a purpose of punishment (French Penal Code, Article 130–1), although the transcripts of the parliamentary debates reveal no particular reason for this amendment and certainly no moral one.

Nonetheless, since the historical analyses and philosophical writings of Michel Foucault,[8] Paul Ricoeur[9] and Vladimir Jankélévitch[10] on confessing, guilty conscience, remorse and pardon, very few empirical studies have analysed the possible influence on sentencing practices of 'emotional deviance': feelings or the expression of feelings that are socially inappropriate.[11] The reason legal researchers have, with few exceptions,[12] shown little interest in this topic is that

[2] R Merle, *La peine et la pénitence. Théologie, droit canonique, droit pénal* (Paris, Cerf/Cujas, 1985).

[3] M Ancel, 'Science pénitentiaire. Notes bibliographiques' (1953) 1 *Revue de Sciences Criminelles* 181.

[4] M Ancel, 'Responsabilité et défense sociale' (1959) 1 *Revue de Sciences Criminelles* 182.

[5] The Constitutional Council is a court charged, inter alia, with review of the constitutionality of legislation.

[6] Decision No 93-334 DC of 20 January 1994.

[7] Decision No 2002-461 DC of 29 August 2002.

[8] M Foucault, 'Mal faire, dire vrai, fonction de l'aveu en justice' in F Brion and BE Harcourt (eds), *Cours de Louvain, 1981* (Louvain, Presses universitaires de Louvain, 2012 [1981]).

[9] P Ricoeur, *Philosophie de la volonté, Tome II, Finitude et culpabilité* (Paris, Flammarion, 1988 [1960]).

[10] V Jankélévitch, *La mauvaise conscience* (Paris, editions Aubier-Montaigne, 1966).

[11] P Thoits, 'Self-labeling Processes in Mental Illness: The Role of Emotional Deviance' (1985) 91 *American Journal of Sociology* 221.

[12] M Herzog-Evans, *Le juge de l'application des peines: Monsieur Jourdain de la désistance* (Paris, L'Harmattan, 2013).

it is hard to assess by close analysis of case law the influence these feelings have on sentencing and its means of execution. Except for judgments issued by the criminal chamber of the French Court of Cassation,[13] the publication of case law is very patchy in France. This is a legacy of France's inquisitorial past. The courts have traditionally been granted complete discretion, and the criminal chamber of the Court of Cassation has held that, except where required to by statute,[14] the courts do not have to explain why they have chosen a particular punishment (neither the length of the sentence, nor the type of punishment). In the future, however, access to the courts' reasoning will be made easier thanks to several cases which have reversed the established jurisprudence[15] and have been reinforced by the new Articles 365–1 and 485–1 of the Criminal Procedure Code requiring the courts to explain their reasoning, albeit briefly.

Despite the limited number of published decisions, an examination of legal databases revealed more than 450 decisions, mostly handed down after 2005, that include the terms 'remorse', 'regret' and, less frequently, 'repent' or 'repentance'. These decisions are primarily from courts of appeal and the Court of Cassation, which leaves us in the dark with regard to the great mass of those made by first instance trial courts, especially at the post-sentencing phase.[16] Nonetheless, empirical research conducted with colleagues over the past 10 years[17] has shed light on the repercussions that regret, remorse, shame, guilt and empathy for the victim have at all stages of criminal procedure, from arrest to serving the sentence. Even though these feelings are not cited as criteria in assessments and decisions, they are a source of interest and interrogation not only for judges, but also for police officers, officials responsible for investigations into social background, probation officers, psychiatric experts, psychologists and even some therapists who have offenders as patients.

Although we were unable to do this for the writings of all these professionals, nor for the available case law, we tried to provide more objective evidence of this influence by (re)using case-file material. This had been collected in the course of two recent quantitative and qualitative research projects focusing on how the courts handle cases that involve psychopathological problems or problems perceived as such, including by ordering treatment. While that research might at first glance seem irrelevant here, the fact is that French treatment programmes are shaped by a penal and moral requirement to reflect upon the factors that have led to the commission of the crime.

[13] This is the highest and final court of appeal in relation to matters of law in criminal cases in France.

[14] Crim 19 December 1996, No 96-81.647.

[15] Crim 1 February 2017, Nos 15-85.199, 15-84.511 and 15-83.984; Constitutional Council, Decision No 2017-694 DC of 2 March 2018.

[16] After an offender is convicted, a specialised judge called the *juge de l'application des peines* (sentence implementation judge) is charged with determining how the sentence will be carried out – in custody or not. This judge has the power to adjust sentences handed down by the court and decide on the obligations that will accompany a grant of probation.

[17] In addition to the two research projects relied on specifically for this chapter and discussed below, there was an initial quantitative and qualitative investigation into how the French courts handle middle-ranking offences (2008–12), based on a representative sample of 7562 case files and 60 interviews. J Danet (ed), *La réponse pénale. Dix ans de traitement des délits* (Rennes, PUR, 2013).

Our first exploratory research project (2014–16) consisted of a review of the files of probation officers with respect to 99 offenders subject to socio-judicial monitoring (SJM), which is a supplementary punishment that includes monitoring, surveillance and treatment measures that begin when the offenders (mainly sex offenders) are released.[18] The files included the initial judgment, the decisions of the *juges de l'application des peines* (JAPs; sentence-implementation judges), probation officers' reports, expert assessments completed before and after conviction, and reports by the coordinating physicians.[19] We made a systematic inventory of the references in all these files to shame, remorse, regret, feelings of guilt and empathy specifically for the victim (rather than in general).

We then reproduced this process in a second research project (2016–21), for which we compiled a sample of 2698 cases that include alternatives to prosecution (warning, mediation, etc) determined by the prosecutor's office (651), middle-ranking offences (*délits*) (1344) and serious offences (*crimes*) (703).[20] We focused our inventory on the psychiatric and psychological assessments contained in 889 of the files in the hope of being able to measure, all other things being equal, how the feelings described influenced the courts' decisions. These assessments, which are not systematic except in criminal cases, were required to be carried out on sex offenders (53 per cent) and perpetrators of homicides and fatal blows (*coups mortels*) (22.8 per cent), as well as with respect to criminal damage to property (14.2 per cent) and, less frequently, domestic violence (2.1 per cent), violations of drugs laws (2.8 per cent) and other offences (5.1 per cent).

Taking an approach based on interpretive sociology and further influenced by the recommendations and methods of sociologists in professional documents,[21] we also examined the professionals' cognitive frameworks, perception structures, methods of categorisation and practical reasoning. Studying the written methods for institutionally supervising individuals makes it possible to understand the administrative code that consists of 'translating profane judgments into professional judgments'.[22] To determine whether and, where applicable, how these feelings help professionals categorise the situations they must deal with and serve as grounds for their assessments and decisions, we also conducted nearly 100 semi-structured interviews with 127 professionals. These included 33 judges and prosecutors, 31 probation and social integration officers, and 57 psychologists and psychiatrists acting as experts, coordinating physicians

[18] V Gautron, *(Se) soigner sous la contrainte: une étude du dispositif de l'injonction de soin* (Paris, Mission de Recherche Droit et Justice, 2017).

[19] A coordinating physician is a psychiatrist responsible for making sure orders for the post-release treatment of offenders are properly carried out and for reporting to the *juge de l'application des peines* through yearly or half-yearly reports.

[20] For a presentation of the research in English, see https://repeso.hypotheses.org/.

[21] C Coton and L Proteau (eds), *Les paradoxes de l'écriture. Sociologie des écrits professionnels dans les institutions d'encadrement* (Rennes, Presses Universitaires de Rennes, 2012).

[22] D Serre, 'Une écriture sous surveillance: les assistantes sociales et la rédaction du signalement d'enfant en danger' (2008) 4 *Langage et Société* 39.

and therapists treating patients who are in custody or on probation. None of the questions we asked or reminders we sent out in the two research projects mentioned above explicitly targeted the subject of the feelings felt or expressed by the suspects or the accused. However, open questions were asked about assessment and/or decision-making criteria. These questions were followed by a single reminder concerning the subject of concern to us here, but that reminder was purposely much more neutral and focused on the influence of admitting the crime. This gave the respondents the opportunity to discuss (or not) the affective components of a confession.

With the help of these materials, this contribution aims to highlight what is still a major assessment and decision-making criterion in the French criminal justice system. It will first clarify the extent and the nature of the methods for detecting the feelings associated with committing a crime (section I), then show that even though these feelings are hidden by the rules governing the judicial process, they exert a certain amount of influence on sentencing practices (section II).

I. A CONTINUING EXAMINATION OF THE FEELINGS ASSOCIATED WITH THE COMMISSION OF THE OFFENCE

In France, as elsewhere, suspects are required to show respect at trial, express regret, acknowledge the victim's suffering and promise to reform. These expectations are not limited to judges, but are often shared by all the professionals advising them and whose functions include detecting potential emotional deviance (A), using relatively similar indicators (B).

A. Paying Attention to Emotions Throughout the Criminal Procedure

Reflecting the 'emotional burden the observer feels almost physically',[23] especially during a trial before the French *cour d'assises*,[24] the courtroom has its own 'emotional ecosystem'.[25] A recent (2008–12) ethnographic study carried out in France shows that jurors at the trials for the most serious offences share the

[23] C Besnier, *La vérité. Une ethnologue aux assises* (Paris, La découverte, 2017) 35.

[24] The *cour d'assises* in France deals with only the most serious offences, and judgment is rendered by a mixed panel of jurors and professional magistrates. For further analysis, see S Field, 'The Enactment of Political Cultures in Criminal Court Process: Remorse, Responsibility and the Unique Individual Before the French *cours d'assises*' in S Field and C Tata (eds), *Criminal Justice and the Ideal Defendant in the Making of Remorse and Responsibility* (Oxford, Hart Publishing, 2023) ch 10.

[25] S Bandes, 'Share Your Grief but Not Your Anger: Victims and the Expression of Emotion in Criminal Justice' in J Smith and C Abell (eds), *Emotional Expression: Philosophical, Psychological, and Legal Perspectives* (Cambridge, Cambridge University Press, 2016).

judges' reasoning and are 'attentive observers who say they do not lose a scrap of the discussions to discern something through emotions, ... on the lookout for whatever they can grasp from a furtive or fleeting look that might betray a feeling'.[26] In addition to the many trials we have attended over the past 20 years, the hastily scrawled trial notes of judges found in the files reveal the extent to which they are interested in what suspects say about the alleged offences and their relationship to the victims: 'I regret what I did, I ask for her forgiveness', 'I'm ashamed and disgusted with myself and I regret doing it'.

Lawyers play a large role in this courtroom drama. Whether representing the civil party[27] or the accused, they try to influence the court when they plead by acting as spokespersons for their clients' feelings. Prosecutors do the same when they argue for punishment, regularly justifying it by referring to the degree of contrition and realisation that the offence is serious. We detected the same thing when reading the 450 decisions identified in the legal databases, even though these feelings appear essentially in descriptive form, with no indication of why they are mentioned or how they influenced the decision. The judges limit themselves to noting that the accused or the convicted offender apologised and/or expressed regret at trial, sometimes through their lawyer, thereby asking the court for leniency. In the post-sentencing phase, especially in cases of sexual violence or other serious violent offences, many JAPs still hope that the offender will show 'clear signs that they assume responsibility and are relatively contrite'.[28]

Beyond the judges and prosecutors, police reports, investigations into defendants' social background, expert assessments and probation officers' reports regularly contain passages devoted to what Paul Ricoeur called the emotional component of 'confessional language'.[29] Police officers are very often the first to start this moral construction. In almost routine fashion, especially when the suspect is a minor, their reports end with open questions similar to an 'invitation ... to begin a self-critique with respect to what they did, and to show remorse'.[30] These questions are regularly followed by the transcription of statements such as 'I realise that it was unacceptable and I regret it' or 'I am sorry for [the victim]'. While the police officers' comments are generally informative and factual, and do not offer an account or interpretation, investigators occasionally add more personal interpretations: 'The investigators thought they saw the

[26] Above (n 23) 79; see also C Gissinger-Bosse, 'L'instruction des émotions. Le jury populaire dans l'institution judiciaire' in L Blondiaux (ed), *La démocratie des émotions. Dispositifs participatifs et gouvernabilité des affects* (Paris, Presses de Sciences Po, 2018) 119–44.

[27] In the French criminal process, victims can join themselves as civil parties to criminal proceedings to seek compensation. In the process, they acquire participation rights which go far beyond the role of the victim in Anglo-American courts (including the right to legal representation, to put questions and to make representations to the court).

[28] M Herzog-Evans, 'Exécution des peines, délinquance sexuelle et positionnement quant aux faits: enjeux juridiques et criminologiques' (2012) 12 *Actualité juridique. Pénal* 632.

[29] Above (n 9) 170.

[30] A Cicourel, *La justice des mineurs au quotidien de ses services* (S Bordreuil trans, Geneva, IES/HETS, 2017 [1968]) 256.

offenders taking a certain delight in relating the details of what they did, coldly and without the appearance of remorse.'[31]

Before the judgment, but after prosecution has begun, social background reports frequently include similar assessments, even though these investigators theoretically play no role in establishing the truth about the crime: their task is to reconstruct the suspects' personal, family, social and employment histories:

> Concerning the crime of which he is accused, Mr. X has progressed on his responsibility and thinking about the commission of the crime. In the beginning, he described having given 'just a little slap,' minimising the violence ... He has progressively called himself into question and was able to discuss this issue more freely. 'I regret everything. I didn't want things to happen that way. It was a mistake. I was stupid.'[32]

In our sample of 99 files of offenders sentenced to socio-judicial monitoring, most of the probation officers, coordinating physicians and experts expressed opinions on the degree to which the offenders acknowledged having committed the acts of which they were accused. They did so in a form that is at first glance devoid of any subjective assessment, without the slightest emotional colouring, but which distinguishes three degrees of admission: denial, full confession or partial admission (see Table 2.1). In addition, many of them probed the offenders' souls to see if there were any feelings of guilt (mentioned by at least one professional in 68.7 per cent of the files), empathy for the victim (69.7 per cent), shame (43.4 per cent), regret (48.5 per cent) and, more rarely, remorse (16.2 per cent).

Table 2.1 Frequency with which feelings associated with committing the crime appear ($n = 99$)

	Psychiatric or psychological assessments (%)	**Probation officers' half yearly reports (%)**	**Coordinating physicians' reports (%)**	**All files (%)**
Regret	40.6	12.1	7.9	48.5
Remorse	13.5	4	1.3	16.2
Feeling of guilt	63.5	17.2	21.1	68.7
Shame	31.3	10.1	13.2	43.4
Empathy for the victim	64.6	24.2	19.7	69.7

While one may infer from these figures that experts are more sensitive than probation officers or coordinating physicians, these differences must not be over-interpreted. On average, an expert assessment by psychologists or psychiatrists contains four or five pages, while the reports of probation officers and coordinating physicians are much shorter (one or two pages). The vocabulary

[31] Summary report of the national police, F201.
[32] Rapid social investigation, socio-judicial association, F1353.

and reasoning are therefore developed to a greater or lesser extent depending on the length of the document. Moreover, in almost all cases, the expert assessment is made before the offender is released, whereas the reports of probation officers and coordinating physicians concern supervision while on parole. These professionals may therefore pay much less attention to this aspect because, although offenders initially denied or only partially admitted committing the crimes, the vast majority of them ended up confessing.

With respect to pre-sentence expert assessments alone, our second survey reveals that feelings are mentioned less frequently, but with regard to much more diverse offences, some of which are significantly less serious. However, an analysis confined to the 105 files of offenders sentenced to SJM reveals that our two samples converge, confirming heightened interest among experts when particularly serious violent offences have been committed (Table 2.2).

Table 2.2 Frequency with which feelings associated with committing the crime appear

	Files containing at least one psychiatric or psychological assessment		**Offenders sentenced to SJM**	
	Number	**Frequency (%)**	**Number**	**Frequency (%)**
Regret	144	16.2	23	21.9
Remorse	55	6.2	11	10.5
Feeling of guilt	257	28.9	44	41.9
Shame	65	7.3	21	20
Empathy for the victim	200	22.5	49	46.7
Repentance	3	0.3	1	1
Total	889		105	

These feelings appear as alternatives or together, without it generally being possible to determine the precise meaning the professionals are giving to each of them – especially since they often consider 'regret', 'remorse' and 'guilt' to be synonymous. Other than brief comments, the narrative is often purely descriptive. These writings also blend the writer's narrative with the suspect's quoted language, which makes analysis more difficult. Some professionals take a neutral stance, limiting themselves to quoting the suspects without interjecting the slightest personal opinion as to whether the emotions being displayed are genuine. Others leave things to the interpretation, if not imagination, of the reader, who is occasionally puzzled by mere insinuations. Their doubts about whether the suspect's or the offender's statements are genuine are expressed through adverbs and adjectives expressing levels of intensity ('some remorse', 'vague regrets' or 'a certain feeling of guilt'). Sometimes, small adjustments in written expression, particularly the type of punctuation used, may 'transform' the meaning of what is written: for example, where ellipses are used by the author to suggest doubt without explaining why, 'through an effect of presumed closeness with the reader'.[33] All of these professional documents, which add to each other but also regularly refer to each other, will be linked by the judges and prosecutors when they read the file, both to assess the objective characteristics of how the crime was committed and 'the moral and social seriousness' of the person being judged.[34] The emphasis on such expressions of emotion in these documents may seem surprising, because our interviews reveal consistent scepticism regarding offenders' expressions of contrition. Like confessions, the emotions suspects or convicted offenders display or claim to be feeling are therefore 'put to the test'.[35]

B. Process of Objectifying Emotional States

Many practitioners underscore the trouble they have deciphering the meaning of offenders' discourse, whether it be through verbal or physical expression of their inner turmoil, and say they approach this highly subjective task with caution. They believe that some suspects and offenders are aware of the influence the expert assessments and reports of probation officers and coordinating doctors have on their journey through the penal system. They are therefore tempted to structure their statements so as to feign repentance and provide evidence of real improvement.[36] Confronted by professionals who say they are not 'fool[s] because [they], too, know very well what it is better to say',[37] suspects and offenders use language designed to meet, point by point, the 'expectations of the person they're talking to'.[38] They seek to build an 'accumulation of evidence in [their] favour',[39] with the help of arguments that are 'highly moralizing [while] not necessarily reflecting [their] feelings and underlying emotional experiences'.[40] They are then accused of merely 'putting on a show' of remorse in the hope of obtaining leniency:

> There's the accused's prepared statement but we don't believe it, there. Afterward, it's the lawyer who comes and says 'don't forget to say this.' It's clear to us when the sentence comes at the end and is totally insincere. Especially since there are 5 of them and they all say the same thing, using the same words.[41]

[33] N Sallée and G Chantraine, 'Observer, consigner, tracer. Les usages d'un cahier électronique controversé en établissement pénitentiaire pour mineurs' (2014) 56 *Sociologie du travail* 64, para 13.
[34] F Vanhamme and K Beyens, 'La recherche en sentencing: un survol contextualisé' (2007) 31 *Déviance et Société* 199, 204.
[35] O Macchi, 'Le fait d'avouer comme récit et comme évènement dans l'enquête criminelle' in R Dulong (eds), *L'aveu. Histoire, sociologie, Philosophie* (Paris, PUF, 2001) 184.
[36] We were not able to examine this particular hypothesis due to a lack of interviews with or comments from suspects or offenders. Only the professionals' opinions are reported here.
[37] F59.
[38] F92.
[39] F18.
[40] F59.
[41] Trial judge, I73.

More understanding than suspicious, the professionals also report on those who completely and continually deny having committed the crime for reasons related primarily to their desire to protect their self-esteem, to not lose face in front of their family or close friends, for fear of being rejected by them. Despite these reservations and at the risk of essentialising emotions,[42] we note that the expert assessments, judgments and probation officers' reports we read show that many of these professionals try to find objective evidence of offenders' emotions before validating them or refuting their genuineness. Given the consistency we observed, the social conventions that characterise this evaluation process seem largely shared by these different professional groups. Like practices elsewhere, the nature of the feelings expressed and the extent to which they are genuine are assessed according to the main expressive modes identified by Proeve and Tudor: first, the language; secondly, the behaviour and attitudes associated with that language; and finally, the actions that express or are motivated by remorse.[43]

As the first and principal source of information, professionals examine the defendant's discourse, but they also consider the conditions under which discourse arises, paying attention not only to the words used, but also to the ease and spontaneity with which the suspects or offenders agree to talk about the crimes of which they are accused. They criticise those who are 'not very talkative', 'reserved', 'terse', 'unclear', 'ambiguous', 'elusive' or 'evasive', and 'spontaneous' conversation is regarded as a much better sign, as a proof of genuineness, which counts in the speaker's favour. Variations in their statements and any disagreement between the official version of the events and the evidence that has been gathered are deemed signs of feigned remorse. Therefore, the professionals test the interviewees' ability to maintain similar, consistent explanations throughout the interview or throughout all of their interviews with professionals, using arguments that must match the information in the criminal file on all points: 'In fabricated remorse, there is always a little sentence that comes and negates what was said. I've noticed that, because it's very surprising: everything holds together and then there is something that slips out and makes it'.[44]

Moreover, they must not simply give purely factual information, but must take a critical approach and show that they are really examining themselves. This requirement of self-reflection is risky for them. Suspects and offenders are expected to talk about the crimes they committed and their reasons for committing them, but every explanation they offer may be interpreted as an attempt to escape responsibility through 'specious arguments with pseudo-psychological overtones',[45] while the professionals transcribe every sign of 'minimization', 'banalization',

[42] S Karstedt, 'Emotions and Criminal Justice' (2002) 6 *Theoretical Criminology* 299; K Rossmanith, 'Affect and the Judicial Assessment of Offenders: Feeling and Judging Remorse' (2015) 21 *Body & Society* 167.

[43] M Proeve and S Tudor, *Remorse: Psychological and Jurisprudential Perspectives* (Farnham, Ashgate Publishing, 2010).

[44] Expert psychologist, I116.

[45] Excerpt from an expert assessment, F16.

'rationalization' and 'shirking responsibility'.[46] As Weisman[47] and Ward[48] noted, their affects must not be self-centred, but related directly to the victims' harm rather than, primarily, the consequences for the offender and their family. Shame plays a special role in this regard, which distinguishes it clearly from other emotions. Feelings of dishonour, humiliation or indignation are regularly criticised for being self-centred, so that before they can be viewed positively, they must be combined with and even surpassed by other emotions focused on the victim.

Spoken statements alone are insufficient when individuals face 'the judicial economy of suspicion'.[49] To clarify the meaning of information given orally, the professionals check whether the form and the content of the message are consistent by comparing it with the non-verbal communication the offender 'exudes'.[50] On the lookout for paralinguistic clues, they scrutinise facial expressions, posture, what people do with their hands, their intonation, eye contact, crying and other signs of emotion.

In one interview, a psychiatric expert encouraged us to 'beware of people who give you what you expect. Personally, I prefer a voice that is suddenly hoarse, a fleeting emotion. It is much more important than the guy who comes and says, 'oh, I was a real bastard'.[51] In another, a judge told us that:

> Sometimes there are facial expressions that say the opposite of the words ... It's true that personally, I have developed a habit of having my clerk take notes on how the scene has been staged, writing things down, so that the way the situation has been acted out is noted somewhere. Because it really says a lot, in fact.[52]

In short, all these non-verbal signs colour the speech, 'thus offering contextual interpretation keys to those who perceive them', based on typification and a 'common-sense understanding of how to behave, express oneself, laugh or cry':[53]

> The events are related with emotion, the subject often being on the edge of tears, holding his head between his hands, or his hands trembling uncontrollably. He is feeling guilt, guilt that is in fact clearly more evident with respect to his last victim. The feeling of guilt, the regret and remorse he verbalises seem sincere and genuine, but they arise only after the fact.[54]

[46] See also C Tata, *Sentencing: A Social Process* (London, Palgrave Macmillan, 2020) especially 104–07; I van Oorschot et al, 'Remorse in Context(s): A Qualitative Exploration of the Negotiation of Remorse and Its Consequences' (2017) 26 *Social & Legal Studies* 359.

[47] R Weisman, *Showing Remorse: Law and the Social Control of Emotion* (Farnham, Ashgate Publishing, 2014).

[48] BH Ward, 'Sentencing without Remorse' (2006) 38 *Loyola University Chicago Law Journal* 131.

[49] F Fernandez, and S Gariépy, 'Les failles affectives. Ethnographie politique de l'enquête sur remise en liberté' (2018) 23 *Tsantsa* 43, 47.

[50] A Ogien, *Sociologie de la déviance* (Paris, PUF, 2012) 251.

[51] I71.

[52] I73.

[53] J Colemans, 'Ce que les émotions font faire aux professionnels du droit: Jalons pour une approche praxéologique des expressions émotionnelles dans la sphère judiciaire' (2015) 54 *Social Science Information* 525, 530.

[54] Expert assessment, F92.

The documents examined show how a laugh, sarcasm or signs of nonchalance or arrogance are enough to refute any feelings of guilt, despite a confession. For example, some experts mention when an offender expresses regret but 'stretches out nonchalantly on the chair, yawning'[55] or 'accompanies his words with large hand gestures while his gaze is shifty and he never looks at the person he's speaking to'.[56] As is the case in other jurisdictions,[57] lack of visible emotion is often interpreted as a lack of any emotion at all. Many professionals downgrade the significance of the words when the narration of the events 'is generally devoid of affect',[58] 'without apparent emotion',[59] 'droning'[60] or 'in an utterly impassive and emotionless tone'.[61]

As for actions that are likely to constitute indirect, external evidence of the inner experience, the experts, probation officers and coordinating physicians are sensitive to actions that have some compensatory dimension, including sending a letter to the victim as well as apologising at trial. Compensating the civil parties is still, however, the most tangible sign, and can even indicate implicit acceptance that the facts are true, despite a denial:

> Because we find that it's a sign, someone who says he is innocent but agrees to pay the civil parties. We wonder. Is it to please the judge, or might it mean that he's saying, 'this is my way of saying I'm responsible, but I won't tell you that I'm responsible.'[62]

For judges and prosecutors, these actions do in fact constitute 'perhaps the most valuable evidence of offender remorse', because 'due to the somewhat pragmatic nature of the legal world … actions very often speak louder than words'.[63] In addition to French standards for writing judgments, which encourage brevity and thus limit access to judges' criteria for determining whether offenders genuinely feel remorse, for evidentiary reasons judges generally avoid setting out their reasoning with regard to subjective criteria such as body language. With rare exceptions, they favour more consequential factors based on the suspect's actions and behaviour, such as turning themselves in to the police immediately, quickly admitting to the crime in custody and repeating that admission to each judge they encounter as the criminal procedure progresses. The more time that passes between the commission of the crime and the adoption of a contrite attitude, the more the judges tend to doubt the suspect's sincerity: 'delayed remorse' cannot 'mitigate the seriousness of the crime'.[64]

[55] F83.
[56] F52.
[57] S Bandes, 'Remorse and Demeanor in the Courtroom: Cognitive Science and the Evaluation of Contrition' in R Hunter, P Roberts, D Young and D Dixon (eds), *The Integrity of the Criminal Process* (Oxford, Hart Publishing, 2016).
[58] F16.
[59] F49.
[60] F26.
[61] F87.
[62] Probation officer, I122.
[63] Proeve and Tudor (n 43) 96.
[64] Crim, 26 November 2014, No 13-87.899.

Like experts and probation officers, judges hunt for inconsistences in what has been said to each of the various professionals. 'Regrets expressed in court' can thus be 'totally negated by statements made to the psychiatrist'.[65] Moreover, on the day of the hearing, suspects are still expected to accept and take part in the 'degradation ceremony'[66] that awaits them; failure to appear is proof of their lack of remorse. When offenders challenge certain points on appeal, judges also weigh the failure to contest the provisions related to compensating the victim. On the other hand, challenging the reality of a victim's financial loss, including 'marginally', is 'somewhat inappropriate and indecent coming from an individual … whose financial reasoning evidences little empathy for their victims'.[67] Whether they are affirmed or discredited by the various professionals, these affects are a major indicator (albeit not the only one) of a person's morality and dangerousness, and have non-negligible effects on the judicial decisions concerning suspects.

II. THE CRIMINAL PROCESS: RESPONDING TO EMOTIONAL DEVIANCE

Once we identified the frequency with which various emotions appeared in our two samples, we analysed the professionals' cognitive and perceptual frameworks, methods of categorisation and practical reasoning. We note that they draw conclusions about a suspect's or an accused's emotional state from medical, criminological and moral inferences (A). These are not without effect on the practical decision-making of judges and prosecutors: our results show clearly the punishment of emotional deviance (B).

A. Overlapping Medical, Criminological and Moral Inferences

The assessment of expressed emotions is a key semiological criterion for the experts that shapes diagnosis more or less directly, whether the emotions are expressed at the moment of the offence itself or later during the course of the criminal process. One naturally thinks of psychopathy or antisocial personality disorders because lack of remorse is a symptom of both according to international disease classifications. However, the expert reports in our samples reveal that emotional deviance is being used to justify diagnoses of perversion, psychosis or schizoid personality disorder, cognitive distortions or, more broadly, what may be seen as constituting evidence of character flaws. To varying degrees, the professionals associate these different disorders with an increased risk of

[65] Crim, 3 November 2016, No 15-87.245.

[66] H Garfinkel, 'Conditions of Successful Degradation Ceremonies' (1956) 61 *American Journal of Sociology* 420.

[67] Crim, 8 November 2016, No 15-83.225.

recidivism. Beyond that, and even though they do not all agree on this issue, many experts believe that, like not feeling guilt or empathy, denying accusations is in itself an indication of future dangerousness.

The sociometric analyses we conducted on the 889 files in our sample, including expert reports, confirm the influence, all other things being equal,[68] of the extent to which a suspect recognises the facts and the emotions associated with committing the offence. When an expert writes that there is no shame, regret, remorse, guilt and/or empathy for the victim, the probability of a negative prognosis is 2.6 times higher, which is statistically very significant (Table 2.3).

Table 2.3 Estimation of the probability of an expert prognosis of dangerousness or of risks of recidivism (other than low risk)

					95 per cent confidence intervals	
Modality to be explained	**Independent variables**	**Significance**		**Odds ratio**	**Lower limit**	**Upper limit**
Prognosis of dangerousness or risk of recidivism (other than low) according to the expert (n = 866)						
	Little or no guilt, shame, regret, remorse and/or empathy for the victim					
	No			1		
	Yes	0.000	***	2.598	1.852	3.645

Moreover, the attention they pay to variations in what the offender says is not intended simply to detect any artifice or manipulation when conducting a medico-psychological or predictive analysis. Although closely related to these two types of analyses, the analysis of how the narrative evolves has a broader, procedural dimension, as it is designed to measure the extent of the offender's moral transformation over the course of their sentence and, indirectly, the effectiveness of the respective professionals' interventions – hence the regular use, in the professionals' writings and during our interviews, of the words 'evolution', 'change', 'movement' and 'progression' in connection with the offender's perception of the alleged offences.

In this regard, the degree to which the offender realises the seriousness of the crime and accepts the punishment is another major indicator. This realisation, and the willingness to make amends by being punished, are perceived as sign of submissions to the authority of the law and the justice system, and that the penal 'lesson' has been learned.[69] Associated with remorse and regret, they are deemed

[68] The explanatory variables in our statistical regressions include the year of the judgment, the type of offence, the number of victims, prior convictions and the suspect's or accused's sex, age, nationality and employment status.

[69] F Vanhamme and K Beyens, 'La recherche en sentencing: un survol contextualisé' (2007) 31 *Déviance et Société* 199.

to show the offender's 'moral awakening':[70] an inclination to take part in their own readjustment through an active, genuine commitment to the rehabilitation process,[71] which supposedly improves their tendency to conform to social norms and criteria for moral rationality in the future. They are therefore seen as constituting a guarantee of readjustment, desistance and future social integration, and even, in the words of a probation officer we interviewed (I112), a sign of the offender's 'healing'. These medical, criminological and moral inferences, then, influence the harshness of the sentence, with a lack of remorse increasing the judges' severity in sentencing.

B. Punishing Emotional Deviance

While we cannot include all prior research results in this chapter, our most recent quantitative research revealed that the position suspects take with respect to the facts influences decision-making at every stage of the criminal process. For example, the extent to which they recognise the facts of the offence affects the decisions of prosecutors, who, depending on the seriousness of the offence, are more likely in the case of a full confession to opt for an alternative to prosecution, such as a caution (*rappel à la loi*) followed by a dismissal. In a previous collective research project,[72] prosecutors also indicated that they take suspects' behaviour at arrest into account, in the light of the emotions they expect of them at that time: 'While acting as duty prosecutor [by telephone], I get [the police officers] to tell me, I always ask how he has behaved since the arrest … When you're caught red-handed, you generally stay humble, discreet or sheepish.'[73]

The extent to which the suspect recognises the facts also affects the decision to place them in pre-trial custody, which occurs much more frequently when there is only a partial admission and, for some offences, in the case of denial. In the sentencing phase, the relevance of remorse flows from the combined weight of all philosophies of punishment, whether backward- or forward-looking.[74] Beyond the inferences judges draw in terms of dangerousness, suspects' feelings are also taken into consideration for retributive purposes, in defining their perceived degree of moral culpability. Case law provides frequent examples of this. In our corpus of decisions, we identified 67 judgments and decisions in which the degree of contrition appears explicitly among the criteria underlying the sentence. These decisions generally concern cases involving violent offences

[70] H Lu and TD Miethe, 'Confessions and Criminal Case Disposition in China' (2003) 37 *Law and Society Review* 551.

[71] DS Medwed, 'The Innocent Prisoner's Dilemma: Consequences of Failing to Admit Guilt at Parole Hearings' (2008) 93 *Iowa Law Review* 491.

[72] Danet (n 17).

[73] Prosecutor, I25.

[74] CD Bennett, 'The Role of Remorse in Criminal Justice' in M Tonry (ed), *Oxford Handbook Online in Criminology and Criminal Justice* (Oxford, Oxford University Press, 2016).

that impact upon the victims' body and their sense of intimacy and sexuality. As our materials contain essentially information drawn from appellate decisions, these references are regularly used when the appellate court upholds the sentence pronounced at first instance (16 decisions), to justify either leniency when the suspect has perfectly followed the 'emotional conventions' or 'feeling rules' that prevail within the courtroom, or harshness when the court attributes blame on the basis of emotional deviance.[75] Emotional deviance may also lead to a harsher sentence on first instance, ie a custodial sentence or a longer sentence. Conversely, if remorse or regret is found to be genuine, the court may deny the prosecutor's appeal seeking a more severe application of the law, may suspend a custodial sentence or may apply the criminal law generously[76] by reducing the length of a custodial sentence or even ordering simply a 'punishment of principle or a warning',[77] such as exemption from punishment or a simple fine. While mentioning emotional deviance is not enough by itself to justify a sentence,[78] the Court of Cassation has regularly upheld this type of argument,[79] including when defence lawyers argue that their clients could not express remorse because they denied committing the crimes, and so taking emotional deviance into account represented a violation of the law against self-incrimination.[80]

The multivariate empirical analyses we conducted confirm, all other things being equal,[81] the influence of both the extent to which the facts are recognised and the feelings mentioned by the experts. Other than in cases of acquittal, relative to a full confession, partial admission increases the probability of a custodial sentence by 2.1 and denial increases it by 2.3. In the files that include expert reports, we also see very significant differences with respect to the sentences handed down, depending on whether or not the experts note feelings of guilt, empathy for the victim, etc or a lack thereof. All else being equal, the mention of emotional deviance in an expert assessment also doubles the incidence of custodial sentences, and increases by 1.5 the probability of being sentenced to a prison term of at least 10 years in serious offences (crimes) cases (Table 2.4). These results must be viewed with caution, however, because we did not have access to what the suspects said or how they behaved during the hearing, which may have differed markedly from what the experts reported before trial.

[75] RA Hochschild, *The Managed Heart: Commercialization of Human Feeling* (Berkeley, University of California Press, 1983).

[76] Court of Appeal of Chambéry, 30 September 2009, No 09/00269.

[77] Court of Appeal of Caen, 6 September 2010, No 09/01088.

[78] Crim 27 September 2011, No 10-81.848; 23 February 2011, No 10-83.461; 11 July 2017, No 16-83.311.

[79] Crim 2 April 1997, No 96-82.528; 6 October 1999, No 98-86.975; 3 March 2004, No 03-82.843; 1 March 2017, No 15-87.069; 5 January 2017, No 15-81.079.

[80] Crim 4 March 2003, No 02-85.678; 23 May 2012, No 11-85933; 4 November 2015, No 14-84.009; 9 September 2015, No 14-86.423; 3 November 2016, 15-87.245.

[81] Once again, the explanatory variables are: the year of the judgment, the type of offence, the number of victims, prior convictions and the suspect's or accused's sex, age, nationality and employment status.

Table 2.4 Estimations of the probability of receiving an unsuspended custodial sentence

					95 per cent confidence intervals	
Modalities to be explained	**Independent variables**	**Significance**		**Odds ratio**	**Lower limit**	**Upper limit**
Unsuspended custodial sentences – all prosecuted cases, excluding acquittals (n = 1711)						
	Full confession			1		
	Partial admission	0.000	***	2.100	1.556	2.835
	Denial	0.000	***	2.354	1.669	3.321
Unsuspended custodial sentences – prosecuted cases that include expert assessments, excluding acquittals (n = 805)						
	Little or no feeling of guilt, shame, regret, remorse and/or empathy for the victim					
	No			1		
	Yes	0.002	***	2.073	1.326	3.239
Prison sentences greater than or equal to 10 years – criminal cases that include expert assessments, excluding acquittals (n = 621)						
	Little or no feeling of guilt, shame, regret, remorse and/or empathy for the victim					
	No			1		
	Yes	0.038	**	1.500	1.018	2.209

Moreover, in the post-sentencing phase, the rare published decisions handed down by the JAPs – 10 in our entire corpus – reveal that some judges take these emotional states into account when granting or denying sentence adjustments, as well as other types of privileges. For example, these judges have explicitly denied temporary leave from prison due to, among other reasons, the refusal to admit the crime by an offender 'little moved by remorse',[82] or denied such leave to others who admitted the crimes but '[did] not seem to really realise how serious they were' or '[made] statements devoid of remorse'.[83] The same was true for an offender who continued to 'minimise his participation', acceding only 'with difficulty to feelings of remorse and guilt' and who did not exhibit 'eagerness to compensate the victims, thus confirming a lack of empathy'.[84] Other decisions concern the refusal to reduce a sentence or limiting the reduction of

[82] Court of Appeal of Rouen, 12 June 2006, No 85/02006.
[83] Court of Appeal of Rouen, 24 March 2011, No 11/00406.
[84] Court of Appeal of Rouen, 20 July 2006, No 111/2006.

a sentence.[85] As it has done at the sentencing stage, the Court of Cassation has upheld such reasoning, especially the need for the offender to 'realise the consequences his actions [may have had] on the victim'.[86]

While a few judgments of the criminal chamber seemed to have signalled a reversal in judicial reasoning in the late 2000s,[87] this impression was short lived. Even though suspending a sentence for medical reasons has both medical and humanitarian foundations, in 2011 the chamber upheld a decision to deny such a suspension based on the fact that the expert had noted 'an inability to self-critique and underscored that the regrets, like the guilt, were superficial', the offender's dangerousness being partially linked to the fact that he 'only very superficially criticised his actions'.[88] In 2018, it also upheld the denial of conditional release for an offender serving a life sentence that was based on the report of the prison's social integration and probation department, which said that the offender claimed that 'his trial was purely conducted with a view to incrimination and that he is "as innocent as Christ," showing no empathy for the victim'.[89] After listing the reasons given by the lower courts, the Court of Cassation found that those reasons were 'wholly adequate' and within the courts' discretion.

Some authors tend to downplay the influence such criteria have in the post-sentencing phase, at least as concerns denial.[90] However, our sample of 99 socio-judicial monitoring files reveals that in 20 cases, the JAPs mentioned or explicitly relied on the extent of the recognition of the facts and the varying emotional forms that that recognition might take.[91] It is hard to determine the specific influence of these criteria, however, because they never appear alone but are always combined with other factors likely to weigh in the assessment of dangerousness and the potential for reinsertion (employment, housing, family support, etc). While the small size of our sample does not allow us to make any conclusive claims in this regard, sentence adjustments were granted slightly more often to those who had made a full confession (54.1 per cent, versus 20 per cent of those who denied the accusations) or who exhibited remorse or regret (66.7 per cent, versus 57.9 per cent in cases where such emotions were invalidated) or showed feelings of guilt (57.1 versus 45.7 per cent), shame (57.7 versus 38.5 per cent) or empathy for the victim (61.5 versus 42.9 per cent).

[85] Court of Appeal of Rouen, 26 August 2010, No 10/01083.

[86] Crim 4 April 2002, No 01-87.416.

[87] Crim 25 November. 2009, No 09-82.971; 3 February 2010, No 09-84.850.

[88] Crim 2 March 2011, No 10-81.070; see also Crim 9 April 2014, No 13-84.290.

[89] Crim 31 October 2018, No 17-86.660; 21 October 2015, No 14-86.990; 7 September 2016, No 15-81.679.

[90] Herzog-Evans, *Le juge de l'application des peines* (n 12) 100.

[91] Note, however, that only 45 files contain orders in which the reasons for granting sentence adjustments or temporary release are cited.

III. CONCLUSION

Despite the fact that contrition has progressively been eliminated as a requirement under French law, the materials reviewed in this chapter show that the expectation of contrition is far from having disappeared from the criminal justice scene. Like judges, police officers, social background investigators, psychiatric and psychological experts and probation officers all watch for signs of emotional deviance. They all look for them, not only in the suspects' words – always deemed unreliable – but also in their demeanour and non-verbal clues. They then draw inferences about the personality and psychological profile of the offender, and their dangerousness. The confirmation of emotional deviance by multiple professionals at each stage of the criminal process results in multiple penalties, from the procedural choices made by prosecutors and placement in preventive custody to the sentences handed down and the terms on which they are carried out.

These are not the only manifestations of the influence of emotional deviance. As suggested in the introduction, there should be equal emphasis on the issue of 'penal healthcare', which is one of the aspects of our ongoing collective research into the combination of healthcare and criminal justice. The vast majority of experts, judges and probation officers see therapy as a means to examine the commission of the crime and to treat emotional deviance, such that treatment is becoming a 'backup for legal mechanisms'.[92] The primary risk is that therapy will become a medicalised version of the old moral treatment.[93] The difference between the legal mechanism of conviction and treatment is that conviction concerns individuals only superficially. It requires formal actions, such as compensating victims and serving sentences, but cannot force offenders to feel 'certain emotions, change their inner relationship to such and such an act'. Treatment, however, involves 'techniques that are supposed to bring about real, deep-down change in the subject's relationship to their crime, their guilt, the victim and their punishment'.[94] This perspective is not so far removed from the reasoning behind punishment if, like Nietzsche, one believes that 'its value' is that it 'awakens a feeling of wrongdoing in the guilty person [and] views it as a genuine instrument [for triggering] the psychological reaction called "bad conscience," "remorse"'.[95]

[92] CO Doron, 'La volonté de soigner. D'un singulier désir de soin dans les politiques pénales' in L Benaroyo, C Lefève, JC Mino and F Worms (eds), *La philosophie du soin* (Paris, PUF, 2010) 287.
[93] Gautron (n 18).
[94] Doron (n 92) 287.
[95] F Nietzsche, *Généalogie de la morale*, II-14 (Paris, Flammarion, 1996 [1887]) 93.

3

Constructing Remorse: Interactional Dimensions of Finding an Emotion

SHARYN ROACH ANLEU* AND KATHY MACK†

Emotion, including remorse, is generated, recognised, labelled, interpreted and managed through social interaction in different settings. An important location for understanding remorse is the sentencing process in a courtroom, a social as well as legal setting. Sentencing law tends to assume remorse is a quality residing within and experienced by an individual that must be demonstrated in court, so its genuine presence (or absence) can be perceived and considered by the judicial officer. Using interviews with judicial officers, in-court observations and transcripts of sentencing hearings, this research investigates the ways remorse is expressed or claimed and how judicial officers assess these performances. The research shows how remorse, like other emotions, is constructed through social relations and interactions in the courtroom that are shaped by legal institutional requirements and everyday judicial practices. This construction of remorse, and of the ideal defendant, is a collective project involving the judicial officer, the defence representative and the defendant.

* Matthew Flinders Distinguished Professor, College of Humanities, Arts & Social Sciences, Flinders University, Australia.

† Emerita Professor, College of Business, Government & Law, Flinders University, Australia.
We appreciate the funding, financial and other support from the Australian Research Council (LP0210306, LP0669168, DP0665198, DP1096888, DP150103663), Flinders University, as well as the Australasian Institute of Judicial Administration, the Association of Australian Magistrates and many courts and their judicial officers. We are grateful to several research and administrative assistants over the course of the research, especially Rhiannon Davies, Colleen deLaine, Jordan Tutton and Rae Wood. All phases of this research involving human subjects have been approved by the Flinders University Social and Behavioural Research Ethics Committee. Earlier versions of this chapter were presented at the International Workshop 'Remorse & Responsibility in the Constructions of the "Ideal" Defendant: Comparing Cultural Expectations in Criminal Process', Cardiff University, 27–28 September 2018 and at the 30th Anniversary International Conference of the International Sociological Association Research Committee on the Sociology of Law (RC 12), Oñati, 19–21 June 2019. We appreciate the comments and suggestions made at those events. We also appreciate the guidance of Stewart Field and Cyrus Tata as editors in the development of this chapter.

I. INTRODUCTION

EMOTION, INCLUDING REMORSE, is generated, recognised, labelled, interpreted and managed in social settings. Feelings and emotion displays are shaped by the informal and formal norms that govern a situation or setting, with sanctions for emotions deemed inappropriate or out of place. The sociological concept of 'feeling rules' refers to these expectations about the emotions participants should feel and display in a situation. Feeling rules are integral to all social settings and interactions; they 'inform the sense of what is "proper" feeling in the performance and reading of emotional expression'[1] and 'prescribe (or discourage) certain emotions'.[2] These rules vary at different times and in different situations, and with different kinds of participants.[3]

This research draws on interviews, court observations and court transcripts to investigate judicial officers'[4] strategies to assess and manage expressions or claims of remorse from or about the defendant. It finds that judicial officers adopt a range of strategies shaped by the legal setting, the social relations and the interactions within that context, including feeling rules. These strategies convey expectations for demonstrating remorse and, by implication, the ideal defendant.

This chapter takes a sociological approach, emphasising the social relations or the 'interaction order'[5] as the context in which emotions are generated, identified, interpreted and managed. From this perspective, 'Emotions are not primarily seen as individual phenomena; instead, emotions are understood as *patterns of relationship*'.[6] Understanding emotion requires considering the

[1] M Scheer, 'Are Emotions a Kind of Practice (and Is That What Makes Them Have a History)? A Bourdieuan Approach to Understanding Emotion' (2012) 51 *History and Theory* 193, 216.

[2] S Shott, 'Emotion and Social Life: A Symbolic Interactionist Analysis' (1979) 84 *American Journal of Sociology* 1317, 1319; AR Hochschild, 'The Sociology of Feeling and Emotion: Selected Possibilities' in M Millman and RM Kanter (eds), *Another Voice: Feminist Perspectives on Social Life and Social Science* (New York, Anchor Books, 1975).

[3] S Bergman Blix and Å Wettergren, *Professional Emotions in Court: A Sociological Perspective* (Abingdon, Routledge, 2018); KJ Lively, 'Status and Emotional Expression: The Influence of "Others" in Hierarchical Work Settings' in J Clay-Warner and D Robinson (eds), *Social Structure and Emotion* (New York, Elsevier/Academic Press, 2008); KJ Lively and DR Heise, 'Emotions in Affect Control Theory' in JE Stets and JH Turner (eds), *Handbook of the Sociology of Emotions: Volume II* (Dordrecht, Springer, 2014).

[4] In this chapter, the terms 'judicial officer' and 'judiciary' are used to refer to any member of the judiciary, regardless of court level or type. In Australia, the term 'magistrate' refers to members of the judiciary who preside in the lower state and territory courts, except in the Northern Territory, where magistrates were given the title 'judge' in 2016. Australian magistrates are paid judicial officers, with legal qualifications, and are appointed until a fixed retirement age, in contrast to magistrates in England and Wales. The term 'judge' indicates those who preside in the intermediate and higher state and territory courts and all national courts.

[5] E Goffman, 'The Interaction Order' (1983) 48 *American Sociological Review* 1.

[6] I Burkitt, 'Decentring Emotion Regulation: From Emotion Regulation to Relational Emotion' (2018) 10 *Emotion Review* 167, 168.

context, the social relations, the interactions and the norms (formal and informal) that govern feelings and their outward display.[7]

Courtrooms are places of considerable emotion for participants, including the judicial officer. These emotions may involve multiple, even conflicting, feelings. Like all social settings, the courtroom is bounded by social norms regarding appropriate behaviour, interaction, language and emotion. Judicial norms require a detached and emotionless judicial demeanour. This aligns with the image of the impartial, independent judge focused only on facts and law.[8] Other participants, including defendants, are expected to observe norms of courtroom decorum and to display respect for judicial/legal authority. Thus, all participants must engage in considerable emotion regulation.[9] Nonetheless, at some moments in the courtroom, outward bodily display or expression of emotion can be appropriate, expected, even required. An example is remorse. Defendants are expected to feel remorse and to demonstrate this emotion through their statements and demeanour in court, as well as by their post-offence actions. Signs of remorse also have to be perceptible by others, especially the judicial officer, who must interpret such signs as (sufficient) evidence of remorse. This chapter investigates the social construction of remorse as part of the practical task of sentencing, which does not sharply delineate this emotion from others such as contrition, regret or shame.

After briefly describing the research design and data, the chapter addresses remorse as an allowed or expected emotion. It then investigates the ways in which remorse is constructed, expressed and interpreted by various legal actors in the course of determining sentence. The feeling rules used in these legal practices to assess the presence of remorse anticipate an ideal defendant who 'accepts responsibility and acknowledges voluntarily and sincerely her own criminal culpability'.[10]

II. RESEARCH DESIGN AND DATA

This chapter relies on three kinds of data, collected within a research programme investigating the everyday work of the Australian judiciary.[11] First, interviews were undertaken as part of a project examining social change in the judiciary,

[7] AR Hochschild, *The Managed Heart: Commercialization of Human Feeling: Updated with a New Preface* (Berkeley CA, University of California Press, 2012 [1983]).

[8] A Remiche, 'When Judging Is Power' (2015) 3 *Journal of Law and Courts* 95.

[9] S Roach Anleu and K Mack, *Judging and Emotion: A Socio-Legal Analysis* (Abingdon, Routledge, 2021).

[10] C Tata, *Sentencing: A Social Process: Re-Thinking Research and Policy* (Cham, Palgrave Macmillan, 2020) 97.

[11] Interviews were conducted with 38 judicial officers – 17 magistrates, 21 judges; 19 men and 19 women – in state courts throughout Australia in 2012–13. For more detail of the methods and research design of this research conducted as part of the Judicial Research Project at Flinders University, see S Roach Anleu, S Bergman Blix and K Mack, 'Researching Emotion in Courts and the Judiciary: A Tale of Two Projects' (2015) 7 *Emotion Review* 145; S Roach Anleu, S Bergman Blix, K Mack and Å Wettergren, 'Observing Judicial Work and Emotions: Using Two Researchers' (2016)

one facet of which was to investigate the role of emotion in everyday judicial work. Questions were open-ended, allowing judicial officers to discuss a full range of issues from their own perspective and in their own words. In these interviews, judicial officers describe emotion on the part of others, their own feelings and emotion display, and how they manage and respond to emotion.

Second, observations of non-trial criminal proceedings – including bail applications, adjournments, guilty pleas and sentencing – in Australian lower courts were undertaken to examine the ways magistrates deliver decisions, and their demeanour, time management and interaction with other participants. The study included observations of 30 court sessions involving 27 different magistrates in 20 different locations – capital city, suburban and regional – across Australia, from August 2004 to July 2005. The unit of observation was the 'matter', defined as an event in which the magistrate dealt with some element of a defendant's case, whether the defendant actually appeared or not. The study generated data on 1287 matters.

Third, where court proceedings were recorded, transcripts of the sessions observed were obtained, either directly from the court or as audio tapes or electronic audio files transcribed by the Judicial Research Project. This produced almost 2000 pages of transcriptions covering 1111 matters across 27 court sessions. (Three observed sessions were not recorded by one jurisdiction.)

III. REMORSE: EMOTION IN LAW

The place and interpretation of remorse is especially important in sentencing decisions.[12] In many jurisdictions, remorse is a mitigating factor a court must

16 *Qualitative Research* 375; S Roach Anleu, J Elek and K Mack, 'Researching Judicial Emotion and Emotion Management' in SA Bandes, JL Madeira, KD Temple and E Kidd White (eds), *The Edward Elgar Research Handbook on Law and Emotions* (Cheltenham, Edward Elgar, 2021); S Roach Anleu and K Mack, *Performing Judicial Authority in the Lower Courts* (London, Palgrave Macmillan, 2017); S Roach Anleu and K Mack, 'Law and Sociology' in N Creutzfeldt, M Mason and K McConnachie (eds), *Routledge Handbook on Socio-Legal Theory and Method* (London, Routledge, 2019) https://sites.flinders.edu.au/judicialresearchproject/.

[12] SA Bandes, 'Remorse and Criminal Justice' (2016) 8 *Emotion Review* 14; S Bandes, 'Remorse and Demeanour in the Courtroom: Cognitive Science and the Evaluation of Contrition' in J Hunter, P Roberts, SNM Young and D Dixon (eds), *The Integrity of Criminal Process: From Theory into Practice* (Oxford, Hart Publishing, 2016); L Presser, 'Remorse and Neutralization among Violent Male Offenders' (2003) 20 *Justice Quarterly* 801; K Rossmanith, 'Getting into the Box: Risky Enactments of Remorse in the Courtroom' (2014) No 12 *About Performance* 7; K Rossmanith, 'Affect and the Judicial Assessment of Offenders: Feeling and Judging Remorse' (2015) 21 *Body & Society* 167; I van Oorschot, P Mascini and D Weenink, 'Remorse in Context(s): A Qualitative Exploration of the Negotiation of Remorse and Its Consequences' (2017) 26 *Social & Legal Studies* 359; I van Oorschot, *The Law Multiple: Judgment and Knowledge in Practice* (Cambridge, Cambridge University Press, 2020); R Weisman, 'Showing Remorse: Reflections on the Gap between Expression and Attribution in Cases of Wrongful Conviction' (2004) 46 *Canadian Journal of Criminology and Criminal Justice* 121; R Weisman, 'Being and Doing: The Judicial Use of Remorse to Construct Character and Community' (2009) 18 *Social & Legal Studies* 47; R Weisman, *Showing Remorse: Law and the Social Control of Emotion* (Farnham, Ashgate, 2014).

take into account when formulating a sentence.[13] For example, South Australian legislation provides that 'the extent of the defendant's remorse for the offence' having regard to whether he or she 'accepted responsibility' and 'acknowledged any injury, loss or damage … or voluntarily made reparation'[14] must be considered in determining the appropriate sentence. Assessing remorse, and so fitting the penalty to the offender and the offence, is part of the individualisation process.[15]

Sentencing legislation anticipates that the defendant will actually experience and somehow adequately demonstrate or display remorse to the court, and that the judicial officer imposing sentence will interpret this information correctly from or about the individual being sentenced. However, the legislation provides little guidance on *how* to accomplish this. Rossmanith suggests that 'There is an implicit belief on the part of judges that, when it comes to assessing the genuineness of a person's remorse, they can read external signs for internal feeling'.[16] In this legal context, remorse is framed as an internal, individual emotion that the judicial officer can decipher and distinguish from an insincere or instrumental display.

Case law on sentencing is clear on *who* is thought to be best placed to identify remorse and assess its performance: 'the person who is best qualified to find the presence or absence of remorse is the original sentencer, whose findings in this respect, in the absence of glaring error, will rarely be interfered with by an appellate court'.[17] The sentencer has the opportunity to observe the offender in the courtroom, or in the witness box during sentencing (and perhaps during the trial, if there was one), and can interpret and assess direct, visual and personal information – or signs – regarding any claim or display of remorse. Bodily presentation, including posture, facial expression, gestures and tone of voice, can be directly observed, though they are unstable markers of emotion and heavily context dependent.[18]

Interpreting emotion is difficult because 'apparently contradictory bits of information … have to be accommodated and brought into a framework that makes sense. It is also complicated by the practical knowledge that expressions may not correspond with what is felt "inside".'[19] Assessing remorse is, therefore,

[13] G Mackenzie, N Stobbs and J O'Leary, *Principles of Sentencing* (Sydney, Federation Press, 2010); M Proeve and S Tudor, *Remorse: Psychological and Jurisprudential Perspectives* (Farnham, Ashgate, 2010).

[14] Sentencing Act 2017 (SA), s 11(1)(g).

[15] C Tata, '"Ritual Individualisation": Creative Genius at Sentencing, Mitigation and Conviction' (2019) 46 *Journal of Law and Society* 112.

[16] Rossmanith, 'Getting into the Box' (n 12) 17; see also LF Barrett, *How Emotions Are Made: The Secret Life of the Brain* (Boston, MA, Houghton Mifflin Harcourt, 2017).

[17] *R v Whyte* [2004] 7 VR 397, [21].

[18] Barrett (n 16).

[19] Scheer (n 1) 214; H Dillon, 'Cranking the Sausage Machine: A Magistrate's Perspective on Remorse Assessment' in S Tudor, R Weisman, M Proeve and K Rossmanith (eds), *Remorse and Criminal Justice: Multi-Disciplinary Perspectives* (Abingdon, Routledge, 2022).

relational: the defendant's performance of remorse relies on the judicial officer's capacity to perceive (markers of) remorse and an assessment that the outward signs are reliable indicators of genuine remorse.

There can be a wide disjunction between the defendant's outward demeanour – facial expression, body language, gestures, display of affect – and the judicial officer's inference, interpretation and assessment of emotion. Defendants might feel embarrassed, be inarticulate or lack confidence to display their (genuine) remorse according to the feeling rules that may or may not have been articulated by the judicial officer or conveyed by legal representatives.[20] An offender awaiting sentence might not have the opportunity to communicate their remorse in the formal, possibly intimidating, often busy courtroom. Alternatively, the incentives to express remorse in order to achieve a lesser penalty may not align with actual feelings.[21] 'Offenders may present themselves as remorseful at sentencing for the purpose of avoiding lengthy prison terms.'[22] This suggests 'surface acting', a focus on outward demeanour or presentation of self that may not be connected with an actual experience of the emotion.[23]

The 'performances of remorse'[24] or explicit 'expressions of remorse'[25] have to be enacted, interpreted and assessed against feeling rules, that is, expectations about appropriate emotions and their display attached to a model of the ideal defendant. A strong theme in case law and scholarship is the quest to distinguish true remorse, deep regret and contrition from feigned remorse and to provide guidance on the indicators of remorse, which typically relate to the offender's post-offence actions and behaviour. 'True remorse or genuine regret for wrongdoing is capable of being expressed in more ways than simply pleading guilty and thereby admitting all the elements of the offence … An exhaustive list of matters would be difficult to state.'[26] Remorse can be communicated through different kinds of information; it can be both 'a showing and a telling'.[27]

Courts have identified evidence that might indicate offender remorse: the guilty plea; a letter to victims; confessions to significant others; statements of regret and remorse to others, including on social media; statements to police officers acknowledging wrongdoing; cooperation with police; restitution or apology to victims; and/or assisting the victim in various ways.[28] These actions

[20] T Booth, 'Victim Impact Statements and the Nature and Incidence of Offender Remorse: Findings from an Observation Study in a Superior Sentencing Court' (2013) 22 *Griffith Law Review* 430; Dillon (n 19); K Rossmanith, S Tudor and M Proeve, 'Courtroom Contrition: How Do Judges Know?' (2018) 27 *Griffith Law Review* 366.

[21] Bandes, 'Remorse and Demeanour' (n 12); J Gormley and C Tata, 'Remorse and Sentencing in a World of Plea Bargaining' in Tudor et al (n 19).

[22] Presser (n 12) 805.

[23] Hochschild, *The Managed Heart* (n 7) 37.

[24] van Oorschot et al (n 12) 2.

[25] Weisman, 'Being and Doing' (n 12) 48.

[26] *R v Starr* [2002] VSCA 180, [26].

[27] van Oorschot (n 12) 98.

[28] Judicial College of Victoria, 'Victorian Sentencing Manual, Fourth Edition' (2020) https://resources.judicialcollege.vic.edu.au/article/669236; H Maslen and JV Roberts, 'Remorse and Sentencing: An Analysis of Sentencing Guidelines and Sentencing Practice' in A Ashworth and

can be, or be accepted as, signs of remorse. All entail reports of out-of-court action, including words and statements, rather than descriptions of internal states or feelings. They provide little guidance on how to assess the defendant's presentation of self, which the judicial officer observes in the courtroom.

To focus on 'true' remorse – as a discoverable 'thing', which just needs precise indicators to enable accurate identification – diverts attention from the social, relational and interactive nature of emotion experience and display. Judicial officers are active in the process of constituting remorse. Rather than being passive recipients of visible, objective information, judicial officers actively interpret claims and classify information as signs of remorse.[29] They must assemble pieces of information to interpret actions and behaviour as evidence of a feeling – remorse. Moreover, they may use emotion language in interaction that elicits in the defendant feelings of shame, embarrassment, guilt or remorse. To approach remorse as a thing ignores the reflexivity and reliance on a judicial officer's own emotion needed to assess another person's emotion display and feeling as appropriate.[30]

Approaching emotion as a relational process means that finding remorse is much more than registering or correctly labelling an emotion as present, absent or sufficient. It entails a process of construction that is embedded in the courtroom context shaped by the structural relations and interpersonal interaction between judicial officers and other courtroom participants. This process can entail ambivalence, ambiguity, uncertainty and opaqueness.

IV. CONSTRUCTING REMORSE

In this section, findings from interviews, observations and transcript analysis disclose judicial attitudes, practices and strategies directed towards identifying remorse. Understanding what judicial officers do with information presented by or about the defendant, including any emotional display and the inferences they draw about the 'actual' emotion, reveals the norms and feeling rules which inform their construction of remorse.

In interviews, judicial officers were asked about emotion, but not directly about remorse. While very few interviewees explicitly talk about remorse, they describe their perceptions of defendants' various emotion displays (and experiences), especially in relation to sentencing. They rely on such displays, along with other evidence, to assess a defendant's remorse in accordance with normative constructs of the ideal defendant. This construct contains feeling rules

JV Roberts (eds), *Sentencing Guidelines: Exploring the English Model* (Oxford, Oxford University Press, 2013); N Thomas-Evans, 'Assessing Indicators of Remorse in Sentencing: Can Courts Now Turn to Facebook and Twitter?' (2017) 1 *Western Australian Student Law Review* 38; Rossmanith et al (n 20).

[29] Bandes, 'Remorse and Demeanour' (n 13); Weisman, 'Being and Doing' (n 12).

[30] M Holmes, 'The Emotionalization of Reflexivity' (2010) 44 *Sociology* 139.

prescribing how the defendant ought to feel, what emotions they should experience, and to whom and how these should be demonstrated. As one judge states: 'my view is to allow people a reasonable latitude for the expression of relevant emotions'.[31] Remorse is a 'relevant' emotion. Adopting strategies to manage what he defines as appropriate or inappropriate expression and experience of emotion actively constitutes feeling rules and reinforces notions of the ideal defendant. This does not occur in a vacuum, but in the complex interactional setting of the immediate courtroom context, the inter-professional relations and the wider socio-legal context.

A. Judicial Interpretation of Observed Offender Demeanour

The judge interviewed above continues by emphasising the importance of direct judicial observation of a defendant's demeanour, including emotion display:

> [I]n sentencing I like to hear and see the accused. I know that I'm no better at judging whether they're little liars than anyone else and sometimes they are and sometimes they're smart but you do get a bit of a sense of what people are like and you know, whether they're genuine often or not and to see them express their emotions can be quite, you know, if they do break down in the witness box, that's a good sign that this is really, you know, a matter of great emotion for them and therefore you're, you're meeting them at a vulnerable place where you've got an opportunity to actually do something that will build on that opportunity.[32]

This comment indicates that this judge is well aware of potential dissonance between expressions of remorse and a genuinely felt subjective emotion. He suggests one value of direct observation – hearing and seeing the accused person – is that it enables the judge to interpret an intense outward emotion display – a 'break down' – as an expression of true feelings, perhaps of remorse or regret. He believes that (some) judges can 'sense', by observing and listening to an offender's testimony, whether or not an offender is 'genuine'. In the courtroom, where overall feeling rules require control and emotional restraint, 'to see them express their emotion' and 'break down in the witness box' may enhance the judge's (confidence in) assessment of genuineness, and perhaps finding remorse. 'That demonstrations of remorse are often described as "breaking down" or "losing control" or as symptoms of emotional collapse fits well with its perceived involuntary character.'[33]

[31] I 11. This data is indicated by the code 'I ##', in which the letter I identifies this as interview data and ## is the number assigned to the individual interviewee (from 01 to 38). Quotations are used verbatim and all identifying, or potentially identifying, details have been deleted. For more information on this phase of the research, see Roach Anleu and Mack, *Performing Judicial Authority* (n 11) 192–96.

[32] I 11.

[33] Weisman, 'Showing Remorse' (n 12) 125.

Such a display of strong emotion and vulnerability could be regarded as an implied acknowledgement of the legitimacy of the court and acceptance of the sentencing process. It suggests compliance with the normative requirements of the ideal defendant. The judge viewing this vulnerability as an opportunity to 'build on' perhaps suggests the potential for rehabilitation, a sentencing goal. On the other hand, a person who does not comply with the feeling rules and appears to be without emotion or as expressing the wrong emotions may be viewed as rejecting the authority of the court.[34]

In the lower courts, sentencing mostly proceeds after a plea of guilty, and after oral submissions by prosecution and the defence. (For unrepresented defendants, see the discussion below.) Judicial sentencing remarks are usually spoken aloud, in the defendant's presence, immediately after hearing submissions, in a crowded courtroom in which many other defendants are present, waiting for their cases to be heard. Time pressures are intense. The average sentence in the court observation study took 7 minutes, 15 seconds (ranging from 28 seconds to 41 minutes, 20 seconds), and the median time was 5 minutes, 25 seconds. Dillon, a former magistrate, describes this as a '5-minute dance that characterises sentencing in high volume criminal courts'.[35] Yet these courts must 'take into account … the extent of the defendant's remorse for the offence'.[36]

When sentencing proceeds after a guilty plea, the judicial officer has not had the opportunity to assess the defendant's behaviour during the presentation of evidence. If, as is usual, sentencing proceeds only on submissions from legal representatives, there will be no direct display of remorse from the defendant as in the higher courts as described above (and detailed in other research). Nonetheless, there may still be some opportunity for the judicial officer to observe the defendant's demeanour during the submissions and in response to any questions the judicial officer might ask. This demeanour is a source of information to be considered when looking for signs of remorse and formulating the sentence.

The demeanour or 'outward countenance'[37] of defendants, represented and unrepresented, was recorded in the court observation study (Table 3.1).[38]

[34] We are grateful to Cyrus Tata for this insight.
[35] Dillon (n 19) 17.
[36] Sentencing Act 2017 (SA), s 11(1)(g).
[37] Hochschild, *The Managed Heart* (n 7) 7.
[38] Two observers (typically the co-authors) each separately assessed and recorded the demeanour of each defendant, who was present in court, on a pre-printed template, selecting from: no apparent emotion; anxious/fearful; defiant/aggressive; and relaxed/at ease. At the end of the session, the observers discussed their assessments together, reaching agreement where there were differences, to enable data entry. For more detail, see Roach Anleu et al, 'Observing Judicial Work and Emotions' (n 11). The observers' assessments relied on external signs such as facial expressions, bodily movements, posture, tone of voice if the defendant spoke, and the content of any statements or responses to magistrates' questions. These assessments represent a brief summary of a defendant's apparent emotion and are subject to the various challenges of deciphering emotion. While the discussions between the two observers about these assessments aided consistency of interpretation, they remain perceptions of others' emotions, as are the judicial officer's perceptions, which may not be accurate: Barrett (n 16).

In these observations of non-trial criminal matters in lower courts, about half of the defendants were assessed as displaying no apparent emotion when appearing in court (Table 3.1). The next most frequent demeanours were anxious/fearful, and then relaxed/at ease. Very few displayed a defiant or aggressive manner. The absence of emotional display does not, in itself, indicate that no emotion was being experienced or that no remorse was felt, but may indicate high levels of emotion management.[39]

Table 3.1 Demeanour of defendant by type of decision

Demeanour of defendant	Sentencing decision	Non-sentencing decision
No apparent emotion	51%	60%
Anxious/fearful	30%	16%
Relaxed/at ease	15%	14%
Defiant/aggressive	4%	10%
*n**	260	526

Source: National Court Observation Study 2004–2005.

*These numbers only include matters where defendants were present in courtroom either physically or via video-link.

Defendants' displays of emotion changed with different types of decisions, reinforcing the expectation that sentencing is an emotionally demanding dimension of judicial work in court. When sentencing decisions are being delivered, almost one-third of defendants were recorded as displaying anxiety or fear. In all other decisions, this was less than one-fifth. Although defendants' displays of defiance or aggression are very rare, there is a slight reduction in this kind of demeanour when being sentenced compared with non-sentencing decisions.[40]

These findings may reflect defendants' practical concerns that a display of defiance will elicit judicial anger, whether justifiable or not, and negatively affect the sentence imposed.[41] However, the most frequently displayed demeanour by defendants when being sentenced is no apparent emotion (Table 3.1). From their interviews with defendants, Jacobson et al quoted descriptions of feelings during sentencing as being 'in a bit of a daze', 'your mind is kind of blank … a surreal experience', which the authors conclude indicate a 'profound sense of

[39] S Bandes and JA Blumenthal, 'Emotion and the Law' (2012) 8 *Annual Review of Law and Social Science* 161; AR Hochschild, 'Ideology and Emotion Management: A Perspective and Path for Future Research' in TD Kemper (ed), *Research Agendas in the Sociology of Emotions* (New York, State University of New York Press, 1990); Hochschild, *The Managed Heart* (n 7); AS Wharton, 'The Sociology of Emotional Labor' (2009) 35 *Annual Review of Sociology* 147.

[40] S Roach Anleu and K Mack, 'Performing Authority: Communicating Judicial Decisions in Lower Criminal Courts' (2015) 51 *Journal of Sociology* 1052.

[41] TA Maroney, 'Angry Judges' (2012) 65 *Vanderbilt Law Review* 1207.

unreality and numbness'.[42] The absence of emotion display suggests that there might be fewer signs the judicial officer can rely on to 'find' remorse.

These findings concretely identify sentencing as a situation requiring emotion work by the judicial officers, who must analyse or interpret any emotion display (or lack thereof) on the part of the defendants.[43] A judicial officer might interpret the absence of expected signs of felt emotion as disengagement from the court proceedings or lack of respect for the sentencing process, or it may not be significant in light of other signs of remorse, especially as presented by submissions from a defence representative. Indeed, the defendant may evince emotionlessness so as not to risk being inconsistent with the defence representative's submissions. A judicial finding of remorse in the absence of an expected emotion display suggests that locating remorse may be less a quest for a subjectively experienced emotion and more for appropriately displayed signs of remorse.

B. Defence Representative Presentation of Client's Remorse

In the lower courts, direct performance of remorse may be limited – defendants might not give evidence from the witness box, their time in court may be relatively brief – so it is necessary to look for signs of remorse apart from the defendant's demeanour. In the sentencing proceedings, submissions from the defence representative to the magistrate relay information about the defendant's apology, guilty plea or other post-offence actions, to provide a basis for a finding of remorse. Moreover, when defendants are unrepresented, a magistrate may not hear about their remorse at all.[44]

Typical statements to the magistrate fall into four overlapping themes,[45] in which the defence representative:

1. describes the offender's sentiments and actions, using feeling words that might convey remorse without using the term remorse or may describe additional emotions to strengthen evidence of remorse;
2. indicates that the offender shows remorse by changed behaviour or specific actions, such as participating in a rehabilitation programme;
3. maintains remorse has been demonstrated by the guilty plea, especially if early; and/or
4. undermines the claims of remorse by offering explanations or justifications for the offending behaviour or suggesting other reasons for apparent remorse.

[42] J Jacobson, G Hunter and A Kirby, *Inside Crown Court: Personal Experiences and Questions of Legitimacy* (Bristol, Policy Press, 2015) 195.

[43] Roach Anleu and Mack, *Judging and Emotion* (n 9).

[44] Dillon (n 19).

[45] These factors are not exclusive to the lower courts; the same markers may be relied on in assessments of remorse in higher courts, as indicated by case law and other empirical research, but that analysis is beyond the scope of this chapter.

The magistrate's remarks imposing sentence ordinarily include reasons. These remarks have (at least) two functions. First, they are responsive to the submissions received and so confirm or reject the signs of remorse presented. Indeed, it appears that the magistrate often does little more than agree that remorse has been demonstrated or state that there is remorse, referring to the early guilty plea as the main indicator. Second, they signal to others in the courtroom – defence representatives, prosecutors and other defendants waiting for their cases to be heard – what the judicial officer expects to hear and will accept as signs of remorse in other cases. This reinforces the importance of the social, interactive context in the construction of remorse.

(i) Feeling Words as a Sign of Remorse, without Using the Term Remorse

In several examples, the defence representative refers to the defendant's regret, or other emotions, without using the word remorse. For the magistrate, these submissions might imply (genuine) remorse, or they may sufficiently establish expected signs of remorse. In one case, where the offence arose out of a fight with a bouncer, the lawyer states: 'He deeply regrets this action because he's trained as a soldier to fight and to be disciplined and not overreact'.[46] Here, the regret is presented as magnified by the military training not to 'overreact', but that was not sufficient to deter the defendant from the criminal offending. In response, the magistrate provides extended sentencing remarks, speaking directly to the defendant, then links remorse to a sentence reduction, rather than relying only on the guilty plea for the discount:

> While I accept there is a full measure of contrition and remorse justifying a 25 percent discount in terms of the sentence which might otherwise have been imposed as a consequence of being found guilty, as opposed to pleading guilty ... I am prepared, at the age of 33, to regard your conduct on this occasion as an isolated incident unlikely to be repeated.[47]

Another defence representative claims: 'He's expressed regret for what he's done ... he did a very very stupid thing and as a result he was involved in a very serious accident and is lucky to be alive.'[48] The regret is made more authentic by the recognition that the defendant's actions were 'very very stupid' and he is 'lucky to be alive'. The defence representative's lengthy plea in mitigation is followed by the magistrate's brief statement without any detail of emotion assessment: 'I accept that – the reasons why the plea was entered, the other matters'.

[46] 960. Each matter is allocated a discrete number (from 1 to 1287). All names have been changed or deleted, participants provided with pseudonyms, where necessary, and all other identifying information removed. For more information on this phase of the research, see Roach Anleu and Mack, *Performing Judicial Authority* (n 11) 187–92.

[47] 960.

[48] 338.

Defence representatives also name other emotions allied to remorse, such as embarrassment or sorrow: 'He's feeling embarrassed and sorry that he finds himself before the court.' In the following excerpt, the defence representative describes a potent, specific emotion ('hates') and a general emotion state of being 'upset'. The defence comments further:

> She understands that in engaging in this act – this one-off act – she has essentially become in this one moment, everything that she hates about her husband and what she's upset about is that she's let herself essentially dragged down, or be dragged down, to this level, and that is part of the reason why she's resolute that this sort of thing will never happen again.[49]

There is a strong implication that the defendant feels shame, mortification and embarrassment, and expresses determination to desist, all presented to the judicial officer as possible signs of remorse, consistent with the applicable feeling rules and emotion display expected from the ideal defendant. However, while there was some interchange between the magistrate and the defence representative, the magistrate did not mention the guilty plea or remorse in sentencing.

In the following example, the defence representative describes a situation that suggests emotional collapse and emotions as involuntary and difficult or impossible to control.

> Ultimately, Your Worship – and it's to her credit – her own innate sense of honesty and responsibility came to the surface and she could not continue with the lying .... As your Worship will appreciate from the statement provided by her, she broke down in tears, called her mum and admitted that she indeed was the person who was driving the car ...[50]

The use of words conveying instinct and a pre-social state – 'innate sense' – and describing behaviour usually associated with emotion – 'broke down in tears' – suggests deep-seated, painful feelings which 'came to the surface'. It also suggests the dissonance between the surface acting, the feigned emotions and the deeply felt emotions could not be maintained. The claim that 'she could not continue with the lying' might imply she was remorseful, and experienced feelings of guilt, regret, shame, embarrassment. Although the word remorse is not used here, her admission to her mother that she was the driver accords with the kind of actions associated in law with remorse, as perhaps 'the ultimate expression of responsibility' – a characteristic of the ideal defendant.[51] The magistrate does indicate he finds signs of remorse:

> There's no doubt in my mind that Ms Wieler covered up her error, which was an error of judgment, and I put it down to the fact that she panicked and her youth and inexperience were a contributing factor to her conduct. ... the defendant attended the

[49] 359.
[50] 54.
[51] Tata, *Sentencing: A Social Process* (n 10) 106.

> police station with her mother, extremely remorseful and regretting and telling the police that she told them a lie ... I am persuaded by counsel that this is a matter that I need to have regard to the factors I've just indicated. She has pleaded guilty and she will get credit for that.[52]

(ii) Changed Behaviour as a Sign of Remorse

In the following excerpt, the defence representative emphasises remorse, reinforcing its existence and extent by describing the defendant's actions to help himself and to acknowledge the harm caused to the victim:

> Mr Jackson is certainly remorseful for what he's done ... so much that he's gone to get some assistance from the Health Commission and, also really, the apology, I think shows – my submission would be that it shows that there is some certain remorse there.[53]

This comment suggests a view of remorse as variable, and the more evidence of action or different activities – seeking medical advice, an apology – the stronger, deeper, more sincere the remorse. The magistrate turns to the defendant and asks: 'Is there anything you wish to say about this?' He responds:

> I just like to say that it doesn't look right on the record there and I have made a lot of mistakes, this being the biggest that I've ever made, more for the fact of my family and my wife, putting her and the family in the position. Work wise it's going to be very difficult because I do travel throughout all of Australia. I have to live with what I've done and I can assure you that I'll never appear before any court in Australia again.[54]

This offender acknowledges wrongdoing, accepts full responsibility and emphasises a commitment to change by promising 'never [to] appear before any court in Australia again'. This person describes actions past and future, and the harm done to family members, but does not use specific feeling words. 'I have made a lot of mistakes, this being the biggest ...', while a statement of fact, given the circumstances, seems tinged with regret, shame, guilt and contrition, even remorse. His first statement, 'it doesn't look right', might also intimate shame and embarrassment. The magistrate directly addresses the defendant: 'you seem to have – to your credit – take[n] this ... programme on board', and characterises this as 'a big wake-up call'. This emphasis on steps towards rehabilitation as part of the justification for a relatively light sentence may imply the magistrate's view that some degree of remorse existed, as a spur towards change.

Another defence representative describes the defendant's participation in a traffic programme, emphasising his 'punctuality', good attendance and completion, which suggests an 'ideal' defendant who not only complies with the

[52] 54.
[53] 59.
[54] 59.

programme's requirements, but is a model student. The programme is presented as integral to rehabilitation and 'a turning point', which suggests change, reform and rehabilitation – key elements of remorse.

> He is again sorry and remorseful for what has occurred, but he just doesn't understand what possessed him ... Further to what has occurred Your Honour is this; he's availed himself of the traffic offenders' programme and he has attended on eight sessions and has been marked good for punctuality; his attendance at lectures and so on is good; and participation in the programme good, and he has completed all the projects. All I can say Your Honour – I hope that this is now as the turning point in this young man's life.[55]

Yet in this matter, the magistrate did not accept the representations about remorse or the participation in a traffic programme as sufficient. Indeed, the magistrate's comments suggest frustration as a response to the representations:

> Mr Cavan please stand up for me. I can't lecture you. I'm just so tired of seeing traffic matters in this court. You've just dug an enormous hole for yourself on this occasion. You drove once during the period of de-merit points suspension. You got twelve months off the road and you've driven during that period as well. The court ... disqualifies you for a period of two years ... Now Jack you might feel inclined to drive in that period. If you do, you're going to be in serious trouble. Firstly, you're likely to go to gaol. Secondly, you're going to get another two years disqualification as a minimum. Thirdly you're going to get five years on top of that ... Now it's a savage penalty and you'll just have to not drive in that period. Do you understand me?

Forecasting penalties for non-compliance with the court orders may be the magistrate's attempt to alter the defendant's emotions, to induce more sincere remorse, regret, shame or fear, as motivation for the driving behaviour to change.

In some instances, the defence representative relies on emphatic language, almost entreating the magistrate to recognise or agree that there is (sufficient) remorse:

> Your Honour I cannot emphasise enough how much – how remorseful my client is, in relation to this incident. She has gone to seek counselling, she's put herself as an inpatient [at private psychiatric hospital dealing with mental health and alcohol and drug dependency], as soon as the claim was made for traffic accident damage ... if I can only stress the point, your Honour, the remorse that she has incurred and she instructed me that she wanted to send a letter to the person involved in the motor vehicle accident ...[56]

In this plea in mitigation, the lawyer enumerates the client's actions that are presented as signs of remorse: seeking counselling, admission as an inpatient, dealing with drug/alcohol problems, wishing to send a letter to the injured person (perhaps the insurer or lawyer advised against this). The defence

[55] 337.
[56] 1229.

representative's insistent claims of remorse bookend these statements: 'I cannot emphasise enough how remorseful my client is' and, in closing: 'if I can only stress the point'. While not explicitly mentioning the defendant's actions or feelings, the magistrate responds directly to her: 'Ms Morgan, I take into account what has been said on your behalf. You are convicted and fined'.

In these examples, defence representatives assert their clients' remorse, reinforced by describing activities and felt emotions which align with normative expectations of the ideal defendant, who accepts responsibility and undertakes self-work and discipline to remove factors that contributed to the criminal offending or to rehabilitate and reform themselves. Magistrates' responses to these submissions are not necessarily expressly linked to a finding of remorse or its absence; sometimes magistrates simply state acceptance.

(iii) Guilty Plea as a Sign of Remorse

Defence representatives often highlight the guilty plea as evidence of remorse, sometimes almost nonchalantly or in an automatic or routinised manner: 'and he shows his remorse by his plea of guilty in respect of the matter';[57] 'I'd ask you to take into account his plea of guilty at the first available opportunity and in my submission that shows a degree of remorse and contrition'.[58]

Interestingly, appeal courts and legislation are clear that a simple plea of guilty does not necessarily demonstrate remorse. Indeed,

> [a guilty] plea may have little, if any, component of remorse. Yet it seems regularly to be assumed by defence counsel that the sentencing judge will simply accept that, because a plea of guilty has been entered, the fact of remorse is established. That assumption is unsound.[59]

Perhaps recognising this, defence representatives may highlight benefits of an early guilty plea, such as saving costs or moving matters out of the busy court system.[60] These advantages are then reframed as relevant to remorse.

> Your Honour, in relation to sentence, his pleas of guilty demonstrate remorse and contrition. The facts demonstrate that my client made admissions to the police and certainly saved the community some dollars in not pleading 'not guilty' and having all these matters dealt with by way of what might well have been a two-day hearing and I ask from you some benefit for that.[61]

In the next example, in addition to a guilty plea, the defence representative relies on a pre-sentence report prepared by a probation or parole officer, or other

[57] 294.
[58] 886
[59] *Barbaro v The Queen* [2012] VSCA 288, [35]. See, eg Sentencing Act 2017 (SA), ss 39, 40 and 41.
[60] A Flynn and A Freiberg, *Plea Negotiations: Pragmatic Justice in an Imperfect World* (Cham, Palgrave Macmillan, 2018); K Mack and S Roach Anleu, 'Sentence Discount for a Guilty Plea: Time for a New Look' (1997) 1 *Flinders Journal of Law Reform* 123.
[61] 307.

professional (ie it is filtered), to reinforce that the client 'is truly remorseful'. Combining this material with the client's instructions to the defence representative suggests that the defendant's consistent claims of remorse across two professional settings are stronger or more credible than a personal emotion display, or claims of remorse, in court.

> Your Honour, the Pre-Sentence Report is a very full report and there's probably no need for me to go through it ... Insofar as these offences are concerned, it is indicated of course in the report that she is truly remorseful for her part in these matters in what she told the probation and parole officer in relation to these matters and also in my instructions. And her remorse and contrition of course is indicated by her plea of guilty.[62]

The magistrate addresses the defendant directly with lengthy comments and seems unpersuaded by the defence claims, in light of the defendant's 'not insignificant record ... and now you seek to minimise or trivialise your conduct as being somehow referable to matters in your past and how you were feeling at the time'. The assertions of remorse are diminished by the criminal record. The magistrate does not accept visible body movements as signs of remorse: 'You can shake your head and say that that's not likely to happen, but history tells us that from time to time that's exactly what does happen.'[63] The final statement, that the guilty plea 'of course' indicates remorse, is almost an add on, a statement of the obvious. This resonates with Gormley and Tata's notion of 'thin' performances of remorse that are attached only to the plea of guilty,[64] perhaps suggesting surface acting and less credible than corroborated claims for deeper, more authentic feelings.

In another example, the defence lawyer builds a picture of the offending as out of character for the defendant: 'he is a man that's not of a violent nature ... [this] case is a one-off situation ... he seems very pleasant – a shy young man normally'.[65] The magistrate states:

> I am prepared to accept of the plea of guilty entered in the cold, hard – and dare I say it – sober light of day, justifies the court accepting that there is a full measure of contrition and remorse for your conduct ... I accept that the plea of guilty entitles you to a discount in this matter, and I accept that the contrition and remorse began from the very beginning when, having waived your right to silence, you voluntarily told your side of the story and acknowledged your conduct when interviewed by police. Those are factors to be taken into account in mitigating the penalty; none of them justify the conduct for its own sake.[66]

This magistrate treats the guilty plea and remorse as complementary and distinct, though not completely: they point in the same direction. The guilty plea

[62] 994.
[63] 994.
[64] Gormley and Tata (n 21).
[65] 973.
[66] 973.

is not the only indicator of remorse. Because 'the contrition and remorse began from the very beginning', it is a distinct source of mitigation. The suggestion that the 'plea of guilty … justifies the court accepting that there is a full measure of contrition and remorse' ties the two together. The guilty plea is directly connected to the sentence discount (as per statute) and treated as a separate marker of remorse in addition to the actions before the guilty plea.[67]

(iv) Claimed Remorse Undermined by Explanation or Justification

If key components of remorse, and of the ideal defendant, are accepting responsibility, admitting the offences without justification or excuse and seeking rehabilitation or change, then offering explanations for the actions or behaviour can undermine the claims of remorse. As Presser found: 'The violent male offenders I interviewed excused or justified their violent actions. Remorse was generally precluded by these accounts.'[68]

In one case, the defendant phoned the police after hearing loud noises and screams at his neighbour's house, only to find that when police arrived, they were arresting his son. From the defence submission, it is not clear what actions the defendant regrets most – phoning the police in the first place or hindering the police as they sought to arrest his son.

> My client actually understands – he understands the seriousness of this matter. He tells me he understands the foolishness of his conduct on that night. He is very remorseful and regrets his actions … everyone was yelling at the police and basically my client was shocked and didn't believe his eyes when he actually saw his own son, Joshua, being arrested by police, because he was the one who called triple zero to come and help the neighbours … he is very remorseful … it was just an impulsive reaction as a father to protect his son and he was actually involved in hindering the police as is in the facts. He basically – if I can explain it this way Your Honour – it is similar to a father seeing his son being attacked by a lion.[69]

The defence lawyer offers an explanation for the defendant's actions as motivated by involuntary emotion: 'an impulsive reaction'. This description of the circumstances surrounding the client's offending suggests the situation generated several feelings, which are presented as normal, instinctual, parental reactions of protection. Perhaps the subtext is that, as the defendant's actions were normal given the circumstances, the client is not entirely responsible for his actions, so that there is no need for evidence of rehabilitation or change, which are normally required to demonstrate remorse. The repeated assertions

[67] Case law and legislation in many jurisdictions establish that the sentence discount for an early guilty plea is not related to remorse. While remorse can justify a reduced sentence, an early guilty plea is a distinct basis for a sentence discount, even if the defendant is not remorseful: see eg Sentencing Act 2017 (SA), ss 39, 40 and 41.

[68] Presser (n 12) 818.

[69] 301.

that the client is 'very remorseful', 'regrets his actions' and 'understands the foolishness of his conduct' suggests the defence representative considers this sufficient evidence of remorse, with nothing more. The magistrate does not directly address the claims of remorse, but concludes the sentencing remarks by addressing the defendant directly: 'Perhaps in future, take your time to explain your position and not – not enter the fray.'

In the next example, the lawyer identifies post-offence actions that may indicate remorse, especially desistance from illegal drug use, and offers several explanations or justifications for the criminal offending: depression, unemployment, bills to pay:

> Having had the opportunity to discuss these matters with him he certainly appreciates just how serious these offences are. He expresses to me that he is very remorseful for it and that it was at a time in his life that he was labouring a depression due to losing family members … He was unemployed at the time, had bills to pay, made the decision that this was the way he could make some quick money. He accepts now that that was the wrong action to take … He instructs me that he has been abstinent since November and has turned his back and mind and life away from any form of illicit drug use.[70]

In this brief submission, the defence representative presents the judicial officer with various kinds of information: the defendant's own subjective feelings, employment status, financial pressure, mental health, recognition of having made a bad decision, understanding of the seriousness of the offences and adopting a lifestyle change: the defendant 'has turned his back and mind and life away from any form of illicit drug use'. The judicial officer must interpret this information to assess what does or does not constitute remorse and formulate the sentence. However, the magistrate makes no particular comment about remorse, and imposes a fine and a good behaviour bond, adding: 'If probation and parole want you to do some counselling, even though in their report they think it may be unnecessary, you are to do it.'

In another matter, the offender's concern for her 'ability to pursue … [her] career to the fullest extent' somewhat undermines the claim of 'true' remorse.

> her main concern is that a conviction will affect her ability to pursue that career [business and accounting] to its fullest extent, and in this regard wanted me to highlight the fact that she was genuinely remorseful. She cooperated with the police, located and clearly admitted that the implement and the contents were hers.[71]

This submission presents fragments of the ideal defendant. The client's main concern seems to be anxiety about implications of a criminal record for her future career, rather than remorse for the offence. Even though the defence representative says she claims she was 'genuinely remorseful', perhaps she regrets

[70] 374.
[71] 1157.

finding herself convicted of the charges rather than feeling sorry for her criminal conduct. Evidence of post-offence actions – cooperating with police, making admissions – may not necessarily point to remorse, but derive from more individual and instrumental motivations, such as desire to get the matter over and done with, expectation of sentencing leniency following cooperation with police or having a no conviction recorded. In this matter, despite the legal representative, the magistrate turns to the defendant and directly seeks information about her studies, employment, income, residential address. In addressing these questions, the defendant says: 'I was hanging around a bad group of people and I – I have stopped doing everything [drug use].' Such changed behaviour can signal remorse.

C. Unrepresented Defendant Presentation of Remorse

In cases where defendants are without legal representation and provide their own plea in mitigation, they tend not to use the term remorse, for example:

D:[72] I'm sorry that I drove without thinking of the consequences –

M: All right

D: – and it won't happen again. I've got rid of the vehicle as well.[73]

***

M: Yes, Mr Windsor. Anything you wish to say?

D: Just sorry for my actions and probably glad I got caught before I injured myself or somebody else.[74]

The following example includes an express apology, as well as showing some empathy or consideration of the perspective of others, and the difficulties that were or could have been caused to them:

M: What do you wish to say, Mr Darby?

D: I'd just like to apologise to the cab driver for my behaviour and the police for wasting their time, I'm sure they've got better things to do than look out for people like me.

M: I think that's a good idea; are you prepared to write a letter of apology?

D: Yes

M: And pay $11.70?

D: Yes, and more if he wants it.[75]

[72] Transcripts have been given a consistent format: 'D' indicates defendant; 'M' indicates magistrate.

[73] 413.

[74] 517.

[75] 63.

The magistrate's response accepts these qualities as signs of remorse, and requests further concrete action as necessary for demonstrating genuine remorse.

In a different matter, a judicial officer's sentencing remarks explicitly identifies a letter of apology as demonstrating remorse: 'I [the magistrate] note that he has written what presents as a genuine, sincere letter to the victims, expressing his remorse for his behaviour'.[76] However, as articulated in criminal law, remorse involves more than an apology.[77]

The next example contains elements of justification and denial, as part of an admission of calling the police 'gutless', as well as feeling words relating to remorse:

> Your Honour, I'd like to say that a lot of those words I didn't actually say. I did say they [police] were gutless but I certainly didn't continue on as much as what was explained in there ... And I am very ashamed of what I have done. My – caused a lot of aggravation with my wife and I am very, very embarrassed and sincerely sorry for my actions and I was intoxicated that evening as well.[78]

The defendant uses emotion words relating to remorse, including 'very ashamed', 'embarrassed' and 'sincerely sorry'. The statement aligns with feeling rules regarding the display of remorse, yet they are undercut by justifications or denial of the offences: 'I didn't actually say', 'I certainly didn't continue' and 'I was intoxicated'.

These examples present unrepresented defendants using emotion words to describe emotions typically associated with remorse, such as regret, shame, embarrassment. They offer apologies, say they are sorry or describe post-offence actions that suggest a desire to atone for the wrongdoing and desist from future offending. These statements are similar to the representations made by defence representatives. Unrepresented defendants also express concern for the results of their conduct or empathy for those adversely affected, especially their own immediate family members. However, assertions of remorse are sometimes diluted by justifications or denial of their offending behaviour. This may result from their status as outsiders in the courtroom context, unfamiliarity with sentencing requirements, unawareness of the need to display remorse and less than full appreciation of the normative requirements of the ideal defendant.

V. DISCUSSION

Interview data, comments from appeal courts and other research suggest that, in the higher courts or in more serious cases, there is sufficient opportunity for defendants to express remorse directly through their demeanour and statements

[76] 70.
[77] Tata, *Sentencing: A Social Process* (n 10); *Barbaro* (n 59).
[78] 1254.

in court. In these cases, judicial officers allow and even require a space for emotion expression. The Victorian Court of Appeal states:

> A person wishing to rely on remorse as a mitigating factor needs to satisfy the court that there is genuine penitence and contrition and a desire to atone. In many instances, the most compelling evidence of this will come from testimony by the offender. A judge is certainly not bound to accept second-hand evidence of what the offender said to a psychiatrist or psychologist or other professional, let alone testimonials from family or friends, or statements from the Bar table.[79]

Judicial officers believe they can correctly identify emotion, especially remorse, when they see it, according to feeling rules they adopt and construct. The extent to which judicial officers can do this accurately is the subject of much discussion.[80] These feeling rules may be explicit, as in the legal requirement for remorse to be considered, or implicit as part of wider norms about courtroom decorum, judicial performance and notions of the ideal defendant who accepts their guilt.

In contrast, in busy, time-pressured, high-volume lower courts, the judicial officer's reading of remorse is less from a defendant's direct verbal or bodily expression in the courtroom and more from actions or feelings attributed to or claimed for the defendant by the defence representative. Emotion is read off action or behaviour, often from the guilty plea: 'I accept the pleas of guilty as an acknowledgement of contrition and remorse.'[81] In cases where remorse is not read exclusively from a guilty plea, the two might be interpreted as mutually reinforcing: 'I take into account the fact that you've pleaded guilty at the first opportunity and you've expressed remorse for your conduct.'[82]

In these courts, during the sentencing hearing, most references to remorse are from the defence representative to the magistrate, sometimes relaying information about the defendant's apology or other actions. Analysis of sentencing transcripts shows that the magistrate often does little more than agree that remorse has been shown or state that there is remorse, referring to the (early) guilty plea or other conduct, such as an apology or expressions of regret, as key indicators.

While some judicial comments, and defence submissions made in relation to sentencing, use emotion words, it may be that judicial officers, especially in the lower courts, do not think about remorse primarily as an emotion. Remorse appears to be identified through behavioural markers or actions: an apology, the assertion of remorse, efforts to change behaviour and an early guilty plea. The extent to which such signs – actions and demeanour – are reliable and valid indicators of remorse as a subjective feeling is unknowable.[83] Nonetheless, they can be observed, perceived, described and accepted by the judicial officer as sufficient signs of remorse to meet sentencing requirements.

[79] *Barbaro* (n 59) [38].
[80] Bandes, 'Remorse and Criminal Justice' (n 12); Rossmanith et al (n 20).
[81] 986.
[82] 412.
[83] Barrett (n 16).

This transcript data suggests the defence representative, the defendant and the magistrate operate within a set script: the early guilty plea, perhaps an apology and/or steps towards change, are key indicators of remorse rather than any overt, observable emotion display interpreted as remorse by the magistrate in court. These elements are also perhaps markers for the ideal defendant: one who pleads guilty (preferably early), apologises, expresses remorse and acts to demonstrate a reduced likelihood of future offending.

VI. CONCLUSION

These findings suggest several insights about the place of remorse in judicial practice. Perhaps the quest for 'real' remorse is less important or less possible in lower courts, or magistrates may accept the impossibility of assessing true remorse in most cases and adopt a more time-efficient formulaic approach.[84] The judicial officer's treatment of remorse in lower courts may be simply part of the routinisation of justice in these courts, with shorthand assessments made against a notion of the ideal defendant and associated feeling rules.

Regardless of court level, findings indicate acceptance (or assumption) of the capacity of judicial officers to recognise the signs of remorse. These signs may derive either from the defendant's demeanour – facial expression and bodily displays – or from post-offence actions and behaviour – principally the guilty plea – as well as claims of allied feelings: regret, embarrassment, shame. By accepting these signs, remorse is being legally constituted, though there may be no confirmed or confirmable link to any subjective feeling of remorse on the part of the offender. It may be that the feeling rules being employed to assess remorse are less about any actual feeling and more about the performance of remorse in court.

Judicial officers implement and constitute an image of the ideal defendant that contains feeling rules which establish the presence or absence of an emotion – remorse. This ideal defendant and performance of remorse is matched by the actions and claims of the defence representative and/or the defendant when making submissions on sentence. However, these judicial practices and the feeling rules they incorporate contain several questionable assumptions: that the outward display is directly connected to the appropriate internal feeling of remorse; that judicial officers can accurately assess bits of information – demeanour, post-offence actions, claims of remorse and assertions of other feelings – to conclude the presence or absence of remorse. This chapter shows how formal, legal sentencing requirements are translated through everyday interactional practices by participants in the courtroom process to constitute remorse and the ideal, remorseful defendant.

[84] Dillon (n 19).

4

Constructing Ideal Defendants in the Pre-sentence Phase: The Connection between Responsibility and Potential Remorse

LOUISE VICTORIA JOHANSEN*

Expectations surrounding defendants' emotive responses have been studied most extensively in the context of courtrooms as spaces that invite very limited emotional expressions while categorising others as entirely undesirable. This chapter, however, takes its point of departure at an earlier stage in the criminal process: at the probation service, where pre-sentence reports are issued to be used by judges in court as a basis for sentencing. The chapter argues that these reports constitute an important element in co-constructing emotional knowledge about the defendant. I analyse the interview that the Probation Service conducts with the defendant as a specific 'opening technique' to reveal the inner core of the defendant, as well as the defendant's stance towards the crime and the reasons underlying its perpetration. Probation workers' efforts to discern defendants' emotions work as a temporal prism, denoting a movement from the past of the deed and the reasons for it, to the responsibility of the present and the vision of a possible non-criminal future. The defendant's recognition of problems, and acceptance of eventual future treatment options, is argued to constitute a sign of 'indirect remorse'. The chapter therefore focuses on the ways in which temporality constitutes an integral part of constructing and anticipating emotional acts.

I. INTRODUCTION

THIS CHAPTER EXPLORES the pre-trial criminal process in Denmark, focusing on the ways in which the production of personal investigation reports constructs defendants as specific moral persons in relation to the

* Louise Victoria Johansen, Associate Professor, JUR Centre for Interdisciplinary Studies of Law, University of Copenhagen, Denmark.

criminal act in question. While the role of remorse in criminal cases has often centred on the courtroom itself – its communicative logics and constrained emotional frame[1] – other studies have explored how probation services document defendants' reactions at the initial stages of the criminal process.[2] The chapter thus attempts to connect two strands of research, on remorse and personal investigation reports, respectively. Based on a multi-sited ethnographic study that followed specific violence cases through the Prosecutors' Office, the Probation Service and the District Court, it asks how probation workers elicit and communicate defendants' attitudes and emotional reactions to the courts through personal investigation reports.

In Denmark, personal investigation reports are generally issued in minor criminal cases, where the defendant, if convicted, will be likely to receive a suspended sentence, often implemented with measures such as community service or treatment conditions. In these cases, the personal investigation reports are read aloud in the courtroom prior to the final remarks being made and before the question of guilt has been assessed. Judges then deliberate on the question of guilt and subsequently determine the sentence. This particular situation puts restraints on the probation workers. The reports are not allowed to address questions of guilt if defendants plead not guilty. However, probation workers are also expected to provide in-depth information on the relation between the alleged offence and the personal and social situation of the defendant. This makes both the conversation with the defendant and the subsequent reporting a balancing act in which probation workers weigh their words carefully in order not to compromise the defendant. More indirectly, though, they search for and convey connections between person and offence on multiple levels that express more subtle indications of possible guilt. Nevertheless, most legal actors regard the production and use of the personal investigation reports as an unproblematic and even mitigating element in the defendant's case. This perception makes it possible for courts to use the reports in order to gain a holistic understanding of each particular case and defendant,[3] and to extract explicit as well as tacit knowledge about the possible explanations for the offence.[4] Although personal investigation reports do not determine any particular sentencing outcome, they

[1] SA Bandes, 'Introduction' in S Bandes (ed), *The Passions of Law* (New York, New York University Press, 1999) 1–16; S Bergman Blix and Å Wettergren, *Professional Emotions in Court: A Sociological Perspective* (London, Routledge, 2018); S Roach Anleu and K Mack, 'A Sociological Perspective on Emotion Work and Judging' (2019) 9 *Oñati Socio-Legal Series* 831.

[2] LV Johansen, 'Between Standard, Silence and Exception: How Texts Construct Defendants as Persons in Danish Pre-Sentence Reports' (2018) 29 *Discourse & Society* 123; C Tata, N Burns and S Halliday, 'Assisting and Advising the Sentencing Decision Process: The Pursuit of "Quality" in Pre-Sentence Reports' (2018) 48 *British Journal of Criminology* 835; I van Oorschot, P Mascini and D Weenink, 'Remorse in Context(s): A Qualitative Exploration of the Negotiation of Remorse and Its Consequences' (2017) 26 *Social and Legal Studies* 359.

[3] C Tata, 'A Sense of Justice: The Role of Pre-Sentence Reports in the Production (and Disruption) of Guilt and Guilty Pleas' (2010) 12 *Punishment & Society* 239.

[4] Johansen (n 2).

do offer a possibility for courts to take the defendants' eventual remorse and ability to reflect on their own actions into account.[5]

A. Vocabularies of Motive: Responsibility and Acceptance as Indirect Remorse

In the courtroom context, 'moralising' is often understood as the act of asking somebody for a moral explanation or reaction. Scheffer[6] adds to this understanding of moralising in the space of the courtroom by referring to 'moralising outsourced' in the work of psychologists, probation workers and other experts who feed courts with additional information about defendants, collected in other institutional settings and within other knowledge frameworks. These experts add temporal layers to the courts' knowledge about the defendant through their biographical approach and their quest for signs of moral engagement during conversations. The process of moralising means that defendants are encouraged to reflect on their past in terms of admitting, explaining or excusing not just the acts, but their causes as well. In the present chapter, this point of view is translated into the term 'indirect remorse', because probation workers use the conversation with the defendant to probe into personal and social reasons for their crime that may be communicated as 'repentance' to the court at a later stage. Sarat[7] has argued that an offender's first step towards expressing remorse is to be able to act responsibly in relation to the offence. Sarat defines this responsibility as the awareness to acknowledge that one *could* have behaved differently. These specific ways of talking about responsibility are analytically coined in the chapter as 'vocabularies of motive'.

According to Mills,[8] vocabularies of motive constitute a framework of meaning that appears to provide adequate reason to explain a person's behaviour. Motives thus provide acceptable justifications within a group for individual and collective acts. Sarat and Felstiner[9] elaborate on Mills's concept in their analysis of lawyer–client interactions by highlighting its relational and negotiation dimensions. They state that vocabularies of motive serve to co-construct the past, present and future in a joint attempt to make sense of life events and interpret conduct. This meaning-making process always takes place in specific contexts and situations in which some vocabularies of motive seem more

[5] van Oorschot et al (n 2).

[6] T Scheffer, *Adversarial Case-making: An Ethnography of the English Crown Court* (Amsterdam, Brill, 2010).

[7] A Sarat, 'Remorse, Responsibility, and Criminal Punishment: An Analysis of Popular Culture' (1999) in Bandes, *The Passions of Law* (n 1).

[8] CW Mills, 'Situated Actions and Vocabularies of Motive' (1940) 5 *American Sociological Review* 904.

[9] A Sarat and WLF Felstiner, 'Law and Social Relations: Vocabularies of Motive in Lawyer/Client Interaction' (1988) 22 *Law & Society Review* 737.

appropriate than others. Transposed to the analysis of personal investigation reports, we may uncover the vocabularies of motive that the probation staff and institutional context make available to defendants and which appear legitimate in this particular conversation situation, and further contextualise defendants' own responses. This also implies that vocabularies of motive are constructed on an assumed 'normality' since some emotional reactions may seem more appropriate than others in explaining criminality. 'Motive' is thus more than a *reason* for crime in this particular context; the concept encompasses other aspects, such as responsibility, personal and social problems, or treatment options. I use 'vocabularies of motive' to analyse how defendants and probation workers can meet expectations to talk about possible relationships between person, social context and crime. This raises specific issues as to the reports' role in knowledge production to be used when judges decide on sentencing. Firstly, probation workers expect specific *ideal* defendant reasons and emotions to be expressed while considering other forms invalid. Secondly, the probation conversations and subsequent reports address and link past, present and future scenarios based on the defendant's emotions. This temporal dimension of emotions has attracted limited attention in a criminological context, but may deepen our understanding of how the criminal justice system uses emotions to understand defendants' present situations in light of the past and to facilitate an imagined non-criminal future.[10] Taking into account this temporal interconnectedness of reasons, responsibility and remorse in the process of report production, the analysis elaborates on the specific Danish social and cultural context in which it makes sense for the Probation Service (and courts) to perceive defendants' responsibility and remorse in terms of an acknowledgement of personal problems (such as addiction) and the acceptance of correspondent treatment options that it offers them. Research on pre-sentence reports has investigated issues such as how the reports reflect broader tendencies within contemporary sentencing[11] and, on a comparative note, how they may be constructed differently according to the penal system and penal ideologies in question in a particular country.[12] Following this line of thought, the chapter ends with a discussion of how 'remorse' may potentially be understood and articulated in this Danish legal context, guided by specific penal rationales and expectations regarding ideal defendant emotions.

[10] C Mattley, 'The Temporality of Emotion: Constructing Past Emotions' (2002) 25 *Symbolic Interaction* 363; R Weisman, *Showing Remorse: Law and the Social Control of Emotion* (Farnham, Ashgate, 2014).

[11] K Beyens and V Scheirs, 'Encounters of a Different Kind: Social Inquiry and Sentencing in Belgium' (2010) 12 *Punishment & Society* 309; K Hannah-Moffat and P Maurutto, 'Re-contextualizing Pre-Sentence Reports: Risk and Race' (2010) 12 *Punishment & Society* 262.

[12] S Field and D Nelken, 'Reading and Writing Youth Justice in Italy and (England and) Wales' (2010) 12 *Punishment & Society* 287.

II. METHODS AND DATA

Personal investigation reports[13] were first introduced in the Danish Penal Code of 1930 in order to identify and decide on supervision conditions in suspended sentences. They have since been used to address shifting penal policies such as community service, and recently to target an increasing amount of possible measures relating to a fine-grained risk assessment. Despite these shifting penal rationales, the structure of the report itself has remained remarkably identical regarding relevant topics that have to be addressed by probation workers.[14] At the time of this study, they were organised into seven topics: upbringing, family relations and friends/leisure time; housing situation; health conditions, different kinds of misuse; education and work; economic situation; future plans and probation officer's impression of the defendant; and documentation. These topics have been quite consistent since 1930, although worded differently over the years.

The present analysis is based on observations of conversations between probation workers and defendants, the writing process that the workers engage in afterwards and document analysis of the final reports themselves. Although this delimited phase of the penal process is the focus of the chapter, it views the production of personal investigation reports as being interconnected with other parts of the criminal justice institutions. Probation workers conduct the interview with the defendant and subsequently write the report while taking into consideration what other professional actors in other contexts and localities, for instance the court, might expect from these documents.[15] Research in European countries often describes judges' ambivalent stance regarding the quality and impartiality of the information conveyed in these documents.[16] However, Danish judges consistently find reports useful when sentencing, and they seem to trust the information given by the Probation Service.[17] Since they have pled not guilty, many defendants are reluctant to be interviewed for the personal investigation report, but are persuaded to do so by their defence lawyers on the grounds that it may benefit their case. Both defendants and probation workers thus participate in this 'conversation project' with the awareness that it may be part of a future trial in which other criminal justice actors will possibly make use of the information in the report.[18]

[13] These reports can be compared with pre-sentence reports in other jurisdictions, but they are read aloud in court in minor cases *before* the question of guilt has been assessed.

[14] Freelance 'investigators' usually prepare these reports and are not considered 'staff'. They are often students or retirees. I have chosen to use the term 'probation worker' (PW) instead of 'probation officer' to capture their non-committal status.

[15] J Gubrium and J Holstein, *Analyzing Narrative Reality* (London, SAGE, 2009).

[16] J Phoenix, 'Pre-Sentence Reports, Magisterial Discourse and agency in the Youth Courts in England and Wales' (2009) 12 *Punishment & Society* 348; Tata et al (n 2).

[17] Johansen (n 2).

[18] *cf* C Tata, *Sentencing: A Social Process: Re-thinking Research and Policy* (London, Palgrave Macmillan, 2020).

I draw upon 32 cases of assault in which the defendants all pled not guilty, in the sense that most of the defendants did not deny having had some sort of contact with the alleged victim, but disagreed on the sequence of events and with the way in which blame had been attributed. Crimes concerning violence were selected because a suspended sentence with retributive measures is a possible but not necessarily expected sentencing outcome in relation to these crimes in Denmark. Reflecting the general pattern in violence cases, men heavily outnumbered women in the sample of defendants (in fact, only one out of the 32 defendants included in the study was a woman); the average age of the defendants was 23, the youngest being only 15 and the eldest 65.

In the cases I observed, probation workers usually interviewed defendants at the offices of the Probation Service. The interviews lasted between one and a half and two hours on average. I was allowed to observe the interviews and to take notes, which appeared inconspicuous as the probation worker was also taking notes of the defendant's responses. Among other details, my notes focused on both the defendant's and the probation worker's emotional expressions concerning both the violence in the case and the interview situation itself, as communicated both orally and bodily. For instance, the defendant's anger, sorrow, discomfort or unwillingness to participate or answer certain questions were noted, as was the probation worker's eventual disapproval or irritation, which could lead to critical, targeted follow-up questions. I followed up on these conversations by interviewing the probation workers about their impressions of the defendant immediately after their meeting. These comments formed part of my field notes. The probation workers were later interviewed more formally with a view to connecting the specific observations I had made during their conversations with defendants and the workers' more general experiences and views. Nineteen probation workers were interviewed formally. The probation workers spanned an age range of 25–65 years, with a predominance of people aged over 50. While many of these workers were women, I conducted one-third of my interviews with probation workers who were men. The interviews lasted approximately one hour and were recorded and transcribed.

The Probation Service provided access to all 32 personal investigation reports issued on the basis of the conversations I had observed. In addition to these reports, I was given access to another 28 reports from the archives concerning violence cases. For the purposes of this chapter, all field notes, interview transcripts and reports were anonymised, read and coded in order to identify the use of emotional expressions and evaluations in their immediate conversational contexts.

III. THE CONVERSATION

This section analyses probation workers' specific techniques for handling conversations with defendants, including the underlying assumptions that guided their work. Probation workers approached the conversation with the defendant from the stance that they possess an inner core and emotional self which the worker should be able to access in order to elucidate personal problems indicating reasons for the crime. Since non-guilty pleas had been entered in all the violence cases, probation workers were not able to target culpability directly but needed to explore possible relations between the violence case and the person by probing into the relationship between the victim and the defendant, as well as issues such as uncontrollable anger or provocation. These problem identifications that are clearly crime-related were complemented by other foci such as substance abuse, general state of mind and addiction to gambling, pointing to a more general problem-identification strategy. Discussing the risk/needs nexus in contemporary correctional practices, Hannah-Moffat[19] suggests that professional knowledge of these issues is fluid and flexible in the sense that needs are categorised dynamically in order to meet targeted interventions. Setting the scene for the conversation, probation workers frame it as a specific situation that presupposes sincerity and unequivocal openness about a very broad range of issues that may be of potential interest for the identification of problems and possible actions.

A. Expecting Openness

Probation workers characterised the conversation as a particular situation in which the defendant must open up and reveal an inner self, if they wished to come across in a positive way in court. It is presupposed that this knowledge about the defendant will only be relevant *if* the court finds the defendant guilty, but the rest of the interview puts this issue aside and probes into possible relationships between the defendant's personal and social characteristics and the offence. It demands that the defendant scrutinise their personality and problems *as if* the violence in question had been admitted to.

Because probation workers sometimes experienced resistance from defendants during their initial conversation, they were very keen to explain that the report is in the best interests of the defendant and hinges on their cooperation. When beginning the interview, many probation workers would state the importance of acting with this degree of honesty and openness, as evidenced in the following quotations from four conversations documented in my field notes:

> PW: 'We have to find out what kind of person you are, what personality you have, so we can find an adequate punishment for you. It goes like this: I ask you a lot of questions … and you can decline to answer, but then again, the more sincere you are, the better you look.'

[19] K Hannah-Moffat, 'Criminogenic Needs and the Transformative Risk Subject: Hybridizations of Risk/Need in Penality' (2005) 7 *Punishment & Society* 29.

Defendant Michael, 35, says, 'Yeah, fine.'

***

PW: 'It's about peeling everything off you and seeing what's inside of you. What do you contain?'

Defendant Noah, 16, nods and looks down at the table.

***

Defendant Ejnar, 38: 'What do those questions have to do with my case, anyway?'

PW: 'It's because I have to make a description of the entire person. I also have to assess if there's a need for support.'

***

PW: 'I'm describing you and collecting as much as possible about you.'

Defendant Hans, 19, nods.

By using the term 'we' in reference to the relationship underlying the conversation, the probation worker speaking in the first quote indicates a common project between himself and the defendant. Their conversation will be characterised by the sheer amount of information shared, conveyed through the pains that workers take to 'collect' as much as possible in order to be able to describe the 'entire' person comprehensively. Other significant words in the quotes include 'peeling off', 'seeing inside' and 'personality', reflecting the fact that probation workers are required to really dig into the defendant's supposed inner self. The probation workers evidently assumed there was a core or inner layer existing within the defendant that they would be able to access during the conversation. The idea of an inner self presupposes that the defendant has to open up in order to grant access to this self, and this openness is achieved by bringing emotions into play as an opening technique. One probation worker explained how he perceived the relationship between himself and defendants during the conversation:

> Many [defendants], they also say, 'It's so nice that I get to talk about myself – for once, somebody is listening. And I seem to get a grip on some issues.' And sometimes, some of them break down crying. And where I say, 'Was it that bad?' 'No, it was okay, because I got to put into words, or to get closure on issues that I haven't, that I've had on my mind.' This way, you often get recognition for the fact that somebody shows interest for another person.

This quote describes the conversation as a space that sparks defendants' interest and elicits engagement from them. Mik-Meyer and Haugaard[20] document similar expectations in their study of labour activation-enabling services: the staff's goal to engage with their clients only seems achievable if clients reflect upon their emotions and difficult situation. Emotions thus become pivotal for

[20] N Mik-Meyer and M Haugaard, *The Power of Citizens and Professionals in Welfare Encounters: The Influence of Bureaucracy, Market and Psychology* (Manchester, Manchester University Press, 2017).

probation work itself. The probation workers in my study often used an element of persuasion to foster this emotional openness – the conversation is voluntary, but defendants should explain themselves comprehensively and open up for their own sake. This gives rise to a situation in which the defendant must exhibit openness and expose very personal matters as a prerequisite to fulfilling the aim of the conversation and in order to be viewed positively in court. Having assessed how probation workers tried to address and tease out the defendant's emotions as an entry point to facilitate the conversation and obtain relevant information, the next sections analyse how criminal reasons are brought into play by using specific temporal dimensions of emotions and, more indirectly, repentance.

IV. THE PAST: CRIMINAL REASONS

Mills[21] noted that 'vocabularies of motive' can serve as both an excuse for and an ascription of guilt, and can justify or reject certain actions. Even though the defendants in the present study had pled not guilty, probation workers searched for, and tended to find, potential explanations for the violent actions. Having set the scene for the conversation and its purposes, probation workers proceeded to ask about the alleged crime. Many probation workers would ask the defendant a leading question, such as 'Would you care to explain the background to the incident?', and most defendants were actually happy to recount their version of events, often finding reasons for them in the personal relations between offender and victim, such as being partners or friends. Probation workers also tried to find explanations in the defendant's suspected addiction(s), psychological instability or violent temper. The handbook that prepares probation workers for conducting these conversations, for instance, states that probation workers should pay attention to 'defendants' personal and/or social problems', and should ask if 'there may be eventual links between the crime and these problems, so that the risk of recidivism may be reduced if the problems are remedied'. This entails that probation workers should search for personal, typological or crime-related motives for the violent, criminal reactions.

These expectations for finding a connection between person and offence were obviously not always met. If the probation worker had tested all possible reasons – the result of drunkenness, provocation, jealousy, etc – without receiving any concessions from the defendant, then the report would often quite negatively conclude that the defendant seemed unrealistic or immature, or did not take responsibility for their actions. In the following paragraphs, two examples of conversations are cited, one which the probation worker reflected positively upon in our subsequent interview and another in which the probation worker's

[21] Mills (n 8).

initial positive stance towards the defendant was reversed. The two examples are then used to show how probation workers and defendants are expected to talk about reasons for crime.

> Frans, 19 years old, is charged with hitting another young man in the street late at night. Before their conversation, Officer Kirsten has read the indictment and remarks that it seems to be a violent assault. She thinks Frans sounded unpleasant during their phone conversation. Frans is then shown into the conversation room and sits in front of Kirsten clothed in a big hoodie; his hair is crewcut and he has large tattoos on his arms and hands. Kirsten: 'You are pleading not guilty?' 'Uh, yeah, part of it at least,' Frans answers. Kirsten: 'Well, you can't get community service if you haven't been through us. I take it you would prefer community service to prison?' Frans smiles and nods: 'Yes.' After giving some practical information and encouraging him to be open, Kirsten proceeds to talk about Frans's childhood. Frans tells her about his parents, who are both early retirees; they've both been to prison once. Kirsten asks how he grew up, and Frans talks about a caring family that he talks with every day. They know about the indictment.
>
> Frans: 'I've always been comfortable with by parents.' Frans smiles while he talks about his parents. Kirsten proceeds to ask about his girlfriend, whom he has been with for several years. He tells Kirsten about her and her family, whom he spends a lot of time with and gets along with very well, and concludes that her parents have been 'my second parents.'
>
> … Kirsten: 'How about your psychological well-being?'
>
> Frans: 'I've always been quite grown-up and taken care of myself.'
>
> Kirsten: 'Are you the type that gets into a lot of brawls?'
>
> Frans: 'I kind of liked it before, but now that you're older you just want to talk about things instead.'
>
> Kirsten: 'What about alcohol?' Frans says that he does not drink that often.
>
> Kirsten: 'Did you drink that night [of the crime]?'
>
> Frans: 'I can't remember that much, I was pissed. In fact, I haven't been drinking since that day.' Frans describes that he remembers both parties as engaging in the violence against each other, but he thinks it was stupid for his part and does not want to drink and put himself in that situation once more.
>
> Kirsten asks about his drug use, and Frans says that he has used hash maybe 10 times, and nothing else. 'I don't want to take anything to feel better about myself. I'm fine with myself.'
>
> They talk about Fran's job situation and future. He states that he just wants a driver's licence and some work. He mentions his tattoos and thinks it was stupid of him to get them. He is saving up in order to get them removed. Kirsten agrees with him and notes down under the section 'Future plans' that Frans wants to have his tattoos removed.
>
> After the conversation, Kirsten remarks to me that Frans was quite nice. 'It's a criminal family, but he seems mature in many ways. So they must have been able to give him warmth because he is not unfeeling.'

The probation worker moves from an initial negative impression of Frans, formed on the basis of the violence committed and their phone conversation, to an assessment of him as being mature and emotionally aware. This ultimately positive view of Frans comes from his openness and smiling attitude, among other things. Additionally, he reacts ideally when talking about his family, drug and alcohol consumption, work situation and future, in which he wishes to remove his tattoos in order to be eligible for a job. Even the fact that his family is 'criminal' does not change the probation worker's impression of him as being responsible and mature. He speaks about these issues within a comprehensible 'vocabulary of motive', recognising his reasons for the crime and responding appropriately; he was drunk, became involved in a public brawl and has therefore not drunk alcohol since. The probation worker deems him eligible for community service and does not have any further treatment suggestions.

In another conversation, the opposite development took place. The probation worker initially had a positive impression of the defendant, but this changed substantively during the conversation:

> Officer Mette says that Sune sounded very nice on the phone. She looks into the indictment and reads that Sune is charged with hitting a woman, Lillie Olsen, in the face with his fist in an electronics shop at four in the afternoon some months ago. Mette is a bit surprised when thinking about her phone conversation with Sune and thinks that he might have hit his girlfriend.
>
> When Sune arrives, Mette tries to understand the indictment: 'You're charged with hitting a woman in the head with your fist?' Sune: 'Yes, it was at an electronics shop where I work.' Mette: 'Did you know her?' Sune: 'No, in fact.' He says that he was depressed four years ago and received treatment for a short period of time. Mette goes on: 'Were you under influence of alcohol, then?' Sune says no. Mette: 'Did you hit a customer?' Sune: 'Yes.' Mette: 'Did she provoke you?' Sune: 'Yes, but that's no excuse, I was a customer myself at that point.'
>
> Mette then probes into his family life. He lives with his mother and sibling and is happy with this situation. He says he does not abuse drugs, and he is currently planning an education that could eventually lead him to a job as a pilot.
>
> After Sune has left, Mette comments to me: 'He did get some medical treatment but that was four years ago! He also seems unrealistic about his future. He doesn't take any responsibility for himself, either. I sense that he doesn't say everything about his childhood … But I think he can manage community service, he isn't ill. But something's quite wrong with him, hitting somebody in a shop, and he doesn't even know her!'
>
> When writing up her report, Mette remarks under the section 'PW's impression': 'Sune seems of average intelligence … It does not seem as if Sune takes any responsibility for his circumstances, and he seems unrealistic as to his future.'

The negative assessment of Sune and his actions is tied to the lack of emotional relation he has to his victim. Mette tried, unsuccessfully, to find a reason for his deed; the positive impression Mette got from the phone call led her to probe quite rigorously into possible reasons for the crime, but she would not accept his explanation that he is psychologically unstable since his doctor has declared him well and he does not take medicine. Mette moved from her impression of 'a nice young man' to one of lack of responsibility. She connected information from the doctor with the indictment, the conversation and Sune's apparently unrealistic future plans, to reach a conclusion of possible insincerity and inexplicable action. Even though Mette declared Sune suitable for community service, her negative comments about his irresponsibility and lack of sense of reality would eventually add layers to the court's impression of this particular defendant.

Both examples elucidate how the initial impressions and even family context of the defendant mean less for the probation workers' assessment of the defendant than their demeanour during the conversation and their reasons for the crime do. There is a difference between being drunk and fighting with another man, and inflicting violence upon a random (female) victim in a shop. The latter example does not seem to fit into an acceptable 'vocabulary of motive'.

Both defendants had probably felt provoked, but only one kind of provocation constitutes a suitable reason. The suitability is also linked to the defendants' reactions *after* the incidents. While Frans had stopped drinking, Sune did not seem to reflect on his own role in the violence sufficiently to actually change anything about himself. There is an important difference in the degree of responsibility each defendant takes, as Mette remarked in the report about Sune: he does not take any responsibility for his circumstances. Conversely, Frans did so to the extent that the probation worker characterised him as 'not [being] unfeeling', implying that she related his responsibility with his emotional capability. Not being unfeeling points to a self-awareness regarding one's role in the crime, suggesting the possibility that one could have acted differently.[22] This is a crucial step towards possible remorse.

Both conversations touch on the reasons for crime as a dimension of the past, and the ways in which the defendant reflects on his situation at present. This latter aspect is elaborated on in the section below.

V. (SELF-)DIAGNOSIS BETWEEN PAST AND PRESENT

As implied in the preceding examples, reasons for crime include issues relating to temper, drugs, alcohol or psychological state. In the following, I focus on the *ways* on which these kinds of information were elicited from defendants during the conversation.

'Self-diagnosis' analytically refers to the parts of the conversation in which the defendant is encouraged to reflect about themselves in relation to criminality, psychological conditions, etc. Rose[23] remarks that 'psy' disciplines – like

[22] Sarat (n 7).

[23] N Rose, *Inventing Our Selves: Psychology, Power, and Personhood* (Cambridge, Cambridge University Press, 1998).

psychology and psychiatry – have contributed to making people conscious about their inner selves. Modern institutions increasingly encourage people to reflect upon themselves. This 'self' does not exist in a vacuum, but is continuously defined and redefined on the basis of shifting historical perceptions of normality and deviance. The relationship between diagnosis and self-diagnosis is apparent in the ways in which probation workers, for instance, shift between providing their own evaluations of the defendant during the conversation and prompting the defendants to reflect critically on themselves. One probation worker explained his (working) strategy this way:

> Jan: Like, using this, under the part about psychological conditions, to say to them: 'How are you, and how's your temper?' I think it's a good idea myself, because sometimes it doesn't match with my [perception], and then I note that down under the part about 'my observations', but at least that's how *they* perceive themselves.

Jan's approach implies testing the defendant's self-perception against the probation worker's professional evaluation. This self-diagnosis highlights a related aspect of the conversation: the probation worker is not the only one to extract information from the defendant; the defendant should ideally also engage in self-presenting their lifestyle, habits and weaknesses. The techniques for obtaining this information may be more roundabout, as in this example in which the worker tries to coax out a defendant's self-perception:

> Probation worker (PW): 'How do you feel psychologically?'
>
> Ernst: 'Generally well, I think. I'm working on some problems right now.'
>
> PW: 'Are you seeing a psychologist?'
>
> Ernst: 'No, I haven't talked to a psychologist.'
>
> PW: 'I've read your personal investigation report from back in 2001, where I read you as a peaceful, non-criminal person, are you still that way?'
>
> Ernst: 'Yes.'
>
> PW: 'How is Ernst?'
>
> Ernst: 'Relatively extrovert, I think.'
>
> PW: 'Is he a happy person, or sad?'
>
> Ernst: 'Generally happy.'

Several of the probation workers used this third-person style when asking the defendant about their inner state, for instance: 'If you were to describe Ole Hansen [defendant's name], how is he?' or 'What does David Jensen's future look like?' The defendants often answered in the third person themselves. Probation workers thereby directed defendants' attention inwards to their 'self' by framing it as a third person that defendants might then reflect on.[24]

In addition to creating this personal level of reflection, 'self-diagnosis' was also a dimension in assessing the criminal act, and probation workers therefore

[24] ibid.

tended to ask specific questions to invite an evaluation of the offence that defendants were charged with. In violence cases, 'temper' was always addressed, for instance through questions such as: 'Do you often lose your temper?' or 'Do you blow up easily?' Probation workers often urged defendants to reflect even more deeply on the issue of temper, as in the following example from a conversation:

> PW: 'Do you have a lot of temper?'
>
> Idrisse: 'No, I don't get into a temper.'
>
> PW: 'Now I'm using stereotypes: "Idrisse" – is it an Italian …'
>
> Idrisse smiles and interrupts: 'It's Tunisian.'
>
> PW: 'Is it your genes? Is this why you think you have a bad temper?'
>
> Idrisse: 'I don't have a temper.'

While this probation worker quite openly admitted his prejudices, he wanted Idrisse *himself* to make the connection between the offence and his personality and/or culture, even though Idrisse had pled not guilty. By giving the defendant the possibility of diagnosing himself ('Is this why you think you have a bad temper?'), he is encouraged to embrace his ideal role as a self-conscious criminal. Fox[25] uses the concept 'criminal self' in her analysis of inmates and the ways in which expert staff within cognitive programmes try to get inmates to realise the connections between their inner selves and the offence. In order to redress their criminal inclinations and predispositions, the inmates must acknowledge that their inner self is criminal, violent, etc.[26] Probation workers similarly work with the relationship that is established between the defendant's self-regulating abilities and the expertise that the worker may offer.[27]

If a defendant has pled not guilty, the probation worker cannot insist on their recognition of a violent temper, but this lacking concession does not seem to influence the probation worker's conclusions as to the defendant's suitability for treatment. Probation workers instead diligently test the defendants' *willingness* to take part in the dialogue about their eventual problems and to scrutinise themselves. Acting responsibly (and cooperatively) during this problem identification process is crucial and reflects the adequate 'vocabulary of motive' in a present-time scenario. Self-reflection on the part of the defendant is also paramount to finding solutions for the future.

VI. ACCEPTING FUTURE TREATMENT

The reasons for the criminal actions as well as the processes of self-diagnosis may lead probation workers and defendants to a possible next step: for the

[25] KJ Fox, 'Self-Change and Resistance in Prison' in FF Gubrium and JA Holstein (eds), *Institutional Selves, Troubled Identities in a Postmodern World* (New York, Oxford University Press, 2008).

[26] ibid.

[27] Rose (n 23).

defendants to acknowledge their weaknesses and to accept the treatment options offered by the Probation Service. A crucial element of any personal investigation report is the defendants' willingness to cooperate with the Probation Service and, in the event that a probation worker has identified a possible problem, to react appropriately to it by either admitting an issue, proposing a solution or accepting treatment. For instance, the aforementioned defendant Frans admitted that he had had a hard time finding work and was now considering having his very visible tattoos removed from his body in order to appear more suited to and eligible for the job market. This was written up in his report as a sign of willingness to change his situation – he was taking responsibility. Similarly, drug or alcohol addiction can be framed almost positively if the defendant expresses willingness to enter into a rehabilitation programme. This emphasis on acceptance as a positive trait and a proper way of addressing problems hinges on the fact that the penal system can only prescribe treatment if the defendant is willing to accept it. The problem, however, seems to be that defendants do not always agree with the diagnosis underlying the treatment option, but may feel compelled to accept treatment in order to be eligible for a suspended sentence. Another issue arises from the fact that institutional solutions can become guiding for the diagnoses. Research about the relationship between staff and clients has shown that the goal of betterment may be influenced by the often limited institutional solutions available to staff.[28]

The overlap between these two problems is explored in the quotes below, in which the probation worker's knowledge about treatment options has a decisive impact on the proposal made to the defendant, irrespective of his non-compliance. During a formal interview with PW Peter, he explained to me how some of the issues in the personal investigation report are ultimately less important to him than others, although they may contribute to the selection of a certain treatment option:

> Peter: 'One thing I find less important is their financial situation, for instance – well of course, if they have a huge debt and a lot of expenses, and maybe they're compulsive gamblers, then you can see that there are some limitations in their possibilities ... Sometimes, when considering compulsive gambling, you may find a relation since some people need special conditions [to the sentence], and I've discovered that quite a lot suffer from this compulsive gambling ... And it's particularly important to dig into in order to find out if there are some measures that we should propose. After all, we have this treatment option in Middelfart [Danish city], and you can direct them to it ...'

Even though Peter does not view a person's finances as a core issue in the report, and certainly not in cases of violence, some situations demand a more thorough investigation into the connections between finance and compulsive gambling.

[28] Gubrium and Holstein (n 25); Hannah-Moffat (n 19); RP Hummel, *The Bureaucratic Experience: The Post-modern Challenge* (Armonk, NY, ME Sharpe, 1977).

Peter feels that he sees an increasing number of 'cases' of compulsive gamblers and links them to the available treatment options. Later during my field work, Officer Peter conducted an interview with a 29-year-old defendant charged with violence during which he tried to pinpoint this specific weakness in the defendant. During the conversation, Peter began inquiring into the issue of 'compulsive gambling' after having asked about the defendant's debts, amounting to the equivalent of £10,000, incurred due to a long trip to the Far East. The probation worker proceeded with the following questions:

> Peter: 'Do you play poker online?'
>
> Tarhan: 'Yeah, sometimes.'
>
> Peter: 'How much do you lose?'
>
> Tarhan: 'It differs.'
>
> Peter: 'Can you quit?'
>
> Tarhan: 'Yes of course.'
>
> Peter: 'Do you think you have a problem you should have treatment for?'
>
> Tarhan: 'No, not at all.'
>
> Peter: 'Do you know that you can get treatment for compulsive gambling?'
>
> Tarhan: 'Yes, but I don't suffer from compulsive gambling.'
>
> Peter: 'Is it a problem for you?'
>
> Tarhan: 'No, I don't think so.'

Peter almost insists on making Tarhan accept that he has a problem with compulsive gambling, and even though Tarhan denies it, he ends up accepting an eventual treatment option for this 'addiction', knowing that he will be closer to a suspended sentence if he does so. This approach is textbook in staff management of client needs since the institutionally available treatment options tend to shape their diagnosis of client problems. Peter has recently discovered a new treatment paradigm, including treatment for compulsive gambling, and applies it to conversations with defendants regardless of their indictment for violence and not guilty plea. Hannah-Moffat[29] describes how the act of assessing risk and need leads practitioners to define needs according to the availability of resources to resolve them and to disregard problems with no solutions, such as unemployment. Popularly stated, 'if there's no solution, there's no problem'.[30] While also noticeable in a Danish context, one might argue this correlation the other way around in the sense that the availability of resources or programmes may lead probation workers to search for and find problems in the defendant that are not overtly obvious but are underpinned by the desire to use specific programmes and interventions. This might

[29] Hannah-Moffat (n 19).
[30] ibid 42.

be readily explained as 'if there's a solution, then there's probably also a problem'. Categorising problems is thus inextricably related to treatment options – options that may change over time.[31]

Acceptance appears to be an ideal way for defendants to talk about the future. Interestingly, defendants do not even have to admit a specific vulnerability, as long as they accept treatment options and show willingness to participate in them.

VII. COMMUNICATING POSSIBLE REMORSE IN REPORTS

Personal investigation reports in Denmark are not expected to communicate the defendant's possible remorse, and it has been put forth that a moral account of the defendant and their level of responsibility is actually absent in reports.[32] Although this is in line with the official articulation of expectations for report writing, a different picture emerges when observing the specific conversations at the probation office as well as the subsequent report writing. They point at more or less subtle ways of communicating the defendant's moral abilities and possible remorse. The quotes below point at the translation from the conversation situation to encoded messages in the report that I argue may convey precisely morality and remorse. I focus on one of the seven obligatory sections in the report: the probation worker's impression of the defendant during the interview. Probation workers' expectations for openness in defendants are honed in this section on their own impressions, and consistent terms that characterise a 'good' conversation are often used. For instance, Probation workers will state that:

> NN tells openly and very eloquently about his personal circumstances.
>
> NN reflects on his situation … He seems thoughtful and mature.
>
> NN seemed honest about his circumstances.

The opposite situation might, however, lead to evaluations such as:

> NN answers the questions more or less cooperatively. At the beginning of the conversation, he seems uptight and difficult to establish contact with.
>
> NN showed hostility towards a conversation that he was probably not able to discern the meaning of.

These descriptions of the defendant consolidate the importance of being open and honest in order to be considered an *ideal* defendant. Some probation

[31] S Jöhncke, MN Svendsen and SR Whyte, 'Løsningsmodeller. Sociale teknologier som antropologisk arbejdsfelt' in K Hastrup (ed), *Viden om verden. En grundbog i antropologisk analyse* (Copenhagen, Hans Reitzels Forlag, 2004).

[32] RH Wandall, 'Resisting Risk Assessment? Pre-Sentence Reports and Individualized Sentencing in Denmark' (2010) 12 *Punishment & Society* 329.

workers expressed that they would put in a substantial effort to present the defendant as positively as they could if they had experienced this openness. Officer Esther explained this in an interview: 'If I've had good contact with them during the conversation I always write that "He seemed very honest", or something like that'. Openness is linked quite automatically with sincerity in this quote. Another probation worker, Lars, asked defendant Tom, 17 years old: 'How *good* a boy are you, when it comes to it? Do you have anything to say?' Tom said that he was sorry and that he repented what happened. Lars did not document this exchange because of the non-guilty plea, but he deliberately wrote his impression that 'Tom seems very mature and honest'. This quote conveys that the defendant has reacted *properly*. Even though the report does not often engage in direct moral language, the preceding conversation is laden with morality. In line with this, probation workers' overall positive impression of a cooperative defendant may lead them to connect this openness and cooperation with defendants' emotional response to the crime they are charged with. Almost one-third of the 60 reports I had access to conveyed defendants' attitude towards the crime as part of the probation worker's 'impression'. The following examples, taken from this part of the reports, describe the defendant's emotional reactions to the offence, even though the defendant had pled not guilty:

> NN has contributed positively and in a friendly way to the interview. He is very sorry about the case and what the victim perceives as having been subject to.
>
> NN underlines that he feels very badly about the case and looks forward to settling it, because it has given him big personal consequences.
>
> NN answers politely, very openly and cooperatively to the questions. A good rapport is established … As for the reasons for the present indictment, NN explains that he was very frustrated and had lost a lot in his life.

The examples illustrate how the reports try to convey the defendant's emotional reactions to the case, expressed through words such as 'feeling badly', 'being sorry' or 'frustrated'. Probation workers try not to incriminate the offender directly and choose to use phrases such as 'what the victim perceives having been subject to' or, more neutrally, 'he feels very badly about the case'. The remarks about possible remorse serve as an open invitation for defence lawyers to encourage defendants to elaborate on these feelings later in the courtroom. More importantly, statements about the defendant's openness, responsibility and acceptance of treatment options seem to link with these more explicit remarks about possible remorse. The expectation for specific emotional reactions represents a vocabulary of motive through which the defendant's actions are made comprehensible in light of their timing in the past, present and future. They presuppose being moral – and consequently open – about the past, responsible in the present and accepting of the future, constituting three layers of temporality that together convey an ideal defendant demeanour.

VIII. CONCLUDING DISCUSSION: THE TEMPORAL PRISM OF MORAL EMOTIONS

Research has set Danish personal investigation reports at the nexus between different penological considerations, drawing on both a modernist-welfare account and a more recent penal change towards risk assessment.[33] This is in line with international research stating that one should regard shifts between old and new penologies as coexisting and partly overlapping penal rationales.[34] For instance, Moore[35] states that the criminal subject may be defined quite differently now than in the 1960s, while the focus on rehabilitation seems to endure. My analysis has tried to add to this discussion about different penologies by showing how the interpretation and communication of defendants' emotional reactions play a mediating role for the relation between crime and punishment. It might be tempting to assume that a previous focus on defendant emotions such as repentance and morality has been abandoned in favour of actuarial risk assessment in present-day personal investigation reports. Although the language of repentance may be less protruding in these written reports, it still seems to thrive in the probation conversation and to be encoded in the report writing. Probation workers try to tease out adequate emotional reactions in the shape of openness, responsibility, self-reflection and a project of change, translating them into issues of cooperation, maturity, honesty and possible repentance in the report. This 'responsibilized subject'[36] indicates that the criminal can *choose* to change. The defendant is expected to embrace the need for normalisation because of their deviations from an imagined norm.[37] As Tata remarks[38] this process entails that defendants align themselves with the image of the 'ideal' offender who takes responsibility and acknowledges culpability. My examples from non-guilty pleas accentuates this issue since culpability is denied by defendants. The personal investigation report as 'technique', though, succeeds in transforming the issue of guilt into a therapeutic goal of motivation[39] that the defendant can accept regardless of the plea.

Field and Nelken[40] argue that 'the social construction of problems and solutions in relation to crime may be highly culturally specific, relating closely to the institutional relations and the social and political cultures of particular jurisdictions'. Danish judges seem to accept the validity of personal investigation reports,

[33] ibid.

[34] Field and Nelken (n 12); Hannah-Moffat (n 19); D Moore, *Criminal Artefacts: Governing Drugs and Users* (Vancouver, UBC Press, 2007); P O'Malley, 'The Risk Society Implications for Justice and Beyond' (1999) Report Commissioned for the Department of Justice, Victoria, Australia.

[35] Moore (n 34).

[36] ibid.

[37] ibid; Hannah-Moffat (n 19).

[38] Tata, *Sentencing: A Social Process* (n 18).

[39] Moore (n 34) 106.

[40] Field and Nelken (n 12).

and they similarly attach greater importance to defendants' acknowledgement of issues of addiction, uncontrollable temper, etc than to direct expressions of remorse. This is a tendency possibly sparked by a political and cultural understanding of how to prevent crime in Denmark.[41] The Danish penal system emphasises rehabilitation and treatment. To be able to offer treatment, however, one needs an offender who openly reflects on and copes with personal problems and accepts treatment. This necessity is met by interweaving emotions in the 'time–space'[42] surrounding the defendant and the criminal act as presented in the personal investigation report. Probation work is structured so as to enable workers to move back and forth between past, present and future events. Hannah-Moffat[43] similarly links present and future perspectives in correctional work by quoting Rose in saying that 'calculations about tomorrow should and must inform decisions made today'. This means that the professional power and assumed capability of calculating possible recidivism constitutes knowledge that has to be put to use in order to guide interventions in the present to avert a criminal future. Past, present and future dimensions should not, however, be understood as unidirectional, but rather consist of many decisions that are made by going back and forth in time.[44] If a defendant does not respond appropriately regarding their future plans, this may lead probation workers to revisit the indictment, for instance. The temporal aspect instead works to structure probation work itself and to ascribe meaning to defendant actions, risks and needs.

Added to this, and in light of the present analysis, one should also pay attention to the power of time in identifying and making the defendant's criminal deeds *emotionally* understandable, in that they serve to identify the defendant's emotional reactions and to situate them in time and space. Probation workers evaluate defendants' moral culpability and pathology in order to find a match between the defendant and the available institutional solutions. In order to be assessed as needy and worthy of these solutions, defendants are required to express an appropriate moral stance towards their flawed past, an active responsibility in the present by acknowledging the reasons for their problems and acceptance towards the future solution that the probation service makes available, even if they do not recognise the diagnosis or problem that it seeks to address.[45] This happens within a narrowly defined institutional vocabulary of motive that comes to exercise control over a limited range of acceptable moral reactions. Since these vocabularies are 'unofficial' and even discouraged by official politics of rehabilitation, they work inconspicuously in classifying defendants as more or less morally *ideal*.

[41] Johansen (n 2); Wandall (n 32).

[42] Scheffer (n 6).

[43] Hannah-Moffat (n 19).

[44] AV Cicourel, *The Social Organization of Juvenile Justice* (London, Heinemann, 1976 [1968]); Tata, *Sentencing: A Social Process* (n 18).

[45] N Mik-Meyer and D Silverman, 'Agency and Clientship in Public Encounters: Co-constructing "Neediness" and "Worthiness" in Shelter Placement Meetings' (2019) 70 *British Journal of Sociology* 1640.

5

The Paradoxical Uses of 'Culture' in Judicial Assessment of Defendant Demeanour and Remorse

IRENE VAN OORSCHOT*

This chapter examines how practising judges in a Dutch context mobilise the concept of 'culture' to make sense of defendants' in-court demeanour and their demonstrations of regret and remorse. It approaches the notion of culture as an everyday resource that judges use to make sense of individual defendants. In such practices of sense-making, culture operates in two contrasting ways: first, as a lens focusing on the defendant, in which 'culture' sharpens judges' understanding of the unique person and helps explain specific courtroom performances; second, as a 'veil' that clouds their understanding of the defendant as a unique individual. In so examining the paradoxical use of the idea of culture in actual judicial practices, this chapter suggests that culture as an explanatory concept has specific uses as well as misuses. As such, it is a double-edged sword, capable of illuminating as well as obscuring our socio-legal worlds.

I. REMORSE AND CULTURE: INTERPRETATIVE PUZZLES

IN MANY, IF not all, Western jurisdictions, remorse plays a crucial role in judicial decision-making. Understood as an authentic expression of regret and a willingness to make amends, 'signs of remorse'[1] tend to be understood as a sentencing mitigating factor in practices of 'judgecraft'.[2] However, a growing body of work has demonstrated that remorse is far from a stable 'sign'.

* Assistant Professor at the Department of Public Administration and Sociology, Erasmus University Rotterdam, the Netherlands. The author wishes to express her gratitude to reviewers, Prof Cyrus Tata and Prof Stewart Field for their careful reading of various draft versions and their invaluable comments and feedback.

[1] J Tombs and E Jagger, 'Denying Responsibility: Sentencers' Accounts of Their Decisions to Imprison' (2006) 46 *British Journal of Criminology* 803.

[2] C Tata, 'Sentencing as Craftwork and the Binary Epistemologies of the Discretionary Decision Process' (2007) 16 *Social & Legal Studies* 425.

Instead, it is increasingly understood to be a situated and variable accomplishment, demonstrated both in *words* – for instance, through apology or through story-telling and narrative – and in *actions* – by bettering one's life. As such, remorse is increasingly thought of as a doing and a telling.[3] Recent studies, furthermore, also point out that remorse does not exert a stable or uniform influence across offence and offender types; indeed, as a narrative the defendant tells about themself, it is in turn embedded in wider case-specific narratives, as well as broader discourses surrounding certain types of offences.[4] While the status of remorse as a mitigating factor is far from uncontroversial, these studies have made important strides towards explaining how, where and when remorse matters to judicial decision-makers. These observations have also broadened the scope of the social study of remorse to include issues of performance – in other words, how remorse is physically expressed – as well as issues of legibility and interpretation.[5] How, in other words, do judges *know* the offender is remorseful?

The answer to this second question – how do judges know – remains somewhat mysterious, not least to judges themselves. Rossmanith et al[6] point out that judges expect themselves to 'know it when they see it'. From contemporary studies of remorse, we learn that this 'knowing it when one sees it' is shaped not only by the narratives put forward by defendants in court, but also by defendants' physical demeanour and the extent to which they show themselves to be affectively invested in the proceedings and their role in the facts. Drawing out just how judges 'know it when they see it', Rossmanith et al[7] show that the performance of remorse is also an embodied accomplishment, the expectation being that 'the remorseful person will often express their remorse, whether consciously or unconsciously, through their physical demeanor, be it distressed, downcast or withdrawn'.[8] Johansen[9] similarly shows remorse to be an affective accomplishment: judges actively look out for the (performance of) feelings on the part of defendants. At the same time, judicial actors may also characterise such performances of emotions as strategic 'gamesmanship' instead of authentic expressions, a dynamic worsened in many instances by the very institutional context in which such expressions are elicited and demanded (for instance, in

[3] R Weisman, *Showing Remorse: Law and the Social Control of Emotions* (Farnham, Ashgate, 2014).

[4] I van Oorschot I, P Mascini and D Weenink, 'Remorse in Context(s): A Qualitative Exploration of the Negotiation of Remorse and Its Consequences' (2017) 26 *Social & Legal Studies* 359.

[5] K Rossmanith,'Cultural Sensitivity Training, Judicial Feelings, and Everyday Practice: conversations at the edge of research' in in S Field and C Tata (eds), *Criminal Justice and the Ideal Defendant in the Making of Remorse and Responsibility* (Oxford, Hart Publishing, 2023) ch 6.

[6] K Rossmanith, S Tudor and M Proeve, 'Courtroom Contrition: How Do Judges Know?' (2018) 27 *Griffith Law Review* 366.

[7] ibid.

[8] ibid 374.

[9] LV Johansen, '"Impressed" by Feelings – How Judges Perceive Defendants' Emotional Expressions in Danish Courtrooms' (2019) 28 *Social & Legal Studies* 250.

plea bargaining).[10] Indeed, the emphasis on authentic remorse may also clash directly with defendants' rights and interests, eg when they seek to contest or deny (parts of) the charges and, as such, run the risk of appearing to take insufficient responsibility for the events in relation to which they are charged.[11]

Importantly, studies point out that defendants' readiness and ability to perform remorse in ways legible to judges may not be distributed evenly over various defendant populations. Rossmanith et al[12] point out that there are several reasons for these differences. Whether or not defendants 'perform' remorse adequately may be a function of limited cultural and social resources and means (one has to know how to speak to a judge, a skill that may take a specific class background, for instance). But studies also point to ethnic and racial differences between ideas and practices of 'showing the self' and its emotions. Johansen also suggests that the legibility of remorse is to be thought of as tied up with cultural differences, and emphasises the way judicial understandings of cultural difference shape their interpretation of remorse.[13] Drawing on an intersectionality framework, she untangles how social categorisations shape the legibility of specific performances of emotions. Importantly, Rossmanith[14] similarly addresses the issue of legibility, suggesting that such differences may contribute to judicial unease when interpreting remorse in different defendants. Rossmanith especially stresses the centrality of affects like anxiety, frustration and unease in judicial encounters with defendants they find 'illegible', connecting these affects to the desire of judges to do right by the defendants. Cultural differences, in other words, may interfere with the taken-for-granted confidence judges experience when judging people's motives and interior feelings, and in that capacity disrupt the sense that they are doing a good job. Both the academic literature and the judges themselves – not least the judges I studied in the Dutch context – have yet to fully disentangle how conceptions of, and expectations about, cultural others shape judicial assessments of remorse. The nagging suspicion, here, is that what *looks* and *feels* like remorse to a judge may very well fail to resonate with other cultural registers within which the self articulates and communicates with authorities. So how, then, may we begin to think about the relationship between different cultures and remorse? And what do judges *themselves* have to say about this?

In this contribution, I take up this challenge. I want to zoom in on the ways Dutch lower court judges evaluate the remorse of defendants they perceive to be culturally different. Here, I am especially interested not in culture as an *analytical category*, with which we, as researchers, may try to understand what goes

[10] J Gormley and C Tata, 'Remorse and Sentencing in a World of Plea Bargaining' in S Tudor, R Weisman, M Proeve and K Rossmanith (eds), *Remorse and Criminal Justice* (London, Routledge, 2022).

[11] Van Oorschot et al (n 4).

[12] Rossmanith et al (n 6).

[13] Johansen (n 9).

[14] Rossmanith (n 5).

on in legal settings, but rather in culture in its informal, vernacular usage as an *everyday sense-making resource*, that is, a category judges mobilise themselves when they seek to understand what this case is about, and crucially, *who* this case involves. These questions are urgent for judges in the Dutch context as, typically, the legitimacy and fairness of a sentence is thought to depend on an accurate understanding and weighing up of the 'person of the defendant', including their circumstances in life, some sense of their biography, as well as their outlook and attitude. As such, these questions about the 'person of the defendant' are also instrumental in the enactment of individualised justice.[15]

In approaching 'culture' less as an analytical category and more as an everyday sense-making resource, I am indebted to anthropological theorising and critique of the concept of culture. As a discipline with a large stake in the culture concept, anthropology's engagement with the notion of culture is instructive, as we will see that anthropological approaches to culture and their criticism are reflected in the sense-making practices of the judges I studied.

In section II of this chapter, then, I will elaborate on these theoretical, anthropological debates on the culture concept, showing how anthropological theorising has increasingly started to approach it as a word people themselves use, mobilise, as well as contest. In so doing, I set the stage to start exploring 'culture' as a local sense-making resource in judges' sense-making and individualisation practices. In section III, I will then introduce my ethnographic fieldwork in more detail and comment specifically on the practice-based approach to judging I have developed, which is indebted specifically to an ethnomethodological concern with the local production of (social and legal) order, and to Tata's notion of 'judgecraft'.[16] I then move on to an examination of the way judges mobilise the culture concept to make sense of defendant demeanour and demonstrations of remorse (or, indeed, lack thereof) in section IV. In other words: *what* does the notion of culture help judges do? *How* does it help them to make sense of defendants' remorsefulness? And where does it *fail* to help them? In that section, I show how this cultural 'reading' becomes a way to attend to the unique individual – the 'person of the defendant' – in their sentencing decisions, for instance when judges frame a defendant's neglect to demonstrate remorse as a 'typically Moroccan' way to deal with the court. Yet at the same time, I also show how the notion of 'another culture' may also be seen to bar access to the unique individual, for instance when judges feel they cannot get a grip on the unique person because that person's 'culture' makes their 'real' and authentic motives thoughts and emotions illegible to them. In such cases, judges do not only suggest that the defendants' 'culture' may make them difficult to read, but also that seeing defendants through the lens of culture is still an impoverished way to attend to the unique individual 'behind' the culture. As such, judges both

[15] See especially C Tata, '"Ritual Individualization": Creative Genius at Sentencing, Mitigation, and Conviction (2019) 46 *Journal of Law and Society* 112.

[16] Tata, 'Sentencing as Craftwork' (n 2).

use and contest culture as an everyday sense-making resource. Culture, then, plays a paradoxical role: it can be mobilised as a way to get to know the unique individual – a lens – but it can also be taken as a barrier to such attempts to read the defendant – a veil. In section V, I comment on this paradoxical operation of the culture concept in judicial practice, commenting specifically on the way judges' understandings of culture may reproduce broader ethnic and racial disparities.

II. THE PROMISE OF CULTURE: LESSONS FROM ANTHROPOLOGY

In order to situate my account of the uses of culture, a brief discussion of its uses and theorisation is helpful. The following discussion will show that the notion of culture has become saturated with a set of specific analytical meanings, in that it refers to both symbolic and bodily performances. But this discussion will also make room for an appreciation of the idea of culture as a local resource. People – including judges – draw on culturally-informed sense-making practices. These sense-making practices are symbolic and performed bodily. In this section, I will trace in particular the genealogy of the notion of culture in the discipline of anthropology – the discipline most closely associated with its conceptualisation. Of course, I will be unable to do justice to the complexity of this history (or rather, multiple histories); instead, I want to draw on several disciplinary debates and criticisms in order to situate my attention to culture as an everyday resource.

The discipline of anthropology has a particularly fraught history as a colonial science.[17] The physical anthropology of the nineteenth century in particular was deeply tied up with Western efforts to measure and theorise relative levels of human development. The notion of biological race initially played an important role in accounting for such differences. Incorporating ideas about physical as well as temperamental differences, the race concept helped buttress Western self-conceptions as innately superior to colonised people. Slowly, however, the notion of culture made its entrance, although it did not at first wrestle free from its implications in Western-centric narratives of progressive development.[18] Boas, rejecting such evolutionary perspectives, is usually credited with proposing the word 'culture' in an attempt to leave biological race behind.[19]

For Boas, culture is 'an integrated system of symbols, ideas and values that should be studied as a working system, an organic whole'.[20] This emphasis on the

[17] EC Eze, 'The Color of Reason: The Idea of "Race" in Kant's Anthropology' in EC Eze (ed), *Postcolonial African Philosophy: A Critical Reader* (New York, Wiley, 1997).

[18] See, eg EB Tylor, *Primitive Culture* (Cambridge, Cambridge University Press, 1871).

[19] F Boas, 'The Instability of Human Types' in G Spiller (ed), *Papers on Interracial Problems Communicated to the First Universal Races Congress Held at the University of London* (Boston, MA, Ginn & Co, 1912).

[20] Boas, cited in A Kuper, *Culture: The Anthropologists' Account* (Cambridge MA, Harvard University Press, 2003) 56.

symbolic dimension of culture – the way culture manifests itself in texts, words, concepts and visual materials – resonates with later variations on the culture concept. In his seminal *The Interpretation of Cultures*,[21] Clifford Geertz would draw heavily on textual metaphors to render culture intelligible as an object of investigation: culture, for Geertz, is 'an ensemble of texts, themselves ensembles, which the anthropologist strains to read over the shoulders of those to whom they properly belong'.[22] This understanding of culture-as-text has been criticised in many ways,[23] not least because it tends to treat not only fieldworkers, but the people they study too, as readers of cultural scripts. As such, this metaphor fails to account for the improvisational, uncertain, even playful character of cultural life: the fact that culture is something done, enacted in complex interactions, as a matter of 'an interplay of voices, of positioned utterances'.[24] This emphasis on culture as a poetic, improvisational practice would soon be accompanied by a focus on the body. Moving further away from understandings of culture as a script, this turn towards the body opened up space to re-evaluate the anthropological canon as well as broaden its horizon once again. Drawing on a Maussian understanding of the body as 'man's first and most natural instrument',[25] the body was conceptualised not only as a surface onto which cultural meanings are inscribed and projected (see Turner's evocative notion of the 'social skin'[26]), but as itself shaping the way people inhabit space and interact with others and the self.[27] The body, to bring Butler into mind, *matters*.[28] The body, its surfaces as well as its gestures, is active in cultural practices.

Just as the 1990s, within anthropological theory, saw a turn to the body, so it also witnessed an emerging strand of criticism of the culture concept *tout court*. Kuper is an especially interesting critic here, for his approach to culture moves away from culture as an analytic, explanatory concept towards an understanding of culture as a word and idea that people themselves use to understand and order their social world.[29] He writes in a context in which culture is far from the benign, relativistic concept it was meant to be. Instead, he emphasises that the notion of culture, precisely in drawing borders between different cultures, has the capacity to reify and buttress group-based forms of power, and to gloss over historically and politically situated forms of inequality. An example from the Netherlands,

[21] C Geertz, *The Interpretation of Cultures: Selected Essays* (New York, Basic Books, 1973).
[22] ibid 452.
[23] See especially RM Keesing et al, 'Anthropology as Interpretive Quest [and Comments and Reply]' (1987) 28 *Current Anthropology* 161.
[24] J Clifford, 'Introduction: Partial Truths' in J Clifford and G Marcus (eds), *Writing Culture: The Poetics and Politics of Ethnography* (Berkeley, University of California Press, 1986).
[25] M Mauss, 'Techniques of the Body' (1973[1934]) 2 *Economy and Society* 70.
[26] TS Turner, 'The Social Skin' in J Cherfas and R Lewin (eds), *Not Work Alone: A Cross-cultural View of Activities Superfluous to Survival* (London, Temple Smith, 1980).
[27] TJ Csordas, 'Embodiment as a Paradigm for Anthropology' (1990) 18 *Ethos* 5.
[28] J Butler, *Bodies That Matter: On the Discursive Limits of 'Sex'* (New York, Routledge, 1993).
[29] A Kuper *Culture: The Anthropologists' Account.* (Cambridge MA, Harvard University Press, 2003) Kuper (n 20).

for instance, would be the way in which 'culture', together with 'ethnicity', has over the last 30 years become a powerful device to explain and justify inequalities in education and employment, as well as legal outcomes between the native population and various migrant groups: it is 'their culture' that is seen as the problem, for instance, when 'their culture' does not value democratic rights or the duties that come with citizenship. In so doing, such political uses of the culture concept also help to gloss over processes of discrimination and racism. In that capacity, the notion of culture is not a neutral, descriptive concept, but orders realities in specific ways – often by glossing over real conflicts and differences in (institutional) power. In a way, culture takes on the former duties of the race concept in legitimising relations of hierarchy and power,[30] especially so in former colonising nations and their governance of cultural others.

It is against this background that Kuper calls for attention to the various uses to which the notion of culture may be put, to the situations in which it is mobilised as an explanation or justification, and the limitations it introduces in our apprehension of, and possibilities for action in, the world. In so doing, Kuper's approach is reminiscent of the pragmatist dictum that concepts should first and foremost be tested according to their uses. In the words of William James,[31] in order for a concept to work as it should, it should help us 'hop, skip, and jump over the surface of life', that is: move, go about and *get things done*.

It is with this pragmatic sensibility in mind that I want to turn to the notion of culture and examine how judges use it to 'get things done' in practice. I am interested in what the appeal to 'culture' helps judges do, how it helps them make sense of defendants' remorsefulness, but also where it fails to help them, or actively works against their own stated goals of reading and accessing the unique person. Tracing these everyday uses of culture helps to show that we need to approach the cultural dimension of performances of remorse carefully and cautiously – both theoretically and politically.

III. METHOD: TRACING JUDGING IN PRACTICE

My exploration of the notion of culture in these sentencing practices is rooted in extensive ethnographic fieldwork in a Dutch lower court. Gaining access to the court in 2013, I started reading case files, conversing with clerks and judges, observing court sessions and, importantly, 'shadowing' judges. This meant that I read the case files of their appointed cases, which involved minor cases of petty theft up to cases of assault and domestic violence; sat next to the judges when they were working on and with these files prior to the court session; and again sat at the judicial bench (properly attired in robe and bib) during the court session.

[30] ibid. See also especially K Visweswaran, 'Race and the Culture of Anthropology' (1998) 10 *American Anthropologist* 70.

[31] W James, *Some Problems of Philosophy* (Cambridge MA, Harvard University Press, 1991) 247.

In doing so, I was able to trace the development and unfolding of roughly 250 court cases from case file to judicial decision.

The approach taken throughout this ethnographic project was characterised by a focus on the practical, ongoing and situated character of judicial 'case-making'.[32] Emphasising that 'doing justice' is as least as much a mundane practice of shuffling documents and talking with defendants as it is an esoteric intellectual practice of navigating sentencing philosophies, the project aligned itself theoretically with the idea of social and legal life as an ongoing accomplishment. In so doing, the aim was not to assume a priori a certain logic of practice, but to study how actors themselves order their practices in ways that make sense to them. Here, I was especially informed by practice theory, ethnomethodology, and science and technology studies.[33] Methodologically, I also took inspiration from Annemarie Mol's notion of praxiography:[34] a mode of paying attention not only to humans – the *ethnos* – but also to objects and the way these objects (eg case files, case summaries, written reports and verdicts included) shape practices.[35] Particularly relevant to the project has been Tata's critique of a series of binary distinctions characteristic of legal scholarship focusing on judicial practices.[36] Rather than adopting certain explanatory distinctions – rules versus discretion, rationality versus emotion, extra-legal and legal case factors – I was helped by conceiving of these practices as a craft and as a social process.[37] This emphasis on local ways of 'getting things done', and getting them done legally, translated into an approach that aimed to take seriously the way judges make sense of defendants, and particularly the way defendants' actions and words in court inform judges' appraisals of their willingness to take responsibility. Here, I was especially interested in the narrative character of these sense-making practices and focused on the way judges relate and 'story-tell' their way through their caseloads.

[32] See especially I van Oorschot, *The Law Multiple: Judgment and Knowledge in Practice* (Cambridge, Cambridge University Press, 2021); I van Oorschot, 'Ways of Case-Making' (Dissertation, Erasmus University Rotterdam, 2018).

[33] See especially H Garfinkel, *Studies in Ethnomethodology* (Englewood Cliffs, NJ, Prentice-Hall, 1967); TR Schatzki, K Knorr-Cetina and E Savigny, *The Practice Turn in Contemporary Theory* (London, Routledge, 2001); B Dupret, M Lynch and T Berard, *Law at Work: Studies in Legal Ethnomethods* (Oxford, Oxford University Press, 2015).

[34] A Mol, *The Body Multiple: Ontology in Medical Practice* (Durham, NC, Duke University Press, 2002).

[35] For examples of such analyses focused on case files, see I van Oorschot, 'Het Dossier-in-Actie: Vouw- en Ontvouwpraktijken in Juridische Waarheidsvinding' (2014) 10 *Sociologie* 301; I van Oorschot, 'Seeing the Case Clearly: File-Work, Material Mediation, and Visualizing Practices in a Dutch Criminal Court' (2014) 37 *Symbolic Interaction* 439; L Wissink and I van Oorschot, 'Affective Bureaucratic Relations: File Practices in a European Deportation Unit and Criminal Court' (2021) 39 *Environment and Planning C: Politics and Space* 1049.

[36] Tata, 'Sentencing as Craftwork' (n 2).

[37] C Tata, *Sentencing: A Social Process. Rethinking Research and Policy* (London, Palgrave Macmillan, 2020).

In tracing these sense-making practices, I learned that the individual defendant occupies a central position in these judicial practices. Dutch law requires of judges that they tailor their sentences not only to the gravity and circumstances of the offence, but also to the personal circumstances of the defendant, and concerns with defendants' attitude take centre stage when judges have to weigh different sentencing options against each other. Judges frequently look for signs that the defendant has bettered his or her life, and are generally sensitive to the morally charged narratives of wrongdoing, regret and reparation that defendants may offer them in court.[38] At the same time, these practices take place against a background of high caseloads, so that judges face limited time and resources to get to know the defendant.

As I hope to show, this dynamic – on the one hand, the demand that judges get to know the person; on the other, the reality of high caseloads – introduces the necessity to draw not only on outside information like pre-sentencing reports,[39] but also on certain cognitive short cuts. Some of these short cuts, I learned, have a narrative character, for instance when judges draw on a set of narrative typification practices that connect the individual defendant, the offence and the circumstances of the offence, as well as the defendant's remorsefulness, into a typified whole (eg the 'typical' angry young man accused of physical assault, the typical drug addict charged with petty theft or the typical explosive couple involving a male partner charged with domestic violence).[40] But judicial references to culture – 'their culture', a 'different culture', different 'cultural expectations' – also seemed to acquire dimensions of these cognitive short cuts, allowing judges to account for and understand variations in the way individual defendants speak and act in court. The following is an examination of the informal, vernacular use of 'culture' as an everyday explanatory resource to make of the individual defendant.

IV. THE CULTURAL FIX: SEEING THE INDIVIDUAL MORE CLEARLY – OR NOT?

Among the judges I shadowed, remorse tended to be thought of as – in Weisman's phrase – a 'doing and a telling'.[41] Defendants, for these judges, tend to appear remorseful if they manage to say they are sorry and look authentic doing so, and if they show themselves to have taken steps to 'better their life'. A crucial

[38] van Oorschot et al (n 4); Rossmanith et al (n 6); Weisman (n 3).

[39] See, eg C Tata, 'A Sense of Justice: The Role of Pre-sentence Reports in the Production (and Disruption) of Guilt and Guilty Pleas' (2010) 12 *International Journal of Behavioral Development* 338.

[40] For such whole-case narratives, see especially Tata, 'Sentencing as Craftwork' (n 2); van Oorschot et al (n 4).

[41] Weisman (n 3).

dimension of such performances, I came to realise, is also communicative and embodied: in order to appear authentically remorseful, they also have to appear engaged with the court proceedings. For instance, defendants who appeared withdrawn tended to be thought of as 'just sitting there' (*er maar een beetje bij zitten*), a phrase judges use to describe a certain listlessness or lack of urgency on the part of the defendant. However, this phrase is also evocative of a variety of performances that judges have difficulty 'reading' and interpreting.

These performances, I will show below, trouble judges' preferred mode of relating to defendants – one that emphasises frank, conversation-like speech, which they recognise as authentic – and as such may interfere with their confidence in having got to know the defendant. 'It's just, you don't always know what is going on', one judges sighs sheepishly as she comments on a defendant's seemingly non-committal and brief answers to her questions in court. *You don't always know what is going on*: the formulation here suggests that what is at stake is the legibility, or lack thereof, of certain words and actions. At the same time, judges continue to emphasise the necessity of 'getting to know the person', even if only in a pragmatic sense.

It is precisely here that a cultural idiom makes its entrance. Culture, in other words, can be mobilised to *account for* and at times *excuse* certain words and actions that do not fit judges' preferred mode of communication. It is a pragmatic notion, offering judges a quick cognitive short cut, an epistemological 'fix' in cases in which defendants diverge from a largely silent norm. To demonstrate what is at stake for the judges, I want to zoom in on three culturally and ethnically circumscribed types of defendants in particular, as these are the three groups that judges in this Dutch criminal court tend to distinguish. These groups are typically 'Hindustani' defendants; defendants of Moroccan or, less frequently, Turkish descent; and defendants with roots in the former colonies of the Dutch Antilles. These groups, judges perceive, come with their own, separate 'cultures', which are either nationally grounded in the sending country (Surinam, Morocco or Turkey, and the Dutch Antilles, respectively) or – especially in the case of Moroccan youth – are thought to be rooted in them findings themselves 'in between cultures' or a part of 'street culture'. While most of these defendants are, in terms of their citizenship, fully Dutch, the ease with which judges categorise using the idea of culture already demonstrates the hegemony of the idea of culture in the way judges perceive their defendants. But in these practices, I will show, the idea of culture nevertheless plays a paradoxical role as both something that illuminates the 'person of the defendant' and as something that obscures judges' understanding of the defendant.

While I will use these cultural categorisations – 'Morrocan', 'Hindustani' and so on – in the following to structure my discussion and, for ease of reading, will not continue to parenthesise them, it should be borne in mind that these terms have the status as local, 'emic' terms and do not make up part of my own analytical repertoire in this text.

A. Making Sense of Courtroom Performances: Culture as Lens

I will start with judicial perceptions of Hindustani defendants. The Hindustani minority is, in the Netherlands, to be traced back to migration from Surinam, a former colony in South America with a large Hindustani minority, itself rooted in the colonial mobilisation of Indian indentured labour in the Dutch colonies. Typically, Hindustani defendants strike judges as excessively deferential to the court: they tend to 'speak with two words' (*spreekt met twee woorden*, a Dutch idiom used to denote someone who shows his respect by always including a 'sir' or 'madam' after a yes or a no). This formulation is suggestive of limited talkativeness and overt deference to the court, particularly when it comes to the court's definition of the situation and its demand for a public expression of guilt and remorse. In terms of their embodied performance, one judge in particular told me that these defendants, in his experience, tend to be dressed to the nines (*jasje*, *dasje*), and always try to make an engaged impression in court while not necessarily 'looking me in the eye'. In both words and (embodied) action, we see here the two dimensions of what is perceived of as a typically Hindustani cultural mode of being. And while this Hindustani performance in court may not strike the reader as particularly problematic for judges, the judges themselves are not always quite at ease with it. To them, these defendants' (perceived) overt deference may also bar authentic and frank communication: sometimes 'one gets the impression they'd agree with about *anything* you say', one judge comments. Deference, then, is not always a good thing. When it becomes excessive, it can come across as inauthentic, making these defendants' expressions of remorse difficult to weigh appropriately.

Another troubling performance of remorse – or, rather, the lack thereof – is associated largely with Moroccan, and to a much lesser extent, Turkish defendants. If the desired mode of engaging with the court proceedings is one of frank and authentic speech, a typically Moroccan performance of culpability in these cases, for judges, has a much more equivocal character. 'It's their sense of honor, you see? *He* knows he did it, *I* know *he* knows he did it, but he's never going to *say* so in court', one judge explains his perspective. This sense that Moroccan and sometimes Turkish defendants cannot be entirely trusted to tell the truth, either about the offence or about their own perspective on the offence, is also communicated in a joke I heard a few times during my time in the court. It goes as follows:

Q: What is a 'Moroccan confession'?

A: It's when he doesn't file for an appeal directly after your verdict!

The joke suggests that Moroccan defendants show 'they know *I* know' by accepting their verdict without filing for appeal, further underlining the conception that Moroccan defendants have a rather flexible relationship with the truth. This generates specific problems for judges, especially because equivocal answers can also be read as ways to externalise responsibility for the offence – something judges tend to hold against the defendant when it comes to gauging their remorsefulness.[42] Here, my data resonate with Weenink's,[43] who showed that judicial actors in juvenile justice find it difficult to deal with what they perceive as these Moroccan youngsters' (supposed) cultural tendency to equivocate, that is, to speak in half-truths, to 'talk around' the point and to externalise responsibility. In these cases, the idea that these Moroccan defendants 'have a different culture' allows judges to understand these performances, although it does not necessarily make them more prone to excuse them: 'Listen, if they come in here all making excuses for themselves and avoiding responsibility, I'm done quite quickly', one judge comments on four defendants charged with a burglary turned violent.

The last group judges may comment on in terms of 'their culture' are Antillean defendants. Strikingly, this conception includes not only men, but Antillean women too: 'you don't want to get into a fight with them, I can assure you!', a judge laughs, referring to a female defendant accused of shoplifting. Here, Antillean defendants are thought to be quick to anger in court, their speech uncensored, undirected, 'all over the place'. In that way, they are also seen as disrespectful, of not showing the court the respect it is due. Concretely, this perceived 'aggressiveness' in court may lead judges to have to 'correct' defendants: '*I* am the boss here, you understand?', Judge Peters interrupts one of his defendants as he is protesting against the charges.

B. Everyday Critiques of the Culture Concept: Culture as Veil

At the same time, judges are also aware of the limited use of the notion of culture. They know that defendants who appear equivocal may 'turn around' in court. Frank defendants can become more aggressive or withdrawn over the course of the proceedings. Defendants who start out engaged and seemingly regretful may be caught in a lie, which will cast doubt on the authenticity of their professed remorsefulness. But the culture concept may also come with the sense, for judges, that while they try to use it to see the individual defendant more clearly, it actually clouds their understanding of the unique individual and their unique circumstances. In the following, I want to zoom in on these anxieties with regard to the culture concept, treating them as everyday forms of criticism of that concept that tell us something about the darker and less benign role culture plays.

One problem judges attach to the culture concept is the distinction between explanation and excuse. The notion of culture may explain certain behaviours, but it may not excuse them. Not looking the judge in the eye, for instance, is seen as a relatively benign cultural quirk that can be excused, especially because

[42] Tombs and Jagger (n 1).

[43] D Weenink, 'Explaining Ethnic Inequality in the Juvenile Justice System: An Analysis of the Outcomes of Dutch Prosecutorial Decision-Making' (2009) 49 *British Journal of Criminology* 220.

it is thought of as a culturally specific sign of respect: 'It's just the way they show respect', one judge explains. Here, like the judges in Rossmanith's study, judges may use the idea of culture to deliberately '[bracket] out physical behaviours that they would otherwise class as "shifty" and lacking respect'. Aggressive speech, however, is not as easily excused, nor is equivocation. An example of a judge's growing irritation with what he perceived as a defendant's equivocating 'process attitude' (*proceshouding*) is the case involving defendant Jalal, in which the judge was quick to interpret the defendants' confused answer to a question as a sign of his untruthfulness:

> Judge: So, have you indeed insulted this police officer?
>
> Jalal: Well what can I say? It was all very stupid.
>
> Judge: You'd been drinking, is that right?
>
> Jalal: yeah, I had a few. And those cops were just messing with me, getting up in my face …
>
> Judge: And does that happen more often?
>
> Jalal [visibly confused]: No, not at all!
>
> Judge [piqued now]: Yes it does. I see you've been arrested for an insult just like this before, have you not?
>
> Jalal: Well, that was in the past, wasn't it …

When witnessing this exchange, I remember the defendant get visibly confused when replying to the judge's question whether 'this happen[s] more often'; he seemed to interpret the question as pertaining to the regularity with which police officers harassed him and not – as the judge intended it – as a question about his criminal record. In such cases, the 'cultural fix' offers the judge a way to understand what he perceives to be Jalal's equivocations, but it does not excuse them: the judge later sentenced him in accordance with the prosecutor's demands, hence not mitigating his sentence.

A second problem judges associate with the culture concept is the question of the broader institutional and social context. With increased public attention being paid to police practices of racial and ethnic profiling in the Netherlands, some judges also point to the role of the police in causing or escalating specific encounters in cases of disorderly conduct or assault of a police officer. Interestingly, Judge Starr, judging a case very much like Jalal's, pointed out that

> The bigger issue that plays a role here is also of course the fact that many Moroccans feel they're treated badly by the police. Meanwhile we know the police does in fact seek out certain groups, people with a bit of a color.

Here, the judge presents an alternative 'reading' of the situation: the problem may not lie so much – or not solely – with the way Moroccan youth comport themselves, but rather with discriminatory attitudes and practices on the part of law enforcement. Here, the idea that certain actions (or lack thereof, for instance the lack of showing remorse in a way that resonates with judges) can be explained by means of 'culture' is deemed incomplete without a fuller understanding of the power relationships and lived realities of marginalisation as these affect migrant communities.

The last central problem with the culture concept, judges point out, specifically has to do with their investment in practices of individualised sentencing. Whether or not individualisation is best conceived of as a reality or a myth – or, indeed, a ritual with very real institutional and performative effects[44] – the judges I worked with emphasise their concern with 'getting to know the defendant' and 'getting their story', in order to tailor their sentences accordingly. While, on the one hand, culture may help them explain and understand specific embodied and discursive performances in court, some judges also express the anxiety that, when mobilising the culture concept to understand a defendant, they are nevertheless missing out on the 'person *behind* the culture' (*de persoon achter de cultuur*). While the appeal to 'their culture', then, allows judges to make sense of certain performances of culpability and remorse, 'their culture' also functions as something the judge may have to look behind in order to arrive at a sense of the real defendant.

In summary, then, this account of the way culture operates in judicial practices, and is criticised in such practices, shows that culture plays a crucial, if paradoxical, role in individualising sentencing, particularly in the way it informs judicial interpretations of remorse. The pragmatic and local appeal to culture allows judges an appreciation of the individual even if the individual 'gives off' impressions that do not resonate well with judicial understandings of what constitutes frank and authentic communication. 'It is because of their culture', then, is a way to place between brackets a performance of remorse that would otherwise fail to register as remorse. However, judges know that culture is always an imperfect way to understand and apprehend individual differences; there is always a 'person *behind* the culture'. Here, culture functions less as an interpretative tool that renders certain performances more intelligible than as a screen behind which hides the 'real' defendant. In precisely this double sense, they *see through culture*: on the one hand, they can use it as a lens to see the individual defendant more clearly; on the other, it operates as a veil that the judge needs to strive to see through or beyond, to either see the unique individual or the power relationships that shape that individual's life. My analysis here resonates with the way visual studies scholar WJT Mitchell understands race to operate within certain contexts: on the one hand, as a lens through which we can try to apprehend social life and, on the other hand, as a veil that continually defers encounters with the individual subject presumed to exist 'behind' it.[45]

In this sense, this chapter is productively read in conversation with Rossmanith's chapter in this book.[46] Emphasising the desire for judges to be

[44] Tata, 'Ritual Individualization' (n 15).
[45] WJT Mitchell, *Seeing through Race* (Cambridge, MA, Harvard University Press, 2012).
[46] Rossmanith (n 5).

competent at 'reading people', her chapter highlights the potential of cultural sensitivity training to contribute, if not to a more accurate assessment of remorse, then at least to a heightened sense of adequacy and competence on the part of judicial professionals. At the same time, and as demonstrated in this chapter as well, the conceptual tools this cultural sensitivity training offers may not always work in the desired way. As Rossmanith[47] elaborates:

> When judges receive training about 'other cultures', they may have the sense that a code has been cracked and that they now possess tools with which to read people. However, judges may experience frustration and a degree of anxiety when the offender sitting before them in court remains illegible.

Rossmanith notes that in these cases, productive uncertainty about the defendants' motives and remorse may turn into frustration, and that judges caught in this position may seek to blame the defendant for 'failing to make himself understood'. The dilemma outlined in this chapter similarly pivots on the legibility of defendants, but highlights an additional problem with a reliance on culture, which is rooted in judicial professionals' investment in individualised sentencing. Not only may a cultural register fail to render a defendant legible; culture itself may be perceived to stand between the judge and an accurate sense of the 'individual behind the culture'. Paradoxically, *more* cultural sensitivity training may in fact make judges *less* able to access the individual defendant in terms they themselves are comfortable with.

In the conclusion, I want to take this paradoxical operation of culture and examine what we, as social scientists, can learn from it. How may we use the notion of culture in our research in explaining differences in jurisdictions? And, crucially, what may be arguments *against* the adoption of the notion of culture?

V. SEEING THROUGH CULTURE: NOTES TOWARDS THE CULTURAL STUDY OF CULTURE AND REMORSE

There are a few ways to theorise these insights into the local and everyday use of the culture concept in judicial practice. Firstly, it is important to note the way judicial perceptions of culture explicitly resonate with anthropological understandings of culture, which similarly emphasise both symbolic and embodied actions. For the judges, too, 'culture' shows itself in the way people speak and act, and in that capacity is able to illuminate as well as obscure the 'real' defendant. Secondly, and in the context of this international edited volume, it is perhaps useful to situate these judges' ideas about culture culturally: that is, to try to give a culturally informed account of *why* these Dutch judges react the way they do to Hindustani, Moroccan and Antillean defendants. If I wanted to explain the data I presented here in cultural terms, what would such an explanation look like?

[47] Rossmanith (n 5).

In line with scholarship concentrating on the production of Dutch national identities, such an account would probably highlight the rather specifically Dutch emphasis on egalitarianism, embodied in this case in judges' implicit norm of frank and direct speech as markers of authenticity.[48] Such a cultural explanation would allow us to understand why particularly Hindustani and Antillean defendants' performances in court would be deemed problematic. After all, if the implicit Dutch norm emphasises egalitarian speech, the overt deference shown by Hindustani defendants does not only come across as evasive, but also may confront judges with the institutional power relationships between court and defendant that structure their communication but that they prefer to ignore. Meanwhile, their encounters with Antillean defendants, who tend to be deemed 'aggressive', may require them to exercise their institutional power (as in the example above), which again disrupts frank and egalitarian speech – or, as the court remains a highly unequal discursive space, the illusion thereof.

However, such explanations, cast in a cultural register, also have their limitations – limitations also evident to the judges I worked with throughout my fieldwork. For instance, while it is tempting to draw on the notion of culture to understand and account for observed differences, it is also a notion that may also be used in a totalising and reifying way, glossing over differences *within* cultures while magnifying those *between* them, as well as neglecting the agency of individual actors. As amateur anthropologists, judges know that culture can help them get to know defendants better, but that it can equally obscure their understanding.

Moreover, the use of the notion of culture may also be one way to remain silent about the more structural embeddedness of institutions and behaviours. While culture may explain differences in court behaviours, culture also plays a more odious role in the study of crime and in society more broadly. For instance, in the late 1990s and early 2000s, Dutch criminologists increasingly started explaining crime among migrants with reference to 'their culture',[49] which strongly resonated with a more general rise of xenophobia in Dutch politics. This development also entailed a shift away from more structural explanations of crime, and in that capacity further strengthened individualised, neoliberal imaginations of personal responsibility. Here, cultural others come to the fore as yet to be emancipated, yet to be fully modern subjects: people who, because of the dictates of 'their culture', have not quite managed to catch up to 'our' Western freedoms and values.[50] As a result of these processes, the fact that Dutch society has not been especially welcoming to migrants, and that discrimination

[48] R van Reekum, 'Out of Character: Debating Dutchness, Narrating Citizenship' (Dissertation, University of Amsterdam, 2014).

[49] See, eg H Werdmolder *Marokkaanse Lieverdjes* (Amsterdam, Balans, 2005); F Van Gemert, *Ieder voor Zich: Kansen, Cultuur en Criminaliteit onder Marokkaanse Jongeren* (Apeldoorn, Maklu Uitgevers Nederland, 1998).

[50] S Boersma and W Schinkel, 'Imaginaries of Postponed Arrival: on Seeing "Society" and its "Immigrants"' (2018) 32 *Cultural Studies* 308.

and racism continue to affect the lives of non-native Dutch people, conveniently disappears from view. Culture, in this context, has become a very good way to *not* talk or think about structures of power.

Similarly, the cultural explanation of the implicit norm that seems to guide judicial expectations offered above glosses over longer histories of Dutch colonial relations and race-based oppression. The notion that Antillean defendants are particularly 'aggressive', for instance, is not some innocent accident of chance, but is connected to these broader histories. Indeed, an understanding of black people as being particularly prone to 'flares of the passions', including aggression, has a long pedigree in knowledges produced by Western anthropologists[51] – which knowledges, we must remember, were crucial instruments in the administration of the colonies and powerful legitimisations of colonial oppression. Similarly, understandings of Muslim others as particularly deceitful have their roots in Western imperialism in the Middle and Far East,[52] for instance with Dutch missionaries – apparently blind to the obvious reasons why colonised peoples would not be entirely honest with their oppressors – describing the colonised as especially deceitful.[53] Indeed, if culture may originally have been devised as a way to move away from biological race (as discussed in section II of this chapter), there is evidence that in Western European contexts, particularly when applied to people with recent migration histories, the notion of culture tends to operate functionally as race once again, emphasising what are presumed to be stable and enduring differences between host societies and migrant communities.[54]

When drawing on the notion of culture, then, we do well to remember its paradoxical role as both lens and veil. Promising us to illuminate and order the social world, it also has the power to obscure, and as such is a particularly tricky concept. Because the knowledge we produce as investigators of legal practices tends to travel and inform the practices of the actors we study by a variety of means – reports, lectures, teaching – it is imperative to handle 'culture' with caution; to tease out its possibilities while keeping its limitations in clear view.

[51] Eze (n 17).

[52] EW Said, *Orientalism* (New York, Pantheon Books, 1978).

[53] M Kruithof, 'Shouting in the Desert: Dutch Missionary Encounters with Javanese Islam, 1850–1910' (Dissertation, Utrecht University, 2014).

[54] E Balibar, 'Racism Revisited: Sources, Relevance, and Aporias of a Modern Concept' (2008) 123 *PMLA* 1630.

6

Cultural Sensitivity Training, Judicial Feelings and Everyday Practice: Conversations at the Edge of Research

KATE ROSSMANITH*

It is widely assumed that professional training programmes promoting cultural awareness and sensitivity produce increased awareness regarding the concerns and practices (and even comportments) of people from minorities. This chapter aims to initiate a discussion regarding how cultural sensitivity training plays out in actual practice. Using as a case study the work of criminal court judges in their assessments of offender remorse, it considers potential paradoxes that occur in the operationalisation of 'culture' training. Examining how this training can function in judges' working lives allows us to better understand how judges might 'read' those people who come before them in court as being more or less 'ideal defendants': in this case, 'legible defendants'. The chapter argues that the implementation of 'culture' training needs to be understood through judicial emotions, including through feelings of competence, of doing a good job. It argues that, in order to assess whether training is effective, *we need to understand how it works* affectively.

I. INTRODUCTION

THESE DAYS, PROFESSIONAL training programmes that promote cultural awareness and sensitivity are being rolled out across numerous professional arenas, the intention being to promote equality and justice for marginalised groups. There is a widely held view that this training produces

* Associate Professor, Australian Research Council Future Fellow (2022–2026), Department of Media, Communications, Creative Arts, Language and Literature, Macquarie University, Australia. I thank the editors, Cyrus Tata and Stewart Field, for their generous, insightful feedback (and superhuman patience) as I developed this chapter; Hugh Dillon and Peter Doyle, for their deep engagement with my work; Kawsar Ali, for her research assistance; and the participants at the workshop held at Cardiff Centre of Law and Society, Cardiff University, 27–28 September 2018.

increased awareness regarding the concerns and practices (and even comportments) of people from ethnic minorities.[1] This chapter considers how cultural sensitivity training plays out in actual practice – how it is applied by professionals in their everyday work – and the potential paradoxes that occur.

By way of a case study, I consider the work of criminal court judges. I raise several issues for discussion regarding the ways in which cultural sensitivity training can and might be operationalised in their working lives. Studies of judicial work have raised questions regarding the role of implicit bias when judges encounter witnesses and victims from culturally and linguistically diverse backgrounds.[2] This has resulted in more research and guidance for judges in understanding the testimonies of diverse witnesses and defendants, such as differing approaches to eye contact, language barriers and cultural approaches to guilt. While the goal of such education is to promote cultural awareness and sensitivity when encountering people from 'other cultures', it is unclear how such training is applied in judges' daily work.

Examining how this training can function in everyday practice allows us to better understand how judges might 'read' those people who come before them in court as being more or less 'ideal defendants'.[3] By 'ideal defendant', I mean the person proceeded against by the state who is shown to accept freely, sincerely and wholeheartedly her culpability for the alleged (or proven) offences and the impending punishment. Stewart Field and Cyrus Tata point out that the defendant's expression of remorse is the ultimate exemplar of that ideal.[4] A person's remorse powerfully legitimises the criminal justice process: remorse 'shows to state officials that they not only have the right, but are right, to punish'.

This chapter explores the question of cultural sensitivity training in relation to the practical assessment of defendants' remorse. I consider how potential outcomes of such training for judges might be both variable and unexpected. In some cases, the training can indeed produce its intended result: ie the improvement of judges' capacities for self-reflexivity in their working lives, helping in the deconstruction of harmful cultural stereotypes. In other cases, though, the training may lead to paradoxical outcomes that should be guarded against. The chapter considers how the operationalisation of this training might work in

[1] For example, a psychological study has proposed that people infer deception when the 'communicator' violates expected social norms, and that 'cross-cultural biases in deception judgments' may be prevented by providing appropriate information to those people who are encountering 'communicators' from cultures different to those observers. P Castillo and D Mallard, 'Preventing Cross-Cultural Bias in Deception Judgments: The Role of Expectancies in Nonverbal Behavior' (2012) 43 *Journal of Cross-Cultural Psychology* 967.

[2] J Kang et al, 'Implicit Bias in the Courtroom' [2012] *UCLA Law Review* 1124.

[3] I use the terms 'defendant' and 'offender' interchangeably throughout this chapter. The terms broadly cover the various formal legal statuses of the person to be sentenced, and how the person proceeded against by the state is expected to admit and explain their guilt. See S Field and C Tata, 'Locating the Ideal Defendant: Punishment, Violence and Legitimacy' in S Field and C Tata (eds), *Criminal Justice and the Ideal Defendant in the Making of Remorse and Responsibility* (Oxford, Hart Publishing, 2023) ch 4.

[4] ibid.

relation to the affective experiences of judges, and it reflects on the ideal of 'the legible offender'.

By examining how training for professionals is interpreted and played out, we can better equip ourselves to identify unintended consequences and to genuinely improve such programmes. In the criminal court system, for example, the improvement of cultural sensitivity training would, in turn, improve judges' everyday working experiences and, most crucially, improve outcomes for defendants.

II. THE CUTTING ROOM FLOOR

This chapter does not present 'research findings'; there are no 'findings' to present. Rather, I wish to draw attention to something very curious that emerged at the edge of my research on remorse in the courts – something that merits further reflection and empirical research.

A little over a decade ago, I commenced a study of the ways in which offenders' remorse is assessed in the criminal justice system. Over the course of several years, I conducted ethnographic research. I conducted more than 100 interviews. I spoke with judges, as well as parole authorities, lawyers, support workers, offenders and victims of crime. I spent time in court hearings and parole hearings, and in people's places of work. I asked them how they could tell if someone was sorry for what they had done. I asked them what they thought remorse was, and what they thought it could or should do.

The project took place in the state of New South Wales, Australia. Access to judges was difficult to secure. The New South Wales judiciary was wary of researchers.[5] I was approaching the question of remorse evaluations from an anthropological perspective, not a legal one, although during our discussions questions of law, of course, arose. At the time, I interviewed 25 New South Wales judges and magistrates.[6] I conducted follow-up interviews over the years with a small number, several of whom are now my close friends.

This is by way of saying that ethnographic fieldwork produces intimate relationships. As anthropologists have recognised for more than half a century, human life is inherently relational,[7] and ethnographic research is research in the context of human entanglements. For this reason, I have often felt uncomfortable

[5] I have sometimes wondered whether I was granted permission to interview judges because I didn't, and still don't, have a law degree.

[6] In most states and territories in Australia, the term 'magistrate' refers to members of the judiciary who preside in the lower courts, while 'judge' indicates those who preside in the intermediate and higher courts, and all federal courts. This contrasts with the way 'magistrate' is understood, for example, in England and Wales, where the term refers to a layperson. For the benefit of international readers, in this chapter the term 'judges' and 'judicial officers' are used to refer to both judges and magistrates.

[7] PG Blasco and H Wardle, *How to Read Ethnography* (London, Routledge, 2007).

when the time comes to present my 'findings'. That I am obliged to present 'findings' is perfectly appropriate: I am an academic whose job it is to produce new knowledge. And, it is true, when I pore over and analyse interview transcripts and fieldnotes, patterns emerge and findings are arrived at. But framing my work like this can feel strange – work that involves deep, exploratory conversations with people; exchanges that are profound and complex.

In designing my study on remorse, I developed the following questions to ask judges:

How do you assess if someone is remorseful?
How can you tell if someone feels remorse?
What is remorse?
Why is remorse a mitigating factor?
Does an offender's remorse, or lack of remorse, affect victims of the crime? In what ways?

During the interviews, these open-ended questions allowed judges to reflect at length. When thinking about remorse in the law, judges introduced, and tended to talk about, the following topics:[8] the relationship between remorse and responsibility; forms of remorse evidence; genuine versus non-genuine remorse; remorse and demeanour assessment; remorse and an offender's personal story; remorse and rehabilitation; truth-telling in the courts; and emotion and judicial decision-making.

Such conversations recurred during the interviews. But other sort of talk arose in our conversations too, talk that crept in at the edges; talk that, were my project a feature film, would be relegated to the cutting room floor. Interesting points emerged in this talk, but I do not have sufficient data to know their extent. The offcuts to which I refer concern the issue of 'culture'. Judges spoke of 'cultural problems' and 'cultural communication difficulties'. It was in the context of trying to 'read' the comportment of offenders whose ethnic backgrounds differed from those judges.[9] Occasionally, judges referred to the cultural sensitivity training they had received. The exchanges we had were awkward. Remarks made by some judges were surprisingly strident and made me uncomfortable. Other judges grasped for language to describe the struggles they

[8] For an exploration of these topics, see K Rossmanith, *Small Wrongs: How We Really Say Sorry in Love, Life and Law* (Melbourne, Hardie Grant Books, 2018); K Rossmanith, 'Getting into the Box: Risky Enactments of Remorse in the Courtroom' (2014) 12 *About Performance* 7; K Rossmanith, 'Affect and the Judicial Assessment of Offenders: Feeling and Judging Remorse' (2015) 21 *Body & Society* 167; K Rossmanith, S Tudor and M Proeve, 'Courtroom Contrition: How Do Judges Know?' (2018) 27 *Griffith Law Review* 366; M Hall and K Rossmanith, 'Imposed Stories: Prisoner Self-Narratives in the Criminal Justice System' (2016) 5 *International Journal for Crime, Justice and Social Democracy* 38; M Hall and K Rossmanith, 'Long Haul Remorse: The Continuous Performance of Repentance throughout Prison Sentences' in S Tudor, R Weisman, M Proeve and K Rossmanith (eds), *Remorse and Criminal Justice: Multidisciplinary Perspectives* (London, Routledge, 2022) 156–74.

[9] One judge who I interviewed reflected: 'The judiciary is so monochrome. Most of the judiciary are of European background. There aren't many middle eastern, Asian, Aboriginal magistrates and judges. We've got a long way to go.'

encountered in the courtroom, their attempts to truly understand the offender sitting before them.

Now, years later, when I look back on my transcripts and my fieldnotes, I regret not pursuing this line of questioning further. I felt compassion for the judges and did not want them to feel attacked nor criticised. Judges are not unique in this regard. When any of us – no matter our profession – try to put professional training into action, we are faced with a much more complex world. Implementing such training is mediated through a myriad of feelings, especially amongst an occupational group of which so much is expected, and expects of itself. To be honest, I felt a bit lost for words myself when it came to questions of 'cross-cultural remorse assessment', 'other cultures', 'race' and 'ethnicity'. I did not want to use such loaded terms. Nor did I want to say the wrong thing, or for the judges to feel that I was trying to catch them out. (I am not alone in finding myself in such a situation. Irene van Oorschot has usefully reflected on what she calls 'the ghosts that haunt a practice',[10] which I revisit at the end of this chapter.)

When it comes to my research data, I am left only with offcuts, outtakes, fragments. How to think about them? They are what John Law, in his book *After Method*, might call 'mess'. [11] I do not wish to approach this 'messy talk' – talk-at-the-edge-of-research – through a social science lens. As Law suggests, social science is not very helpful when it comes to describing things that are complex and diffuse. 'This is because clear descriptions don't work when what [social sciences] are describing is not itself very coherent.'[12] Instead, I wish to use my 'not very coherent' exchanges with judges about 'cultural communication' to raise questions regarding the potentially curious outcomes, in judicial everyday working practice, of cultural sensitivity training. In doing so, I hope to identify an area worthy of further study.

III. 'CULTURE' IN THE CONTEXT OF REMORSE ASSESSMENT

Groundbreaking work has been done, and continues to emerge (from a range of disciplinary perspectives[13]), on the ways in which the criminal courts make decisions concerning offenders' remorse. This includes, but is not limited to, discursive analyses examining how offender remorse figures in sentencing judgments;[14]

[10] I van Oorschot, 'Culture, Milieu, Phenotype: Articulating Race in Judicial Sense-Making Practices' (2020) 29(6) *Social & Legal Studies*, journals.sagepub.com/doi/10.1177/0964663920907992.

[11] J Law, *After Method: Mess in Social Science Research* (London, Routledge, 2004).

[12] ibid 2.

[13] For an exploration of remorse from multidisciplinary perspectives, see S Tudor, R Weisman, M Proeve and K Rossmanith, 'Remorse: Multidisciplinary Perspectives on How Law Makes Use of a Moral Emotion' in S Bandes, JL Madeira, K Temple and E Kidd White (eds), *Research Handbook on Law and Emotion*. (Cheltenham, Edward Elgar Publishing, 2021) 131–45; Tudor et al, *Remorse and Criminal Justice* (n 8).

[14] See, eg R Weisman, 'Being and Doing: The Judicial Use of Remorse to Construct Character and Community' (2009) 18 *Social & Legal Studies* 47; L Wood and C McMartin, 'Constructing Remorse: Judges' Sentencing Decisions in Child Sexual Assault Cases' (2007) 26 *Journal of*

interviews with jurors regarding how they evaluate remorse;[15] philosophical discussions concerning remorse in the law;[16] psychological approaches in relation to remorse assessment;[17] sociological studies;[18] ethnographic methods, including interviews with the judiciary;[19] and creative practice approaches that apprehend affective dimensions of remorse in criminal justice.[20] Scholars agree that, while remorse is a mitigating factor in many jurisdictions of the world, how judges, juries and parole boards[21] assess remorse remains unclear. The consensus is that a myriad of factors inform how decisions are made concerning a person's apparent remorse (or remorselessness). And, especially relevant for this chapter, scholars agree that the evaluation of emotion is unavoidably interactive.[22]

In such scholarship, researchers often raise the issue of 'cross-cultural' or 'cross-racial' remorse evaluations. They posit that cultural differences may affect judges' and lawyers' ability to perceive genuine remorse when it is expressed differently than in their own culture;[23] that, for example, cultural and social norms and display rules create a problem for those evaluating the remorse of adolescents who are accused of serious crimes;[24] and that

Language and Social Psychology 343; BH Ward, 'Sentencing without Remorse' (2006) 38 *Loyola University Chicago Law Journal* 131.

[15] See W Bowers, 'The Capital Jury Project: Rationale, Design and Preview of Early Findings' (1995) 70 *Indiana Law Journal*; S Sundby, 'The Capital Jury and Absolution: The Intersection of Trial Strategy, Remorse and the Death Penalty' (1998) 83 *Cornell Law Review* 1557.

[16] See S Tudor, 'The Relevance of Remorse in Sentencing: A Reply to Bagaric and Amarasekara (and Duff)' (2005) 10 *Deakin Law Review* 40; H Maslen, *Remorse, Penal Theory and Sentencing* (Oxford, Hart Publishing, 2015); J Murphy, 'Well Excuse Me! – Remorse, Apology, and Criminal Sentencing' (2006) 38 *Arizona State Law Journal* 371; J Murphy, 'Remorse, Apology, and Mercy' (2007) 4 *Ohio State Journal of Criminal Law* 423; M Proeve and S Tudor, *Remorse: Psychological and Jurisprudential Perspectives* (Farnham, Ashgate, 2010).

[17] M Proeve and K Howells, 'Effects of Remorse and Shame and Criminal Justice Experience on Judgements about a Sex Offender' (2006) 12 *Psychology, Crime and Law* 145; J O'Donahoo and JG Simmonds, 'Perceptions of Remorse in Forensic Patients' in Tudor et al, *Remorse and Criminal Justice* (n 8); R Zhong et al, 'So You're Sorry? The Role of Remorse in Criminal Law' (2014) 42 *Journal of the American Academy of Psychiatry and the Law* 39.

[18] See, eg R Weisman, 'Showing Remorse: Reflections on the Gap between Expression and Attribution in Cases of Wrongful Conviction' (2004) 46 *Canadian Journal of Criminology and Criminal Justice* 121; Weisman, 'Being and Doing' (n 14); R Weisman, *Showing Remorse: Law and the Social Control of Emotion* (Burlington, VT, Ashgate, 2014).

[19] Rossmanith, 'Affect and the Judicial Assessment of Offenders' (n 8); I van Oorschot, P Mascini and D Weenink, 'Remorse in Context(s): A Qualitative Exploration of the Negotiation of Remorse and Its Consequences' (2017) 26 *Social & Legal Studies* 359; Rossmanith et al (n 8).

[20] See, eg Rossmanith, *Small Wrongs* (n 8); K Rossmanith, 'Unnatural Deaths: The Emotional Power of Forensic Photographs (video)' *The Guardian* (18 February 2018); K Rossmanith 'Ditching the *New Yorker* Voice' *Sydney Review of Books* (21 February 2022).

[21] K Young and H Chimowitz, 'How Parole Boards Judge Remorse: Relational Legal Consciousness and the Reproduction of Carceral Logic' [2022] *Law & Society Review*, https://doi.org/10.1111/lasr.12601.

[22] Bandes et al (n 13); see also Weisman, *Showing Remorse* (n 18).

[23] RS Everett and BC Nienstedt, 'Race, Remorse and Sentencing Reduction: Is Saying You're Sorry Enough?' (1999) 16 *Justice Quarterly* 99.

[24] MG Duncan, '"So Young and So Untender": Remorseless Children and the Expectations of the Law' (2002) 102 *Columbia Law Review* 1469; S Bandes, 'Remorse, Demeanor, and the Consequences

'Reading remorse across ethnic, racial or cultural lines is fraught with the possibility of error'.[25]

Scholars are also interrogating the very category of 'culture' itself, and studies have looked at how judges articulate culture and race in their sentencing work.[26] Irene van Oorschot's chapter in this volume, for instance, considers how 'culture' in the courtroom is a powerful tool and a problematic concept.[27] Drawing on the work of Adam Kuper, among others, she suggests that 'culture' is not a neutral, analytical concept, but a 'local vernacular' with specific uses, and that the concept 'culture' (as it is used in everyday judicial practice) allows for and can perpetuate certain ideas.

Hovering behind some of the discussions regarding problems of cross-cultural and cross-racial remorse assessment is the idea that judges require more training; that if only they received more training, many issues would be resolved. The assumption is that cultural sensitivity training increases judges' respect for, and understanding of, people from other cultures or social groups, and makes them realise that other cultures are rich and complex. This is the paradigm case. But, in reality, things are more complicated.

IV. CULTURAL SENSITIVITY TRAINING: IN SEARCH OF THE LEGIBLE OFFENDER

Here, I wish to introduce a more nuanced understanding of the responses that judges might have to cultural sensitivity training. The exploration is a conceptual one: I briefly sketch four conceptual outcomes of such training. My aim is to initiate a discussion, not set down a definitive account. And I am not suggesting that judges *themselves* might be categorised in the following ways; rather, that judges' *operationalisation of judicial education* could fall into one or more of these categories.

A. Self-Reflexivity and Uncertainty

Judges may practise insightful self-reflexivity and express uncertainty regarding their ability to 'read' other people. Cultural sensitivity training might produce in such participants the deeper realisation that they are more ignorant than they thought regarding the complexities of the lives and experiences of members of

of Misinterpretation: The Limits of Law as a Window into the Soul' (2014) *Journal of Law, Religion and State* 170.

[25] S Bandes, 'Remorse and Judging' in Tudor et al, *Remorse and Criminal Justice* (n 8).

[26] See, eg van Oorschot, 'Culture, Milieu, Phenotype' (n 10); I van Oorschot, 'The Paradoxical Uses of "Culture" in Judicial Assessment of Defendant Demeanour and Remorse' in Field and Tata, *Criminal Justice* (n 3) ch 5; D Eades, 'Telling and Retelling Your Story in Court: Questions, Assumptions and Intercultural Implications' (2008) 20 *Current Issues in Criminal Justice* 209.

[27] Van Oorschot, 'The Paradoxical Uses of "Culture"' (n 26).

some cultural groups. In their courtroom exchanges with, and assessments of, offenders, judges may carry an epistemological modesty and an understanding that they will never be truly certain how another person is thinking and feeling – especially regarding an offender's remorse.

Sometimes this ongoing uncertainty may be constructive and judges approach courtroom evaluations with a continual self-reflection regarding their decision-making practices.[28] Other times, though, the doubt judges carry may play on their minds and impact their ability to make decisions with complete confidence.

B. 'Making Allowances': Benefit of the Doubt

This category follows on from the one above. Judges may indeed be deeply self-reflexive and modest in how they view their own ability to 'read' people – and they 'accommodate' offenders with cultural backgrounds that differ from themselves. Judges may be of the belief that the fair and just approach is to 'make allowances': that, say, when it comes to assessing a person's remorse, judges accept that the person might be unable to perform 'the signature tunes of remorse'[29] because that person is not steeped in the dominant culture and is unable to produce behaviours that count as signs of remorse. Having participated in cultural sensitivity training and been exposed to information regarding the comportments of certain cultural groups, judges, in their interpretation of people's demeanour, may deliberately bracket out physical behaviours that might otherwise be classed as disrespectful. This, in turn, opens up the possibility, in their minds, that the offenders are remorseful. The offenders are, perhaps, 'sort of remorseful'.

Steven Tudor has written of 'sort of remorseful' offenders who fall somewhere within 'the wide grey zone' between clear cases of remorse*ful* offenders and clear cases of remorse*less* offenders: they 'inhabit the shadows of the paradigms of remorse'.[30] He offers a philosophical exploration of this grey zone, including a discussion of the 'remorseful but reticent' offender who does not

[28] In my essay 'From Here to There', I attempt to evoke, through in-depth interviews and creative writing techniques, a judge's affective experience of arriving at a sentencing decision. K Rossmanith, 'From Here to There' *Sydney Review of Books* (27 June 2022).

[29] One especially reflective judge used this phrase. He spoke with great insight regarding his dealings with defendants in the courtroom, and his recognition that he himself was steeped in the dominant culture's ideas of what remorse was and how it ought to be expressed. He spoke about encounters with young Lebanese men in the courtroom and the 'posturing' thing that these young men do. He said: 'Over time I came to see [the posturing] as a manifestation of them feeling as if they didn't fit into society. I came to see it as discomfort. And I saw how this discomfort overrode any ability [of them] to perform the signature tunes [of remorse].'

[30] S Tudor, 'Reflections on the Grey Zone: "Sort of" Remorseful Offenders' in Tudor et al, *Remorse and Criminal Justice* (n 8) 97–113.

display their remorse during their journey through the criminal justice system, other than by simply pleading guilty.[31] Tudor suggests that the 'remorseful but reticent' offender:

> might feel unable to express their remorse because they lack the relevant skills in self-presentation. They are in fact remorseful but don't have the social or communicative skills to know how to convey that, especially in the formal legal setting. They feel remorse, but cannot articulate that feeling, and, aware of their limitations, venture nothing.[32]

Significantly, Tudor suggests that this problem 'will often be exacerbated by gaps between the culture of the offender and the culture of the legal system (both the system's own culture and the broader culture it is part of)'.[33] He gives the example of offenders who come from 'marginalised or subordinated indigenous or migrant communities' and who 'may be uncertain how to navigate or conduct themselves in a criminal justice system they encounter as alien and disempowering, and that uncertainty then translates into reticence'.[34]

C. Enduring Confidence

Judges may, from the outset, feel very confident in their ability to 'read' people (regardless of ethnicity or social group), and the added cultural training or guidance simply heightens that self-confidence.[35] Here, the training propagates judicial expectations regarding offender legibility. Some judges may at times make declarative statements about people, with reference to people's internal states, generalised external bodily indicia and simplistic metaphors of 'legibility',[36] thus advancing oversimplistic attitudes. Attitudes may include, for

[31] See also J Gormley and C Tata, 'Remorse and Sentencing in a World of Plea Bargaining' in Tudor et al, *Remorse and Criminal Justice* (n 8) 40–66.

[32] Tudor, 'Reflections on the Grey Zone' (n 30).

[33] Amanda Carlin argues that 'baselines for proper courtroom communication still map onto white norms and expectations'. A Carlin, 'The Courtroom as White Space: Racial Performance as Noncredibility' (2016) 63 *UCLA Law Review* 450, 469.

[34] Tudor, 'Reflections on the Grey Zone' (n 30).

[35] Johansen has shown that offenders are expected to express feelings according to their category membership. Ethnic minorities, for example, may be described as reacting in specific ways according to their 'culture'. She quotes a judge from her interviews: 'Ethnic minorities are a bit like, well, they don't understand the game. It's no use that they enter with a big chain around their neck and tilted cap and all that. They don't show any humility. It's more Danish to do it this way: with the face of an undertaker to show that you understand it's serious.' LV Johansen, '"Impressed" by Feelings – How Judges Perceive Defendants' Emotional Expressions in Danish Courtrooms' (2019) 28 *Social & Legal Studies* 250. See also van Oorschot, 'Culture, Milieu, Phenotype' (n 10).

[36] As Eve Hanan writes: 'Accurately assessing nonverbal behaviour … is difficult. We erroneously assume that certain expressions, postures, and gestures have universal meaning' (E Hanan, 'Remorse Bias' (2018) 83 *Missouri Law Review* 300, 321). Meanwhile, van Oorschot has written of the ways in which 'culture' functions as a tool for understanding people. She discovered that Dutch judges have the option to attend post-vocational training days in which they are taught about ethnic minorities in the law. The courses were titled 'Turkish and Moroccan People in the Practice of Law' and 'Antillean

example, that people from certain cultural backgrounds 'won't look you in the eye'[37] in court and that this should be 'read' in a certain way. In this context, cultural and ethnic stereotypes may perhaps be unintentionally reproduced.[38]

D. Confidence Turning to Frustration and Blame

This category is perhaps the most paradoxical of all. Some judges may feel confident at reading people – but it is a confidence that, in the courtroom, can lead to frustration and the attribution of responsibility. When judges receive training about 'other cultures', they may have the sense that a code has been cracked and that they now possess tools with which to read people. However, judges may experience frustration and a degree of anxiety when the offender sitting before them in court remains illegible. The tools the judges have been given are not working. (One judge I spoke with talked of her frustration at her inability to read people's remorse: 'I find Chinese men impossible to read', she said. Another talked of trying to interpret offenders' courtroom demeanour: 'You can certainly see whether a person in the dock is distressed. But distressed about *what*? The immediate consequences for them? Or about what they've done?').

This frustration may turn into annoyance. This is understandable: in our workplace, when any of us become frustrated we can become irritated, especially if we are under a lot of pressure and expect so much of ourselves. In part, this may be because of the heavy weight of almost impossible expectation placed on judges and which they expect of themselves – what Tata identifies as 'the trope of the heroic individual professional'.[39] In the courtroom, when judges grow

and Surinamese People in the Practice of Law'. She points out that the courses 'draw on a wide variety of criminological and social–psychological knowledges that suggest that certain forms of deviance (honor-related violence) as well as certain forms of interaction (especially evasive behavior) are to be understood as rooted in offender's "culture".' Van Oorschot, 'Culture, Milieu, Phenotype' (n 10).

[37] One judge I interviewed said: 'Everyone knows about Aboriginal people – for example the cultural significance of them not looking you in the eye.' Another said: 'Aborigines, we're told, and it's certainly borne out in my experience, sometimes have difficulty, culturally, looking people in the eye. They can look shifty. It would be very wrong to discount their evidence because they didn't measure up to the standard test for whether someone's telling the truth: that is, whether they look you in the eye' (note: the term 'Aborigine' is offensive to Indigenous Australians because it is connected to Australia's colonial past. Preferred terms are 'First Nations people', 'Indigenous people', 'Aboriginal people').

[38] Three decades ago, Sherene Razack pointed out that 'white judges' are 'being urged to be culturally sensitive', and that 'Sensitivity in this context means learning how to read culturally specific behaviour in the courtroom setting'. Razack showed how a concept of 'culture' in this context is understood, problematically, as a set of readily identifiable values, practices and responses that categorise all members of a particular group. S Razack, 'What Is to Be Gained by Looking White People in the Eye? Culture, Race, and Gender in Cases of Sexual Violence' (1994) 19 *Feminism and the Law* 894, 898.

[39] Cyrus Tata points out that individual professionals like judges are charged with having to address on an individual basis the effects of what are systemic social problems. So, in the case of the courts, judges see every day the palpable effects of poverty, addictions, homelessness, discrimination, neglect, etc. Like other professionals, responsibility for the effects of these systemic social

frustrated at being unable to 'read' the offender sitting before them, they may sometimes blame the offender. In such situations, instead of judges framing the situation as not understanding offenders, judges view offenders as 'not making themselves understood'. ('He did not make himself understood', one judge told me.) The offender is considered responsible for their 'unreadability'.[40] Thus, the culture training for judges – designed to promote access to justice for marginalised groups – may, in this instance, have paradoxical consequences regarding the construction of, and attitudes towards, the people being sentenced.

V. DESIRING 'LITERACY', THE FEELING OF DOING A GOOD JOB

In this chapter, I am arguing that it is naive to assume that the training of any professionals (not only judges) could ever be simply applied, unmediated by social, psychological and other situational factors. We must instead seek to understand the subtle and complex dynamics of its operationalisation. Dedicated research is needed regarding relationships between judicial cultural sensitivity training programmes and the lived, affective experience of judging.[41] Of course, different training programmes are different. Some are more effective than others. To measure their effectiveness, and to make improvements to them, it is crucial to examine how they are operationalised in daily practice.

The implementation of training needs to be understood through judicial emotions such as pride/satisfaction, confidence, doubt/worry, frustration and even shame; it needs to be understood through judges' feelings of competence, of doing a good job. Put simply, to assess whether training is effective, we need to understand how it works affectively. The 'ideal offender' is the 'legible offender' and judges want to feel 'literate',[42] including those judges who maintain a constructive uncertainty regarding the interpretation of offenders in court. Judges want to have a 'feelingful' sense of literacy when 'reading' people. While this is surely something we all wish to feel in our working lives, it is perhaps especially so for judges. Judges, Tata argues, bear a triple weight

problems is delegated by governments to the discretion of individual judges. They are expected (and may expect themselves) to shoulder an almost impossible burden in addressing the effects of these chronic social problems. C Tata, *Sentencing: A Social Process* (Switzerland, Palgrave Pivot, 2020).

[40] See also van Oorschot, 'The Paradoxical Uses of "Culture"' (n 26), which discusses judges encountering defendants in court 'who just sit there'. She writes: 'A crucial dimension of such performances, I came to realise, is also communicative and embodied: in order to appear authentically remorseful, they also have to appear engaged with the court proceedings. For instance, defendants who appeared withdrawn tended to be thought of as "just sitting there" (*er maar een beetje bij zitten*), a phrase judges use to describe a certain listlessness or lack of urgency on the part of the defendant. However, this phrase is also evocative of a variety of performances that judges have difficulty "reading" and interpreting.'

[41] Tata (n 39) calls for a deeper understanding of the reality of daily sentencing work.

[42] Recall the quotation of Foucault, cited by Field and Tata: 'judges need to believe that they are judging a man as he is and according to what he is', see Field and Tata, 'Locating the Ideal Defendant' (n 3).

of responsibility.[43] They are aware of themselves as (i) a human being with an immediate responsibility for the suffering of another;[44] (ii) a 'professional' (people who identify as 'being a professional' tend to claim ethicality, altruism, honour, etc); and (iii) a professional self-consciously responsible for 'justice'. This weight, together with what Tata terms the burden of 'the heroic individual professional' who is expected to address the effects of what are in fact systematic social problems, may mean that judges, far more than other people, have a great need to feel that they can 'read' people. And this, too, explains why judges may become frustrated and annoyed when a person's legibility remains elusive.

This chapter has aimed to initiate a discussion. Dedicated empirical research on the subject is required. How might a researcher conduct possible future research regarding relationships between cultural sensitivity training programmes and everyday experiences of judges? One prism through which a study might develop is the concept 'emotive-cognitive judicial frame'. In their sociological study of the role of emotions in the work of the Swedish courts, Stina Bergman Blix and Asa Wettergren use this term to conceptualise the framing of judicial practice. They point out that our ideas concerning wisdom and sound judgement are concerned with morality: that is, what is 'good' (sound) and what is 'bad' (unsound). The emotive-cognitive judicial frame is one against which the professional performance, actions and decisions of judges are measured as 'good' or 'bad'. Such performance is noticed by colleagues and by the performing (judicial) self; crucially, a judge's performance is felt at an affective level: 'The way the self becomes informed about his or her ongoing performance (crucially in the sense of how it is valued by others) is through emotions of pride/satisfaction (good) and shame/embarrassment (bad).'[45]

The way judicial competence is set up in sentencing entails a capacity to 'read' individual character in order to do justice in each individual case, to treat defendants as 'unique individuals'.[46] This enables judges to assess dimensions they are required to assess: for example, offenders' culpability, remorse/remorselessness and potential to change. Ideally, judges want to feel confident when conducting their work. How might cultural sensitivity training inform judicial experiences of competence?

In the previous section of this chapter, categories A and B – judges who practise self-reflexivity, judges who may feel uncertain and judges who may 'make allowances' – present training outcomes whereby judges are attempting to balance confidence and varying degrees of doubt in their decision-making.

[43] Thanks to Cyrus Tata, who, during our discussions, offered this insight, including what the 'triple weight' might consist of.

[44] In this sense, a judge's role might be viewed as a sort of perversion of Emmanuel Levinas's philosophy.

[45] S Bergman Blix and A Wettergren, *Professional Emotions in Court: A Sociological Perspective* (London, Routledge, 2018) 7.

[46] Tata (n 39).

What does this look like in practice? In category A, I described a training outcome whereby judges come away with more questions than answers; where they view the lives and experiences of members of some cultural groups as more complex than they first thought. On the one hand, this is an ideal outcome. Effective cultural sensitivity training needs not just to expand judges' knowledge of different cultures, but must also promote uncertainty and doubt in relation to that knowledge. At the same time, however, this is not what we normally expect 'training' to do. Training equips you with the knowledge to *do* something (certainly in employment contexts). How, then, might the promotion of uncertainty (when it comes to 'reading' people) play out in the courtroom? How does this form of doubt operate in judges' experiences of decision-making?

Does an extremely confident attitude – the sort I outline in category C (enduring confidence) – afford judges an ability to process cases especially expeditiously? Does it spare them the feeling of doubt about the legitimacy of the decisions they make?[47] Judges need to feel they are being fair and just, that they are performing a legitimate role, ie delivering justice. The job of sentencing people is challenging if you are feeling uncertain about your competence to do it because it entails inflicting penalties and control on behalf of the state. The conceptual outcome I present in category D (confidence turning to frustration and blame) is one in which judges grow frustrated and annoyed, and then shift the responsibility for being legible to offenders. Is this a case of judges being forced to question their own ability to satisfactorily perform their job (and, by extension, to question their legitimacy as penal decision-makers)? Or is it something else?

Studying the operationalisation of culture training will involve a particular methodological sensitivity. Irene van Oorschot's insights regarding what she calls 'a sociology of ghosts' are useful here. When reflecting on interviews she conducted with judges in the Netherlands, she writes of her efforts 'to uncover those things that are not said, or only said with embarrassment, a sense of anxiety', and that her conversations with judges 'meant staying with and wading through affects such as discomfort, embarrassment or perhaps even shame on the side of the judges … some of whom felt easily attacked'.[48]

Any future empirical study on the ways in which judges apply cultural training in their daily work must recognise the very human dimension of judicial decision-making. It is important to better understand the complex practical and affective dimensions of this aspect of judicial work. Indeed, such a study would come at a time when scholarship is seeing an explosion of interest more generally in human skill and practical expertise.[49]

[47] Field and Tata, 'Locating the Ideal Defendant' (n 3) write: 'Decisions must be made, rapidly. To do so, uncertainty and doubt about the legitimacy of such decisions have to be minimised.'

[48] Van Oorschot, 'Culture, Milieu, Phenotype' (n 10) 17.

[49] See, eg E Fridland and C Pavese (eds), *The Routledge Handbook of Philosophy of Skill and Expertise* (Abingdon, Routledge, 2021); K Bicknell and J Sutton (eds), *Collaborative Embodied Performance: Ecologies of Skill* (London, Bloomsbury Publishing, 2022).

In this chapter, I have drawn attention to potential paradoxes in the application of cultural sensitivity training in judges' working lives, articulating four conceptual outcomes. Not only is it vital to examine how these (and other outcomes) play out in the courtroom, but it is also important to consider a dimension that may perhaps be irreconcilable: the potential tension between ideal education about 'other cultures' and the requirements involved in being a sentencing judge.[50] If an ideal programme for judges promotes greater complexity (and therefore a lack of certainty) when it comes to 'reading' people from diverse backgrounds, how can this possibly be compatible with the confidence required to send a person to prison?

[50] Thanks to Stewart Field, who, during our discussions, identified this potential tension.

Part 2

Beyond Remorse

7

'Remorse Is Not Enough': Disentangling the Roles of Remorse and Insight in the Construction of the Ideal Defendant

RICHARD WEISMAN*

This chapter analyses the relationship between remorse and insight as concepts that play parallel but distinguishable roles in the sentencing of offenders in criminal law in Canada and the USA. Both concepts are deployed in law to prescribe standards that offenders must meet in order to demonstrate that they are no longer the same persons who committed the crimes for which they were convicted and hence, purportedly, are less likely to reoffend. But, to date, the academic bodies of literature on remorse and insight have been analysed in isolation from each other, with remorse looked at in relation to its impact on sentencing and insight looked at in relation to its impact on parole decisions. The goal of this chapter is to draw from a population of cases in which both concepts are applied to the same offenders to show where they overlap, where they differ and where they conflict. More specifically, the analysis shows that the decision to focus on remorse or insight affects both the sequence of transformation that the offender is enjoined to demonstrate to show that they are fit to return to society and the manner in which offenders communicate their relationship to the crime. The central finding of the analysis is that the focus on insight gives greater emphasis to cognition and verbal agility, whereas the focus on remorse gives greater emphasis to spontaneous emotional display. How these differences affect the population of offenders – whether they confer advantages to some groups over others – is taken up in the conclusion of the chapter.

*Professor Emeritus, York University, Law and Society Programme, Department of Social Science, Canada.

I. INTRODUCTION

TWO DECADES AGO, in his posthumously edited collection, *Remorse and Reparation*, Murray Cox could lament the neglect of remorse as an object of academic inquiry despite its ubiquity in law and social relationships and despite its crossing of disciplinary boundaries.[1] In the intervening 20 years, many of the gaps that Cox identified have been addressed in an ever-growing body of research. This has shown that considerations of remorse enter into decisions at every phase of the criminal justice process from the moment of arrest to the pre-trial preparation between defendants and their counsel, to trials by judges and by juries, and then on to post-trial deliberations regarding probation and parole. At the core of this process lies a ritual repeated in the many jurisdictions where remorse plays two central roles. First, the offender communicates how they feel about the transgression for which they have been convicted, and second, a body of decision-makers then evaluates this communication according to both explicit and implicit criteria, with significant consequences for how the offender is disposed.

While the substance of this ritual takes a particular form in the legal domain, its origins and affinities with quotidian remedial exchanges as practised in the everyday world remain intact. In its most basic formulation, the showing of remorse is a moral performance that demonstrates a separation between the real self and the self that committed the transgression. The question it poses to the audience before whom this performance is addressed – whether the victim or the court as surrogate for the victim – is which is the more real and true self. Is it the self that breached the norm or the self that now joins in condemnation of the breach?[2] Because the transfer of these rituals from the public domain to the courtroom attaches them to decisions about sentencing with significant consequences for the offender, they have now been subjected to increased scrutiny in terms of how different kinds of performances are connected to different outcomes.

The result is a literature that does not simply observe and track the ubiquity of remorse in the conduct of the criminal law, but also helps to explain its continued expansion as a feature of modern criminal justice. For one, it is clear that the credit given to remorse is a driving force in the rapid disposition of criminal law cases through guilty pleas that would otherwise proceed to trial.[3] Add to this the widely prevalent belief[4] that the presence or absence of remorse

[1] M Cox (ed), *Remorse and Reparation* (London, Jessica Kingsley Publishers, 1999) 13.

[2] For fuller elaboration of this formulation, see R Weisman, *Showing Remorse: Law and the Social Control of Emotion* (New York, Ashgate, 2014) 9.

[3] For nuanced analysis of how attributions of remorse work systemically to accelerate the production of 'closed' guilty pleas, see C Tata, ''Ritual Individualization': Creative Genius at Sentencing, Mitigation, and Conviction' (2019) 1 *Journal of Law and Society* 112.

[4] I use the term 'belief' advisedly. What systematic investigation has been undertaken to test the proposition that there is a correlation between remorse and successful rehabilitation has yielded mixed results. See, eg MJ Proeve, DI Smith and DM Niblo, 'Mitigation without Definition: Remorse

is directly related to the likelihood of reoffending and one can readily appreciate another reason for its ubiquity on the promise that it will further public safety. But even apart from these arguably instrumentalist uses, courts do not act in isolation from the larger moral communities where they have jurisdiction. Expressions of remorse where they are expected signify agreement with the standards of the community and attract goodwill, just as the lack of remorse when remorse is expected evokes anger and adverse judgement. Judges and other legal actors are not immune from the passions that abound in society at large. Even a cursory survey of judgments in Canadian courts will bring up recurrent phrases such as 'absolutely no remorse' or 'devoid of remorse', which can be taken as a damning recognition of the gap between what is shown and what was expected.

Yet despite the service that the showing of remorse and its attribution renders to criminal justice systems in numerous jurisdictions, a parallel language has emerged in the past few decades, at least in Canada and the USA, that can variously be described as a replacement, a supplement or even a way of disqualifying claims to remorse.[5] This language uses the concept of 'insight' as the standard for evaluating the performances of offenders. I refer to it as parallel to remorse because it provides another way of prescribing, measuring and validating the changes an offender must demonstrate in order to have their sentences mitigated or to meet the criteria necessary to achieve parole. In this chapter, my purpose is to describe the interrelationships between the showing of remorse and the demonstration of insight as alternative approaches to the classification of offenders. In both discourses, the court creates expectations that offenders must meet in order to show that they are no longer the same persons who committed the crimes for which they were convicted. My analysis will address the question of whether these expectations are compatible or incompatible, or at times compatible and at times incompatible. Thus far, the bodies of academic literature dealing with the impact of how remorse and insight, respectively, affect sentencing and parole have evolved separately, with the one making little or no reference to the other. The primary task of this chapter is to bridge that gap.

To accomplish this objective, I have assembled a population of Canadian judgments issued over the 10-year period from 2010 to 2020, all of which include

in the Criminal Justice System' (1999) 32 *Australian and New Zealand Journal of Criminology* 16; M Bajaric and K Amarkkehara, 'Feeling Sorry? Tell Someone Who Cares: The Uselessness of Remorse in Sentencing' (2001) 40 *Howard Journal of Criminal Justice*, 364; M O'Hear, 'Appellate Review of Sentences: Reconsidering Differences' (2010) 51, *William and Mary Law Review* 2123. O'Hear writes at fn 127: 'Indeed, one prosecutor suggested that, in his experience, recidivism rates were higher among defendants pleading guilty than going to trial.' While this is anecdotal, it indicates scepticism by one of the foremost researchers into the judicial guidelines in US law regarding how remorse should affect sentencing.

[5] For discussion of role of insight in parole decisions in Canada, see K Hanna-Moffitt and C Yule, 'Gaining Insight, Changing Attitudes and Managing "Risk": Parole Release Decisions for Women Convicted of Violent Crimes' (2011) 13 *Punishment and Society* 149; for the USA with a focus on California parole hearings, I have relied primarily upon H Aviram, *Yesterday's Monsters;*

references to remorse and insight.[6] This population consists of all cases in which the word 'insight' is mentioned at least 10 times and the word 'remorse' is mentioned at least five times. I have intentionally over-represented references to insight in my population since there is a dearth of analyses of how this concept is applied in Canadian sentencing decisions.[7] For the purposes of this analysis, I have confined the population to cases drawn from criminal law, although there are other areas of the law, such as disciplinary hearings and child custody hearings, where the degree of contestation also helps to provide clarification on how these two concepts are distinguished in legal discourse.[8]

But first, I want to place the relationship between remorse and insight in the larger context of their usage outside of law, examining how they have been incorporated into legal discourse and the consequences of choosing either of these frameworks or using them in combination as a way of regulating the lives of offenders.

II. INTERRELATIONSHIP BETWEEN THE CONCEPTS OF REMORSE AND INSIGHT

If we draw from popular usage, or even from the more precise discourse of moral philosophy, one might easily conclude that the overlap between the feeling and expression of remorse and the awareness of self that is implicit in the

The Manson Family Cases and the Illusion of Parole (Berkeley, University of California Press, 2020); VL Shammas, 'The Perils of Parole Hearings: California Lifers, Performative Disadvantage, and the Ideology of Insight' (2019) 42 *Political and Anthropological Review* 142; L Paratore, '"Insight" into Life Crimes: The Rhetoric of Remorse and Rehabilitation in California Parole Precedent and Practice' (2016) 21 *Berkeley Journal of Criminal Law* 99; J Izard, 'Under the Cloak of Brain Science; Risk Assessment, Parole, and the Powerful Guise of Objectivity' (2017) 105 *California Law Review* 1223.

[6] My population consists primarily of sentencing decisions. Canadian sentencing decisions provide a richer source of information on the interplay between remorse and insight than parole decisions, which frequently do not even mention remorse – as exemplified in the decision on Robert Latimer – see n 18 below.

[7] I have used different weightings of the two terms in order to balance between two objectives that pull in opposite directions. On the one hand, the greater the number of cases, the more opportunity there is to identify patterns in how the concepts are used. On the other hand, the more frequently the term is used in a case, the more it is likely to be elaborated and clarified. But the greater the frequency, the fewer the number of cases. The setting of these different thresholds is intended to capture as many cases as possible while ensuring the inclusion of those cases in which the relationship between remorse and insight is most fully expounded.

[8] I used two legal data bases to generate a total of 66 cases that met my criteria of judgments that mentioned 'insight' at least 10 times and 'remorse' at least five times between 1 January 2010 and 31 May 2020. My primary database was Lexis Nexis and my search term was – 'atleast10(insight)' and 'atleast5(remors!)'. This search generated 65 cases, of which 48 were applications of criminal law. I then supplemented this population with cases drawn from the legal database CanLaw ii. Because this database does not have a search function that allows sorting by frequency of mention, I used search terms 'remorse insight' and specified the same time period arranged by relevance. I then went through the cases in order of relevance and stopped when the mentions of remorse and insight were less than 10 for insight and five for remorse. This generated 18 additional cases for a total population of 66 cases.

concept of insight is such that one is not possible without the other. As Proeve and Tudor write in their unpacking of the meanings attached to remorse, there is a cognitive component as well as an affective component to this moral emotion that they refer to as 'remorse's beliefs'. Central to these beliefs is the awareness that one's actions have harmed another person and that these actions were wrongful according to some agreed-upon moral standard.[9] For the most part, this conceptual proximity between doing a wrong, feeling that it is a wrong and understanding that it is a wrong is reflected in the legal usage of these terms: more often than not, they are merged using phrases such as 'remorse or insight'.

It is all the more surprising, then, that a gap between the legal uses of these concepts that was already discernible in parole hearings two decades ago in numerous jurisdictions in North America has since widened to include decisions about sentencing as well. There are two dimensions to this shift towards distinguishing insight from remorse: the more obvious is that it focuses attention less on how the offender feels about their crime than on their understanding of why they committed the crime. As Victor Shammas has expressed it, to qualify for insight, 'The inmate must be able to show why a crime occurred, that is, to produce a causal account of the crime and show how these causes have been curbed by a labor of self-improvement'.[10] Hadar Aviram has shown in her recent analysis of parole proceedings in California over the past 50 years that the shift to insight, while not fully eclipsing concerns over the prisoner's remorse, has moved the battleground in parole hearings from inquiry into how fully the inmate accepts responsibility for their crime to how deeply they understand the causes of their crime.[11] No matter how fully documented the inmate's efforts to renounce the self that perpetrated the original transgression, parole presentations can still falter if they do not articulate what those in authority have concluded are its root causes. Thus, for example, the inmate who participated in the highly publicised kidnapping of schoolchildren for ransom in California in the 1970s must, after 40 years in detention, come up with a deeper understanding of his motivation than simply admitting that his primary motive was greed no matter what other efforts at reparation have been made. As expressed by the deputy director of the parole board in the hearing that denied him parole:[12]

> After 34, 35 years in prison, when asked about the causative factors, all you can tell is greed … But after all the years of therapy that you say you have done, the self-help that you have done, the fact that you're a facilitator now in Alternatives to Violence, we expected more than that, more insight on your part, more understanding of what is it that would allow you to commit such a horrendous crime.

[9] M Proeve and S Tudor, *Remorse: Psychological and Jurisprudential Perspectives* (Farnham, Ashgate, 2010).

[10] See Shammas (n 5) 152.

[11] Aviram (n 5) 94–108 describes the birth of insight in the mid-1980s in California as an increasingly important part of parole board discourse. See also the commentary on the use of insight in the California system in D Slater, 'How to Get Out of Prison – California Changed Its Laws to Give More Inmates Serving Life Sentences a Chance' *New York Times Magazine* (5 January 2020) 32.

[12] *Woods v Valenzuela*, 28 April 2014, Petition for Writ of Habeas Corpus, 279.

Under the regime of insight, the inmate's account of the reasons for their crime are closely scrutinised according to how well they match an ever-evolving standard of self-understanding.

But I would argue that the other dimension of this change is equally significant. The move from remorse to insight involves not just a shift in emphasis, but also a change in discourse.[13] No matter what its other instrumentalities, law's inquiry into the offender's remorse is a moral discourse that judges how the offender feels about what they did according to a standard of how they should feel about what they did. The discourse of insight purports to elevate the findings of the court to a more exacting actuarial standard of risk and the likelihood of reoffending. The impact of this change in discourse is to invest attributes that might previously have been classified under the rubric of deficiencies in the expression of remorse with greater evidentiary weight when reclassified as deficiencies in insight. This hierarchy of credibility is explicit in an Alberta Court of Appeal judgment rendered in 2012:[14]

> Remorse is subjective. A lack of insight, on the other hand, compares the accused's state of mind to an objective standard. The convicted person can only apologize for and be remorseful with respect to what he realizes he has done. That remorse may be entirely sincere and deeply felt, even if objectively the accused does not fully appreciate what he has done. It is flawed reasoning to equate the objective measure of the accused's perception of his culpability with the sincerity of his apology.

More recently, the Supreme Court of Canada held that

> remorse gains added significance when it is paired with insight and signals that the offender has come to realize the gravity of the conduct, *and as a result has achieved a change in attitude or imposed some self-discipline which significantly reduced the likelihood of further offending.*[15]

Both of these judgments give recognition to the practices of courts to distinguish insight from remorse and to inscribe it within a discourse that suggests greater predictive power for lack of insight than for deficiencies in the showing of remorse. Increasingly, it is this language of risk and dangerousness, as well as that of remorse and recidivism, that guides the changes an offender must undertake to demonstrate that they are no longer the same person who transgressed.

In the next section, I want to compare the judicial uses of insight and remorse as attributions that variously overlap, compete and complement each other in the disposition of the offender. However much resemblance these terms bear to their conventional usage outside of law, once inserted into the legal domain,

[13] For further discussion of the relationship between discourses that emphasise remorse and discourses that focus on risk, see LV Johansen 'Constructing Ideal Defendants in the Pre-sentence Phase: The Connection between Responsibility and Potential Remorse' in S Field and C Tata (eds), *Criminal Justice and the Ideal Defendant in the Making of Remorse and Responsibility* (Oxford, Hart Publishing, 2023) ch 4.

[14] *R v Andrukonis* (2012) ABCA 148, para 37.

[15] *R v Friesen* 2020 SCC 9, para 165.

they assume a power over the lives of those to whom they are applied that can be managed in different ways but never avoided. At the same time, both concepts are so fluid and ambiguous that it is impossible to know with any precision what they mean apart from their usage.[16] The expectations for showing remorse can vary from the most perfunctory of gestures, such as a guilty plea, to an undefinable standard of self-condemnation and self-transformation. So, too, insight embraces a wide span of behaviour that can be expanded from a simple assent to what others have concluded is the 'true' cause of the criminal misconduct to a demand for self-examination with no fixed boundaries. As Aviram has suggested, the introspection demanded of insight 'can be a bottomless pit'[17] – hence the need to look more closely at decisions that distinguish between remorse and insight to bring out how they differ, what impact these differences have on how offenders are classified and what differences these distinctions make with respect to sentencing.

To facilitate this comparison, I will draw on one of the most famous cases in recent Canadian history to serve as a framework for the analysis to follow. Perhaps no decision by a parole board in Canada ever attracted as much public commentary by the national press as that handed down by the National Parole Board of Canada on 5 December 2007. The offender to whom the parole board denied day parole was Robert Latimer, a farmer from Saskatchewan, who had already served seven years in prison for a conviction for second degree murder for the 'mercy killing' of his severely disabled 12-year-old daughter in 1993.[18] But what made this case stand out from other mercy killings were Latimer's refusal to show remorse for his actions and his defence in court and to the public that he was justified in ending his daughter's life to spare her from the ordeal of excruciating and unrelenting pain, for which there was no medical remedy. Latimer's lack of remorse had been noted in the Supreme Court judgment that would affirm the conviction and sentence rendered by the Saskatchewan Court of Appeal. When asked by the parole board how he felt about his crime, he repeated what he had said earlier: 'I still don't feel guilty because I feel it was the best thing to do.'[19]

But this time it would not be for lack of remorse that Latimer would be refused parole. Instead, the parole board concluded that despite the lack of institutional problems, his compliance with all conditions while on bail and

[16] Indeed, one researcher who attempted to identify the usage of insight in California parole hearings concluded that 'Despite repeated discussions among coders, an evaluation of insight could not be reliably coded. For similar reasons, the degree of remorse was not used as a variable in the regression. Evaluations of insight and remorse are markedly subjective; if they track measurable features that can be reliably identified by a diverse group of people, these features were undiscoverable by the author.' See K Bell, 'A Stone of Hope: Legal and Empirical Analysis of California Juvenile Lifer Parole Decisions' (2019) 54 *Harvard Civil Rights – Civil Liberties Law Review* 478.

[17] Aviram (n 5) 104.

[18] For the final verdict, see *R v Latimer* (2001) SCC [85].

[19] Quoted in G Bauslaugh, *Robert Latimer* (Toronto, James Lorimer, 2010) 79.

his positive family support, he had developed 'little insight into the factors which contributed to (his) decision to murder (his) daughter'.[20] How did the parole board arrive at this conclusion? First, he did not acknowledge what they perceived as the true causes of his offence: 'You denied any connection between your personal phobias for blood or infections and your difficulties coping with the medical care required by your daughter.' But this lack of insight was also reflected in how he answered the questions that were directed to him: 'You struggled throughout the hearing to provide any coherent explanations of your thoughts, feelings, or beliefs, frequently not answering the questions asked or providing rambling responses that conveyed little relevant information.'[21] Given this absence of insight, what would be required to bring about the changes necessary to allow Latimer the day parole for which he had applied? 'It appears to the Board that you require further intervention to help you in developing a better understanding of your motivations for this crime to ensure you are prepared to manage your risk for future offending.'[22]

I will use this decision as a template to identify the major points of contrast and continuity between the attributions of remorse and insight. First, it is apparent that the invoking of insight as the primary basis for denying parole to Latimer alters the crime narrative as had been articulated by the courts and by Latimer up to this point. Hitherto, the clash between Latimer and the state had been framed as one of principled opposition to the legal prohibition against ending someone's life for any reason, including the prevention of irrevocable and extreme suffering. The shift from remorse to insight redefines his crime from one of defiance of the law to what is asserted as the true underlying causes for his crime – namely, Latimer's perceived phobias 'for blood or infections' and his difficulties in 'coping with the medical care required by [his] daughter'. This power of insight to reshape the crime narrative away from the commission of the offence to what are ascribed as its underlying causes will be the first category for the comparison with the attribution of remorse.[23]

Second, the decision refers to how Latimer performed insight – that is, how successfully or unsuccessfully he was able to explain why he had committed the act for which he was convicted. I am using performance as a generic term to refer to the presentation of self before an audience. I refer to the showing of remorse and the demonstration of insight as moral performances because the outcome of these presentations results in the elevation or degradation of the status of the offender, depending on how their performance is judged. The most

[20] NPB (National Parole Board) Pre-Release Decision Sheet (5 December 2007) 4.
[21] ibid.
[22] ibid 4–5.
[23] For more general discussion of the constraints imposed on offenders in terms of how to think about their crime and how to describe their crime, see M Hall and K Rossmanith, 'Imposed Stories: Prisoner Self-narratives in the Criminal Justice System in New South Wales, Australia' (2016) 5 *International Journal for Crime, Justice, and Social Democracy* 38.

apparent difference between the attributions of remorse and insight is contained in the very categories we use to describe them: that insight can be demonstrated, explained or expressed suggests that what is uppermost in this performance is its verbalisation. The objection of the parole board that Latimer's performance 'lacked coherence' or that he 'struggled' to express himself is taken as a failing in the demonstration of insight in contrast to how it might be viewed through the lens of remorse, where spontaneous emotional display and incoherence might connote authenticity. This difference in emphasis between the affective and cognitive aspects of moral performance will be the second category of contrast to be analysed in the comparison between the attributions of remorse and insight.

III. CONSTRUCTING THE REMORSEFUL AND INSIGHTFUL OFFENDER

A. Controlling the Crime Narrative

As mentioned above, the use of insight in place of remorse reframes the crime narrative in two distinguishable ways. The first involves the positing of two distinct sequences of personal transformation by which offenders are enjoined to demonstrate that they are fit to return to society. The second way – to be considered below – consists of the substitution of insight for remorse and the corresponding shift from an overtly moral discourse to the more specialised language of risk and dangerousness. What I will call the remorse-driven sequence focuses attention on the criminal act for which the offender was convicted. One of the cases from the population under investigation can be used to illustrate this difference. In this instance, the offender pleaded guilty to a charge of manslaughter. The forensic psychiatrist assigned to the case described the offender as 'feeling a sense of guilt and remorse', stating that 'she cannot stop thinking about the victim and the victim's parents and she is very tearful when describing this'.[24] Moreover, he reported that she had written a letter to the family of the victim stating that 'I do not want another day to pass without trying to express to you and your family the remorse and regret that overtakes my heart and invades my mind every single day'.[25] Here, the emphasis is on establishing the change in the offender from someone who committed an act of criminal misconduct to someone who now shows at a deep level of feeling that she condemns her own actions.

From the vantage point of insight, however, transformation is incomplete unless it is complemented by proof that the offender has successfully addressed the underlying causes of their criminality. In the insight-driven sequence, the

[24] *R v Doolan* [2018] BCPC 28, para 73.
[25] ibid para 74.

crime is viewed as a symptom of an underlying cause and the offender is reconstituted not just as someone who committed a crime, but as someone whose crime is an expression of more fundamental and enduring characteristics. Hence, in this instance, the offender can be given credit for remorse but not for insight, since she is viewed as 'having limited insight into her "need for treatment" for "alcohol addiction" necessitating intensive and ongoing counselling so that (she) can begin to comprehend what her past has been and how it is driving her current conduct'.[26] So, in this regime in which remorse and insight are differentiated, it is quite possible, as in this case, to be credited with remorse but not with insight.[27] Similarly with respect to the remorseful perpetrator of fraud who lacks insight into her gambling addiction[28] or the remorseful offender who pleaded guilty to sexual assault claiming that 'I have no right to treat women like that' but who lacks insight into 'his delusional disorder'.[29]

But control over the crime narrative goes deeper. It is clear from the reactions of the court to initiatives by the offender that certain types of explanations of criminal misconduct are unacceptable. Those who assert that their crime was the result of situational factors are apt to encounter a stern dismissal. In the following case, when the offender who had pleaded guilty to possession and distribution of child pornography mentioned that situational factors such as stresses in his life and 'incremental desensitization to adult pornography' contributed to the commission of the offence, the court responded:[30]

> Mr. W, I have known many people engaged in destructive or self-destructive behaviours who have stopped what they are doing and sought help. You could have erased your computer and sought professional help. That option was available to you. You did not take it. This is no one else's fault. You have pleaded guilty, you have accepted responsibility, however, I am not at all certain as to the level of your insight. I think that you are still quite far from comprehending that the problem is you and only you. I think that you are still trying to rationalize your behaviour to yourself and to others in the face of society's reaction to what you have done.

In another, more high profile case, in which the offender was convicted of two counts of first degree murder and 10 counts of sexual assault for knowingly infecting his sexual partners with HIV virus, his listing of 12 situational factors as explanations for why he failed to disclose his condition elicits a similar judicial response: 'While the offender has provided a variety of reasons for not disclosing his HIV status to the victims in this case, he has little insight into

[26] ibid para 92.

[27] This category of offender, who is attributed some but not all the qualities of conscience and control that the courts consider in sentencing, is analysed further by S Tudor, 'Reflections on the Grey Zone: 'Sort of Remorseful' Offenders' in S Tudor, R Weisman, M Proeve and K Rossmanith (eds), *Remorse and Criminal Justice* (Oxford, Routledge, 2022).

[28] *R v Penttila* [2020] BCJ 262, para 42.

[29] *R v Eamer* [2017] OJ 2181, paras 103 and 303.

[30] *R v Wysom* [2018] ONCJ 450, para 14.

his offending behaviour or his need for treatment.' Elsewhere he described the offender as having 'an incredible lack of insight into his conduct'.[31] Offenders who invoke situational explanations for their transgression are described as engaged in 'minimization and justification of their behavior' and hence lacking in insight.[32] As with the decision of the parole board regarding Robert Latimer, demonstrating insight requires that offenders accept that the causes of their criminal misconduct are disturbances internal to themselves and for which they bear sole responsibility to correct.

But the separation of insight from remorse has come to play another potentially significant role in the sorting of offenders into those who are safe to return to the community and those who are not. Consider the following case, in which the offender pleaded not guilty to sexual assault of an underage victim:[33]

> The absence of remorse is not an aggravating factor. But the lack of empathy of insight is important when considering specific deterrence and rehabilitation at it may '*indicate a lack of insight into and a failure to accept responsibility for the crimes committed, and demonstrate a substantial likelihood of future dangerousness*'.

Here, the very acts of pleading not guilty or pleading guilty but not communicating 'enough' empathy for the victim are reframed not just as a failure to show remorse, but as a deficiency in insight, and hence as indicators of risk and dangerousness to the community. What is noteworthy here as well is the disclaimer that while the court is not increasing the offender's sentence because they exercised their right to a trial by pleading not guilty and thereby did not show remorse, the very same act of pleading not guilty does not exempt them from being attributed a lack of insight, which can be used to increase their sentence. The same approach can be extended to those offenders who plead guilty if the court decides that their insight or awareness of the impact of their crime falls short of expectations. Thus, the offenders who pleaded guilty to trafficking in drugs, although credited with remorse, are nonetheless faulted as follows:[34]

> I accept by their guilty pleas and brief addresses to the court that the accused are remorseful for their conduct ... I am concerned that the accused do not have true insight into the gravity of their offences. They have not expressed empathy for the people likely harmed by their sales of [prohibited drugs]. Neither accused indicated to the court that they have lost any sleep wondering how many overdoses or deaths they are connected to by trafficking in these noxious substances.

[31] *R v Aziga* [2011] OJ3525, paras 132 and 139. Some of the factors listed were 'Fear of rejection; Stress related to son's autism, stress related to marital breakdown, HIV stigma' at para 53.

[32] *R v CAP* [2020] BCJ 764, paras 75 and 161. This is consistent with Aviram's observations regarding how insight is used by the California Parole Board: 'efforts to contextualize the crime are perceived as 'minimization and lack of insight' (para 104).

[33] *R v Sohail* [2018] ONCJ 566, para 36.

[34] *R v Mann* [2018] BCJ 1237, para 68.

Similarly, insight is invoked as a standard for rejecting other guilty pleas where the harm that the offender acknowledges is widely at variance with the harm the court expects the offender to acknowledge, such as the offender who pled guilty to sexual assault with underage victims but contended that the harm he caused was mollified because of his 'love for the victim'.[35] Likewise, a lack of insight is attributed to defendants who use language that is perceived as understating the impact of their criminal misconduct, such as referring to a collision that caused permanent injury to a victim as an 'accident'[36] or describing the impact of an aggravated assault that resulted in a victim's brain damage as 'a massive butterfly effect',[37] thereby purportedly absolving the perpetrator of intent to cause the damage that resulted. In all these cases, insight substitutes for remorse as the measure of the offender's failure to meet expectations of taking responsibility for the impact of the crime on the victim. As mentioned above, it also shifts discussion about the offender from concern about the credibility of their expression of remorse to their risk of future dangerousness.[38]

Notwithstanding the separation of insight from remorse as an alternative category for evaluating the character of the offender and their prospects for rehabilitation, there are substantial points of continuity in the judicial use of these attributions. Both the remorseful offender and the insightful one are expected to take full responsibility for their misconduct without invoking situational factors to mitigate culpability. Both are also expected to show an empathetic understanding of the impact of their crime on the victim. What in the language of remorse is referred to as minimisation is transmuted in the language of insight into a lack of awareness. One measure of the overlap between these categories is that while the population assembled for this analysis contained cases in which offenders were attributed remorse but not insight, in no case were any offenders attributed insight without also being attributed remorse.

What does distinguish the two approaches to evaluating character – apart from the emphasis in insight on the 'true causes' of the crime as opposed to the focus of remorse on the crime itself – is the use of two ostensibly dissimilar discourses: on the one hand, an overtly moral discourse that gives precedence to remorse, and on the other, a purportedly actuarial discourse that gives precedence to insight. On closer reading, however, it is probably fairer to say that the moral dimension in remorse is more explicit than it is with respect to the attribution of insight. For, just as the condemnation of a lack of remorse or an insufficient expression of remorse can only occur in relation to an expectation of how a member of the community should feel, so too the attribution of a

[35] *R v JS* [2018] OJ 4095, para 23.

[36] *R v Fairchild* [2017] ONCJ 658, paras 35 and 36.

[37] *R v Sesay* [2019] BCSC 795, para 78.

[38] The question arises whether the substitution of insight for remorse unsettles the tacit understanding between courts, counsel and offender that a plea of guilty will result in mitigation of sentence. It is on these grounds that several of the cited cases have been appealed.

'lack of awareness' can only arise in relation to an expectation of what a member of the community should understand about the impact of their crime.

In sub-section B below, I will identify the dimension that most distinguishes insight from remorse as a way of monitoring the passage from transgressor to member of the moral community. The shift from remorse to insight, I will suggest, entails the elevation of cognition and verbal competence to equal status with the expression of the moral emotion of remorse as a measure of personal transformation. I will now focus on how this shift in performance affects the different categories of offenders that come before the courts.

B. Cognition versus Affect

As the academic literature on remorse suggests, there are reasons to be sceptical about the reliability and validity of assessments of emotions, such as the presence or absence of remorsefulness, for a number of reasons. Prime among these is the fallibility of trying to discern inner feelings from demeanour.[39] Hence, at least one possible rationale for the increased emphasis on the cognition of the offender – their awareness of the causes of their criminality – is the belief that it offers a more trustworthy basis for evaluating their readiness to be returned to the community.

One way of capturing the difference between how insight and remorse are performed is to note the different language used by courts and other observers to describe how offenders communicate these attributes. In only four cases out of the population under review were offenders credited with both insight and remorse.[40] While there is some overlap in word usage, in that both 'remorse' and 'insight' can be demonstrated, what distinguishes the two is that only insight is 'developed' or 'gained' and only remorse is 'expressed'. Hence, remorse can be performed at any point in the offender's trajectory through the criminal justice system, whereas insight is acquired and cumulative. It does not come as an epiphany, as was claimed in one case, that the court rejected as 'bizarre' and unreliable as to 'the implications for … the commission of future violent act'.[41] Only with reference to remorse was one of the criteria for validation that the offender was 'genuine'. With insight, progress and credibility is achieved – the offender improves in their understanding of why they committed the crime. Insight is perceived as learned, whereas the ability to experience remorse is

[39] For discussion of this problem and its persistence, see S Bandes, 'Remorse, Demeanor, and the Consequences of Misinterpretation: The Limit of Law as a Window into the Soul' (2014) 3 *Journal of Law, Religion, and State* 170; S Bandes, 'Remorse and Judging' in Tudor et al (n 27) ch 1.

[40] *R v Inksetter* [2017] OJ 4390; *R v Palacios* [2012] OJ 1535; *R v Woolf* [2019] ONCJ 37; *R v Heffernan* [2012] OJ 6262.

[41] *R v ASD* [2019] BCJ 162, paras 32 and 588.

perceived as intrinsic to the person and less susceptible to change.[42] In all four cases, the offenders were perceived as meeting the expectation for showing remorse by expressing to the satisfaction of the court the feelings that a member of the moral community should have about the offence they committed. They were also credited with insight by putting forward corroborative testimony that they had developed awareness of what were purportedly the true causes of their criminal misconduct.

Where remorse and insight diverge most, however, is in the almost antithetical requirements for successfully performing one or the other. In 14 out of the total population of 66 cases, expert testimony was offered as evidence that the intellectual demands required for the acquisition of insight were beyond the offender's capabilities. For example, here is one psychiatrist's conclusions about the ability of one offender to gain insight:

> Mr. F is drastically lacking in insight into his personality and into his patterns of being hurtful. I don't think we should expect fundamental change from (F) as he is approaching his 50th year. He does not have the background, the education, or the reflectiveness to suggest that kind of thing is going to happen.[43]

In other cases, the offender's unsuitability for insight-oriented therapy is attributed to intellectual limitations: 'PL is not a suitable candidate for insight oriented psychotherapy due to his low level of intellectual functioning.'[44] Even in cases where the offender has pleaded guilty and expressed remorse, expert opinion is quoted as communicating doubt about the capacity of the offender to develop insight:

> Mr. (H) is a youthful first offender. Despite entering guilty pleas and demonstrating an acceptance of responsibility, he has very limited insight into his offending … I recognize, however that that insight, or lack thereof, is very much a product of his cognitive and intellectual limitations and challenges which are well documented.[45]

As Shammas has written, the performance of insight 'hinge(s) on personal capacity to (1) verbally express thoughts and feelings, (2) speak in a reflective manner, and (3) produce linguistic utterances in a socially legitimate form'[46] – skills that are unevenly distributed in the population as a whole.[47]

[42] In two of the cases, the offender's remorse was perceived as a result of having achieved insight into why they committed their criminal act. The following is a quote from an offender attesting to this sequence: 'I want to be accountable. If you say 20 years or if you say life that I gotta do it, I will be accountable. I'll go in there still with the life sentence, I work hard to change. I want to tell the victim that I – they possibly don't care, they possibly don't care about what I feel or what I say today, but I'll go in there and do everything I possibly can. I apologized before. I didn't have the understanding of the impact that I caused on the people in the past, Mr. Simpson. You and Mrs. Durant pushed this. I did it.' *R v Bitternose* (2012) AJ 1223, para 238; see also *R v Eamer* [2017] OJ 218, para 88.

[43] *R v Fontaine* [2014] SJ 464, para 29.

[44] *R v PL* [2017] ABPC 198, para 30.

[45] *R v Hems* [2019] OJ 5541, para 117.

[46] Shammas (n 5) 151.

[47] For adverse impact of using insight as standard for deciding parole for juveniles, see Bell (n 16); for impact on the cognitively impaired in parole hearings, see A Heron, 'Note: An Impossible

Yet the ability to meet these linguistic requirements may itself attract suspicion. Among the cases are offenders who were able to manifest all the verbal skills necessary to convince experts of their insight into their 'dysfunctional behaviour', yet who reoffended shortly after they were released. Here, the observations of experts reflect disbelief that the verbal proficiency of the offender necessary to convey insight corresponds to how they feel. Comments about offenders by court-appointed assessors, such as 'MC says what we want to see – But is he assimilating?',[48] or by the court when referring to another case, such as that the offender 'presents well as having insight – as such he can be deceptive' or that 'he has a history of professing insight',[49] make it clear that the problem of distinguishing between authentic and manipulative displays of personal transformation is as likely to occur with respect to attributions of insight as with attributions of remorse.

Too awkward or inarticulate a performance may define the offender as incapable of achieving insight. Too smooth a verbal performance may reflect a moral incapacity to feel what is required to experience remorse. To escape these disqualifying attributions requires of the offender a very fine balancing between verbal dexterity and the projection of sincerity – what Aviram has called 'rehearsed authenticity'.[50] The paradox at the core of how insight and remorse are communicated is that verbal dexterity is essential to the former but attracts suspicion in the latter.

IV. SCRIPTING REDEMPTION – THE MOVEMENT FROM REMORSE TO INSIGHT

I use the term 'redemption'[51] advisedly to describe the changes that our criminal justice system envisages for those accused and convicted wrongdoers before they can be allowed to return to the community. Whether inscribed in a religious ritual or secularised as a therapeutic intervention targeted to 'risk factors', the movement from condemned wrongdoer to the category of the remorseful or newly awakened or reformed is a rite of passage that cannot be divested of its moral significance. And whether the transformation thus envisioned signifies deep characterological change or merely a shallow compliance with an external standard, it is a passage that marks a shift from estrangement to alignment with the moral standards of the community at large.

Standard: The California Parole Board Process for Inmates with Cognitive Impairments' (2018) 91 *California Law Review* 989.

[48] *R v Caston* [2019] BCJ 1233, para 190.

[49] *R v Eamer* [2017] OJ 2181, paras 177 and 303.

[50] Aviram (n 5) 168.

[51] For a link between secular and theological conceptions of personal transformation, see N Maguire, 'Repentance and the Law: The Intersection of Theological, Legal, and Criminological Perspectives' (2011) 2 *ET Studies* 197; S Maruna, *Making Good: How Ex-Convicts Reform and Rebuild Their Lives* (American Psychological Association, 2001) especially ch 5.

The remorse sequence and the insight sequence discussed above represent distinguishable, but not necessarily incompatible, approaches to this process of transformation. Both sequences root their prescriptions for change in a terminology that retains its links to popular usage and has no precise legal definition – hence the fluidity noted above in the criteria used to validate the claims of a purportedly remorseful or insightful offender. But this is not to suggest so loose a usage as to be without any lines of demarcation. The two sequences direct the attention of courts, parole officers, forensic psychiatrists and psychologists, and ancillary personnel to different aspects of the offenders' performance. If the attribution of remorse creates a template for how the transformed offender is expected to feel about their criminal misconduct, the addition of insight as a condition for mitigation or parole regulates the offender's narrative of why they engaged in criminal misconduct as well as specifying what changes they must make to lessen the likelihood of reoffending. So comprehensive is this control over the offender's life history that personal trajectories that were viewed as acceptable even a generation ago, such as religious conversion, are now subject to increased scrutiny if they do not match this scripting with some exactitude.[52]

The elevation of speech and the corresponding demotion of feeling as evidence of personal transformation does affect the performance of the offender, with arguably greater adverse consequences to those who are socially disadvantaged or suffer from cognitive disability, as previously noted. But just as is the case with remorse, the benefit that attaches to a successful performance of insight raises doubts about whether the performance is genuine or strategic. Equally significantly, the lability of the category of insight leaves open the possibility that expert witnesses can disagree over whether the offender's claim is creditable. In the population under review, in one-third of the cases, witnesses arrived at conflicting opinions about the offender's insight, with the Crown marshalling expert evidence to contest the claim and the defence to support the claim. Comments made in cases where offenders who had previously convinced forensic experts of their insight into their risk factors but who had nevertheless reoffended reveal that the concerns that pervade demonstrations of remorse also extend to performances of insight; in other words, does what is shown correspond to what is felt? Just as in the showing of remorse, this context of suspicion places the offender in the awkward position of having to meet the specifications of insight while also conveying authenticity – a hurdle that only four of the offenders in this population were able to surmount.[53]

At present, the language of remorse is still paramount in the courtrooms of Canada, while the language of insight and risk prevails in the parole boards. What remains are questions about whether the tighter control that insight exerts over how the offender comes to understand the causes of their criminal misconduct is

[52] Aviram (n 5) 13 remarks on the Parole Board's reaction to born-again Christian inmates as varying between 'suspicion of the converts' sincerity and rebuke of their zealousness'.

[53] See n 37.

more effective in preventing recidivism than reliance on remorse as the primary test of whether the offender is ready to return to the community. Other questions follow as well from the foregoing analysis. Does the shift in emphasis away from the power of the moral emotions to the acquisition of a new language to inhibit criminal misconduct – that of insight – have an adverse impact on already disadvantaged populations? If so, should there be remedies to alleviate these effects and what form would they take? In the context of the Canadian criminal justice system, these questions take on a special urgency. Indigenous offenders comprised 3 per cent of the Canadian population and 30 per cent of the total population of federally incarcerated prisoners as of 2020.[54] The use of actuarial tests to determine risk has already been successfully challenged in Canadian courts for possible cultural bias against indigenous populations.[55] How the standards for achieving insight and for communicating remorse are affected by cultural differences and educational disparities are matters of interest both as academic issues and issues of social policy.

[54] Office of the Correctional Investigator, www.oci-bec.gc.ca/cnt/rpt/annrpt/annrpt20192020-eng.aspx#s10.

[55] *Ewert v Canada* [2018] SCC 30.

8

The Construction of the Ideal Defendant: Comparative Understandings of the Normalisation of Guilt

JACQUELINE S HODGSON*

This chapter examines how legal actors contribute to the production of the guilty plea in England and Wales and in France in ways that outwardly satisfy fair trial guarantees of voluntariness and fairness, but which are often at odds with the due process rhetoric of the law and the defendant's own understanding of her responsibility. Through a narrative of due process and defendant choice, guilt is performed and represented to the defendant, and to legal actors themselves, in ways that conceal or simply deny the processes of persuasion. Defendants are modelled by police, lawyers and prosecutors before and at court to accept their guilt and so the legitimacy of their punishment. The chapter explores the legitimating function performed by criminal defence lawyers in England and Wales, and how they square their management of the defendant towards a guilty plea with their professional ethical responsibility to represent the best interests of their client. In France, it is the judicial status of the prosecutor, assumed by courts and lawyers to protect the interests of the accused and guarantee the credibility of the evidence, which masks and legitimises prosecutor-sanctioned pre-trial practices that centre on obtaining a confession. The defence role is limited, but serves to demonstrate compliance with fair trial procedures and so helps further legitimate the process of conviction. In both jurisdictions, legal actors' active engagement in the construction of the ideal – guilty – defendant calls into question the authenticity of the defendant's participation and decision-making, and so the legitimacy of the accused's plea and sentence.

* Professor and Deputy Pro-Vice-Chancellor (Research), School of Law, University of Warwick, UK.

I. INTRODUCTION

DRAWING ON EMPIRICAL studies conducted in England and Wales and in France over several decades,[1] this chapter examines the role of legal actors in the normalisation of the guilty plea in England and Wales and in France – how this is produced and represented in ways that appear to satisfy guarantees of voluntariness and fairness, but which are often at odds with the due process rhetoric of the law and the defendant's own understanding of her responsibility. It explores how defendants are modelled outside of court, and then positioned at trial as individuals who accept their guilt and so the legitimacy of their punishment; and how, underpinned by the language of due process and choice, criminal guilt is represented to the defendant, courts and lawyers in ways that serve to legitimate a legal narrative of fair trial norms, while concealing the uncomfortable processes of persuasion and pressures to plead guilty.[2] In England and Wales, the criminal defence lawyer is at the centre of this, managing the defendant towards an admission and choreographing public expressions of guilt and remorse to produce the ideal defendant.[3]

The chapter also compares the production of guilt in France, an inquisitorial procedure in which legal actors have different roles and responsibilities before and at trial. The defence plays a much smaller role than in England and Wales, though one that is used increasingly to lend legitimacy to the choices made by the defendant.[4] More important is the prosecutor (the *procureur*), whose judicial

[1] The principal studies referred to employ both direct observations and semi-structured interviews, and include, in England and Wales: my own large-scale study of 48 lawyers' firms and three independent agencies, carried out between 1988 and 1992: M McConville, J Hodgson, L Bridges and A Pavlovic, *Standing Accused: The Organisation and Practices of Criminal Defence Lawyers in Britain* (Oxford, Oxford University Press, 1994); the study carried out between 2007 and 2011 by D Newman, *Legal Aid Lawyers and the Quest for Justice* (Oxford, Hart Publishing, 2013); the doctoral research carried out between 2012 and 2016 by J Horne, 'A Plea of Convenience: An Examination of the Guilty Plea in England and Wales' (PhD thesis, University of Warwick, 2017). In France, my own focused, single-country study carried out over 18 months and five field sites in 1993–94 and 1997–99: J Hodgson, *French Criminal Justice: A Comparative Account of the Investigation and Prosecution of Crime in France* (Oxford, Hart Publishing, 2005); my multi-country comparative project carried out between 2011 and 2013: J Blackstock, E Cape, J Hodgson, A Ogorodova and T Spronken, *Inside Police Custody: An Empirical Account of Suspects' Rights in Four Jurisdictions* (Antwerp, Intersentia, 2014); and the empirical work carried out between 2011 and 2016 by L Soubise, 'Guilty Pleas in an Inquisitorial Setting – An Empirical Study of France' (2018) 45 *Journal of Law and Society* 398.

[2] The lawyer's co-opted role as 'double-agent', formally representing the interests of her client whilst serving those of the court and wider criminal process, has long been a feature of criminal courts. See, eg A Blumberg, 'The Practice of Law as a Confidence Game. Organizational Cooptation of a Profession' (1967) 1 *Law and Society Review* 15; McConville et al (n 1).

[3] The term 'defendant' refers to those facing criminal prosecution in court. The 'accused' is a broader, more generic term. Being an accused will trigger pre-trial rights such as access to counsel, even though the person may not go on to be prosecuted at court. I have used the two terms interchangeably here for stylistic reasons.

[4] The rights of the defence appear to be expanding as lawyers have a greater presence in the criminal procedure, but they are very limited in what they are permitted to do. See, eg E Cape and

status and supervisory role are understood to protect the interests of the accused and guarantee the credibility of the evidence against the defendant in the eyes of the court and other legal actors. In both jurisdictions, though in different ways and to different degrees, legal actors play a crucial role in the production and legitimation of the guilty plea, calling into question the authenticity of the defendant's participation and decision-making, and so the legitimacy of the accused's plea and sentence.

II. THE SIGNIFICANCE OF THE GUILTY PLEA AS A FINDING OF THE COURT

Both in England and Wales and in France, the criminal trial is the formal site at which the defendant's criminal responsibility is determined. This might be through the hearing and examination of witness testimony, and arguments made by counsel for the prosecution and defence, but more often it serves as a mechanism that translates the accused's apparent acknowledgement of responsibility into a judicial finding of guilt. How this admission is formalised – as a verification at court of the accused's pre-trial account or as a plea of guilty – and what precedes this admission vary between jurisdictions and offence types. Within law's rhetoric of due process and fair trial, an admission of criminal responsibility at court is understood to be underpinned by a neutral investigation conducted by police or a judicial figure, with the interests and informed decision-making of the accused ensured through a combination of defence representation and judicial guarantees. In practice, there is a system of structured incentives around charge and sentence, designed to abbreviate or avoid investigation and trial, and to encourage an admission at the earliest moment. But reliance is placed upon the defence lawyer or the prosecutor, rather than on the court, to ensure defendants sign up to these incentives, whilst at the same time demonstrating that the accused understands the charges, the evidence and the precise nature of the facts for which they are admitting responsibility. In this way, whether through a guilty plea at trial or an alternative form of case disposition, the court's responsibility for ensuring the voluntariness of the admission is in practice devolved to other legal actors.

In England and Wales, the vast majority of court verdicts are made up of guilty pleas.[5] Although different from the fully contested trial, in which evidence and witnesses are examined, the guilty plea represents a formal, legal determination of guilt by the court, based on a voluntary admission of responsibility by the

J Hodgson, 'The Right of Access to a Lawyer at Police Stations: Making the European Union Directive Work in Practice' [2014] *New Journal of European Criminal Law* 450.

[5] Guilty pleas account for nearly 80% of disposals in the magistrates' court and 73% in the Crown Court: Crown Prosecution Service, *Annual Report and Accounts 2019–2020*, HC 558 (London, HMSO, 2020). In addition to the incentives set out here, there is a growing number of strict liability cases, to which there is no defence.

accused. It exists within a court procedure that is understood to reflect the same fair trial values and guarantees as a contested trial and so carries the same legal consequences and legitimacy. The defendant's statement to the court that she understands the charges and her entering of a guilty plea constitute her acceptance of, and agreement to, the prosecution case against her. However, whilst the guilty plea abbreviates the trial process, it does not extinguish it completely. The defendant's admission through a guilty plea is not determinative – it does not override the court's power to convict: a finding of guilt remains the sole responsibility of the court. The court may (and in practice will) accept the defendant's plea as its own finding of guilt and proceed to sentence,[6] but in theory, it may also reject the plea if it believes that the charges are not in fact made out, or that the plea is equivocal or involuntary.[7]

The core principle underpinning the court's acceptance of the plea as its own finding is that the guilty plea represents a clear and voluntary acknowledgement of guilt. The defence lawyer's role in this process is crucial, both at trial and in the provision of pre-trial advice. Acting as translator and advocate, the defence lawyer is required to ensure that the defendant understands the nature and strength of the prosecution evidence and the consequences of any plea, identifying and building the defence case, and arguing the defendant's case at court. In this way, the lawyer serves as a guarantee for the defendant, the court and the public that the accused is able to make an informed and voluntary choice whether to contest the prosecution case and plead not guilty or to accept the charges and enter a plea of guilty. Party autonomy is a key feature of the values of procedural fairness underpinning the adversarial tradition and legal representation appears to guarantee this autonomy and so strengthen the protection of the accused. By treating the guilty plea as determinative and translating it seamlessly into the legal finding of the court, the court is able to abdicate its fact-finding responsibility. In this way, the defence lawyer's role in advising and representing her client becomes a proxy for the trial itself. Furthermore, the provision of a lawyer representing the interests of the defendant clothes the process with a legal and professional legitimacy, a visible guarantee that due process protections have been adhered to. This guarantee binds the defendant tightly into the process, making it difficult to challenge the grounds of a guilty plea or the legal advice on which it was based – described by Horne as the 'immunising effect of legal advice'.[8] This legitimating function of the lawyer is seen in other parts of the

[6] The Criminal Procedure Rules anticipate this in practice, authorising the court to convict without hearing the evidence if the plea is a clear acknowledgement of guilt. Criminal Procedure Rule 24.7.

[7] Criminal Procedure Rule 24.7 means that, in practice, the court is unlikely to hear the evidence and so will be unable to judge whether the charges are made out. The defendant's behaviour – telling the court that she did not in fact commit the offence despite entering a plea of guilty, for example – may lead the court to question the guilty plea. Or, the court may simply ask the lawyer to instruct her client to remain quiet.

[8] Horne (n 1).

criminal process too. The introduction of custodial legal advice, for example, created a presumption of equality of arms in the eyes of the courts, making challenges to the fairness of police interrogation almost impossible, regardless of the quality of legal representation.[9] In France too, the protective value of custodial legal advice is limited by the passive terms in which it is defined. Legal advisors are permitted simply to be present as observers, causing many lawyers to characterise their role as ornamental, like that of a vase.[10]

This is not to assert that legal representation does not benefit defendants. The court's treatment of the guilty plea when the defendant is unrepresented demonstrates the ways that defence lawyers are able to serve the interests of their clients, but it also shows clearly their value to the criminal process in ensuring the efficient processing of cases and in providing a public assurance of due process that is also protective of the actions of court communities.[11] Cuts to legal aid have resulted in larger numbers of unrepresented defendants coming before the criminal courts,[12] depriving the accused of any legal assistance in understanding and dealing with their case and creating difficulties for the court whose procedures are neither designed for nor easily adapted to unrepresented defendants.[13] Transform Justice's 2016 study found that unrepresented defendants did not understand the charges; were likely to plead guilty when they ought not to have done; were unable to cross-examine witnesses effectively; and received harsher sentences because they did not know how to mitigate – how to present their personal circumstances and those of the crime, and how to set out mitigating factors fitting the sentencing guidelines.[14] Vulnerable defendants were especially

[9] J Hodgson, 'Tipping the Scales of Justice: The Suspect's Right to Legal Advice' [1992] *CLR* 854.

[10] Blackstock et al (n 1). When introduced in France in 2011, lawyers were permitted only to be present, not to speak or advise, and so described their role as ornamental, serving only to legitimate and prevent future challenges to the police interrogation of their client. Lawyers were previously allowed a 30-minute consultation with their client (in 1993 after 24 hours of detention; in 2000 from the start of custody), but not to be present during questioning. Code de procédure pénale, Art 63.

[11] The lawyerisation or professionalisation of justice is not simply a reflection of law's complexity, but also a function of what Larson calls the 'professional project', through which lawyers have successfully marketised their expertise in exchange for enhanced social status and economic reward. Reductions in legal aid rates of pay and the resulting shrinkage of the criminal bar suggest that this is no longer the case for criminal practitioners. MS Larson, *The Rise of Professionalism: A Sociological Analysis* (Berkeley, University of California Press, 1977).

[12] There are no official statistics on the number of unrepresented defendants in the magistrates' court, rendering them invisible in criminal justice policy terms, but magistrates estimate that more than one-fifth of those appearing before them are unrepresented. Transform Justice, 'Justice Denied? The Experience of Unrepresented Defendants in the Criminal Courts' (April 2016) 4. The number of applications for legal aid has fallen significantly. Ministry of Justice statistics show that from 2012–13 to 2016–17, magistrates' court disposals fell by 3%, but legal aid applications fell by 31%. J Peay and E Player, 'Pleading Guilty: Why Vulnerability Matters' [2018] *MLR* 929, 948.

[13] Whilst legal aid cuts represent some financial savings, the overall benefits to the criminal justice system (whether in time or money) were questioned by clerks, magistrates, district judges and prosecutors, who reported the huge impact on staff resources and increased delays as cases take much longer to deal with. Transform Justice (n 12).

[14] The report draws on existing data, court observations and interviews with prosecutors from the independent bar, district judges and magistrates. On the disadvantage suffered by unrepresented

at risk, as vulnerabilities may not be picked up during the court hearing. Without a defence lawyer to smooth the path, the motivations of prosecutors and judges were also more starkly apparent. Some court clerks and prosecutors tried to explain the process and help defendants, but others bullied them into a plea of guilty.[15] Horne reports similar accounts of judges directly challenging unrepresented defendants' decisions to plead guilty: 'Well there it is, there will have to be a trial. I've done my best to avoid it, but I can't see any way around that.'[16] With nobody tasked with representing the interests of the accused, there is no pretence of equality of arms. In the absence of the defence lawyer to bring the client into line in the privacy of the office or consultation room, the court is faced with the unmediated autonomy of the defendant, making all too visible the pressures applied to achieve a guilty plea.

The significance of the defendant's guilty plea as a due process finding of the court is further underlined by the reluctance of the appeal courts to quash a conviction following a guilty plea, even when the voluntariness (and so the reliability) of the plea is in question, or where there is evidence that the appellant is not guilty.[17] Here too, the role of defence counsel is pivotal in maintaining the external narrative of defendant autonomy and choice and so the integrity of the conviction.[18] Guilty pleas entered in order to avoid prison, or in exchange for discontinuing proceedings against family members, for example, are not considered improper pressure in a way that calls into question the voluntariness of the plea provided these have been properly put to defendants by defence and prosecution counsel, thus binding them into the narrative of party autonomy and choice.[19] Indeed, professional rules of conduct allow the defence lawyer to

defendants who do not have lawyers to argue their mitigation and remorse, see also H Dillon, 'Cranking the Sausage Machine: A Magistrates' Perspective on Remorse Assessment' in R Weisman, M Proeve and K Rossmanith (eds), *Remorse and Criminal Justice: Multidisciplinary Perspectives* (London, Routledge, 2021).

[15] See also Horne's account of a 13-year-old boy being pressured into a guilty plea by the magistrates' legal adviser, even with his solicitor present. Horne (n 1) 216.

[16] ibid.

[17] There is no right of appeal from a guilty plea in the magistrates' court, other than on a point of law. A plea of guilty may be appealed successfully if it is involuntary – that is, if it is the result of wrongful pressure to plead guilty; if it is the result of an abuse of process, erroneous legal advice or some other criminal process error; or if there is an exceptional case made that there is significant new evidence that is in the interests of justice to admit and which suggests that the appellant is not guilty. See further ibid 128–75.

[18] See, eg *R v Herbert* [1992] 94 Cr App R 230, 235. The defendant had entered a plea of guilty in order that his wife would not face legal proceedings. This was unproblematic for the court as the defendant 'had the benefit of the most conscientious legal advice'.

[19] In a striking illustration of the potentially involuntary nature of guilty pleas, even by legally represented defendants, in April 2021, the Court of Appeal overturned the convictions of more than 40 sub-postmasters prosecuted for theft and false accounting, referred to it by the CCRC: *Hamilton and others* [2021] EWCA Crim 577. Despite asserting their innocence, many of the accused felt, and were advised, that they had no choice but to plead guilty in order to avoid imprisonment. The prospect of avoiding prison acts as a particularly powerful incentive to plead guilty, especially for those who may be vulnerable in other ways – and rather than diminishing this pressure, legal representation may contribute to or amplify it. S Jones, 'Under Pressure: Women Who

advance a guilty plea and mitigation on behalf of the defendant even when her instructions are that she is not guilty.[20] In *R v Dann*, the appellant was told on the day of trial that charges against his partner and the mother of his two young children would be dropped if he agreed to plead guilty. In his signed statement on the day of trial, he denied any liability for the offence, but agreed to plead guilty in order to avoid the possibility of his partner being sent to prison and his children being without their mother, stating that 'the pressure this offer has put me under leaves me with no choice but to admit to something that I have not done'.[21] The Court of Appeal rejected the argument that the appellant had been placed under improper pressure, ruling that the plea followed a proposal based on the Crown's judgment of the public interest in the prosecution as a whole, and that the defendant had been 'properly and carefully advised by his counsel'.[22] It was unconcerned that the defendant's plea contradicted directly his assertion of innocence, content that the presence and advice of his own defence lawyer acted as a guarantee of procedural fairness. Refracted through the rhetoric of freedom of choice, counsel's advice plays a vital role in ushering the defendant towards a guilty plea and in preventing subsequent legal challenge by demonstrating that the plea has been made in an informed and voluntary way. In *R v Nightingale*, the court stated:

> It is the duty of the advocate ... to point out to the defendant the possible advantages in sentencing terms of tendering a guilty plea to the charge. So even if the defendant has indicated or instructed his lawyers that he intends to plead not guilty, in his own interests he is entitled to be given, and should receive, forthright advice on these and similar questions. These necessary forensic pressures ... and clear and forthright advice from his lawyers do not deprive the defendant of his freedom to choose whether to plead guilty or not guilty; rather the provision of realistic advice about his prospects helps to inform his choice.[23]

III. THE ROLE OF COURTS AND LAWYERS IN NORMALISING THE INEVITABILITY OF GUILT

The criminal defence role in guilty plea cases in England and Wales can be understood as a logical extension of a party-led procedure, in which

Plead Guilty to Crimes They Have Not Committed' (2011) 11 *Criminology and Criminal Justice* 77, 82. Jones's research explored the gender-specific factors that make it more likely that women will make false admissions. For a wider discussion of the risks to vulnerable defendants of the sentence discount guidelines, see Peay and Player (n 12).

[20] Rule 21.20(5) of the Law Society Conduct Rules, now replaced by Solicitors Regulation Authority Handbook. It used to be the case that, as an officer of the court, the lawyer could not represent a defendant on a guilty plea when the client had said they were not guilty. To do so would be to knowingly mislead the court. This led to vaguely comical exchanges where this was spelled out repeatedly until the client understood and finally parroted back the words 'Oh, OK, yes I am guilty'. McConville et al (n 1).

[21] *R v Dann* [2015] EWCA Crim 390, para 5.

[22] ibid para 13.

[23] *R v Nightingale* [2013] EWCA Crim 405, para 12.

prosecution and defence determine the contours of the case put before the court. This might be done through a process of negotiation or bargaining between the two parties, after which the prosecution agrees to put to the court a version of facts to which the accused will plead guilty. Defence lawyers are able to 'sell' these deals to the client and obtain a guilty plea by offering the dropped charge as an incentive, often accompanied by a warning that this will also avoid the harsher sentence that would follow the inevitable conviction should the case go to trial.[24] Alternatively, the need to present the prosecution evidence at court can be dispensed with altogether through the 'basis of plea' procedure, whereby a written version of the facts is agreed by defence and prosecution, signed by both parties (evidencing the autonomous decision-making of the parties and so the fairness of the process) and then handed to the court,[25] with the expectation that the matter will then proceed to sentence without further enquiry.

Outwardly, the lawyer's behaviour in these cases appears to reflect the informed choice of the accused in setting the limits of the case. But it may also mask a more complex and messy process in which the defendant's account is repackaged, better to fit with trial norms and expectations of guilt, reflecting a lawyer–client relationship in which, rather than empowering or advocating for the accused, the defence lawyer seeks only to avoid the possibility of a contested trial.[26] Research has shown that, despite describing their role in often adversarial terms, the starting point for many defence lawyers is a presumption of guilt.[27] Case preparation centres on the extent to which the defendant agrees to the prosecution version of events,[28] and it is rare for lawyers to contact witnesses or to obtain photographs of injuries or of the crime scene, the onus to collect this kind of evidence often being placed on the client. In this way, lawyers understand themselves as having engaged in defence building, knowing that the client, with no expertise or guidance, will fail to present a credible defence case and so come to see the inevitability of a guilty plea. Where the charges are contested, on the day of trial defendants are frequently told by their own lawyer that they will not be believed and so should plead guilty, even where this means having to

[24] McConville et al (n 1) 195.

[25] Attorney General's Guidelines on the Acceptance of Pleas and the Prosecutor's Role in the Sentencing Exercise, revised 2009 (2012) para C1-8.

[26] Efficiency may also serve the interests of the accused, but the tendency is to privilege the interests of the system in producing convictions and wider forms of criminalisation. This is also demonstrated in the appeal cases such as *Dunn*, *Herbert* and *Nightingale*, discussed above.

[27] Newman (n 1); A Mulcahy, 'The Justification of Justice: Legal Practitioners' Accounts of Negotiated Case Settlements in the Magistrates' Courts' (1994) 34 *British Journal of Criminology* 411; McConville et al (n 1).

[28] Tellingly, even the defence lawyer refers to the prosecution case as 'the facts'. McConville et al (n 1) 141–43. Barristers also went on to advise defendants in the Crown Court of the risk of conviction, without any consideration of the client's account. The defence case is simply not relevant. ibid 256.

construct new facts to fit an admission – either explicitly ('I can't say that, it's going against the evidence')[29] or implicitly through a retelling of events.[30]

Mirroring the language of the courtroom, lawyers employ the rhetoric of choice and voluntariness, invoking their own expertise in predicting the likelihood of conviction, firmly asserting that a guilty plea best serves the client's interests in securing a lower sentence, while at the same time telling the client that this is ultimately their decision. In this way, the lawyer understands herself to have fulfilled her professional obligations, providing the defendant with the kind of 'realistic advice about his prospects' to 'help inform his choice' that is so praised by the courts.[31] As legal professionals, these behaviours can be made sense of by lawyers through an appeal to the 'ethical indeterminacy' of advice and representation: if the evidence against the defendant is overwhelming and conviction seems certain, for example, one version of the client's best interests is to advise a plea of guilty and secure a lighter sentence.[32] This reasoning is in turn influenced by the wider features of the criminal justice process, such as sentence discounts for guilty pleas or pressures to avoid contesting evidence where possible.[33] In this way, lawyers can rationalise their behaviour both for their own sense of professional identity and integrity, but also to justify their actions in the eyes of the court. While pressures to avoid trial and a lack of resources inevitably influence the lawyer's behaviour,[34] the functioning of the system and the maintenance of lawyers' own credibility with the courts and fellow professionals depend on this being kept hidden, or at least not articulated explicitly. Legal actors dislike terms such as 'plea bargains' (preferring negotiation) or 'sentence discounts', as these suggest something underhand or unfair, which does not accord with how they understand themselves to be acting – to secure the best outcome for the defendant.[35] Wrapped in the rhetoric of party

[29] ibid 149.

[30] ibid 146–49. C Tata, 'Humanising Punishment? Mitigation and Case Cleansing Prior to Sentencing' (2019) 9 *Oñati Socio-Legal Series* 659 describes this process as 'case cleansing'.

[31] As described in *Nightingale* (n 23) para 12.

[32] See also Mulcahy (n 27) 421–22. This approach is supported by the appeal courts, as discussed above.

[33] T Goriely et al, *The Public Defence Solicitors Office in Edinburgh: An Independent Evaluation* (Edinburgh, Scottish Executive Central Research Unit, 2001) explains that decisions around plea are complex: 'The complexity of the decision [around plea] gives rise to ethical indeterminacy, where ethical practitioners may genuinely differ over the correct course of action' (3); 'in making difficult and evenly-balanced judgements, greater weight is placed on the advantages that flow from a course of action that is in one's own interests' (68–69).

[34] See Thornton's analysis of lawyer behaviour through the interaction of Bourdieu's habitus, field and capital. J Thornton, 'The Way in which Fee Reductions Influence Legal Aid Criminal Defence Lawyer Work: Insights from a Qualitative Study (2019) 46 *Journal of Law and Society* 559.

[35] A Flynn and A Freiberg, *Plea Negotiations: Final Report to the Criminology Research Council* (Canberra, Australian Institute of Criminology, 2008) 19–21 – though one defence lawyer said that their preferred term was 'horsetrading, I'm serious … that's what it is' (19); J Gormley and C Tata, 'To Plead or Not to Plead? "Guilt" Is the Question. Rethinking Sentencing and Plea Decision-Making in Anglo-American Countries' in C Spohn and P Brennan (eds), *Handbook on Sentencing Policies and Practices in the 21st Century* (New York, Routledge, 2020).

choice and autonomy, lawyers can plausibly believe themselves to be acting in the best interests of their clients.

The following example illustrates how the lawyer is able to manage the messy business of guilt, while persuading the client – and then representing to the court – that the plea is their choice.

> Solicitor: All of the witnesses are here – are you still going to plead not guilty?
>
> Client: Yes, why shouldn't I?
>
> Solicitor: Well – I've prepped your case, but self-defence is a hard one to run and it's a very tough bench today.
>
> Client: Are you saying I should plead guilty?
>
> Solicitor: No, not at all – I'm just saying there are two ways of handling this: you can plead not guilty, have a trial – you'll be cross-examined and the prosecution (remember they have three witnesses) will say that you merely stuck one on him, that he hadn't got his fists raised.
>
> Client: Yes but …
>
> Solicitor: Let me finish – or, you can take the *other* course – whereby they won't even *have* a say and I can speak on your behalf I can say that he'd already hit George … it's much better mitigation
>
> …
>
> Client: Well, you're the expert and you say that the bench is tough, shall I plead guilty then?
>
> Solicitor: That's entirely your decision.
>
> Client: … and it would save a lot of time if I plead guilty wouldn't it?
>
> Solicitor: Yes it would – if you have a trial, you'll be here until at least lunchtime, probably after that, whereas if you plead guilty you will be out of here within the hour – but time really isn't the issue.
>
> …
>
> Client: I'll plead guilty – because, as you say, it's a hard bench.
>
> Solicitor: It is, but it's your decision.
>
> Client: I know what these people are like … there are other things, like the people on the bench – and you're the expert, you have inside information about things like that, you know things about the bench and the prosecution that I don't know, so I've listened to you – and I'll plead guilty – but you *will* speak for me?
>
> Solicitor: Yes I will.[36]

While lawyers typically justify their focus on guilty pleas in this way through a reframing of the interests of the defendant, invoking the uncertainty of trials and the inevitability of conviction, especially in the magistrates' court, some lawyers do not even claim to understand their role in these terms, aligning themselves

[36] McConville et al (n 1) 195–96.

instead with wider system goals of pragmatism, expediency and fairness and the achievement of outcomes they perceive as just.[37]

> I think, you know, we are all trying to do justice at the end of the day to everybody. You know, we are all members of the public as well as defendants and lawyers … I don't think there is anything to be gained by running a trial where it's not going to affect the final outcome … much as we would like to live, I think, in the ideal world – I think you've got to say: 'Well, no, we've got to make the system work, and we've got to try and do justice,' and I think that [plea negotiations] does really.[38]

These behaviours are encouraged by the court, framed as reflections of procedural rules, effective case management and the 'proper and careful advice of counsel'.[39] The court's actions in speeding the case along mean that the defendant's guilty plea, even with the benefit of legal representation, is often neither informed nor voluntary. The defendant is required to enter a plea and set out what parts of the case are contested before having had sight of the prosecution case against her, with the papers often being provided on the morning of the court case.[40] Although the possibility exists to put the prosecution to proof to ensure that any conviction is on the basis of credible evidence, the rules of procedure and the practices and expectations of the court militate against this. The defence lawyer as much as the prosecutor is required 'actively to assist the exercise by the court of its case management powers',[41] and lawyers understand the expectation on them, reassuring the magistrates, for example, that they have advised their client of the wisdom of a guilty plea: 'I will once again have some stern advice for my client'.[42] The court is intolerant of defendants and lawyers who challenge this normalisation of guilt, with some judges seeking to press defendants into an admission of guilt with little concern to maintain even the appearance of detached neutrality.[43] Horne reports instances of judges openly offering higher than normal sentence discounts in order to extract a guilty plea, challenging the truth of the defendant's account and asking lawyers repeatedly

[37] This might be understood as an example of the ethical indeterminacy described by Goriely et al (n 33), the lawyer leaning towards their role as officer of the court.

[38] Mulcahy (n 27) 422–23.

[39] Even the court paperwork, such as preparation for trial form in the magistrates' court, requires the defence lawyer to confirm that the defendant understands that they will receive credit for a guilty plea and that this may affect the sentence and order for costs.

[40] Weak cases are prosecuted in the knowledge that most defendants will plead guilty and so the strength and quality of the evidence will not be questioned. The late disclosure of evidence will have a particular impact on vulnerable defendants, who may then be less likely to understand the elements of the offence, the strength of the case against them or the relevance of the exculpatory material. Peay and Player (n 12).

[41] *Malcolm v DPP* [2007] EWHC 363, para. 31.

[42] Horne (n 1) 219. See also Darbyshire's account of the complicity of lawyers and judges in procuring guilty pleas. P Darbyshire, 'Judicial Case Management in Ten Crown Courts' [2014] *CLR* 30; P Darbyshire, *Sitting in Judgment: The Working Lives of Judges* (Oxford, Hart Publishing, 2011).

[43] M McConville and L Marsh, *Criminal Judges* (Cheltenham, Edward Elgar, 2014).

whether their client understood that they would be losing any sentencing credit by going to trial.[44] Judges also sought to put pressure on defendants via the defence lawyer. When indicating at a plea and case management hearing that the defendant would be pleading not guilty, not yet having had the prosecution papers, one solicitor told Horne that the judge went 'ballistic', demanding 'I want a plea right now because he knows whether he's done it or not', and this was not an isolated incident.[45]

IV. THE ROUTINISATION OF GUILT BEFORE THE COURT

The court process itself, assisted by the legal actors at trial, plays an important part in the normalisation of guilt. The formality of court procedures appears to reflect due process safeguards, voluntary and informed decision-making and so a credible and legitimate finding of guilt, whilst often masking the defendant's lack of autonomy and the backstage pressures under which she is placed to admit responsibility. As the accounts above of unrepresented defendants illustrate, the defence lawyer plays a vital part in ensuring the smooth running of the court hearing and that the defendant behaves as the court expects. Beyond answering the charges, any attempts at participation by the accused are seen as unwelcome interruptions. When she does speak, the language of the court is scripted and the defendant is simply invited to adopt it, with no concern to ensure she understands the significance of her words. When asked how she pleads, the defendant is required to answer 'guilty' or 'not guilty', for example; a reply of 'Yes, I stole the bag but …' will not be heard and the accused will be instructed to say only the words of the plea.

Examples from research spanning several decades show that it is difficult for defendants to participate effectively in their trial when pleading guilty.[46] The ways that they are managed through the process, both by the court and by their own lawyer, place little value on defendants' understanding of what is being said about them or what is happening to them.[47] In this instance, for example, no solicitor was available to represent the defendant in court, so the solicitor's

[44] Horne (n 1) 214–17.

[45] Another lawyer confirmed receiving similar treatment at a plea and directions hearing from the same judge 'when he refused to indicate his client's plea because, as he put it, "I've got a case summary without a single statement and I'm not going to assume it's accurate in a case like this, a massive conspiracy. There are going to be more people on the indictment. I don't even know who I'm supposed to be conspiring with".' ibid 218.

[46] McConville et al (n 1); Newman (n 1); Horne (n 1). See also Mulcahy (n 27); Goriely et al (n 33).

[47] The management of clients is not limited to trial. This is part of a wider culture of managing clients towards some form of admission, including alternatives to charge and prosecution administered by police and prosecutors. M McConville and J Hodgson, *Custodial Legal Advice and the Right to Silence* (London, HMSO, 1993); McConville et al (n 1); Newman (n 1); Horne (n 1).

clerk spoke to the client. The defendant was instructed what to say, but with no real explanation of why this was happening or what it would mean for them.[48]

> Clerk: Hello. I've had a word in there – you won't need a solicitor, it's a bind over. The clerk will explain it when you appear just say 'yes I understand'. OK?
>
> Client: I suppose so.[49]

There is no expectation that the defendant will participate other than through her lawyer. This allows lawyers and the court to maintain a fair trial narrative of party autonomy, whilst enabling the defence lawyer to shape the defendant's response. For example, when the court clerk asked the defendant 'Do you understand the charges against you?', on several occasions I observed the defendant, unsure of the answer, turn to her lawyer, who mouthed across the court to her client 'Yes'. The defendant then turned back to the clerk and replied 'Yes'.[50] On other occasions, defendants were unaware that they had entered a guilty plea at an earlier hearing. Lawyers could explain this to themselves and to the client as making the process easier for defendants, but in fact it simply made it easier for the lawyers and the court, whilst alienating the accused from her own process of accusation and conviction.

The defendant's disconnection from her own trial process is part of the lawyer's active management of her client towards the inevitability of a guilty plea, as illustrated by examples such as this exchange outside the courtroom in a case of driving without a licence. The clerk had sought agreement to an adjournment so that the client could obtain the necessary proof and plead not guilty.

> Clerk: Bad news I'm afraid … they're going to oppose our application for an adjournment.
>
> Client: What does that mean exactly?
>
> Clerk: It means they want to deal with it today and they don't think we should stretch it out any longer and that's what they will say to the magistrates.
>
> Client: Well, what does that mean for me?
>
> Clerk: (firmly) It means you will have to plead guilty I'm afraid.
>
> Client: (indignantly) But I'm not guilty!
>
> Clerk: I know, but you see we haven't got any proof have we? … As it is, I think if you plead guilty the magistrates will only fine you.

[48] Clients are seen by a range of legal representatives at the police station and in the office, with solicitors concentrating their work on courtroom advocacy. Busy legal aid firms typically employed a clerk (sometimes known as a 'runner') to run between courts, speaking to clients and court staff so that everything is primed for the solicitor – whose timetable is often dependent on the court business of the day and where her cases appear in the list – to deal with the case as soon as she arrives. McConville et al (n 1) 163–67.

[49] ibid 172.

[50] I observed this during the 1994 Standing Accused study: McConville et al (n 1).

> Client: (outraged) That's not the point – it's not right is it?
>
> Clerk: Well, no – but if you plead not guilty and then they find you guilty you'll get a heftier fine. I know what you're saying – it's not right, but what can we do?[51]

There are exceptions – solicitors who recognise the dangers of incentivising admissions, especially for those more vulnerable to pressure,[52] but in many instances, lawyers consider it a failing if they are unable to avoid conflict and secure a guilty plea. They do not understand themselves to be pressuring their clients, claiming that innocent defendants would not entertain a guilty plea, as this lawyer explained:

> They are guilty of something and what you learn with working in crime for so long is that if you entertain the conversation with a client and you say 'Look, you can get 33 per cent off your sentence, off any sentence, if you plead guilty at the earliest opportunity', the fact that your client wants to engage in that conversation suggests that he's either guilty of the offence or guilty of something.[53]

And while courts and lawyers are prepared to do the necessary dirty work to achieve the desired result – to threaten and persuade the defendant, to adjust the facts to fit the outcome – this must remain hidden in order to protect the appearance of defendant choice and autonomy. Nor is the court concerned to ensure adherence to procedural protections designed to protect the accused and to provide for fair trial standards. In managing defendants towards a guilty plea, magistrates exercise their discretion such that they routinely refuse adjournments requested by the defence and insist on the defendant entering an early plea despite the prosecution's failure to provide evidence disclosure. The right to know the case against you is not taken seriously and there is no expectation that the defence will put the prosecution to proof. The introduction of remote hearings using video technology facilitates this management of the accused by courts and lawyers, making her participation and understanding yet more remote from the trial.[54] Horne gives the following example of a sentencing hearing that took place by video link from prison:

> [T]he court was observed ignoring an equivocal plea from a vulnerable and unrepresented defendant who had serious mental health and drug problems (including schizophrenia and bipolar disorder). He was produced by video link from prison. When the charges were put, the defendant replied 'guilty' to each one but on the last occasion he added, 'I don't know what I've pleaded guilty to!' The court ignored this comment and proceeded to sentence the defendant to ten weeks imprisonment.[55]

[51] ibid 167.

[52] Horne (n 1). We also observed (in McConville et al (n 1)) that a minority of lawyers committed to the adversarial ideals of testing out the prosecution case and going to trial when clients contested the charges against them. Interestingly, these lawyers were often characterised as in some way political, for taking criminal procedure seriously in this way.

[53] Horne (n 1) 198. See also McConville et al (n 1); Newman (n 1).

[54] JI Turner, 'Virtual Guilty Pleas' (2022) 24 *University of Pennsylvania Journal of Constitutional Law* 211. Remote hearings have become commonplace in the USA during the coronavirus pandemic, but there are now calls to maintain them.

[55] Horne (n 1) 244.

V. THE NORMALISATION OF GUILT IN FRANCE

As an inquisitorially rooted procedure, findings of guilt are more firmly rooted constitutionally and procedurally in the decision-making responsibility of the judge both at court and during the pre-trial: it is not for the parties to shape the contours of the case. Fair trial guarantees are in part assured by the centrality of this judicial role, and the judicial supervision of investigations in particular, obviating the need for strong party representation as a means of gathering and testing out the evidence in the way that is central to fair trial protections in the adversarial tradition. Directed towards a search for the truth and guided by a public interest-centred ideology, judicial officers (*magistrats*) are required to investigate exculpating as well as inculpating evidence and all evidence is recorded in the case dossier, later to be confirmed or verified at court. Therefore, understood as the result of a judicially supervised investigation, greater credibility attaches to the dossier of evidence assembled during the pre-trial phase than to the prosecution file in England and Wales.

The ideological power of the dossier as the outcome of a judicially supervised enquiry is important in understanding the construction of the defendant's guilt and the role of legal actors in actively bolstering this. At trial, the solidarity of the judiciary[56] means that the dossier, ratified by a fellow *magistrat*, is assumed to represent a complete account of the truth and one that need not be challenged. For the defence lawyer too, the treatment of the dossier as the product of a judicially supervised investigation means that it is accepted at face value in most instances. If not, rather than challenge its findings, lawyers present an alternative reading of the dossier in a way that is more favourable to the defendant.[57] In this way, both lawyers and trial judges play an important part in legitimating the dossier as an expression of judicial supervision that assures the reliability of the prosecution case and so any pre-trial admission of guilt by the defendant.

However, just as the safeguards of party autonomy and choice that serve to legitimate defendant admissions of guilt in England and Wales are often illusory in practice, so too the legitimating rhetoric of judicial supervision does not withstand close scrutiny. In practice, the vast majority of investigations are carried out by the police, under the supervision of the *procureur* – the public prosecutor, who is also a judicial officer. The police enjoy considerable autonomy in their conduct of the investigation: detention times are limited and written accounts

[56] Often described as judicial corporatism. See, eg A Vallini, *Rapport fait au nom de la commission d'enquête chargée de rechercher les causes des dysfonctionnements de la justice dans l'affaire dite d'Outreau et de formuler des propositions pour éviter leur renouvellement* (Paris, Assemblée Nationale, 2006) 276.

[57] See Field and West's account of lawyers 'pleading the dossier', offering an alternative reading based on the evidence contained in the dossier. Attempts to go beyond the scope of the dossier and challenge the evidence itself are not well received by the court, being seen as an attack on the credibility of the judiciary. S Field and A West, 'Dialogue and the Inquisitorial Tradition: French Defence Lawyers in the Pre-trial Criminal Process' (2003) 14 *Criminal Law Forum* 261.

of the evidence and procedure are required, but statements are not routinely audio recorded and lawyers have a largely passive role. This is in part because police accountability to the prosecutor is considered the primary safeguard for the conduct and outcomes of the investigation. In practice, however, supervision is unable to provide these guarantees, consisting of a largely file-based retrospective form of bureaucratic accountability, focused on the integrity of the evidence presented in the dossier rather than the conditions under which it was produced. There is no expectation that supervision will operate as a close or contemporaneous check on police activity, but like the 'immunising effect' of the defence lawyer in England and Wales, the judicial status and public interest ideology of the *procureur* provides a powerful outward assurance of fairness, protecting the procedure from challenge.[58] The police enquiry is approved by the prosecutor and so is transformed into a judicially supervised investigation, leaving unseen the processes by which the defendant has been encouraged to make an admission whilst in police custody. In addition to the weak and ineffective mechanisms of supervision provided by the *procureur*, the ideal defendant is constructed through a case dossier narrative that, in practice, often equates the search for the truth and the ideology of judicial supervision with the guilt of the defendant.

VI. ENCOURAGING AND LEGITIMATING DEFENDANTS' ASSUMPTIONS OF RESPONSIBILITY: THE ROLE OF PUBLIC PROSECUTORS IN FRANCE

In overseeing the pre-trial enquiry, the prosecutor's role in practice is oriented towards a presumption of guilt, with a firm expectation that police questioning should produce an admission.[59] This makes her a central player in the production and normalisation of the guilty defendant within French criminal justice.[60] The defence role is defined more narrowly than in the adversarial tradition, being seen as less necessary in a procedure understood to be characterised by judicial investigation and supervision.[61] This places the defendant in a very different position from her counterpart in England and Wales, requiring a greater level of participation at trial and leaving her unshielded from the direct questioning of the prosecutor and the trial judge in pre-trial hearings and at court.

[58] The 'immunising effect' of the prosecutor's judicial status is further strengthened by the re-definition of her pre-trial role in a way that more closely mirrors that of the investigating judge, with explicit responsibility for ensuring the investigation is conducted into elements that point to the innocence as well as the guilt of any suspect. Code de procédure pénale, Art 39-3.

[59] Hodgson (n 1).

[60] Oversight of the police investigation rests with the prosecutor, who controls the flow of investigations to the investigating judge, the court and alternative modes of case disposition.

[61] For a detailed account of the auxiliary role of the defence, see Hodgson (n 1) ch 4. See also Field and West (n 57).

In practice, the prosecutor's ideology aligns strongly with that of the police.[62] Detention was extended, and interrogations repeated until suspects confessed. As one prosecutor told me:

> It's true that the *garde à vue* exerts a certain psychological pressure and for some people that pressure may lead to slightly ill-considered admissions ... But that is not the point of view of a *procureur* – there are no innocents in *garde à vue*.[63]

While this contradicts the public interest-centred ideology of the *procureur* as *magistrat*, prosecutors understand themselves to be acting in accordance with their professional and ethical responsibilities. They speak in terms of protecting the public interest and of searching for the truth, but equate this in practice with obtaining a confession. As one *procureur* explained: 'The *procureur* will be excused for being too harsh, but he will be excused much less for an error, a lack of severity.'[64] Investigative oversight focuses on the form and outcome of the enquiry, ensuring the documentation of procedural compliance and enabling the *procureur* to sidestep the methods by which evidence is obtained and her own part in sanctioning these.[65]

The occasions when accused persons were brought before the *procureur* in order to extend the period of detention or to send the accused to trial further demonstrate the guilt-oriented presumptions on which she worked.[66] As one prosecutor explained to a defendant who wished to correct something in the police statement: 'I am paid to read the dossier of evidence. I believe what I read ... This is written and signed.'[67] Allegations of police misconduct were also ignored and, just as with defence lawyers in England and Wales, the undeserving nature of the defendant was key in the *procureur*'s construction of her guilt and the discounting of anything that challenged this assumption.

> You have to bear in mind that he has several convictions and does not respect the law, so his word counts for less than that of the police ... This guy is an addict too and I've seen them at the police station – they are out of touch with reality. If locked in a confined space, they freak out and make things up to get their own back.[68]

[62] Hodgson (n 1) 169–77.

[63] ibid 172. The *garde à vue* is the period of police custody. This view was shared by many *juges d'instruction* too. As one *juge d'instruction* explained: 'The presumption of innocence exists in theory but not in practice ... The search for the truth is quite easy, but they [suspects] just refuse to confess.' ibid 225.

[64] ibid 170.

[65] *Procureurs* accepted that the police would put pressure on suspects, shouting, threatening and even hitting them. ibid 169–77.

[66] The law required that suspects be brought before the prosecutor in order to approve the extension of police custody beyond 24 hours unless there were exceptional circumstances making this impossible. In practice, in many prosecutor offices, exceptional circumstances were relied on as the norm and suspects were almost never seen by the *procureur*.

[67] Hodgson (n 1) 237.

[68] ibid 240.

The *procureur*'s view of the supervision she is required to provide is shaped in part by the sheer volume of cases for which she is responsible, but also by the importance of the trust that underpins her relationship with the police.[69] She identifies strongly with police objectives, whilst maintaining the appearance of detachment as a judicial officer. Operating a presumption of guilt and reluctant to challenge any police behaviour, the *procureur* clothes the police investigation with legitimacy, authenticating rather than regulating the period of detention and questioning. However, while pressure is placed on the accused to confess during the police investigative stage and to maintain their admissions at court, the trial is not a site of negotiation in the ways familiar in England and Wales. An admission at trial is considered less imperative, in part because the difference between contested and non-contested trials is less significant in terms of court time and the appearance of witnesses, but principally because greater reliance is placed upon the findings of the pre-trial investigation contained in the case dossier before the court.[70] In France's time-pressured trial system, the court is unwilling to countenance any challenge to the defendant's earlier admission. Whether conducted by the *juge d'instruction* or overseen by the *procureur*, the investigative phase is characterised as a judicial inquiry and so it is at the pre-trial stage that an admission is of most value, and it is to this that the court will attach the greatest weight.

VII. PUBLIC HEARINGS AND THE JUDICIAL VERIFICATION OF ASSUMPTIONS OF RESPONSIBILITY

The centrality of judicial investigation and decision-making means that French criminal procedure does not allow the accused to substitute her own admission for the court's fact-finding role and determination of guilt. At trial, the defendant does not enter a plea and her evidence, including any admission, is treated as a piece of witness testimony like any other – its significance and credibility to be determined only by the judge. In practice, however, a clear distinction is made between the treatment of cases where defendants contest or admit the charges, and pre-trial behaviours will affect bail, whether a case goes to trial and even sentencing.[71] Pre-trial admissions made in custody to the police are reported to the *procureur* and have an important impact on case disposition. For example, prosecutors' presentation of these admissions will influence judicial decisions on bail. Furthermore, the prosecutor's decision on the procedural track a case will follow is based on conversations with the police about the suspect's demeanour

[69] C Mouhanna, *Polices judiciaires et magistrats. Une affaire de confiance* (Paris, La documentation Française, 2001); Hodgson (n 1).

[70] Hodgson (n 1); Soubise (n 1) 411–12.

[71] Hodgson (n 1); Soubise (n 1); V Gautron, 'Remorse in the French Criminal Justice System: A Subterranean Influence' in in S Field and C Tata (eds), *Criminal Justice and the Ideal Defendant in the Making of Remorse and Responsibility* (Oxford, Hart Publishing, 2023) ch 2.

and any show of remorse or assumption of responsibility.[72] In particular, the rapid summary form of trial known as *comparution immédiate* is used extensively for cases where the prosecutor sees a clear pre-trial admission. And in recent years, a further abbreviated form of procedure has been introduced, the *comparution sur reconnaissance préalable de culpabilité* (CRPC), which is more akin to a guilty plea hearing. What these procedural tracks have in common is that in practice they limit scrutiny of pre-trial evidence (including admissions of responsibility) while in theory retaining the legitimate authority that flows from formal judicial verification of the truth of the dossier.

The *comparution immédiate* procedure, for example, is a hearing scheduled immediately following charge for cases that are ready to proceed,[73] with an expectation that the defendant will be sentenced immediately, often to a term of imprisonment. Whilst going through the motions of a trial, the speed with which the hearing takes place (immediately following the period of police custody) leaves no time for the defendant to consider the evidence, advance a defence or prepare any mitigation. Representation is usually provided by a duty lawyer, but the very short spaces of time between arrest, prosecution and trial mean that there is little opportunity for defence-building or even to take anything more than basic instructions.[74] The credibility attached to the dossier by prosecutors, lawyers and trial judges allows them to rely on the admissions contained within it – treating them not as the result of a police interrogation without a lawyer present, for example, but as the product of a neutral, judicially supervised investigation. In actively treating the evidence in this way, legal actors reinforce and legitimate the production of confessions in ways that fail to protect the rights of the defendant whilst appearing to adhere to procedural safeguards.

In my own observational study, it was clear that lawyers had only been able to take the most rudimentary of instructions from their clients, often having to see three or four over the lunch recess. Yet, the lack of any meaningful defence engagement was never challenged. Defendants inevitably agreed to be tried immediately, with no real understanding of the alternatives, and conviction duly followed. For their part, lawyers played along, as though the defendant had made an informed choice and mitigating on the basis of a cursory glance at the evidence and what little information they had been able to obtain from the defendant. Despite their limited role, lawyers played a part in the normalisation of guilt and in a process that gives the appearance of protecting the interests and choices of the defendant. Prosecutors were under no illusions as to the limited protection the lawyer might afford the defendant in these cases that had essentially been pre-judged on the basis of the case file produced and assembled by the police. The lawyer's value was in providing the appearance of a fair trial and

[72] Hodgson (n 1) 236–37.

[73] Generally, where the accused has admitted guilt, or where the prosecutor considers the evidence to be strong and so a conviction very likely.

[74] Hodgson (n 1) 130–31.

making the accused feel that she had been represented: 'Someone who has been sentenced to imprisonment and has a lawyer will at least feel that they have been defended. That role exists. It is very important.'[75]

In 2004, the first formal plea procedure, the CRPC, was introduced.[76] Seen as a radical reform because of its short-circuiting of judicial examination at court, it is a form of guilty plea hearing, prior to which the prosecutor offers the accused, in the presence of her lawyer, a reduced sentence in exchange for the accused agreeing to forgo the usual trial process in favour of the more rapid CRPC procedure.[77] The conviction is formally a court finding in the same way as a regular trial, but while the judge is required to verify the facts and that the level of criminal charge is made out, she may only ratify or reject the sentence and the prosecutor's prior finding of guilt;[78] there is no power to amend.[79] This represents a radical departure in shifting responsibility for the determination of guilt to the prosecutor to a certain degree, and in making space for defence and prosecution to discuss and agree on the sentence to present to the court for ratification.[80] In this way, like the guilty plea in England and Wales, the CRPC is a procedure through which the finding of the court is, in practice, pre-determined by the parties.

However, the French guilty plea has developed rather differently from that in England and Wales. The impact of the CRPC procedure is felt more strongly at the start of the case, placing additional pressure on suspects to confess during

[75] ibid 129.

[76] See J Hodgson, 'Guilty Pleas and the Changing Role of the Prosecutor in French Criminal Justice' in E Luna and M Wade (eds), *The Prosecutor in Transnational Perspective* (Oxford, Oxford University Press, 2012) 116. The CRPC procedure applies to *délits* (middle-ranking offences) where the accused is over 18 and has admitted the offence. The procedure does not apply to offences carrying a prison term of more than five years – such as sexual assault – or to political offences (eg participating in an unauthorised demonstration) or defamation.

[77] Two-thirds of defendants dealt with through the CRPC procedure receive an immediate or suspended prison sentence. It also differs from the ordinary court process in that it removes the opportunity to ensure that the sentence is 'adapted' or appropriate to the needs of the offender, with a focus on her character and antecedents, as is usually the case. Described further in J Hodgson and L Soubise, 'Understanding the Sentencing Process in France' in M Tonry (ed), *Comparative Sentencing*, Crime and Justice vol 45 (Chicago, University of Chicago Press, 2016) 221.

[78] The procedure applies only to adult defendants and depends upon a prior admission on the part of the accused, so whilst it is an abbreviated trial process, it is not a form of charge or plea bargaining.

[79] The cursory nature of these ratification proceedings has been criticised by V Perrocheau, 'La composition pénale et la comparution sur reconnaissance de culpabilité: quelles limites à l'ominipotence du parquet?' [2010] *Droit et Société* 55; C Saas, 'De la composition pénale au plaider-coupable: le pouvoir de sanction du procureur' [2004] *Revue de science criminelle et de droit comparé* 827.

[80] The procedure was challenged as unconstitutional on the grounds that the court did not make the determination of guilt. This was rejected by the Conseil constitutionnel (Decision 2004-492 DC of 2 March 2004) on the basis that the judge was still required to verify the guilt of the accused and the legal sufficiency of the charges; that the defendant consented to the procedure; and that the sentence was appropriate. If the judge is not satisfied with any of these things, the case can be referred for an ordinary trial.

the investigative stage, with police, supervising prosecutors and even defence lawyers emphasising the benefits of an early admission.[81] However, if it emerges during the preliminary meeting between the prosecutor, accused and their lawyer that the defendant has not in fact admitted the offence, she is simply referred back for an ordinary trial hearing; with no power to amend the charges at this stage, the prosecutor has little incentive to persuade the defendant to change her version or to make an admission before the court.[82] Any bargaining that does take place is around the edges of sentencing.[83] Nor is the *procureur* concerned to test the veracity of any admissions, happy to accept them at face value and to assign the defence lawyer to the role of observer in any discussion with the defendant.[84] In this way, encouraged and condoned by the *procureur*, defendant choice is emphasised while the pre-trial and largely police business of obtaining admissions remains hidden. *Magistrats* do not want to be seen to pressure the accused into a plea of guilty, maintaining the appearance of judicial neutrality and keeping their own hands clean, so to speak.[85]

The CRPC represents a procedural innovation that, for the first time in France, institutionalises a sentencing outcome advantage for the 'ideal' defendant who assumes responsibility. But it does so in a way that retains the trappings of public judicial verification of the dosser (including the usually critical pre-trial admissions) while authorising the judge, in practice, to limit the rigour of that verification. Once again, the real pressures to assume responsibility are obscured by the combined rhetoric of defendant choice (they need not accept the CRPC procedure, opting instead to go to full trial) and the ideology of the prosecutor as judicial officer providing formal judicial scrutiny of the dossier.

VIII. CONCLUSION

To conclude, those convicted in the criminal courts in England and Wales and in France are presumed to have benefited from the guarantees of a fair trial, including the interrogation of evidential sufficiency by prosecutors and the court, and the provision of an effective defence – even after a plea of guilty. The language of court procedure around charge, plea and the sufficiency of evidence, reinforced by the actions of legal actors, serve as powerful and public

[81] The benefits of an early admission were mentioned consistently by those providing custodial legal advice in France. See Blackstock et al (n 1); Cape and Hodgson (n 4).

[82] Soubise (n 1) 407 and 416. However, referring the case for trial, often on the same day, has other consequences, as defendants not qualifying for legal aid were sent for trial without legal representation. Soubise (n 1) 417.

[83] Soubise (n 1) 419–20 notes that prosecutors sometimes proposed a higher sentence at the outset of the discussion where they anticipated a strong defence lawyer who might negotiate them down.

[84] ibid.

[85] See, eg R Lévy, 'Police and the Judiciary in France Since the Nineteenth Century' (1993) 33 *British Journal of Criminology* 167, 181; A Garapon, *Bien Juger: Essai sur le rituel judiciaire* (Paris, Odile Jacob, 1997) 81.

assurances of this. Like the terms and conditions to a contract that we tick without reading, these procedures may serve to give the appearance of conformity, rather than representing the realities of practice. Yet, they also tie the accused into accepting a legal narrative that justifies punishment, but which may have little relationship to their own understanding of the case and their criminal responsibility in it. From the first accusation, lawyers, prosecutors, magistrates and judges actively encourage the defendant to conform to these expectations and to accept responsibility through an admission and a guilty plea. However, this backstage, routinised pressure to publicly assume responsibility is masked by the public display of the guilty plea as a free and voluntary act justifying punishment.

The guilty plea has been less attractive in jurisdictions such as France, where the status of the accused is that of a witness and the decision as to guilt may only be taken by a judicial officer, a *magistrat*. A form of guilty plea now exists in France, but this has not developed into routine plea-bargaining as it has in England and Wales and the USA – in part because the trial is less important as a locus of fact-finding: the dossier on which the prosecution case rests already has the credibility of judicially tested evidence. Instead, this continues to be a *magistrat*-led procedure to speed up the process in order to avoid the resources needed for trial, centring on the agreement of sentence, rather than plea. And crucially, there is no negotiation or persuasion – either by the prosecutor *magistrat* or the defence lawyer. There may be some discussion around sentence, but the door to charge bargaining remains closed as the *procureur* lacks the power to drop or amend charges once the case has been set for trial. As a court process, without the pressures to avoid a contested trial, the guilty plea in France appears to have greater authenticity than that in England and Wales. It is not the product of prosecution or courtroom incentives, but reflects an earlier admission of responsibility on the part of the defendant. However, this procedure shields from the public gaze the pressures placed upon the accused to make an admission during the pre-trial process – through prosecutor-sanctioned police questioning and early defence advice to consider the potential of a sentence discount following a confession to the police and agreed plea of guilty. As a more judicially centred procedure, French criminal justice has developed a rather different form of guilty plea, from which the judge remains distant and which is connected to the pre-trial pressures on the accused to confess through the status attached to the dossier and the role of the prosecutor as *magistrat* in the pre-trial process.

In both jurisdictions, driven by concerns for efficiency rather than truth, justice or the authentic participation of the accused, there are systemic incentives in place to guide the accused towards the inevitability of an admission. Representing themselves to the court, the defendant and to each other, as acting in the defendant's best interests and promoting defendant choice, prosecutors, defence lawyers and judges become complicit in managing the defendant towards the expectation of a plea of guilty as the norm in England and Wales.

The position is slightly different in France, but pressures exist during the pre-trial phase, and there are limited opportunities to contest the prosecution case in a procedure still dominated by the belief in a model of independent judicial supervision. In both jurisdictions, by redefining the interests of the accused in terms that emphasise the importance of an early admission, neither court procedures nor legal personnel serve to ensure the protection of fair trial rights. The ideal defendant, it seems, is a guilty defendant – or at least one who pleads guilty.

9

Looking for the Ideal Parole Applicant?

NICOLA PADFIELD*

The growing empirical literature on the role of remorse at sentencing suggests that sentencers look for 'remorse'. This has been explained in terms of their search for the 'ideal defendant', one who takes responsibility for their offending. Yet much of the academic, or theoretical, literature advises caution: one reason is the philosophical or moral question whether remorse should be a relevant factor. Another (more practical) reason arises from the recognition that whilst expressing *remorse in court is difficult,* assessing *remorse may be even more so. This chapter applies these arguments to English and Welsh parole processes. The chapter reviews both the limited empirical evidence as well as case law decisions and concludes that decision-makers are, in practice, sometimes influenced by apparent remorse (or, more obviously perhaps, by an apparent absence of remorse). What is expected of applicants varies across different places and times, but in England today, whilst the superficial attraction of identifying 'remorse' remains apparent, parole decision-makers' awareness of the ambiguous and complex world of prisons and parole may make them less attracted to the concept. They may also be aware that, having to focus on the assessment of future risk, remorse has little relevance. But these are speculative and tentative conclusions, meriting further exploration.*

I. INTRODUCTION

MANY OF THE chapters in this book usefully explore questions of 'remorse' in relation to the imposition of the initial sentence. Despite the superficial attraction of considering remorse as a relevant factor in sentencing, the academic consensus appears to advise caution on two main grounds. The first is a philosophical argument that questions whether remorse

* Professor of Criminal and Penal Justice, Law Faculty, University of Cambridge, UK.

should be a relevant factor. The other, more practical, ground arises from the recognition that both expressing and assessing remorse are notoriously difficult, with the result that the decision-maker is in reality likely to 'get it wrong'. In this chapter, I argue that the same challenges face decision-makers at parole hearings. I shall explore the very limited evidence, from my empirical work carried out in England[1] and from relevant case law, on the role of 'remorse' (and other expressions of taking responsibility) to conclude that a parole hearing is ill-suited to encouraging either frank displays of remorse or realistic assessments of those expressions. There is no neat conclusion: the extent to which individual parole decision-makers are influenced by 'remorse' remains unclear.

II. 'REMORSE' IN CRIMINAL JUSTICE

In everyday language, we use the word 'remorse' with little concern for its precise meaning. The psychological and philosophical literature, however, distinguishes a number of different but closely related (and overlapping) emotions: remorse, regret, shame, guilt, repentance and so on. Proeve and Tudor suggest that remorse should be distinguished from its more negative cousin, 'shame', which 'involves a greater sense of oneself as flawed, disgraced or discredited, and characteristically involves a desire to cover one's flaw, to hide or to withdraw'.[2] Remorseful behaviours, on the other hand, have more positive interpersonal effects. Having identified many of the characteristics of remorse, they acknowledge that the distinction between one emotional state and another can in reality be blurred. This is an important warning. Parole decision-makers are unlikely to identify 'remorse' accurately.[3] Bandes wisely counsels that we should be more interested in what judges believe remorse to be, pointing out that judges are not working from a consensus definition of remorse: they are 'often working with highly idiosyncratic and unpredictable notions of what remorse is, how to evaluate it, and why it matters'.[4]

[1] N Padfield and A Liebling, with H Arnold, *An Exploration of Decision-Making at Discretionary Lifer Panels* (London, TSO, 2000) Home Office Research Study 213; N Padfield, 'Understanding Recall 2011' (University of Cambridge, 2013) Legal Studies Research Paper Series; N Padfield, 'Parole Board Oral Hearings 2016 – Exploring the Barriers to Release: Avoiding or Managing Risks? Report of a Pilot Study' (University of Cambridge, 2016) University of Cambridge Faculty of Law Research Paper No 62/2017; N Padfield, 'Parole Board Oral Hearings 2016–2017 – Exploring the Barriers to Release: Stage Two of an Exploratory Study' (University of Cambridge, 2017) University of Cambridge Faculty of Law Research Paper No 63/2017.

[2] M Proeve and S Tudor, *Remorse: Psychological and Jurisprudential Perspectives* (London, Routledge, 2010) 3.

[3] See also the distinction drawn between cognitive, affective and motivational elements of remorse in J Pugh and H Malsen, 'Drugs That Make You Feel Bad? Remorse-Based Mitigation' (2017) 11 *Criminal Law and Philosophy* 499.

[4] S Bandes, 'Remorse and Judging' in R Weissman, M Proeve, S Tudor and K Rossmanith (eds), *Remorse in Criminal Justice: Multi-Disciplinary Perspectives, Routledge* (London, Taylor & Francis, 2020) 5, http://dx.doi.org/10.2139/ssrn.3535062.

For the purposes of this chapter, it has been difficult to identify where and whether decision-makers are looking for 'remorse' or simply some other aspect of 'taking responsibility'.[5] In sentencing, it would appear that judges believe that they can identify 'remorse' and they do take it into account (even though it is probably not a predictor of reoffending).[6] Indeed, remorse was the most common mitigating factor mentioned in the Sentencing Council's survey of judges in 2013.[7] Judges may fail to recognise 'real' remorse, especially when cultural barriers get in the way.[8] Courts are difficult 'theatres' in which to express or assess remorse (imposing pressures of time, space and procedure).[9] How do these questions of 'remorse' apply at parole?

III. THE 'IDEAL' APPLICANT FOR PAROLE

The argument that, from the sentencer's perspective, an 'ideal' defendant is one who accepts both their guilt and their sentence/punishment is convincing. Tata's 'ideal' offender 'is seen to accept guilt freely and sincerely'.[10] That is so much easier for the sentencer. It also appears to give the process legitimacy.[11] Tata suggests that sentencing professionals (including judges and lawyers) engage in 'ritual individualization' and 'case normalization', which allows them to identify the person who they must sentence as having a new and 'approved' identify as a 'culpable offender, regarded by the court as freely and sincerely accepting

[5] For example, 'insight' as discussed by R Weisman, '"Remorse Is Not Enough": Disentangling the Roles of Remorse and Insight in the Construction of the Ideal Defendant' in S Field and C Tata (eds), *Criminal Justice and the Ideal Defendant in the Making of Remorse and Responsibility* (Oxford, Hart Publishing, 2023) ch 7.

[6] See J Craissati, *The Rehabilitation of Sexual Offenders: Complexity, Risk and Desistance* (London, Routledge, 2018).

[7] Sentencing Council, *Crown Court Sentencing Survey Annual Publication 2013* (2014) 29. On whether judges should take remorse into account as much as they do, see H Maslen, *Remorse, Penal Theory and Sentencing* (Oxford, Hart Publishing, 2015).

[8] Bandes (n 4); see also LV Johansen, '"Impressed" by Feelings – How Judges Perceive Defendants' Emotional Expressions in Danish Courtrooms' (2019) 28 *Social & Legal Studies* 250: judges' assessments of emotions are mediated through their own cultural understandings, and what counts as 'appropriate' emotion is dependent on how the defendant is culturally and systemically situated.

[9] The possibilities of expressing remorse in English courtrooms seem particularly remote, as the defendant is often placed in a secure box at the back of the room and may well not speak at all during the sentencing 'hearing': see J Jacobson, G Hunter and A Kirby, *Inside Crown Court: Personal experiences and questions of legitimacy* (Bristol, Policy Press, 2015); K Rossmanith, 'Cultural Sensitivity Training, Judicial Feelings, and everyday practice: Conversations at the Edge of Research' in Field and Tata (n 5) ch 6 explores courts as theatres of remorse, showing how judges misread and misunderstand it.

[10] C Tata, *Sentencing: A Social Process: Re-thinking Research and Policy* (London, Palgrave, 2020) 94; see also J Hodgson, 'The Construction of the Ideal Defendant: Comparative Understandings of the Normalisation of Guilt' in Field and Tata (n 5) ch 8.

[11] This is not to argue that sentencing judges get it right! See D Hayes, 'Proximity, Pain and State Punishment' (2018) 20 *Punishment and Society* 235; D Hayes, *Confronting Penal Excess: Retribution and the Politics of Penal Minimalism* (Oxford, Hart Publishing, 2019).

her impending punishment'.[12] Speed and routinisation are important imperatives to these sentencing professionals, working in what Tata describes as 'an assembly-line process, a sausage machine, a factory of mass case-disposal necessitated by overwhelming case volume'.[13] So, he argues, they engage in ritual individualisation.

The criminal process is seen as akin to a rite of passage in which the person's troubling, unsettled status is shown to the professional community (court) to have been resolved because the person is shown to have been treated as a unique individual who now accepts individual moral responsibility for offending. This ritual work reduces the anxiety of sentencing professionals about whether the person has been treated fairly. It reduces the anxiety of their task as sentencer. It is ritual which changes someone's ascribed status from a troubling, ambiguous defendant at the start of the criminal justice process (when their innocence is formally presumed) to that 'of a culpable offender who is *shown* to accept her own punishment sincerely and completely'.[14] Tata then identifies the key stages or transformations in that rite of passage, which realigns the manifestation of the person to be punished so as to be closer to the ideal of fully and sincerely accepting personal culpability. Remorse is the ultimate, but not the only, exemplar of the showing of that acceptance of responsibility and legitimacy of the process.

What may reassure judges and lawyers as a display of individualisation may be experienced very differently by defendants, for whom the criminal justice process can be a ritual in degradation. The stigma of conviction is obvious. The sentencing process is a classic 'status degradation ceremony'.[15] The person changes from citizen to convicted criminal. The judge's sentencing remarks are an act of public denunciation. The court process can be seen to exclude and to humiliate. The defendant plays a peripheral role, an observer in a glass box at the back of the court, marginalised as their fate is decided by the lawyers in front of them.[16] Serious 'offenders' then go to prison. Prison takes people out of 'free' society and, by way of a series of 'status degradation ceremonies', turns them into an 'offender' or 'criminal'. Maruna explores the de-individuation processes involved in institutionalisation,[17] citing Goffman's description of a ritual process

[12] C Tata, '"Ritual Individualization": Creative Genius at Sentencing, Mitigation, and Conviction' (2019) 46 *Journal of Law and Society* 112, 114. See also J Gormley and C Tata, 'Remorse and Sentencing in a World of Plea Bargaining' in S Tudor, R Weisman, M Proeve and K Rossmanith (eds), *Remorse and Criminal Justice: Multidisciplinary Perspectives* (London, Routledge, 2022).

[13] Tata, 'Ritual Individualization' (n 12) 118.

[14] ibid 126.

[15] H Garfinkel, 'Conditions of Successful Degradation Ceremonies' (1956) 61 American Journal of Sociology 420. In the next two paragraphs, I have relied heavily on the work of Shadd Maruna, especially S Maruna, 'Reentry as a Rite of Passage' (2011) 13 *Punishment & Society* 3. See also J Braithwaite and S Mugford, 'Conditions of Successful Reintegration Ceremonies: Dealing with Juvenile Offenders' (1994) 34 *British Journal of Criminology* 139.

[16] See Jacobson et al (n 9).

[17] Maruna (n 15).

of 'mortification' or the depersonalisation of a person's former identity through the 'abasements, degradations, humiliations and profanations of self' common to total institutions.[18] Thus the prisoner undergoes a 'civil death', not only losing former citizen rights and liberties, but also facing ritualistic admission procedures – strip searching, new institutional clothing, cramped living quarters – and 'obedience tests' meant to break his or her personality.

In England and Wales, the Parole Board gets involved after a prisoner has spent a considerable time in prison. Do Parole Board panels look for an 'ideal' applicant? Might the 'ideal' applicant for parole be remorseful? The decision to release can be seen as more difficult for the decision-maker than the original decision to imprison. There is little to 'feel good' about – either one is harsh and punitive in keeping someone in prison who has already served their term or one is taking the risk of public opprobrium when releasing someone in case something 'goes wrong' in the community. But, as we shall see, simply recognising the enormity of the challenge facing the decision-maker does not help us answer our core question.

IV. DOES THE PAROLE BOARD LOOK FOR EVIDENCE OF 'REMORSE'?

No research has focused explicitly on this question. Let us look at two studies, one carried out in 1999 and one in 2016–17.

After huge changes were introduced into the parole system in England and Wales in 1992, with the introduction of oral hearings for some life sentence prisoners (Discretionary Lifer Panels), Padfield and Liebling carried out an exploratory observational study of decision-making by these panels in 1999. Panels were always made up of three people, always chaired by a judge. We carried out 40 formal interviews with participants in the process and observed 52 cases. Panels looked for evidence of change, insight into the offence, evidence of offending behaviour work successfully undertaken and realistic release plans, with the prospect of effective supervision. We concluded that panels were interested in questions of remorse and, in a chapter on the factors considered by Parole Board panels, we included a section on 'attitude towards the victim, denial and the role of remorse':

> What mattered was that prisoners had understood the effect that their offence had upon the victim(s). Remorse, insight into offending behaviour, victim empathy and willingness to engage in offending behaviour courses were linked in actual assessments of risk, although remorse was difficult to assess, particularly many years after the offence. Panels sought an intellectual and emotional understanding of the seriousness of the offence but treated it as 'something where you have to build up a picture over time'. There was an operational consensus that expressions of remorse

[18] I Goffman, *Asylums: Essays on the Social Situation of Mental Patients and Other Inmates* (Garden City, NY, Anchor Books, 1961) 14.

> (those perceived as 'genuine') were an important component of 'making progress' in prison (Tidmarsh, 1999) – 'almost a starting point'. There was less consensus about how far a perceived lack of remorse should hold up the release decision (at page 50).[19]

The relevance of 'remorse' was particularly disputed in relation to sex offenders.[20] Tidmarsh questioned why so many sex offenders deny their offences, asking whether this was due to 'fear of persecution by other prisoners' or 'less obvious psychological mechanisms'.[21] We were well aware that what Tidmarsh called the 'prognostic relevance of guilt' was not well understood:

> There was acknowledgement by several respondents that sex offenders may start their offending careers as victims, and that in these cases 'remorse' is not straightforward … In the end, the term 'victim empathy', 'understanding the effect that their actions had on their victims', was preferred to remorse as it was easier to test. We were given examples of prisoners who refused to discuss their offence for years and then gradually came to terms with the enormity of what they had done. This was regarded as a key stage in the reduction of future risk.[22]

In my 2016–17 study,[23] 'remorse' did not appear to be a factor that was much discussed. This does not mean that Parole Board members were not looking for evidence of change, or 'progress' in prison. Perhaps panels had accepted that remorse was not relevant to future risk assessment, or perhaps they were more focused on practical evidence of 'risk'. Panels were careful to identify continuing risk factors and to test the quality of the evidence, particularly the quality of the risk assessments carried out by professional staff. Panels knew they were testing 'risk' against many uncertainties and imponderables:

> For example, whether a man who has had (and probably still has) a tendency to drink or use drugs to a degree that rendered him dangerous would be released to an environment which would acerbate the risk. Clearly his personal robustness and resolution were important, but so was the likely support available.[24]

Prisoners were generally questioned more gently than professional witnesses, though their accounts were listened to and probed. Panels heard a lot about the difficulty of life in prison, and prisoners pointed out their lack of control in the implementation of any sentence plan. Panels looked for evidence of behavioural change, but largely so that they could be confident that the prisoner had sufficient internal strategies to manage their risk of future violence. Victim empathy might sometimes be relevant, but this did not seem to mean 'remorse'. And even

[19] See n 1.

[20] R Hood and S Shute, 'Paroling with New Criteria: Evaluating the Impact and Effects of Changes in the Parole System: Phase Two' (Oxford Centre for Criminological Research, 1995) Occasional Paper No 16.

[21] D Tidmarsh, 'Necessary but Not Sufficient: The Personal View of a Psychiatric Member of the Parole Board' in M Cox (ed), *Remorse and Reparation* (London, Jessica Kingsley Publishers, 1999).

[22] Padfield and Liebling with Arnold (n 1) 50.

[23] Padfield, 'Parole Board Oral Hearings 2016' (n 1).

[24] ibid 19.

victim empathy was rarely explored in any detail. Thus, I would conclude, based on these small empirical studies, questions of remorse do not play an active role in Parole Board decision-making today, whereas a few decades ago the issue might have been seen to be more relevant. Today, panels are more focused on testing the management of future risk plans and whether prisoners understand their 'risks'. Why is this? In part, it is the changing nature and role of the Parole Board, but it is also the changing political context.

V. PAROLE HEARINGS IN ENGLAND AND WALES

At this point, it is essential to note that parole processes vary enormously from jurisdiction to jurisdiction, and even within the same jurisdiction 'parole' can change massively over time. In England and Wales, structured discretionary early release was introduced in 1967, and the Parole Board, and with it 'parole', was created.[25] At that time, there was a lingering affection for the rehabilitative ideal, which included a belief or feeling amongst many policy-makers that there might be a good time in a prisoner's sentence when they should be released. Prisoners were originally eligible to be considered for early release after they had served one-third of their sentence.

Massive changes were made to the parole process by the Criminal Justice Act 1991. The Parole Board was no longer concerned with the discretionary release of prisoners serving less than four years' imprisonment. For those serving more than four years, there was a parole 'window' (between the halfway point and the two-thirds point in their sentence, when they would automatically be released on conditions, until the three-quarters point). Importantly, the Parole Board was now also to decide on the release of those serving indeterminate (life) sentences.[26] This made the Board's role very different – less focus on releasing less serious offenders early and more focus on 'dangerous' offenders. Might this affect their attitude to remorse?

The next radical changes were made in the Criminal Justice Act 2003. The Parole Board's role in deciding on the release of those serving determinate sentences was removed completely.[27] The Parole Board was now to decide on

[25] For a history, see N Padfield, 'Giving and Getting Parole: The Changing Characteristics of Parole in England and Wales' (2019) 11 *European Journal of Probation* 153. For a longer account, see T Guiney, *Getting Out: Early Release in England and Wales, 1960–1995* (Oxford, Clarendon Press, 2018).

[26] N Padfield *Beyond the Tariff: Human Rights and the Release of Life Sentence Prisoners* (Cullompton, Willan Publishing, 2002). The complexity of the many forms of indeterminate sentence being served in England today are explored in N Padfield, 'Justifying Indeterminate Detention – on What Grounds?' (2016) *Criminal Law Review* 795.

[27] All such prisoners are now released at the halfway point in their sentence, or up to 135 days earlier, on Home Detention Curfew (electronic monitoring; HDC). HDC is not automatic – the rules are applied by prison staff, who make the decision on release. For the current HDC policy framework, see https://assets.publishing.service.gov.uk/government/uploads/system/uploads/attachment_data/file/882216/home-detention-curfew.pdf. See M Nellis, 'Electronic Monitoring, Neoliberalism and

the release of all life sentence prisoners,[28] those serving 'extended' sentences,[29] those considered for release after they have served two-thirds of their sentence and those recalled to prison during the period of their sentence served on licence in the community. Two points to note: the 'diet' of the Parole Board was the decision to release very serious offenders, but also with an increasing number of re-release decisions: 'recall' has become a major part of the parole process, with some prisoners being released and recalled several times.[30]

Thus, we must take particular care with comparisons made with different times or places. The original concept in England and Wales was for 'early' release. Now the Parole Board deals only with 'late' or 'delayed' release: those people who have completed the minimum terms laid down by the sentencing judge, or who have been recalled to prison, and are now being detained beyond that period for questions, largely, of public protection. This fundamental change in function presumably affects its decision-making.

Secondly, the decision-makers have changed very significantly. The original Parole Board had only 17 members, including judges, psychiatrists and criminologists, who worked together quite closely. There are now well over 200 Board members, few psychiatrists and almost no criminologists. In the early days, most members of the Board were appointed because of their relevant expertise; now many have had little experience of the criminal justice process before appointment. Drawing comparisons between 'judges' in different courts, times and jurisdictions has to be done with great care.

Thirdly, the process of parole is now very different to that applied in the early years, when, for example, any prisoner hoping for 'parole' would be interviewed in advance of a 'paper review' by a member of a local review committee. Today, many prisoners will have an oral hearing before the panel, which decides the question of release (within a prison or, increasingly, by video link). But sometimes, after an initial assessment, the decision will be made 'on the papers' and

the Shaping of Community Sanctions' in P Bean (ed), *Criminal Justice and Privatisation Key Issues and Debates* (London, Routledge, 2020); M Nellis, K Beyens and D Kaminski (eds), *Electronically Monitored Punishment: International and Critical Perspectives* (London, Taylor & Francis, 2012).

[28] The law here is extremely complex: there are prisoners serving perhaps 11 different sorts of life sentence in England and Wales today: see Padfield, 'Parole Board Oral Hearings 2016' (n 1). Imprisonment for public protection (IPP) was an option available to sentencing judges only from 2005 until 2012, for example, but there are still many serving the sentence.

[29] There have been many versions of 'extended' sentences, and the release rules have been changed too frequently. The current version may be imposed only on those who the court finds to be 'dangerous', and is a determinate sentence, with a period of 'extended' supervision in the community. There are other complexities relating to those convicted of terrorism-related crimes and other 'offenders of particular concern': see Criminal Justice and Courts Act 2015, and the further changes in 2020 and 2021.

[30] On 31 March 2020, there were 82,990 prisoners in England and Wales. Of these, 9110 (8769 men, 341 women) were indeterminate sentenced prisoners (those serving IPP sentences and other 'life' sentences). Of the population of 2039 people in prison serving IPP, 1328 were on recall. The recall population (8933 of the 82,990 total prison population) increased by 24% over the year leading up to 31 March 2020.

the prisoner's voice will not be heard. Clearly, the procedure followed has a significant impact on both perceptions and outcomes,[31] and yet the impact of parole processes remain little studied.

Fourthly, and finally, the context, the political climate, has changed very significantly. Laws have become more punitive, and the prison population has soared in recent decades. Today, the Parole Board of England and Wales considers the protection of the public to be its primary concern.[32] Parole decision-makers are not immune to the influence of what is often called 'penal populism'.

All these important changes over time must have significant impact on parole practices and decision-making. The extent of that impact on the use of 'remorse' by decision-makers is unknown. I turn now to consider the equally important practical challenges to identifying remorse in prison, which may make Parole Board members cautious about allowing remorse to play a significant role.

VI. THE PRACTICAL CHALLENGES TO SPOTTING REMORSE IN PRISON

Today, parole hearings usually take place only after a lengthy period of custody. Serving a long sentence of imprisonment is deeply challenging.[33] The early years are often marked by anger, emotional turmoil and frustration. Often, prisoners describe or exhibit symptoms that are consistent with post-traumatic stress disorder, including dissociation, numbness and intrusive recollections (eg flashbacks and nightmares). Others are thrown into a state of acute turmoil by the nature of the sentence itself, which, as Crewe, Hulley and Wright argue, 'dislocates' prisoners from their social and family networks, their sense of who they are and the future that they had anticipated.[34]

Most prisoners then learn to cope by going through various stages of adaptation, often with little help from the 'system'. Parole Board members may well be aware of the dangers in 'parking' long-term prisoners during the early years of their sentence: 'if the prison system fails to provide meaningful engagement and

[31] For an excellent analysis of the way English courts can intimidate and alienate, see Jacobson et al (n 9). See also D Drake and A Henley '"Victims" versus "Offenders" in British Political Discourse: The Construction of a False Dichotomy' (2014) 53 *Howard Journal of Criminal Justice* 141.

[32] I am not reviewing the law here, simply commenting on how varied it can be, but I have argued elsewhere that this should not be its top priority, achieved at the expense of other, equally important, priorities such as human rights and the promotion of a crime-free lifestyle. See N Padfield, 'The Function of the Parole Board – Avoiding Failure or Promoting Success?' [2020] *Public Law* 468.

[33] B Crewe, S Hulley and S Wright, *Life Imprisonment from Young Adulthood: Time, Identity and Adaptation* (London, Palgrave Macmillan, 2020). See also B Crewe, 'Depth, Weight, Tightness: Revisiting the Pains of Imprisonment' (2011) 13 *Punishment and Society* 509.

[34] On the pains of imprisonment for women prisoners at this stage, see N Sakande, 'Righting Wrongs: What Are the Barriers Faced by Women Seeking to Overturn Unsafe Sentences in the Court of Appeal (Criminal Division)?' (2020) Griffins Society Research Paper 2019/2, which highlights the unfairness in practice of the rule that appeals should be lodged within 28 days of sentence, given the intense trauma faced by women arriving in prison.

activity, then more extreme and destructive belief systems will fill the gaps'.[35] Importantly, as prisoners get further into their sentences, many are motivated to 'give something back', either to a younger generation of lifers or to society at large. Discussing those convicted of murder as young men, Crewe et al say that

> a large proportion express a desire to work with young offenders on release. These motivations are directly connected to feelings of remorse and are expressed in a language of redemption: a way of making amends, proving moral worth, leaving a legacy that might supersede the act of murder that otherwise defined them and preventing others from making the same mistakes.[36]

So, prisoners may be remorseful, but the reality of prison life does not encourage an 'ideal' applicant for parole.[37] Many English prisons today are violent and frightening places. Rather than educating people for a law-abiding and productive future, 'punishment seems to disable rather than enable, to disintegrate rather than integrate, to injure rather than to remedy'.[38] Crewe et al identify 'the difficulty of preparing for life in the community having been removed from it for so long' and that 'adaptations that are functional within prison are deeply dysfunctional on release, particularly in the realms of social and family life'. They conclude that

> one of the many tragic aspects of imprisonment is that, while it often produces a desire among prisoners to lead a different kind of life, it so often disables the possibility of doing so through the ties that it breaks and the traits that it generates.[39]

Parole Board members will be aware of these tensions.

While preparing this chapter, I initiated a discussion on 'remorse' with a group of long-term prisoners in a category A (ie maximum security) prison, but the discussion did not develop as I had hoped. For the prisoners, the concept of remorse had little relevance as they worked out their way to survive decades in tough prisons. There were so many injustices that they felt they were confronting that they really did not want to discuss 'remorse' with me, a visiting academic lawyer. They wanted, in the brief time available, to discuss the deeply felt unfairness of the penal system, and of their own dehumanising experiences. Prisons, and prison regimes, are not designed to foster empathy, let alone remorse.

[35] M Nussbaum, *Anger and Forgiveness: Resentment, Generosity, and Justice* (Oxford, Oxford University Press, 2016) 285.

[36] B Crewe, S Hulley and S Wright, 'What Should Happen to People Who Commit Murder?' in A Fox and A Frater (eds), *Crime & Consequence: What Should Happen to People Who Commit Criminal Offences?* (London, Monument Trust, 2019) 286.

[37] Crewe et al (ibid) are clear that prisoners should be offered a greater level of psychological and therapeutic support to deal with their circumstances, including more regular and meaningful contact with family members and greater access to the kinds of educational, cultural, spiritual and therapeutic activities that can provide 'narrative lifeboats' (a powerful metaphor used in B Crewe, *The Prisoner Society: Power, Adaptation and Social Life in an English Prison* (Oxford, Oxford University Press, 2009)) – resources for personal change.

[38] F McNeill, 'Righting Wrongs: The Need for Dialogue' in Fox and Frater (n 36) 18.

[39] Crewe et al, 'What Should Happen to People Who Commit Murder?' (n 36) 330.

With hindsight, I decided that it was unrealistic of me to expect them to admit publicly to 'remorse' or even to want to discuss it. Some were many years post-'tariff' (one had served 33 years on a 20-year tariff), others still had many years to serve pre-tariff.[40] Our current system feeds anger, not remorse.[41] In a penal system which is not perceived to be fair or legitimate, showing remorse may be psychologically and politically impossible.

And yet, paradoxically, I have been deeply moved by the insights and expressions of remorse that prisoners have expressed to me in one-on-one private conversations or interviews. Most moving, perhaps, was the prisoner who I interviewed in 2016 straight after his parole hearing, who reflected at length on his huge regret and remorse. This remorse had not manifested itself at all in his parole hearing, immediately before the interview. There, he had simply responded, somewhat defensively, to specific questions from the panel. I noted in my report

> how differently the prisoner came across when talking outside the room, or in interview with me: particularly when discussing their index offence in the hearing, it felt as though they had covered the ground so often that they had little left to say, and they could appear somehow detached or lacking remorse. In the hearing, they simply responded to questions. But in interview with me, the pace of the conversation was slower, the odds less high,[42] and they were perhaps more in control. I heard more expressions of regret, reflection, and sadness.[43]

Thus, even those prisoners who feel remorseful may well not express it at the hearing. Some, of course, were unable to express themselves clearly. But more importantly, perhaps, was the 'atmosphere' of the hearing. So much hangs on this for the prisoner, but he or she is not in control. In terms of physical layout, not all venues are appropriate: some are scruffy, cramped and noisy, and increasingly prisoners will appear only by video link.[44] The layout is very different to the formality of a court, with the participants sitting around a table: the panel on one side, and the prisoner, their lawyer and any witnesses on the other. The process is choreographed by the panel chair. The prisoner, like the other witnesses, responds to questions. He is not in control.

To explore further what role 'remorse' or the 'taking of responsibility' might play in parole decision-making, I searched several legal databases. Parole Board decisions are not published, but there are some avenues through which some

[40] We have shifted from the concept of a tariff, after which a prisoner might legitimately expect to be released, to the concept of a 'minimum term' from which there is no expectation of release.

[41] Nussbaum (n 35).

[42] I meant simply that so much was at stake for the prisoner: either they would 'win' release or lose, and face at least another two years waiting for the next hearing.

[43] Padfield, 'Parole Board Oral Hearings 2016–2017' (n 1) 18.

[44] For current purposes, I am ignoring the huge difficulties provoked by 'virtual' hearings, on which see Padfield, 'Parole Board Oral Hearings 2016' (n 1); Padfield, 'Parole Board Oral Hearings 2016–2017' (n 1).

decisions come to be reported. My first avenue was the 'reconsideration mechanism', introduced in July 2019, in which either the prisoner or the Secretary of State for Justice can apply to the Parole Board for a decision to be reconsidered by a legally qualified member of the Board. The reconsideration decisions are placed on the British and Irish Legal Information Institute (BAILII) website, owned by the Institute of Advanced Legal Studies. Secondly, I searched both BAILII and the Westlaw case law database for relevant reported cases. The most obvious were cases of judicial review of decisions of the Parole Board.[45] Then there were a small number of other decisions concerning prisoners' progression for which 'remorse' could be relevant: most obviously, reviews of minimum terms, permitted only for those convicted of murder when still a child.

First, the reconsideration mechanism. These are very brief reports, following a standard template, and just 52 of the 145 decisions made by March 2020 were available at that point.[46] In one case,[47] the question of 'remorse' was centre stage. The prisoner asked for the Parole Board's decision to be reconsidered on three grounds, one of which was because 'the panel's finding that [he] was not remorseful, insightful or reflective' was irrational. Aged 22, this man had pleaded guilty to five counts of causing or inciting a 14-year-old girl to engage in sexual activity. He had received an extended sentence of 12 years, made up of a custodial period of four years and an extended licence of eight years. The retired judge who reconsidered the Parole Board's decision not to release him simply concluded that 'The assessment of the presentation of a witness at a hearing is a matter exclusively for the panel. A bare assertion to the contrary cannot make the panel's conclusion irrational.' (It is difficult not to sympathise with Mr Hibberd: another of his arguments was that the panel had placed undue weight on the fact that, through no fault of his own, he had not completed a particular course whilst in prison. The judge concluded that 'While it was a matter of regret that the prison had not yet been able to provide this course', this did not make the panel's decision, based on risk, irrational.)

More typical, perhaps, are cases where the person reconsidering a decision comments on the absence of remorse as a further reason for upholding the decision not to release. For example,[48] Vickers was sentenced to indeterminate imprisonment for public protection (IPP) in 2009.[49] He challenged the decision not to release him or to recommend a transfer to open conditions. Remorse had been mentioned as an encouraging sign, but the retired judge concluded that 'the applicant has not shown that in any of the areas about which he complains such evidence would have had a materially significant effect on the

[45] Given the absence of formal appeal mechanisms, applications for a review of the legality of a Parole Board decision by the judiciary have been common.

[46] See www.bailii.org/recent-decisions.html#ew/cases/PBRA.

[47] *Hibberd* [2019] PBRA 61.

[48] See also *Asawah* [2020] PBRA 56.

[49] *Vickers* [2019] PBRA 24.

decision-making process'. This seems to confirm my perception that remorse is not enough.

The reconsideration mechanism was introduced after the publicity and outrage that followed the decision of the Parole Board to release a notorious rapist, John Warboys (now Radford).[50] It was designed to create a mechanism by which victims could ask the government (specifically, the Secretary of State for Justice) to refer a decision to be reconsidered. But, given the cautious approach of the Board, it is of no surprise that most applications have come from prisoners, not their victims. One case referred by the Secretary of State is that of Hawes, an 81-year-old sex offender who had received an indeterminate sentence in 2006 for offences committed in the 1960s and 1970s.[51] He represented himself at both the hearing and in defending against the government's application resisting the decision to release him. In relation to remorse, there is an interesting statement that his 'expressed remorse and victim empathy' had to be put in the context of his refusal to do any work to address his offending. But the retired judge who considered the reconsideration concluded that the decision to release, whilst difficult to make, could not be considered to be irrational.

I turn secondly to judicial review decisions.[52] In recent times, there have been about 40 applications for judicial review of Parole Board decisions a year. Only four applications in the five years reviewed here (2015–20) mentioned 'remorse', and these 'life stories' serve to illustrate why 'remorse' may play such a limited role. One[53] concerns a man convicted of murder committed when he was 16 years old. The trial judge had commented when sentencing that, in his view, 'remorse was not a word in the claimant's vocabulary'.[54] The pre-sentence report had also indicated that he had 'scant insight' regarding his offending. This lack of remorse is used by way of contrast with his progress in prison, seen as a sign of his maturation. (Despite this, he loses his case, a challenge to the Parole Board's public law duty to hold a hearing within certain time limits.) Another[55] involved a prisoner who, in his early 20s, had pleaded guilty to nine assaults occasioning actual bodily harm and two common assaults, all against his female partner, sexual assault of a child under 16 and seven counts of possession of indecent images. He was originally given an extended sentence of 10 years, made up of a four-year custodial sentence and an extension period of six years. The Court of Appeal had quashed that sentence and imposed instead IPP, with a minimum

[50] See the discussion of *R (DSD and others) v Parole Board* [2018] EWHC 694 (Admin) below.

[51] *Hawes* [2020] PBRA 29.

[52] Since there had never been any formal appeal mechanism until the introduction of the reconsideration mechanism, the only remedy for disgruntled prisoners was an application for judicial review. This is not an appeal, but the judge may quash a decision on the grounds of illegality, procedural unfairness or irrationality. If successful, the case is sent back to the body who made the decision to take a fresh decision.

[53] *R (Hussain) v Parole Board* [2017] EWCA Civ 3748.

[54] ibid para 6.

[55] *R (PL) v Parole Board* [2019] EWHC 3306 (Admin).

term of two years.[56] He had a history of self-harm and was diagnosed as having a personality disorder with an anxiety type disorder. It was reported at the time of sentencing (2009) that he had exhibited sadistic behaviour towards his former partner as well as cruelty towards animals; he was fascinated by serial killers; and he had an urge to kill adults. The question of his limited remorse and his minimalisation of his offending behaviour were considered relevant at the time of sentencing and raised in two of the reports before the original sentencing judge. Since 2014, his behaviour in custody had been reported as positive. He had engaged in significant psychological intervention. His tariff expired in 2011. The decision that is criticised did not turn in any way on questions of remorse: the panel had simply not explained its reasoning effectively, and their decision was quashed.

Another example[57] concerned a prisoner who was convicted in 2006, aged 17, of a number of offences, including wounding and robbery, and was sentenced to an indeterminate detention for public protection,[58] with a five-year minimum term that expired in 2011. He has now served more than 14 years. He has clearly had a difficult prison career: he was said to have minimised his role in the index offences, and there were many allegations of poor behaviour (many of which he denied). He had been moved from prison to prison 47 times. Yet he had been illiterate on arrival in prison and was now undertaking a degree course in psychology and criminology. The panel commented, 'it is worthy of note that you are a large, well-built man whose mere presence can at times appear intimidating and aggressive even if that is not your intention'. They refer to a report by a psychiatrist who 'found you lacked genuine remorse, lacked empathy, presented yourself in a positive light and were reckless and impulsive in your behaviour'. The reports all supported a move to open conditions. The Parole Board, however, decided in 2019 that he should not be released or moved to open conditions. The court quashed this decision because the panel had not obviously undertaken the balancing exercise between the risks and benefits of a transfer to open conditions.

My final example is the well-known case of *R (DSD and others) v Parole Board*.[59] This was the challenge (by several different parties: two complainants, the Mayor of London and a media group) to the decision of the Parole Board to release John Radford (previously Worboys), the notorious 'Black Cab rapist'. Here, 'remorse' may have played an interesting role. In 2009, Worboys, as he then was, was convicted of 19 sexual offences, involving 12 victims, committed between October 2006 and February 2008. He had no previous convictions. In April 2009, he was sentenced to IPP with a minimum term of eight years

[56] This was a prosecution appeal: see *Attorney General's Reference (No 12 of 2010)* [2010] EWCA Crim 1212.

[57] *R (Samuel) v* Parole Board [2020] EWHC 42 (Admin).

[58] The equivalent of IPP for children.

[59] [2018] EWHC 694 (Admin).

(the equivalent of a determinate sentence of 16 years). The minimum term expired in February 2016.

Late in 2017, a three-member panel, made up of a chairperson, a psychologist and a lawyer,[60] considered his case. The lengthy dossier, put together, as always, by the Prison Service, gave an account of his sentence, for most of which he had maintained his innocence, including his application for his case to be considered as a miscarriage of justice by the Criminal Cases Review Commission.[61] In May 2015, he changed his position, admitting the offences for which he had been convicted. He then undertook the Sex Offending Treatment Programme Foundation and Core programmes, which he completed in 2016. Reports submitted by his Offender Manager (a probation officer in the community) and his Offender Supervisor (in the prison) did not initially support release or a move to open conditions. One psychologist supported a move to open conditions and another supported release. Very unusually, the panel heard from seven witnesses, as well as from Mr Radford. The Secretary of State (ie the prison authorities) was also represented (again, this is unusual – the 'prosecution' or prison authorities are only represented nowadays in high-profile cases, as this was).[62] The High Court explains:

> The Parole Board requested a further forensic psychological assessment from P9 [a psychologist]. This … was provided … in the form of an addendum psychological report. P9 stated that in all of the assessments of Mr Radford 'he has demonstrated a very good understanding of victim empathy and has expressed remorse and shame for his offending behaviour'. P9 noted that Mr Radford's offending behaviour was linked to his break-up with M1 in 2005/6 and that in the 'build up to his offending he was dwelling on his relationship breakdown with [M1] and during the period he offended he was feeling unhappy and unsatisfied about the lack of intimacy in his relationship with M8' … Mr Radford had problems with intimate relationships and this was an area to monitor for future risk management.[63]

The panel decided to direct his release, subject to several licence conditions. When news of the decision became public early in 2018, it was subject to widespread condemnation in the media. The Court of Appeal held that the Parole Board should have undertaken further inquiry into the circumstances of Radford's offending and, in particular, the extent to which the limited way in which he had described his offending might have undermined his overall credibility and reliability.[64] This high-profile case is relevant as an example of the

[60] As a high-profile case, this was not an oral hearing held by three-way video link, as is increasingly often the case. Video hearings are particularly problematic: see Padfield, 'Parole Board Oral Hearings 2016' (n 1).

[61] The body set up in 1995 to investigate possible miscarriages of justice in England, Wales and Northern Ireland.

[62] It is different in Scotland.

[63] para 34 of the judgment: see n 60.

[64] A new panel of the Board, having considered a huge dossier of 1255 pages, reached the conclusion that Radford should not be released. In May 2019, following a review by the Crown Prosecution

wider context in which the Board assesses 'risk': their original assessment of Radford's remorse was eventually rejected.

Finally, I examined other cases concerning prisoner progression, to discover whether they throw light on questions of 'remorse'. There was a small stream of cases in the early 2000s, after the enactment of Schedule 5 to the Criminal Justice Act 2003, when prisoners serving life sentences all became entitled to a 'minimum term' fixed by a High Court judge. Here, it would appear that 'remorse' was sometimes considered to be relevant: a good example is *Cadman*.[65] In 1988, Cadman was convicted, aged 18, of three murders of elderly people, carried out with a co-defendant during burglaries. Under the process then in place, the Home Secretary fixed a minimum term of 25 years. Under the new law of 2003, this term was to be reviewed by a judge. He noted that the sentencing judge in 1988 had described the murders as 'remorseless'. He had recommended a 15-year minimum term (secretly, as was then the process), but that had been increased to 30 years by the Home Secretary. By 1998, the law had been changed to allow the prisoner to be informed of the minimum term and to make representations: it was then accepted that he was now 'genuinely remorseful for having murdered the three victims'. The tariff was reduced to 25 years. At the hearing in 2005, much was made of both his remorse and his exceptional progress since he was sentenced. At this time, he was aged 37, and the prison staff again commented on his 'deep remorse' and increased maturity. The minimum term was reduced to 19 years.[66]

More recently, there have been cases where those sentenced to a mandatory life sentence for murder when a child (a sentence known as detention during His Majesty's pleasure (!), or HMP) seek a review of their 'tariff'. Since the decision in *R (Smith) v Secretary of State for the Home Department*,[67] HMP prisoners have been entitled to a periodic review of their tariff or minimum term. These are of interest to us for two reasons: they are not initial sentencing decisions nor yet 'backdoor' parole decisions, but something intermediate. They are also of interest because remorse is explicitly relevant. There are three possible grounds on which the tariff may be reduced:

1. The prisoner has made exceptional and unforeseen progress during the sentence.
2. The prisoner's welfare may be seriously prejudiced by his, or her, continued imprisonment and the public interest in the offender's welfare outweighs the public interest in a further period of imprisonment lasting until the expiry of the current tariff.

Service, he was charged with four further sexual offences, alleged to have occurred between 2000 and 2008. He was sentenced to two life sentences with a minimum term of six years for attacking the four women.

[65] [2006] EWHC 586 (Admin).

[66] This expired in 2007. I do not know whether he has been released.

[67] [2005] UKHL 51.

3. There is a new matter that calls into question the basis of the original decision to set the tariff at a particular level.

The current 'Criteria for Reduction of Tariff in Respect of HMP Detainees' lists:[68]

1. An exemplary work and disciplinary record in prison;
2. Genuine remorse and accepted an appropriate level of responsibility for the part played in the offence;
3. The ability to build and maintain successful relationships with fellow prisoners and prison staff; and
4. Successful engagement in work (including offending behaviour/offence-related courses) with a resulting reduction in areas of risk.

A not untypical case is that of Michael Lynch, sentenced for a murder committed when he was 16, for which he received a minimum term of 15 years.[69] In prison, he had matured very significantly. At his second periodic review, the judge reduced his minimum term by six months in recognition of his exceptional and unforeseen progress to date. Similarly, in 2008, Stephen Bonelli, convicted of a murder committed when he was 17,[70] had his original 'tariff' of 18 years reduced to 15 years on appeal. Then, in a tariff review in 2016, the judge decided that 'his progress has not only been exceptional but also, given the low base from which he started, unforeseen' and reduced his tariff by one year, to 14 years. These tariff reviews are carried out many years after sentencing, but are more like a re-sentencing exercise than the risk assessment carried out later by the Parole Board. Remorse is perceived to be relevant, though the minimum term is only ever reduced by a matter of months. This leads us to reflect on the nature of 'parole'.

VII. CONCLUSIONS: JUSTIFYING 'PAROLE'

Most countries appear to have discretionary 'early' release systems, which allow the early or delayed release of some people but not others. These are inevitably controversial, requiring assessment criteria, and people qualified and appointed to make those assessments. We have seen in this chapter how the idea of parole has changed immensely in England and Wales over the last 50 years. Comparative perspectives are also invaluable in allowing us to question why we are committed to a certain process. Field[71] points out that a French sentencing

[68] Para 5.2.5, Generic Parole Process Policy Framework, https://assets.publishing.service.gov.uk/government/uploads/system/uploads/attachment_data/file/1111492/generic-parole-process-policy-framework.pdf.

[69] *Michael Lynch* [2017] EWHC 3180.

[70] *Stephen Bonelli* [2016] EWHC 1293.

[71] S Field, 'The Enactment of Political Cultures in Criminal Court Process: Remorse, Responsibility and the Unique Individual Before the French *cours d'assises*' in Field and Tata (n 5) ch 10 …

court is looking for evidence of the defendant's capacity to give practical effect to their expressions of remorse through personal change. This is very clear, too, in the French method of sentence supervision by *juges d'application des peines* (JAP).[72] For example, one surprise for the English spectator of the French system is the weight given by judges deciding on release to the prisoner's attempts to pay off his compensation order, however slowly. Field has argued that

> in France, the trial is presented as part of a process of rehabilitating the accused as a citizen of the state. The legitimacy of that notion of criminal trial is related to the legitimacy of a positive concept of the citizen against which it is appropriate to judge the character and life of the accused.[73]

This is my experience of the French JAP: more openly empathetic and individualised in their decision-making. The positive concept of the citizen can be seen as the first step towards reintegration. The English and Welsh system does little, even symbolically, to welcome the citizen back – hence Maruna's powerful argument in favour of 'reintegration rituals' to support ex-offenders' re-entry into society as 'citizens' once more. Positive rituals can be potent tools for change.[74]

Any discussion of the use parole decision-makers make of 'remorse' or other evidence of 'taking responsibility' for one's crimes turns, in part, on what the decision-makers assume to be their priorities.[75] There are both utilitarian and retributive arguments for taking remorse into account at sentencing. And these arguments can be applied at parole/release hearings. The remorseful offender has acknowledged their 'guilt'. For the utilitarian, if it could be shown that remorse is linked to decreased recidivism, that would justify taking it into account.[76] But it would appear that remorse has no role in predicting reoffending. Indeed, it has been suggested that shame (so difficult to distinguish from remorse) might increase recidivism.[77] Retributive arguments would appear to have no place, unless one argues that the parole hearing is in effect a re-sentencing exercise. Remorse may well be used at sentencing to reduce an offender's culpability or to show how a crime may be less serious (when the defendant's remorse assuages

[72] M Herzog-Evans and N Padfield, 'The JAP: Lessons for England and Wales?' (Criminal Justice Alliance, 2015).

[73] S Field, 'State, Citizen, and Character in French Criminal Process' (2006) 33 *Journal of Law and Society* 522, 545. See also J Hodgson and L Soubise, 'Understanding the Sentencing Process in France' (2016) 45 *Crime and Justice* 221; N Padfield, 'An Entente Cordiale in Sentencing? Part 1' (2011) 175 *Criminal Law and Justice Weekly* 239–41, 256–58, 271–73 and 290–92.

[74] Maruna (n 15) 22.

[75] For an account from another jurisdiction, see E Ruhland, 'Philosophies and Decision Making in Parole Board Members' (2020) 100 *The Prison Journal* 640, who states that US data shows that 'paroling authorities' value remorse highly, and that 'a demonstration of remorse during the interview is important' (642).

[76] For Tata, *Sentencing* (n 10), remorse may be seen as the 'ultimate expression of the acceptance of responsibility' (106).

[77] See Bandes (n 4). See also S Bandes, 'Remorse, Demeanour, and the Consequences of Misinterpretation: The Limits of Law as a Window into the Soul' [2014] *Journal of Law, Religion and State* 170.

a victim's fear or guilt, for example). This chapter has attempted to explore whether different factors apply to decisions to release offenders, either 'early' or under an indeterminate or discretionary 'delayed' release regime.

The 'ideal' applicant for parole may well be 'sorry' for what they have done. But it is difficult to identify the 'ideal' applicant who appears before a panel of the Parole Board or a 'sentence implementation court'. And this is probably because of the uncertainties which surround the purpose of parole, at different times and in different places.

In this chapter, I started by trying to define remorse and then to situate the concept within the context of 'parole' in England and Wales. This led to a discussion of the reality of life in prison in England and Wales, which concluded that it is both impractical and unrealistic to look for evidence of 'remorse' in the context of people living in what are often brutal and unsafe environments. A review of my studies of parole in practice and a study of the case law revealed little evidence that either Parole Board decision-makers or judges involved in parole decisions put much weight on remorse today.

This is unsurprising, given that the current test the Parole Board of England and Wales applies is simply the risk of reoffending.[78] Perhaps the Parole Board accepts that remorse is of little probative value. There is no evidence that proves a connection between remorse and not reoffending. Indeed, Craissati shows that several studies link 'denial' to reduced recidivism, particularly in higher-risk sex offenders.[79] She argues that denial may be functional because it relates to a number of adaptive characteristics, such as a capacity for shame, distaste for the behaviour and attachment to social networks whose opinion of the offender matters to him. She concludes that this fits with a desistance model whereby those who deny their crimes are allowed to give themselves a redemptive script, which, in turn, promotes pro-social behaviour. If a convicted sex offender may be more likely than not to reoffend if he continues to deny his offence, the same may also be true of other offenders who show no remorse.

Parole decision-makers consider many of the same factors as those who sentence, but not entirely. In England and Wales, where the focus is on the release of those who have been judged 'dangerous' (either thereby receiving an indeterminate or extended sentence, or having been recalled to prison), it may be of comfort to the panel hearing the case that an offender is truly remorseful. It makes their job easier. But they may also be aware that this is not a good predictor of 'risk'. Or they may be 'case-hardened' into a focus on risk, which means that they have no need or space to identify an 'ideal' applicant.

Today's Parole Board is very different to the small body created in the 1960s. Now panels are less likely to include judges and rarely include a psychiatrist.

[78] The Board may not direct the release of a prisoner unless 'it is satisfied that it is no longer necessary for the protection of public that the prisoner should be confined': Crime (Sentences) Act 1997, s 28(6)(b).

[79] J Craissati, 'Should We Worry about Sex Offenders Who Deny Their Offences? (2015) 62 *Probation Journal* 395.

Panels can be composed of one, two or three members. There has been little research on how the characteristics of the decision-makers affects their decision-making. Importantly, too, the function of the Board has changed completely: originally the Board would decide who should get 'early' release; today, the Board is making decisions about 'late' release.

The relationship between the original sentencing decision and that of a Parole Board is inevitably complex. They are doing very different jobs, with very different aims. In England and Wales, a sentencing judge is entitled to consider a broad range of factors. Section 57 of the Sentencing Act 2020[80] provides that any court sentencing an offender must have regard to the following 'purposes of sentencing':

(a) the punishment of offenders;
(b) the reduction of crime (including its reduction by deterrence);
(c) the reform and rehabilitation of offenders;
(d) the protection of the public; and
(e) the making of reparation by offenders to persons affected by their offences.

This provides no priority between these often-contradictory purposes. The Parole Board is much more focused, limited to considering the 'risk' of reoffending. This discussion inevitably provokes questions about whether indeterminate sentences and a system of discretionary release (and recall) can ever be fair. Sentencing is, in practice, a continuing process, with a complex array of purposes. Demonstrations of remorse, whenever and however expressed, may make judges and Parole Board members feel better about their task. But there is little evidence that it has a significant impact on parole decision-makers in England and Wales today. The superficial attraction of identifying a remorseful or 'ideal' applicant for parole who takes responsibility for their offending behaviour is obvious, but my speculative conclusion is that parole decision-makers in England today understand they are making focused decisions on future risk in a deeply ambiguous and complex context. Aware that prisons do not encourage 'remorse', they do not focus on it. Nor is it easy for prisoners to 'make progress' from within a prison setting. This discussion thus raises fundamental questions about the nature of prison regimes and the purposes of 'parole'. If prisons operated according to different priorities, giving priority to helping prisoners take responsibility for their offending, perhaps Parole Board members might look more carefully for evidence of this 'ideal' applicant. But today's 'ideal' applicant need not be remorseful – what they need is a supportive probation officer and secure accommodation on release, and to have addressed their key risk factors, such as managing their anger, or their use/abuse of alcohol or drugs.

[80] Previously s 142 of the Criminal Justice Act 2003.

Part 3

The Political and Cultural Significance of Remorse and Responsibility

10

The Enactment of Political Cultures in the Criminal Court Process: Remorse, Responsibility and the Unique Individual before the French cours d'assises

STEWART FIELD*

*This chapter takes up David Garland's injunction to understand penal practice in cultural terms by examining empirically how different notions of political authority and state–citizen relations are enacted in the courtroom. Based on observations of France's highest ranking first instance criminal courts (*cours d'assises*), it contrasts practice there with that in some Anglo-American jurisdictions, arguing that the court demands far more of both the citizen and the state than is required by (or perhaps even acceptable to) the tenets of Anglo-American liberalism. Before the* cours d'assises*, public expressions of remorse and acceptance of responsibility are part of a broader set of expectations of the 'ideal defendant' or the 'good accused'. The public performance of these expectations by defendants constitutes a symbolic recognition of the legitimacy of state punishment that elicits a reciprocal response from the state in the form of an elaborate demonstration of concern for defendants as unique individuals and a recognition of their continuing status as citizens. Although vestiges of this symbolic exchange can be seen in other courts in other jurisdictions, the forms in which those expectations are framed before the* cours d'assises *are shaped by particular normative conceptions of state–citizen relations that are rooted in French Republican political tradition. Although the chapter emphasises the political resonance of the French state's (implicit) promise of concern for the unique individual that is each French citizen, it ends with doubts as to how far it is delivering on them.*

* Professor, School of Law and Politics, Cardiff University, UK.

I. INTRODUCTION

THIS CHAPTER BUILDS on some of my earlier work that has sought to examine comparatively the interrelations between legal and political cultures.[1] It follows David Garland's injunction to see penal practice not just as a reflection of broader cultural forces, but also as positively constructing and generating cultural relations.[2] Garland argues that through its daily routine activities, penal practices are involved in the production of social meaning in that they provide an interpretative grid through which to make moral sense of conduct and experience. This involves representing and reproducing images not just of individual subjects ('normal persons and normal attributes'), but also of social authority and social relations. Thus, the state, through the penal process, constructs its own public image by representing a certain style of state authority to victims, defendants, court professionals and the public. It also acts out a distinct sense of how social relations are (and should be) constituted in that society, for example by reproducing a particular way of understanding the breakdown of social relations. Thus, for Garland, state punishment is not just about how we deal with a group of people on the margins of society, but about 'how we define ourselves and our society in ways which may be quite central to our cultural and political identity'.[3]

This chapter picks up on Garland's call to examine the way that styles of penal justice construct and represent images of the state's authority. But rather than offering multi-faceted abstract models of relations between political regimes and legal process,[4] it focuses empirically on how images of state–citizen relations may be acted out in the courtroom under the lens of their breakdown. It is based on observation of the French *cours d'assises* (the first-instance criminal court that deals with the most serious cases). It argues that public expressions of remorse and acceptance of responsibility are seen there as part of a broader set of expectations of the 'ideal defendant' or the 'good accused'. The public performance of these expectations by defendants constitutes a symbolic recognition of the legitimacy of state punishment. This elicits a reciprocal response from the state in the form of an elaborate demonstration of concern for defendants as

[1] S Field and C Brants, 'Legal Cultures, Political Cultures and Procedural Traditions: Towards a Comparative Interpretation of Covert and Proactive Policing in England and Wales and in the Netherlands' in D Nelken (ed), *Contrasts in Criminal Justice* (Aldershot, Dartmouth, 2000).

[2] D Garland, *Punishment and Modern Society* (Oxford, Clarendon Press, 1990) ch 11. For excellent examples where the influence of political and social formations on penal practice is the foreground rather than the reverse, see M Cavadino and J Dignan, *Penal Systems: A Comparative Approach* (London, Sage, 2006); N Lacey, *The Prisoners' Dilemma* (Cambridge, Cambridge University Press, 2008). Note also that the broad modelling of regimes in those books is very different from the approach taken here of close observation and reading of particular legal practices.

[3] Garland (n 2) 276.

[4] M Damaska, *The Faces of Justice and State Authority* (New Haven, CT, Yale University Press, 1986).

unique individuals and a recognition of their continuing status as citizens.[5] This symbolic exchange is not the result of a bargain: the state will not negotiate its terms with the defendant. Nor is it the exchange of explicit promises on each side in the sense of vows, undertakings or pledges. Rather, these are promises implicit in the background assumptions about normal underlying relationships between state and citizen. Vestiges of this symbolic exchange centred around defendant expressions of remorse, and acceptance of responsibility may well be seen in other criminal courts in France as well as other jurisdictions. However, the forms in which those expectations are framed before the *cours d'assises* are shaped by particular normative conceptions of state–citizen relations. French republican ideals demand more of both the citizen and the state in public court performance than is required by (or perhaps even acceptable to) the tenets of Anglo-American liberalism. Those ideals have their ultimate public exemplar before the *cours d'assises*.

Thus, this chapter examines the significance of the expression of remorse in a very specific legal context: one in which the constraints of managing a high volume of cases are much less obviously present than in most courts in France and elsewhere. The *cours d'assises* constitute the highest tier of the French first-instance criminal courts. Its caseload is overwhelmingly homicide and rape, but cases of armed robbery and other very serious violence are also sometimes heard there.[6] It has a very unusual formation for France: whereas professional judges determine all cases in the lower first-instance courts, before the *cour d'assises* (CA), six lay jurors decide on both culpability and sentence, together with three professional judges (a president, who has overall authority to direct proceedings, and two judicial assessors).[7] Before the French lower courts, even cases where guilt is contested may well be over in less than an hour. In contrast, before the CA – even where the defendant openly admits guilt from the start – most cases take two to three days (with a minimum of at least a day).[8]

The symbolic political investment of the French state in these courts and these trials is evident not just in the imposing architecture. It is also evident in the considerable public court-time invested in situating the facts (and the defendants' responsibility for them) within the context of their personality and

[5] These ideas were inspired by C Tata, 'Ritual Individualization: Creative Genius at Sentencing, Mitigation and Conviction' (2019) 46 *Journal of Law and Society* 112. Here, however, they are applied to a very different procedural context and political culture.

[6] As a percentage of overall cases tried in the French courts, the *cour d'assises* deals with much less than 1% of cases. For statistical information, see www.justice.gouv.fr/statistiques-10054/references-statistiques-justice-12837/justice-penale-donnees-2019-33704.html.

[7] At the time of the observations upon which this chapter is based, there were a minimum of 12 jurors. Since 2012, the figure has been six. For detailed studies of CA, see D Salas (ed), *La cours d'assises* (Paris, Documentation Française, 2016); H Ancevin, *La pratique de la cours d'assises* (Paris, LexisNexis, 2016); A Jellab and A Giglio, *Des citoyens face au crime* (Toulouse, Presses Universitaires du Mirail, 2012).

[8] C Besnier, *La vérité côté cour: une ethnologue aux assisses* (Paris, La Decouverte, 2017) 14.

life, and encouragement of the most developed forms of expression of remorse and acceptance of responsibility from the defendant. Thus, this is a case study that is highly culturally specific – not just to France, but to a setting that is very particular within France. The argument is that by concentrating on a context where there is a great deal of state investment in the construction of a public ritual around remorse, responsibility and the relationship between state and citizen, we may reveal – in a more developed form – a practice the vestiges of which we might be able to see elsewhere. That public ritual, I will argue, is one in which an implicit political exchange between the individual and the state is being acted out.

The empirical data underpinning the argument was gathered in the course of a study of French defence lawyers based on observation, interviews and case-file analysis conducted in the late 1990s and early 2000s. This included a sample of 25 cases heard before the CA which involved a close reading of the official dossiers and observation of the trials themselves, as well as semi-structured interviews with lawyers and informal conversations in and around the court-room with lawyers, prosecutors and occasionally the senior judges who act as presidents of the court.[9] This empirical data has been supplemented by, and compared with, reports from more recent French ethnographic studies of the CA.[10] Besnier argues that key elements of the culture of the CA as set out here were reinforced from the 1980s through her period of observations from 2001 to 2016.[11]

The rest of the chapter is organised in three sections. Section II situates defendants' demonstrations of remorse and acceptance of responsibility within a broader set of French expectations of the 'ideal defendant'. It shows the way that the public performance of these expectations by the defendant elicits a symbolic response in the state's demonstration of its concern for the defendant as a unique individual. This concern for the individual is manifested in two primary ways: first, by an apparent commitment to a careful and meaningful dialogue with defendants about their responsibilities in the light of the reciprocal responsibilities of the French state and other citizens; and secondly, by offering a viable route back to full citizenship and reintegration into the polity. Section III uses evidence of equivalent practices in England and Wales and in Scotland to compare and contrast the way the roles and relationships around these practices are constructed in these different jurisdictions. It suggests that

[9] For details, see S Field and A West, 'Dialogue and the Inquisitorial Tradition: French Defence Lawyers in the Pre-trial Criminal Process' (2003) 14 *Criminal Law Forum* 261; S Field, 'State, Citizen and Character in French Criminal Process' (2006) 33 *Journal of Law and Society* 522.

[10] Besnier (n 8); M-P Courtellement, *La vie ordinaire des assises* (Paris, Ramsay, 2005); G De Lagasnerie, *Judge and Punish* (Stanford, Stanford University Press, 2016); V Bouillier, 'How Should the Other Be Judged?: Justice and Cultural Difference in French Assize Courts' (2015) 60 *Diogenes* 74; S Weill, 'Transnational Jihadism and the Role of Criminal Judges: An Ethnography of French Courts' (2020) 47 *Journal of Law and Society* S30.

[11] Besnier (n 8) 9–10. Note, however, managerialist concerns that may ultimately lead to some limitations on depth of investigation set out here at 146–49.

differences in legal practices may be explained by differences in political cultures and conceptions of the relationship between citizen and state. Section IV considers some issues about the legitimacy of these symbolic exchanges and the extent to which their underlying implied promises are fulfilled in practice.

II. BEYOND REMORSE: THE CONCEPT OF THE 'GOOD ACCUSED' BEFORE THE FRENCH *COUR D'ASSISES*

Jean Danet, on the basis of many years' practice as a defence lawyer before the CA, has argued that there is a clear concept of '*le bon accusé*', or 'the good accused', which defines a set of expectations of defendants.[12] The expression of remorse is a key part – but only a part – of these broader expectations. The 'good accused' is expected actively to participate in the trial and to see it as part of a continuing personal journey.[13] This is seen as a reflection of their acceptance of responsibility and commitment to personal change. Despite a formal right to silence that has been a part of the Code of Criminal Procedure since 2014,[14] the accused is expected to tell their story openly and honestly, with real detail as to how and why the offence was committed.[15]

Here, we must remember some of the ways that criminal trials in France differ from those in Anglo-American jurisdictions. The court, rather than the parties, calls witnesses in an order determined by the judicial president, with no formal division between prosecution and defence witnesses. The questioning of witnesses is done first and foremost by the president (and only after that is questioning by victim, prosecution and defendant permitted). Much of the questioning is based on readings or summaries of the 'dossier', which is an official record of the pre-trial investigation (containing, for example, pre-trial witness statements and police and expert reports).[16] These differences between the French and Anglo-American traditions impact on the way defendants are expected to participate at trial. Unlike Anglo-American jurisdictions, the court does not simply engage with the defendant at discrete moments or stages of trial designated for questioning of the accused. Presidents continually return to defendants through the course of the trial for their reaction to the testimony of others.[17] Often, this will be used to offer opportunities to the defendant to

[12] J Danet, *Defendre: pour une penale critique* (Paris, Dalloz, 2001) 96–97.

[13] See Gautron's confirmation from French case-file data, V Gautron, 'Remorse in the French Criminal Justice System: A Subterranean Influence' in S Field and C Tata (eds), *Criminal Justice and the Ideal Defendant in the Making of Remorse and Responsibility* (Oxford, Hart Publishing, 2023) ch 2.

[14] Code de procédure pénale (CPP), Art 328. On the difference between expectations of speech and the right to silence, see Besnier (n 8) 125–26.

[15] Besnier (n 8) 133–34.

[16] In the most serious cases, such as those heard before the CA, the pre-trial investigation would be led by a judge.

[17] Besnier (n 8) 43.

go further in accepting responsibility and expressing remorse. This may involve giving the accused the opportunity to confess for the first time in the rare cases in which there has been no pre-trial confession.[18] More frequently, it involves challenging the accused when he or she seeks to row back from pre-trial admissions given weight by their very existence within an official dossier. This applies not just to outright denials (which are rare in court), but even minor attempts to move away from the most damaging accounts of involvement. For example, in cases of violence, attempts to reduce even slightly the number or force of blows or to deny full intent or knowledge of circumstances are countered (sometimes with expressions of judicial impatience) by detailed summary of witness statements from the dossier (including the defendant's own statements) and reminders of the consistency and mutual corroboration of those statements.[19] Judicial questioning demands not just general acknowledgement of the facts by the defendant, but their recall in great detail. Presidents routinely go through each of several allegations, wanting to know exactly what happened, when and how many times. Explanations are sought by presidents for decisions made by defendants at every stage.[20] Failures to recall or provide explanations are seen as failures to engage with the mission of the court. Presidents often greet new explanations offered at trial that contradict known elements of the dossier with incredulity.[21]

Beyond acknowledging the facts in the dossier, the good accused is expected to express remorse and assume responsibility. Presidents picked up and highlighted in positive terms any expressions of remorse (or conversely minimisation of responsibility) made in pre-trial statements or interview with psychiatrists or psychologists.[22] The accused was also encouraged by the president to acknowledge the consequences for victims at the hearing, to recognise their immediate distress and longer-term suffering, and to express remorse.[23] Often, this was first formulated as an open invitation: 'Do you have anything to say?' The good accused was expected to seize such opportunities.[24] Not all defendants – faced with acknowledging innermost secrets in a highly formal public arena – were able to recognise them or react appropriately.[25] If defendants responded by bare expression of regret or remorse, they might be asked to explain these feelings. On occasion, an apparently inarticulate or unreflective accused was unable to say anything.[26] Sometimes an accused said more, but in apparently mechanistic

[18] ibid 131.

[19] SAF06, SAF19, SAF24 and SAF48. The codes refer to cases observed, with the initials of the primary observer.

[20] SAF24 and SAF19.

[21] SAF24.

[22] SAF48.

[23] SAF06; Besnier (n 8) 134.

[24] On the negative consequences for the accused of failing to take those opportunities, see Besnier (n 8) 135–38.

[25] SAF06.

[26] SAF24.

ways that suggested 'coaching' by their defence lawyer and a lack of authenticity and genuineness. Self-reflection and insight were seen as evidence of the 'quality' of remorse.[27]

So, the expectation is that expressions of remorse should be part of a broader examination of self. Presidents made it clear to the accused that they needed to participate in the court's search for the reasons for their behaviour. Why did the sexual abuse take place?[28] In a homicide, why did the assault continue after the victim was clearly incapable of defending himself any further?[29] Perhaps the most dramatic instance of this was a case involving several counts of kidnapping young minors and persuading them to perform oral sex acts.[30] By the time of trial, the accused had essentially admitted the facts and (with some small variations) continued to do so at trial. But he could not or would not admit that this had been done for sexual motives: he continued to argue at trial that he had done this as an experiment because he wanted to see how anyone could derive pleasure from such an act. Throughout the trial, the president went back to this repeatedly, at one point explicitly saying that the defendant must examine himself and indeed confront himself to get beyond this denial. At the next pause in proceedings, the highly experienced *huissier* (usher) of the court commented to the researcher: 'all these denials, he thinks they go for him, but really, they go against him, always against him'.[31]

Similarly, the failure of an accused to engage fully and early in psychological therapy while in pre-trial detention was seen – and explicitly described by the judge – as a failure of the necessary introspection to come to greater self-understanding. Often, the contents of the dossier would be used by the president to push, encourage or help the accused to go further: in a case of sexual abuse of a daughter by her father, where the accused struggled to provide explanations for his behaviour, the president encouraged the accused, in the face of initial reluctance, to talk about the breakdown of his sexual relationship with his wife.[32]

But it is not just down to the president of the court, as the representative of the state, to bring out the behaviour expected of a good accused. Apart from in those rare cases where the accused denies guilt completely, defence lawyers also see it as part of their job to encourage their client at trial to go further in expressing remorse and accepting responsibility.[33] In pre-trial interviews, lawyers generally negotiated with clients an agreed position as to exactly which

[27] SAF20; R Weisman, 'Remorse Is Not Enough: Disentangling the Roles of Remorse and Insight in the Construction of the Ideal Defendant' in Field and Tata (n 13) ch 7.

[28] SAF06; generally, see Besnier (n 8) 127–28.

[29] SAF24.

[30] SAF20.

[31] The *huissier* in France is a professionalised version of a court usher, working under the direction of the President, but with a wider range of functions; see Besnier (n 8) 24–25. Of course, these are not so much denials as evidence of lack of insight; see Weisman, 'Remorse Is Not Enough' (n 27).

[32] SAF06.

[33] Besnier (n 8) 184.

facts would be admitted and which denied.[34] Lawyers seemed to be looking for a defence position on facts and responsibility that they felt was plausible in the context of the established assumptions of the system (not least those of the 'good accused'). They knew that presidents were often impatient with attempts to retreat from assumptions of responsibility acknowledged in the dossier. The French inquisitorial tradition means that surprises at trial have to overcome much judicial scepticism. Thus, defence lawyers would often see the interests of a client who made initial admissions as being furthered by acknowledging guilt and taking responsibility, particularly when the original admissions were detailed and repeated before a pre-trial investigating magistrate.[35]

At trial, lawyers would sometimes encourage their clients not to retreat from the details of their pre-trial statements and to explain variations in accounts as difficulties of memory.[36] It is common practice for lawyers, or sometimes their trainees, to spend hours with the accused in preparation for trial, going through pre-trial statements that the president might use, pointing out inappropriate replies and suggesting appropriate ones. The defendant is schooled in the need to prepare the ground for the lawyer's *plaidoirie* by explicitly expressing remorse and taking responsibility.[37] Clients who resisted that advice were sometimes seen as stupid or '*fantasiste*'.[38] If the accused had expressed remorse or shown empathy for the victims in their statements to police or examining magistrate, that was often explicitly mentioned at trial by their lawyer with an emphasis on how early in proceedings responsibility had been acknowledged.[39] They coach their clients to contrast any initial failures to acknowledge guilt with their current preparedness to go further and the increased sense of self-knowledge that had prompted that. That increased self-knowledge might be linked to therapy that the defendant was undergoing. They would also prompt (and coach) explicit expressions of remorse and acceptance of responsibility from their clients, even thinking strategically about the point of the trial at which such expressions should be made in order to have maximum effect.[40] They would not just provide explanations of the behaviour,[41] but would emphasise in their *plaidoirie* how far the client had come in acknowledging their guilt and the consequences of their acts (even while accepting the client had more work to do).[42] If a client had not been able to express remorse, other conduct, such as attempts at suicide or an

[34] ADW06.

[35] SAF06.

[36] SAF19.

[37] The *plaidoirie* is the defence speech to the court at the end of a hearing. Sometimes it involves an argument that the defendant is not guilty at all. More frequently, the argument will be geared to mitigation of sentence and/or suggesting lack of proof in relation to at least some charges. ARB01.

[38] *Fantasiste* in this context has connotations of a fanciful failure to acknowledge reality. Interview/Av02, SAF19 and ARB01.

[39] SAF03 and ARB01.

[40] SAF03, SAF19 and ARB01.

[41] SAF06.

[42] SAF19.

inability to talk about the facts to a therapist, might be (more or less plausibly) evoked by lawyers as evidence of an acceptance of responsibility.[43]

Lawyers whose clients appeared unprepared for their role as the 'good accused' were judged by other legal actors as either performing badly or struggling with an unhelpful client.[44] In one case, researchers were told that the previous defence lawyer had resigned from the case because the accused would not move to a more plausible account.[45] Sometimes, defence lawyers seemed to struggle to build rich, plausible accounts where their client was apparently unreflective and inarticulate.[46] This was seen as problematic because a jury was more likely to be clement in sentencing if they understood the motivations and broader causes of the act.[47]

Victims also played an important role in the dialogue around remorse. This was given a distinctive dimension by the fact that victims themselves are usually legally represented.[48] This is a consequence of the French *partie civile* system, which allows victims to join their own civil claims to criminal prosecutions. This gives their lawyers full access to the dossier and allows them to ask questions of witnesses and the accused, and to make closing speeches.[49] Victims were sometimes asked about their reaction to expressions of defendant remorse or the lack of them.[50] Their lawyers regularly evoked a failure to confess, to admit responsibility and to express remorse as something that increased the suffering of their clients or failed to help them come to terms with what had happened.[51] This was, unsurprisingly, particularly marked in sexual offences.[52] During their closing speeches, they would emphasise any evidence of failure fully and promptly to admit responsibility in relation to all incidents and any gestures that showed a contempt or lack of regard for the victim's feelings.[53] The fact that only arrest had stopped the abuse – in other words, the accused had not stopped himself – would also be evoked.[54] Even failure to admit to incidents set out in the dossier with unidentified victims might be seen as evidence of a continuing failure to confront one's own offending.[55] At times, lawyers for the victim appeared to be working in tandem with the president of the court to encourage the accused

[43] ARB01.
[44] Interview/Av02 and SAF24.
[45] SAF20.
[46] SAF24.
[47] ADW14 and SAF16.
[48] The term 'victims' has been adopted here because in almost all these cases the defendant is not denying that the 'victim' is a victim. It is who did what and why that is at stake.
[49] Besnier (n 8) 32–37 argues that the space, literal and metaphorical, given to the victim before the CA has developed further since our study in the late 1990s–early 2000s.
[50] ARB01.
[51] SAF16. See Besnier (n 8) 183 and 188 for examples where victims directly press the accused to go further in their taking of responsibility.
[52] ADW14.
[53] SAF16 and SAF48.
[54] SAF06.
[55] SAF20.

to examine themselves more closely to understand their own motives and take fuller responsibility.

Thus, all the legal actors see getting the accused to assume his responsibilities as being an important part of what the trial at the CA is about. But admitting the 'how' and the 'why' is not enough. Courts seek to integrate this within a broader account of 'who' the defendant is and their journey in life. This is linked to the mission of the court in a serious criminal case. One investigating judge described this to a defendant during an interview focused on his life and personality (*comparution sur curriculum vitae*): 'you will be judged on the facts but through the personality'.[56] This is the starting point for trial: usually, even before the alleged facts have been discussed, the president of the court will spend between 45 minutes and two hours questioning defendants directly on their life story.[57] Sometimes defendants speak spontaneously, sometimes the president will drag information out of them by summarising witness statements.[58] Direct questioning of the accused is often supported by several character witnesses called by the court. Sometimes, though by no means always, they offer new insights into the accused's personal development.[59] This can be seen very much as the court building a picture of the 'unique reality' of the defendant's life.[60] Often what emerged over the course of the trial was a reasonably coherent – though often not clearly proven or uncontested – account of the accused's personality and its evolution over time. Coherence and plausibility often flowed more freely from a participating and cooperative accused. And the defendant was expected to participate even if this led to examination of embarrassing or shameful episodes or moments of loss and grief. So suicide attempts, impotence, alcoholism and drug abuse, revenue, timidity and clumsiness with women and absence of sexual relations might all be raised.[61] And the good accused is expected to identify friends and family who can talk about him to the pre-trial investigating magistrate and possibly be called as character witnesses.[62] Defence lawyers encouraged participation by the accused in this process and often seemed to be working with the president at trial in situating the accused's behaviour within a plausible frame of interpretation. This was a key part of defence strategies: selecting character witnesses, getting them to court and coaching their clients as to what kinds of explanations would be both plausible and useful to their interests.[63] Besides the view that this was in the client's interest, defence lawyers

[56] SAF15.
[57] For further discussion, see Field (n 9).
[58] SAF06.
[59] SAF24.
[60] Tata (n 5).
[61] SAF20, SAF19, SAF15 and SAF06.
[62] SAF15.
[63] SAF39, SAF24, ARB01, Interviews/Av02 and Av16. Generally, on the role of the defence lawyer in 'pleading the man in context', see Besnier (n 8) 197–99. Defence lawyers cite witnesses (they ask for them to be called), but within the inquisitorial tradition it is the court that decides (primarily on the basis of relevance and significance).

saw this as part of the legitimate truth-finding mission of the court with which it was proper to cooperate (and, indeed, part of the attraction of working at the CA was to participate in the fullest expression of that mission).[64]

The sense of the underlying personality of the accused that emerged was also critical to presenting an image of positive personal change and coming to terms with offending. Often there will be a period of two or three years between the events at issue and the trial. The defendant will have spent lengthy periods on bail or on remand. The president will routinely start the questioning on the personality by asking the defendants about their experiences during this time: how have they been feeling, have they been undergoing treatment, are they working, training or doing classes, how much contact is there with their family? The court is looking for – and expects the good accused to demonstrate – evidence of personal change or a capacity for such change that could give (now or in the future) practical effect to their expressions of remorse.[65] At the same time, the court is performing state concern for the 'unique individual'. Thus, presidents would routinely question accused about the pattern of prison visits they were having: visits were seen as evidence of supportive family relationships.[66] They might question an accused about having given up psychotherapy in prison or only just having started it. Reasons are scrutinised and encouragement given to persevere.[67] Defence lawyers were keen to chart at trial a positive evolution in the character of their client and link them to plausible explanations (abstinence from drink and drugs, commitment to – and insights from – therapy, a new stabilising relationship or new-found support in an older relationship).[68] To be engaged in no activities in prison was not a positive sign; nor, in particular, was 'not seeing the point' of psychotherapy in sexual abuse cases. Lawyers explain the importance of this image of evolution to their clients.[69] The 'good accused' must tell, but must also 'do'.[70] Presidents also give opportunities to defendants to indicate their plans for the future and to suggest what they have learnt from prison.[71]

Thus, expressions of remorse and broader acceptance of responsibility before the CA are key aspects, but only aspects, of a broader conception of

[64] On the truth-finding role of defence lawyer, see also Besnier (n 8) 84–87. A very experienced defence lawyer at the CA said to the researcher after his retirement that it had been the right time to stop because his final trial was the fullest example of the CA achieving its mission he was likely to experience: he explained that this meant not an acquittal, but the richest possible reflection by all parties on the respective responsibilities in the case. This acceptance of the participation of the defence in a truth-finding mission came from a lawyer who had played a leading role in the most left-wing of the lawyer's professional associations.

[65] For consideration of the way French case files make clear the importance of personal change as 'moral transformation', see Gautron (n.13).

[66] SAF24.

[67] ADW14 and SAF20.

[68] SAF24, ARB01 and ADW06.

[69] SAF06.

[70] R Weisman, *Showing Remorse: Law and the Social Control of Emotion* (Farnham, Ashgate, 2014) esp ch 2.

[71] SAF24.

the 'good accused'. Ideal defendants are expected to talk openly and in detail about exactly what they did and why, and to contribute actively to a broader dialogue that situates their offending and their response to it within the story of their lives. And they are expected to demonstrate 'insight', and a capacity and preparedness for personal change.[72] All these different indicators of acceptance of responsibility are assessed as part of a broader evaluation in court of the character or personality of the accused. Ultimately, the good accused is one who cooperates with the court in its mission to find the truth and determine the appropriate punishment. By doing so, they implicitly acknowledge the legitimacy of that very punishment by the state. In the following section, I will argue that the concept of the good accused is a concept of the 'good citizen', and that the particular pattern of relationships acted out in the CA reflects key aspects of French legal and political culture and its view of the relationship between state and citizen. So far, I have been talking almost exclusively of the state's expectations of the accused. But the relationship between French state and citizen is wrapped in a sense of reciprocal exchange. What is it that the French state implicitly promises in these courtroom exchanges?

III. PERFORMING CONCERN FOR THE UNIQUE INDIVIDUAL: THE SIGNIFICANCE OF ROLES AND RELATIONSHIPS

Cyrus Tata has argued, drawing on his own empirical research into the work of the Scottish intermediate (Sheriff) courts, that more or less detailed pretrial interrogations into character and personal and social circumstances serve to reassure both defendants and the professional court community that the accused defendant is being treated as a 'unique individual'.[73] The practice of the CA seems to provide a powerful example of the French state's investment of time and resources in that demonstration of concern for the individual. From the perspective of the Anglo-American lawyer, simply the time invested in situating the offence within the context of a particular life is striking.[74] Here, for the Anglo-American reader, it is important to remember that there is no abbreviated guilty plea procedure before the CA. Each case will take a minimum of one day to be heard even though the vast majority of defendants are not contesting their guilt.[75] In contrast, before the courts in England and Wales, even very serious uncontested cases before the Crown Court last little more than an hour.[76]

[72] Weisman, 'Remorse Is Not Enough' (n 27).

[73] Tata (n 5).

[74] See the opening example given in Field (n 9).

[75] Fewer than 10% of defendants are found not guilty before the CA: www.justice.gouv.fr/statistiques-10054/references-statistiques-justice-12837/justice-penale-donnees-2019-33704.html

[76] For pre-Covid hearing times, see www.gov.uk/government/statistics/criminal-court-statistics-quarterly-october-to-december-2019/criminal-court-statistics-quarterly-october-to-december-2019#fnref:3.

Much that is discussed before the CA would be excluded as irrelevant or unduly prejudicial evidence of character in a contested Crown Court trial and regarded as unnecessary detail for a sentencing hearing.[77] At a CA, there are usually several character witnesses, some of whom are questioned for as long as 30 minutes. Furthermore, there is considerable investment in expert psychological and psychiatric analysis of the defendants' personality. All cases had at least one psychiatric report and one psychological report, with most experts coming to trial to be subject to questioning.

But these are not just differences in the investment of time: the nature of participation is different. In England and Wales, sentencing hearings are not only short, but are dominated by the lawyers. Defendants are expected mainly to keep their mouths shut and not to disrupt proceedings. Judges are mainly listening rather than talking and they are mainly listening to lawyers. The nature of English practice reflects Tata's account of practice before the Scottish courts, where concern for individual circumstances is largely played out backstage in the pre-sentence phase: it is there that pre-sentence reports are written (by probation officers) and read (by judges). The sentencing hearing itself is rapid, with only superficial engagement with the defendant.[78] In contrast, before the French CA, both the expression of remorse and concern for the unique individual flows from the central relationship between an active judge and a personally participating defendant. This is not work delegated to defence lawyers and probation officers, hidden away in a private pre-trial process; it is on display centre stage, as a dominant theme of a public hearing. Thus, it is not just that much more is expected of defendants in terms of the weight or 'thickness' of admissions of responsibility and professed remorse.[79] Their key interlocutors – the key coordinators of the process – in both pre-trial and trial stages have judicial status. At trial, it is the president of the court who leads a direct, oral dialogue with the defendant. That role builds on the pre-trial role of the *juge d'instruction*. This investigating magistrate controls the pre-trial construction of the *enquête de personnalité*, which provides much of the material in the official dossier for questioning on character at trial.[80]

This provokes some linked reflections. First, by contrast to both Scotland and England and Wales, in the most serious cases, the court – principally in the figure of its president acting for the French state in their judicial truth-finding

[77] The Crown Court is the English court most nearly equivalent to the French *cours d'assises* in that both are first-instance criminal courts that deal with the most serious offences. However, the percentage of cases appearing before the CA is smaller than that appearing before the Crown Court.

[78] Tata (n 5).

[79] J Gormley and C Tata, 'Remorse and Sentencing in a World of Plea Bargaining' in S Tudor, R Weisman, M Proeve and K Rossmanith (eds), *Remorse & Criminal Justice: Multi-disciplinary Perspectives* (London, Routledge, 2021).

[80] The *enquête de personnalité* or 'investigation into character' is part of the pre-trial investigation supervised by the investigating magistrate: documentation and witness statements are compiled that speak to the life course and personality of the accused.

role – is making a much more visible display of its commitment to understanding the unique reality of the defendant. In Tata's account of Scottish Sheriff courts, it is the judges, lawyers and probation officers – the professional court communities – that seek backstage to give a sense of individualised justice to a public process largely focused on rapid sentencing outcomes. In France, an active judge often seems to be speaking publicly for the state on matters going beyond the narrow question of guilt, and in a way that seems to act out a particular notion of state–citizen relations. A French judge can speak for the French state in a way that an English judge cannot speak for the British state. French judges generally enter the Ecole Nationale de la Magistrature immediately after university (and a classic competitive state *concours*) to be trained for more than two years and socialised into a judicial corps distinct from that of the lawyer (*avocat*). This reflects a French variant on the career judiciary system common to many Continental jurisdictions.[81] In contrast, English judges spend most of their careers as barristers (essentially, independent contractors) rather than career state servants. This sense of the judge speaking for the French state and distinct French republican values was most obvious when judges engaged with issues that are marginal to what Anglo-Americans would think of as the core functions of the trial. Presidents emphasised strongly and positively aspects of the defendant's life and character that emerged from the dossier or from the testimony of character witness that showed them as good citizens: doing well in training or education, being a good and reliable worker or father,[82] participating in voluntary associations or activities,[83] even having a diverse range of appropriate interests (sport, history, politics and reading).[84] Presidents often at these moments seemed to subtly but clearly demonstrate the approval of the court and state, and to welcome the opportunity to share values with the defendant. For example, a defendant struggling to get access to her fostered child might be encouraged to continue their attempts and told that such contact was important to both child and mother.[85] There were instances where presidents found time to affirm positive values by, for example, talking at length to the defendant's mother about problems of access to her grandchildren.[86] At these points, judges seemed to display a human and paternalist face of the state, concerned with aspects of the functioning of families that went beyond questions of simple legality. This supports an interpretation that the expressed concern for the unique individual that is the defendant should be seen as part of a broader symbolic relationship.

[81] J Bell, *Judiciaries within Europe: A Comparative Review* (Cambridge, Cambridge University Press, 2006) ch 2; C Guarnieri and P Pederzoli, *The Power of* Judges (Oxford, Clarendon Press, 2002).

[82] SAF06.

[83] SAF48.

[84] SAF03.

[85] SAF16.

[86] SAF39.

Ultimately, the 'good accused' is a dimension of the good citizen. The positive and demanding expectations made of '*le bon accusé*' reflect a positive sense of what it means to be a French citizen that goes beyond simply not breaking the criminal law. It involves defendants not just actively explaining their unlawful acts, but doing so in the light of their life as French citizens.

This argument that the French state is more actively involved in defining the very identity of citizens than may be true of Anglo-American states is consistent with the historical analysis of political scientists.[87] They argue that since the Revolution, the French state has had a particular and distinctive importance in promoting national unity and social cohesion, so that the form and nature of the French state has become central to the way the French see themselves. The significance of the Revolution is that it was not merely a political revolution, but was the sweeping away of an entire established social order.[88] Central to the constituting of the new social order has been the direct relationship between citizen and state. In English, we refer – and always with positive connotations – to many different types of 'communities' as intermediate social groups between citizen and state that provide a sense of belonging.[89] In French, the concept of community is regularly associated with '*communautarisme*', which has pejorative connotations of a sense of belonging to religious, regional and other social groups that cuts across what should be a sense of belonging to the 'one and indivisible' French nation.[90] In the nineteenth century, the French state became critical to establishing the legitimacy of the new social order by defining positive abstract notions of both France and what it means to be a French citizen. Thus, appeals to the normative force of 'the values of the Republic' are a frequent aspect of political discourse in a nation in which the dominant French political tradition of republicanism has been seen as a 'civil religion'.[91] The French state has been key to the defining of a positive notion of French citizenship: a set of 'French' values that are 'deeply particular to, and constitutive of, French national identity'.[92] And the relations between individuals and the state are associated

[87] HS Jones, *French State in Question* (Cambridge, Cambridge University Press, 2002) ch 1; S Hazareesingh, *Political Traditions in Modern France* (Oxford, Oxford University Press, 1994) chs 1, 3 and 6.

[88] See also Field (n 9) 541–42.

[89] For historical development of the meanings of the word, see R Williams, *Keywords* (London, Fontana, 1988) 75–76.

[90] See in particular forum.wordreference.com/threads/communautarisme.7439/. The French revolution saw the absolute sovereign power of the king transferred in theory to the nation rather than individuals or groups. But in practice, that sovereignty is exercised by the state, which personifies the nation and acts as the guarantor of the public interest: see Art 3 of the Declaration of the Rights of Man and the Citizen, 26 August 1789; P Ardant, *Institutions politiques et Droit constitutionnel* (Paris, LGDJ, 2000) 166–70; J Hodgson, *French Criminal Justice* (Oxford, Hart Publishing, 2005) 14–15. My thanks to Laurène Soubise for this point. Note that the search for national unity has managed to coexist with strong regional identities: see S Hazareesingh, *How the French Think* (London, Allen Lane, 2015) ch 6.

[91] Hazareesingh (n 90) 4 and 60.

[92] A Favell, *Philosophies of Integration: Immigration and the Idea of Citizenship in France and Britain* (London, Macmillan, 1998) 83.

with the 'republican contract' in which the demands of integration are not seen as a 'coercive infringement on group or individual autonomy but as the basis of mutuality'.[93]

This positive concept of the French citizen and the place of the state in defining the identity of the nation and its citizens reflects a polity that seems significantly at odds with dominant notions of liberal pluralism as understood in Anglo-American society.[94] Drawing on a variety of historical studies, Nicola Lacey has traced the way that, in England, notions of responsibility based on evaluation of character retreated during the eighteenth and nineteenth centuries. At the start of the eighteenth century, the English judge played an active truth-finding role in a trial based on assumptions of responsibility and the need for defendants to explain themselves in ways that emphasised their law-abiding character and reputation within the local community.[95] But by the beginning of the nineteenth century, the rule of generally excluding evidence of character was established. Lacey attributes this in part to institutional developments within criminal justice associated with the rise of adversarial trial dominated by lawyers and with technical rules of evidence. But she also attributes it to shifts in political cultures and social contexts: industrialisation and urbanisation weakened the trust in local community standards upon which character could be judged. The rise of individualism and liberal notions of autonomy required a legitimation of criminal justice rooted in a more abstract and impersonal mode of judgement in which character was marginalised. The repeated public performance by the French CA of a very different relationship between state and citizen seems to affirm the underlying imperatives of a particular political settlement.

IV. QUESTIONS OF LEGITIMACY: KEEPING THE STATE'S (IMPLICIT) PROMISES?

What is being acted out in the French *cours d'assises* is a symbolic exchange between citizen and state. This is not a negotiated bargain or exchange of explicit promises. Rather, it is based on background assumptions about normal underlying relationships between state and citizen. Practice before the CA suggests that the French state is expecting a broader commitment from the French citizen defendant than would be the case in equivalent Anglo-American courts. But what exactly is the French state offering in return, and is it making good on those (implicit) promises? One reading is that, in return for performing the role

[93] A Crawford, 'Contrasts in Victim–Offender Mediation' in D Nelken (ed), *Contrasting Criminal Justice* (Aldershot, Ashgate, 2000) 218–19.

[94] See Favell's analysis of differences in conceptions of citizenship in France and Britain as they play out in policies around integration and immigration: Favell (n 92).

[95] N Lacey, *In Search of Criminal Responsibility* (Oxford, Oxford University Press, 2016) 116–17.

of ideal defendant (or approximations of it), the state is offering two things: first, to engage in a careful and meaningful dialogue with defendants about their responsibilities in the light of the reciprocal responsibilities of the French state and other citizens; and secondly, to provide a viable route back to full citizenship and reintegration into the polity. Thus, Besnier, on the basis of her observations, salutes the 'collective work' of the CA, to which 'all the actors contribute', as the 'global restoration of the social link' or 'the organic link which unites a human community'. For her, it is the eliciting and acceptance of responsibility that enables this path towards integration and reconciliation.[96]

The playing out of the criminal trial as a symbolic enactment of implicit but reciprocal promises between citizen and state is one which affirms the legitimacy of state punishment. But some researchers have raised doubts as to whether the state in different jurisdictions is really making good on such (implicit) promises. How far is this really an open dialogue around responsibility in which defendants can effectively participate and have their unique circumstances taken into account? In their study of the operation of remorse before the Dutch police courts, Van Oorschot et al emphasised the defendant's limited capacity to participate actively and effectively in dialogue.[97] The defendant faces a dilemma. As with defendants before the CA, judges expect them to tell their story. But what if telling one's story involves identifying the role and responsibility of others in what happened? In Van Oorschot's study, judges often responded negatively when defendants sought to attribute responsibility to others: whether this was acceptable or not depended on judicial stereotypes around cases which defendants could not necessarily anticipate. Often, seeking to attribute responsibility to others was regarded as failure to fulfil the expectation of the 'good accused', who should fully accept their individual responsibility. In this volume, Weisman, drawing on Canadian cases, points out that defendants are expected to demonstrate 'insight' into their responsibilities, but that ascribing a key role to broader 'situational factors' is not regarded as acceptable.[98] Thus, acceptable dialogue about responsibility is closed in significant respects. Tata has raised a different anxiety about practice before Scottish Sheriff courts.[99] He argues that individual circumstances are investigated in the pre-sentence process only to be frequently marginalised or discounted by judges as mere routine background, largely unnecessary to their functions. Why, they complain, should they need to know about the defendant's golf handicap or where they went to school? The routine demonstration of the multiple social disadvantages experienced by defendants is thus nullified: it has little impact on the state's response in sentencing.

How far do these concerns about restrictions in the permitted dialogue around responsibility and the nullification of personal and social circumstances

[96] Besnier (n 8) 182, 190 and 193. My translations.

[97] I van Oorschot et al, 'Remorse in Context(s): A Qualititative Exploration of the Negotiation of Remorse and Its Consequences' (2017) 26 *Social and Legal Studies* 359.

[98] Weisman, 'Remorse Is Not Enough' (n 27).

[99] Tata (n 5).

apply to the French CA? Unlike the rapid oral verification of the dossier in other French criminal courts, the CA is supposed to be different: this is a court where there is time to determine the intersecting responsibilities of the defendant and others (family, school, state) by the interplay of competing oral arguments and varied testimony at trial.[100] There were a number of cases observed where defendants were clearly allowed – and, indeed, supported – in attempts to bring out the responsibility of state, community, family and others in the deep background to the events. The impact of childhood trauma such as sexual abuse, the death of younger siblings or domestic violence and its potential as part of the explanation for subsequent events was regularly explored in some detail using questions to defendants, character witnesses and medico-psychological and psychiatric experts.[101] Soo too were accidents leaving physical and mental scars, parental addiction and failures to provide a supportive environment.[102] And these matters are not just reported in pre-sentence reports, they are matters of close questioning and sometimes often highly emotional exchanges between character witnesses and defendants.[103] Defence lawyers worked throughout trial to build up these mitigating explanations for exploitation in closing speeches.[104] Whether attempts to share responsibility with co-defendants or build mitigatory claims on the actions of victims appeared to be acceptable seemed to depend less on judicial stereotypes around particular categories of case than on conventional ways of judging veracity.[105] They were founded on triangulation with other witness accounts, other sources of evidence and, above all, consistency in defendants' accounts (with a heavy dose of scepticism about self-interest).

However, active participation in a broad-ranging discussion about responsibility in the light of family and social contexts poses risks to defendants and their lawyers. To accept, contest or limit responsibility is a delicate judgement, with profound implications. In adversarial trial, the defence can plead mitigation with very little active participation by the defendant in oral proceedings. Negotiations about plea and its factual basis take place in private, and once decisions are made, the defence lawyer has greater control because the defendant is not expected to say anything. By contrast, the French defendant is expected to participate throughout the trial, reacting in real time to detailed facts, expert reports and witness testimony, and the coherence and consistency of their response is taken as an index of their having a credible discourse around responsibility. Skilled defence lawyers sift through a variety of possible versions of the truth to find the one that will, within the context of this particular process, appear the most plausible and favourable to the client. And that version will have to be negotiated with the client themself, the script maintained through

[100] Besnier (n 8).
[101] ADW14, ARB01 and ADW06. See also Besnier (n 8) 155.
[102] SAF39 and ARB01.
[103] ARB01.
[104] ADW14 and ADW06.
[105] *cf* van Oorschot et al (n 97).

unforeseen challenges and pulled together into a plausible narrative account of psychology and motivation. This process often raised difficult questions about self-advantage. For example, if defendants were drunk, would it be wise to play that up or play it down? If they were afraid of someone or of being implicated, does that help or hinder their case? This construction of plausible narratives is difficult to pull off and its relationship with the 'truth', often years after the event, is very difficult to judge.[106]

Defendants are highly dependent not only on being well coached in the pre-trial process by defence lawyers, but also on their own emotional and intellectual capacities. Visit any CA and you will see a space constructed for grand political statements rather than personal growth and the confronting of inner demons.[107] During our observations, some defendants found ways to intervene that seemed to demonstrate genuine empathy with their victims.[108] Most found something intelligible to say about themselves. But each intervention by the defendant was full of both the potential to demonstrate and the potential to undermine the image of the good accused. A defendant angrily putting questions to his own stepfather as to why the latter was never there for him might come over as self-serving failure to take responsibility. But the next moment, in his response, the stepfather might clearly demonstrate himself exactly as the uncaring and uninterested figure that the defendant was portraying.[109] Not surprisingly, many defendants found these demands a challenge, and came over as confused and/or self-serving. Defendants have unequal personal resources to deliver what is expected of the good accused. Furthermore, medico-psychological and psychiatric reports and testimony often provided very negative character portrayals of defendants expressed in apparently expert language that was often incomprehensible and therefore unchallengeable.[110] More broadly, as elsewhere, the expert psychiatric and psychological focus on personality tended to reframe responsibility in terms of individual rather than collective factors.[111]

Beyond participation in a meaningful dialogue about the fair apportionment of responsibility, the other implicit promise of the CA is that performing the role of the good accused provides a viable route to reintegration into the broader polity.[112] Again, there are questions about whether the French state delivers on its implicit promises. There are sometimes moving moments before the court

[106] SAF16.

[107] A hint of the historical grandeur of some *cours d'assises* can be gleaned from videos on the Ministry of Justice website: www.justice.gouv.fr/histoire-et-patrimoine-10050/architecture-et-chantiers-12268/quel-sens-donner-a-larchitecture-des-palais-de-justice-23348.html.

[108] SAF19.

[109] ADW06.

[110] SAF24 and ADW14. On the role of experts and the practical exclusion of the accused, see Besnier (n 8) 129–30 and 141–45.

[111] De Lagasnerie (n 10) 107 et seq and 164 et seq.

[112] For the view that the CA is a kind of restorative justice, see Besnier (n 8) 135. But restorative justice is traditionally seen as a much more bottom-up process.

where taking responsibility seems to open possibilities for reconciliation and reintegration.[113] But the performance on stage does not receive consistent support when the curtain falls. The *cour d'assises* has no power to respond to the many social inequalities and failures of the state revealed before it. It is set up to sanction named individuals, not the collective responsibilities of states or social groups.[114] The conditions of the French prison system are far from being generally conducive to the reintegration of offenders.[115] And we must contrast the experience of the less than 1 per cent of defendants that appear before the CA with that of the other 99 per cent heard before the lower French courts. While expressions of remorse and responsibility may be important there, the opportunity to explore the nuances of the mutual expectations of citizens and states and the unique reality of defendants' lives is much attenuated. Here, we see again the significance of Doreen McBarnet's 'two tiers of justice': the public image of justice is drawn from the work of the higher courts, but the lower courts deal with almost all the cases.[116]

V. CONCLUSIONS

This chapter has examined the significance of expressions of remorse and their meaning within a particular legal and political culture. Before the CA, the significance of remorse can best be understood as part of broader dialogues around, and assessments of, individual character, responsibility and the potential for personal change. Underpinning these broader dialogues is a politically symbolic exchange between state and defendant. The state is implicitly undertaking to punish only after carefully taking into account not just the facts, but also the personal circumstances and life history of the defendant. These promises are not explicit: they are the underlying background assumptions of a political culture – not just that the state's punishment will be appropriately calibrated, but also that the bond between citizen and state can be recreated provided that each plays the appropriate mutually supporting role. Specifically, state efforts to reintegrate the citizen must be supported by the citizen's recognition of the authority of the state through cooperation with the mission of the court and thus public acceptance of the legitimacy of its punishment. Remorse is a key indicator of that cooperation and acceptance. Thus, the state's preoccupation with expressions of remorse represents its search for the fullest and most complete expression of

[113] ibid 187–90.

[114] De Lagasnerie (n 10) argues that the French CA suppresses and ignores the social determination of action and refuses sociological explanations. That was not true of the cases observed insofar as social contexts were evoked regularly and taken seriously. But it was true in that the penal response was always to act on the individual and not the society.

[115] D Fassin, *Prison Worlds: An Ethnography of the Carceral Condition* (Cambridge, Polity Press, 2017) 126. Most of those judged before the court will be sent back to prison to finish their sentence.

[116] D McBarnet, *Conviction* (London, Macmillan, 1981) 153.

this. In practice, in most cases, the court has to accept, and indeed welcomes, much less than perfect performance of the role of the 'good accused'.[117] Indeed, this is part of a broader paradox: it is not a reciprocal bargain whose moral force can be derived from voluntariness or freedom of choice. Because there is an ever-present danger and frequently clear evidence of rejection in practice by the accused, the penal system provides incentives designed to encourage the accused to behave 'as if' the ascribed roles are voluntary. Yet the very need for incentives suggests that the accused may not feel them to be so.

Some elements of this symbolic exchange may be evident in relations between many states and their citizens. However, this chapter examines the way in which these dialogues around remorse, character and responsibility play out and vary in different jurisdictions, with different actors playing different roles and on different parts of the stage (eg the private pre-trial and public trial phases). In part, that reflects differences in procedural tradition, but it also reflects differences in political culture, particularly different conceptions of the relations between state and individual. English courts invest time differently to the French: they give the defendants much more time to contest their guilt publicly, provided they are prepared to endure various process costs (eg being held longer on remand) and penal costs (eg a harsher sentence if found guilty after pleading not guilty). For the limited numbers who accept those costs, the Crown Court publicly enacts a procedurally elaborate contest in which the defendants appear to be guaranteed a status that involves not just full participation, but also the apparent equality with the state that is inherent in a process built on autonomous parties. But where guilt is not contested, there is much less investment of judicial and public court time in the symbolic enactment of state–citizen relations. By contrast, in France, the 'majesty' of the judge and public court time is more heavily invested in the portrayal of a demanding but potentially paternalist state. Thus, Anglo-American liberalism and French republicanism seem to make different kinds of public investment in the display of the defendant 'as a unique individual, who freely and sincerely accepts the legitimacy of her impending punishment'.[118]

This chapter is a return to previous themes in my work: the interrelations between legal and political cultures.[119] It seeks to follow a path sketched out by David Garland when he advocated the exploration of penal practice not just as something itself shaped by broader social forces but also as a means by which cultural and social relations are themselves constructed and maintained by

[117] The most profound challenge to the French state is that represented by defendants who refuse to speak or recognise the court or reject the primacy of French law: 'Votre loi n'est pas la mienne [Your law is not mine]: au proces de Reda Kriket la justice des hommes face a la justice divine' *Le Monde* (9 March 2021).

[118] Tata (n 5) 115.

[119] Field and Brants (n 1).

the state.[120] Courtrooms are a place where social meaning is produced, where observing and participating citizens are encouraged to understand individuals, their attributes and social relations in particular ways and not others. At the very point of apparently serious breakdown of relations between state and citizen, powerful images of idealised relationships show how those relations may be – indeed, should be – repaired, restored and (by implication) maintained. The appropriate role of both citizen and state in this process is publicly acted out. In showing the way Anglo-American liberal and French republican instincts lead in different directions, the analysis here points to the potential fruitfulness of comparison in the interpretation of penality's varying social meanings.

This is a cross-cultural case study that uses the heightened awareness of a 'cultural outsider' to render explicit the unspoken political assumptions underpinning historically established ways of doing things.[121] In evoking images of legal and political culture, there is always the danger of presenting something that is more unified, coherent or stable than is actually the case. The *cour d'assises* is distinctive even in France, and its practices are under challenge. French commentators are beginning to talk of its 'decline' in the face of a managerial discourse that sees its elaborate symbolism as too costly.[122] But its defenders – from the political right and left – see this as an attack on republican tradition. What that emphasises is that what a particular state puts on display in its highest criminal court expresses a response not just to the fundamental legal and moral dilemmas of state punishment, but also to profoundly political questions about preferred models of state–citizen relations.[123]

[120] Garland (n 2). For excellent examples where the influence of political and social formations on penal practice is the foreground rather than the reverse, see M Cavadino and J Dignan, *Penal Systems: A Comparative Approach* (London, Sage, 2006); N Lacey, *The Prisoners' Dilemma* (Cambridge, Cambridge University Press, 2008). Note also that the broad modelling of regimes in those books is very different from the approach taken here of close observation and reading of particular legal practices.

[121] For my thoughts on theory and method in cross-cultural research, see S Field, 'Making Sense in Cross-Cultural Research in Criminal Justice: Some Reflections on Theory and Method' in D Nelken and C Hamilton (eds) *Research Handbook on Comparative Criminal Justice* (Cheltenham, Edward Elgar, 2022).

[122] There are now plans to expand experiments in deciding such cases without juries but with five professional judges: www.huyette.net/2021/04/la-generalisation-de-la-cour-criminelle-departementale-oui-mais.html?.

[123] I have suggested that there must be real doubts to how far the French state is keeping the implicit promises it is making. Whether the reader thinks it should make good on those promises or stop making them itself depends on a sense of both desired and practicable relations between the individual and the state.

11

Punishment and the 'Blind Symbiosis' of Legal and Rehabilitation Work in the Making of the 'Ideal' Defendant

CYRUS TATA*

Judges, lawyers, probation and other professionals have to see themselves delivering legitimate punishment and control, rather than imposing unjustified coercion. Yet these professionals know they are also obliged to dispose of cases expeditiously. Most scholarly work on this apparent contradiction between 'justice' and 'efficiency' has been limited to a focus on the moral intentions of individual professionals. In contrast to this prevailing approach, and illustrated with examples from empirical research, I argue that the appearance of the contradiction is managed and often resolved in adversarial jurisdictions by the effects of unobtrusive inter-professional casework. Though they are officially separate professional and temporal activities, I show how the guilt-determination casework of judges and lawyers on the one hand and, on the other hand, the rehabilitation practices of probation, social work and other therapeutic professionals tacitly work together symbiotically. This symbiotic case-working realigns with and approximates the person's account and posture to that of the 'ideal' defendant (or penal subject), who is seen voluntarily to accept responsibility and show remorse. This realignment of the person eases for professionals the apparent dilemma of balancing justice with efficiency. However, this symbiosis is not, and could not be, achieved by a planned conspiracy. Instead, it is enabled by the mutual blindness of one profession to the detailed, substantive work of the other. This mutual blindness is based on the depiction of criminal justice in the adversarial tradition as a step-by-step sequence of autonomous

* Professor of Law & Criminal Justice, Law School, University of Strathclyde, Scotland. I owe a debt of gratitude to the following people for their invaluable comments on earlier drafts of this chapter and the ideas contained in it: Stewart Field, Susan Bandes, Loraine Gelsthorpe, Louise V Johansen, Ashley Lennon, Sharyn Roach Anleu, Kate Rossmanith, Sylvie Tata, Elodie Tata, Richard Weisman, Irene van Oorschot and Jacqueline Young.

decision moments, each under the dominion of separate professions. Finally, I explore the implications for future research agendas.

I. MAP OF THE CHAPTER

Section II sets out the perennial dilemma confronting criminal justice professionals: between doing 'justice' by attending to the unique individual on the one hand, and, delivering 'efficiency' on the other. This is why signs of acceptance of responsibility, and ideally remorse, are so sought after: they demonstrate to professionals that their work is legitimate because it is voluntarily shown to be accepted by the person herself. In section III, I will explain how the seemingly autonomous labour by different elements of criminal justice work tacitly together to generate the realignment of the person closer to the 'ideal' defendant (or penal subject).[1] Illustrated by examples from empirical research, I will show how giving the person a voice to tell her story entails its revision and the remodulation of her tone (ie her displayed attitude) towards the legitimacy and authority of the criminal justice process. This, together with the implied promise of future rehabilitation/humane treatment, also enables a symbiosis between apparently autonomous 'legal' and 'therapeutic' professional work. Section IV explores how it is that this symbiosis remains relatively inconspicuous. This is because the criminal process is represented by professional and academic imageries as a linear sequence of segmented and autonomous decision events, each dominated by professional groups. Concluding, section V proposes new research agendas.

II. JUSTICE PROFESSIONALS AND THE PROBLEM OF COERCION

Whatever its motivation, and no matter how seemingly benign, the state's operation of criminal justice is ultimately dependent on the violence of coercion.[2] This distinctiveness of criminal law and justice from voluntary social arrangements

[1] In the context of this chapter, I use the terms 'defendant' and 'penal subject' interchangably. In official and technical terms, this is, of course, inaccurate. However, in the reality of everyday practices, they are synonymous. Technically and officially, a 'defendant' is someone who is prosecuted through court but has not (yet) been convicted (whether or not by way of a guilty plea or trial). However, in this chapter, I am seeking to explore the changing official status of the person proceeded against by the state and how pre- and post-conviction work combine. So, as with other chapters in this book, the term 'defendant' is used expansively to include people pre- and post-conviction. I use the term interchangeably with 'penal subject' because, as I will show here, people proceeded against by the state are, in reality, overwhelmingly expected to be subject to punishment. Because of the overwhelming expectations of guilty pleas and admissions of guilt, the criminal justice court process prior to sentencing is, in reality, geared towards sentencing: the criminal justice process is in that sense also a penal process.

[2] R Cover, 'Violence and the Word' (1986) *Yale Law Journal* 95:1601.

has long demanded the attention of scholars ruminating on the question of how to justify that violence as legitimate punishment. The demand for justification is, however, an immediate question confronting those responsible for inflicting that coercive violence: judges and lawyers in the court sentencing process, and therapeutic professionals (eg probation officers, social workers). I will refer to these two sets of professionals as 'justice professionals' because they are both tasked with responsibility for determining and implementing the coercive acts of the state as matters not of violence, but of 'justice'. Not to regard their own, ultimately coercive actions, as justified would not only be an affront in terms of self-image, but would also negate their own social capital.[3] Justification of that coercion is not, and cannot be, ignored by justice professionals.[4] Devoid of justification, their acts of coercion would be unwarranted violence, morally indistinguishable from those whose conduct they judge. To deny or ignore the need to justify their coercive activities would be tantamount to denying the validity of their role and status.

Uniquely, justice professionals are obliged to regard themselves as discharging a triple weight of duty:[5] first, as human beings aware of their immediate and direct ability to alleviate the palpable distress of those they are faced with every day;[6] second, as professionals ethically and dutifully serving their client and/or the public. Even if research shows a more complex picture of professional behaviour and ethics in which self-interest and altruism are entangled, it is simply unthinkable for a doctor, lawyer, judge, psychiatrist or probation officer to declare publicly that he or she does not care about the person or the wider public good. In other words, the professional has (albeit in varying ways) to be able to see the virtue of her own actions; and third, as, above all (and in contrast to other professionals, like teachers or doctors), the practical custodians of 'justice'. Accordingly, in doing sentencing and penal work, justice professionals have (quite literally) to see (ie observe) themselves enacting justified punishment.

[3] R Lenoir, 'A Living Reproach' in P. Bourdieu et al (eds), *The Weight of the World: Social Suffering in Contemporary Society* (Stanford, Stanford University Press, 1999) 239.

[4] For example, lawyers and especially judges are acutely sensitive to criticism of the practices they constitute, often seeming to take it personally, anxious to justify their personal practices. Defence lawyers express a sense of awkwardness and a degree of embarrassment about the impact of extrinsic (eg legal aid) changes on their ability to spend time with the individual client. Research suggests that most lawyers are willing to observe the deleterious impact of changes to payment structures on the work of *other* lawyers, but refuse to countenance that these same changes have any negative impact on their *own* personal professional practice and find creative ways to justify their practices as ethical. C Tata, 'In the Interests of Clients or Commerce? Legal Aid, Supply, Demand, and "Ethical Indeterminacy" in Criminal Defence Work' (2007) 34 *Journal of Law & Society* 489.

[5] C Tata, '"Ritual Individualisation": Creative Genius at Sentencing, Mitigation and Conviction' (2019) 46 *Journal of Law & Society* 112.

[6] S Roach Anleu and K Mack, *Performing Judicial Authority in the Lower Courts* (London, Palgrave Macmillan, 2017).

A. Professionals' Justice versus Efficiency Dilemma

For these reasons, seeing (ie observing) themselves permitting the defendant fair opportunity to participate in her own case is of particular sensitivity to justice professionals. This includes: allowing the defendant a voice to present her story; treating each case with dignity; and assessing each defendant as a unique individual. These values and principles have to be respected, and be seen to be respected, if the justice professional can believe in her own identity.

Yet there is another discourse at play: efficiency. Justice professionals also feel obliged to dispose of cases expeditiously: with as little time, effort, cost and conflict as possible.[7] These two felt imperatives ('justice' and 'efficiency') are a (perhaps *the*) perennial source of tension and concern preoccupying justice professionals.[8] How is that tension addressed so that professionals can continue to dispose of cases 'efficiently' while also believing that they have not participated in an unjust process?

Taking the professional self-imagery of autonomous individualism[9] at face value, academic work until now has tended to locate the responsibility for addressing this 'justice versus efficiency' conflict at the level of the individual professional. Fuelled by a belief in the pervasive 'cultural trope of the heroic individual professional' (who can save people by ensuring justice despite 'the system' and wider social inequities),[10] much legal and criminological work is more or less critical of the apparent failure of professionals to do their duty by instead preferring to dispose of cases with as little fuss as possible. Explanations for this apparent failure tend to be located at the level of the individual. These explanations are conceived variously as failures of: will; diligence; impartiality; social awareness; and/or ethicality. Justice professionals have been chided by scholars for operating: in bad faith; lazily; selfishly; out of ignorance, prejudice; or self-deception.[11] Governmental policy literature (supported by some scholars)

[7] K Mack and S Roach Anleu, 'Getting through the List: Judgecraft and Legitimacy in the Lower Courts' (2007) 16 *Social & Legal Studies* 341; Roach Anleu and Mack (n 6).

[8] See, eg C Heimer, 'Cases and Biographies: An Essay on Routinization and the Nature of Comparison' (2001) 27 *Annual Review of Sociology* 47.

[9] Here I am referring to the self-image of professionals regulated by autonomous occupational professional groups (independent, self-regulated, etc), but within that composed of individual, autonomous professionals who are expected, and expect themselves, to be independent, self-directed and enjoying a high degree of individual discretion: C Tata, *Sentencing: A Social Process – Re-thinking Research and Policy* (Cham, Springer, 2020). See also TH Marshall, 'The Recent History of Professionalism in Relation to Social Structure and Social Policy' (1939) 5 *Canadian Journal of Economics and Political Science* 325.

[10] Tata, *Sentencing* (n 9) chs 4–5.

[11] eg M McConville and L Marsh, *Criminal Judges: Legitimacy, Courts and State-Induced Guilty Pleas in Britain* (Cheltenham, Edward Elgar, 2014); A Mulcahy, 'The Justifications of "Justice"' (1994) 34 *British Journal of Criminology* 411; D Newman, 'Still Standing Accused: Addressing the Gap between Work and Talk in Firms of Criminal Defence Lawyers' (2012) 19 *International Journal of the Legal Profession* 3; J Tombs and E Jagger, 'Denying Responsibility: Sentencers' Accounts of Their Decisions to Imprison' (2006) 46 *British Journal of Criminology* 803.

tends, on the other hand, to prefer to see 'the balance' tilted towards 'efficiency'. Yet, while the two sides appear to be engaged in passionate disagreement, they in fact share the same implicit assumptions. They both assume that the two values of justice and efficiency are ultimately irreconcilable. In other words, 'justice' and 'efficiency' are regarded as opposing forces, locked in a zero-sum conflict: more of one necessitates less of the other. So it is seen as a matter of striking the correct 'balance' between justice and efficiency. This view, however, rests on an assumption by both sides of the debate that what happens in criminal justice is the result of the aggregate of individual actions by autonomous individual professionals.

By contrast, in this chapter I present a different explanation. Rather than the prevailing individualistic conceptualisation, I argue that to explain adequately how justice professionals confront every day the felt 'justice versus efficiency' contradiction, we need to look beyond a focus on the actions of individual professionals. I will explain how the two competing values of 'justice' and 'efficiency' are shown on a daily basis to professional communities to be reconciled by the displayed presentations of defendants. I propose that we need to study how the seemingly autonomous work of legal and therapeutic professions combine symbiotically (but without any planned deliberation) to accomplish mutually desirable results.

Rather than pointing the finger at professionals for their apparent failures as individuals, I will show how the symbiosis of subtle, inter-professional work enables the management of the apparent contradiction between efficiency and justice. By using the term 'symbiosis', I aim to apprehend the way in which the work of two autonomous professional groups, in the reality of their daily practices, depend on and sustain each other's work, self-belief and goals. I will seek to explain how neither professional group could achieve the making of more or less 'ideal' penal subjects without the work of the other. Within the adversarial tradition, legal and therapeutic work is officially done at distinct, separate stages of the criminal justice process. However, and although carried out at different times by different professional bodies with their different values and practices, legal and therapeutic work is, in reality, mutually sustaining. Without the work of the other, neither legal nor therapeutic work could alone move defendants closer to the characteristics of the ideal penal subject. By 'the ideal penal subject' (also known as 'the ideal defendant'), I mean the image of a person who shows she wholeheartedly and unequivocally accepts full individual responsibility and demonstrates sincere regret, and ideally genuine remorse, for her actions.

At first glance, the proposition that these two professional sets of activities (guilt determination and rehabilitation) operate symbiotically might be met with surprise, even incredulity. After all, the two professional worlds are quite different: different values, different terminologies, etc. In the adversarial tradition especially found in the English-speaking world, a strong emphasis is placed on the importance of the separation of what are regarded as distinct functions of the criminal justice process.[12] Adversarial guilt determination is accepted as the province of law and the courts, while the work of rehabilitation (known in the USA as 'corrections') is the province of the therapeutic professions. These two sets of professional groups (the legal and therapeutic professions) are educated, trained and socialised in distinct values. They see themselves as having distinct functions. For example, lawyers/judges are required and require themselves to uphold due process values, especially the paramount principle of the presumption of innocence. Meanwhile, therapeutic professions emphasise the importance of encouraging and supporting rehabilitation, personal growth and change by helping the person to gain greater self-awareness and insight into the causes of their offending. Yet, as I will argue, in their casework practices, the seemingly separate work of the legal and therapeutic professions is in fact symbiotic: they are mutually assisting and sustaining. One could not successfully conduct its work without the work of the other. They each rely on the other in an unobtrusive, implicit dialogue. In their work, they feed each other with helpful current and anticipated questions, expectations, hints and nudges encouraging the reconstruction of the person's displayed attitude to authority. To the extent it is successful in reconstructing the person's apparent posture, these symbiotic casework practices eventuate in the display of sincere and voluntary admissions of guilt by people who are shown more or less to accept their individual responsibility and the legitimacy of the sentence.

Simply put, the legal achievement of efficient guilt determination (eg through credible admissions of guilt) depends in significant part on the practices of therapeutic professionals. Likewise, rehabilitative achievements (eg the person showing 'self-awareness' and 'insight' and accepting the wrongness of their earlier conduct, which are the seeds of self-change) are contingent on practices securing guilty pleas (the seemingly autonomous province of lawyers and judges).

B. Mutual Professional Blindness

However, this symbiosis is no thought-out conspiracy by a controlling mind. Bearing in mind the importance of professional identity and status,

[12] For further discussion on this comparative point, see S Field, 'The Enactment of Political Cultures in Criminal Court Process: Remorse, Responsibility and the Unique Individual Before the French *cours d'assises*' in S Field and C Tata (eds), *Criminal Justice and the Ideal Defendant in the Making of Remorse and Responsibility* (Oxford, Hart Publishing, 2023) ch 10. Field shows how work examining the person's character is done openly in the higher French courts and is often led by judges rather than being delegated, as tends to be the practices of countries espousing the adversarial tradition. This work examining the individual's moral character 'is not work delegated to defence lawyers and probation officers, hidden away in a private pre-trial process; it is on display centre stage, as a dominant theme of a public hearing'. See also S Field, 'State, Citizen and Character in the French Criminal Process' (2006) 33 *Journal of Law & Society* 522.

inter-professional symbiosis would be unachievable through planned, deliberate intent or malevolence. It is precisely because of the absence of conspiracy or any deliberate plan that this inter-professional symbiotic caseworking operates so subtly and unobtrusively. Legal professionals who are deemed to be exclusively responsible for questions about the determination of guilt must (at least formally and publicly) be seen to be blind to the promises and threats of sentencing and the character of its implementation (eg the prospects for rehabilitation). Similarly, therapeutic professionals deemed responsible for rehabilitation must be seen to disregard the contingencies of guilt determination, including the possibility of false admissions of guilt.

This blindness to the detail of the substantive work of the other profession is crucial in enabling symbiosis to take place. Professions and professional communities are constituted by the self-image of ensuring and protecting certain cherished principles and values (eg for lawyers and judges 'the presumption of innocence' and the free choice of each individual as to how to plead). The purity of these principles and values has to be protected and seen by professionals to be 'uncontaminated' by improper, external pressures. The decision as to how to plead, for example, is expected to be made freely as an autonomous decision in itself. For members of one profession to be very aware of the detailed, substantive work of the other profession would be to witness the contamination of the purity of cherished ideas. I will refer to 'contamination' to indicate the ways in which certain revered values and principles have to be seen to be maintained and untainted by the sullying influence of extraneous pressures.

The symbiotic work by the professions, to which each must be seen to be blind, re-manifests the person subject to punishment so as to seem closer to the ideal penal subject (or defendant). Ideally, the person should be seen to accept her culpability fully and sincerely, and show genuine remorse. For, in doing so, she validates (and so expedites) the work of justice professionals. Nothing legitimates the violence of sentencing and punishment to justice professionals as potently as the voluntary signs of acceptance of its legitimacy by the very person least likely to do so. This is key to understanding why 'signs of genuine remorse' are sought by justice professionals. It is not enough that remorse is an internal state of feeling: the feeling must be externalised. Justice professionals look for whether the person 'shows' remorse:[13] it must be displayed appropriately to justice professionals.[14] This display reaffirms to the court and therapeutic professionals that they not only have the right, but *are* right, to impose and carry out punishment. In other words, the posture (ie displayed attitude) of the person towards the authority of justice professionals and their work is *the* central issue in legitimating what they do. A posture that is shown to approximate that of the

[13] R Weisman, *Showing Remorse: Law and the Social Control of Emotion* (London, Routledge, 2014).

[14] K Rossmanith, 'Affect and the Judicial Assessment of Offenders' (2015) 21 *Body & Society* 167.

ideal penal subject (or ideal defendant) is observed by justice professionals. That observation enables them to convert their work from questionable violence to legitimate and necessary action *because* the subject of it (the very person most likely to object) has been shown to have voluntarily consented to it.

III. THE SYMBIOSIS OF LEGAL AND REHABILITATIVE WORK

Officially, and in conventional academic thought, there are separate stages of the criminal process. Exemplified by the imagery of the criminal justice flow chart, the process is depicted as a linear, temporal trajectory beginning with the commission of an alleged crime as the entry point and (where there has been conviction) ending with the exit point of the completion of the sentence.

A. What Flow Charts Claim

Overviews of criminal justice decision-making in adversarial countries are dominated by images and metaphors emphasising linear travel and segmentation. This is exemplified by the imagery of the criminal justice flow chart. Despite jurisdictional variations, the experience of the person proceeded against is conceived and represented as akin to a logical, linear, sequential journey. Arrows point from one individual decision-moment box to the next.

Flow charts are visual representations of the journey of a case. Individual boxes are used to depict that journey as a series of distinct, individual steps. Typically, these individual boxes are shown to reside within distinct wider phases (eg pre-trial investigation, adjudication, sentencing, implementation of the sentence/corrections).

So commonplace, so authoritative and so seemingly obvious are these visual images of the flow chart that it is easy to take for granted what ideas they represent:

- While following on from the prior one, individual decision moments *exist autonomously*.
- *Each of these decision moments is the province of autonomous professional work*, eg arrest (police), pre-trial (police and prosecution), guilt determination (legal professionals – lawyers/judiciary), sentencing (judiciary), implementation of sentence ('corrections', prisons, social work, probation/therapeutic agencies).
- Decision making is a *logical, sequential, unidirectional, linear journey*.

My argument in this chapter inverts these assumptions. It is through the reality of oblique, symbiotic work that the display of ideal penal subjects (defendants) is curated. The person has to traverse stages in the process which are ostensibly distinct and autonomous, each the province of different professions whose casework is in reality subtly mutually facilitating of the work of the other profession. Nudged by professionals such as defence lawyers, the defendant has to *anticipate* how her self-presentation may impact on subsequent decisions.

This requirement to anticipate the likely effects of one decision on another and across different realms of professional work contrasts with the characteristics of criminal justice flow charts:

> [T]he conventional view is shown as a flow chart, showing a flow from left to right, suggesting that there is a clear direction of flow, rather than a turbulent, jammed-up, multi-level and multi-directional flow. [In the flow chart] it appears that each decision point is one of a series of logical and punctuated series of decisions within this system and its composite various subsystems. *It is organized from the perspective of the institution, not of the citizens who are subject to these processes.* (emphasis added)[15]

Because the representation of criminal justice is organised from the perspectives of the institutions (and the professionals who constitute them) rather than from those of the citizens taken through it, scholarship has tended to suffer from a blind spot. Criminal justice scholarship is dominated by a preoccupation with scrutinising the motives of individual professionals rather than the effects on citizens and their subjective experiences. Enthralled with the 'trope of the heroic individual professional',[16] effects which may occur in the absence of deliberate intent are harder to see, or even recognise.

At first blush, it may seem puzzling that the realignment of the person is achieved in the absence of work by an individual legal or therapeutic professional, but is rather the result of the symbiosis of *formally* separate professional casework practices. While individual legal and therapeutic professionals may each wish to encourage defendants to 'take responsibility' and 'show remorse', doing so alone without the substantive work of the other profession could barely achieve this realignment of their posture (ie displayed attitude to the authority of the process). It is the mutually sustaining casework of one professional group for the casework of the other that secures the realignment of defendants. Members of one professional group being largely unaware of the detailed, substantive work of the other profession enables the symbiosis of legal and therapeutic work. The potential cross-contamination of seemingly autonomous work cannot be too evident without imperilling the conceptual basis (and so the practices) of that professional work. Here, the concept of professions as autonomous occupational groups[17] propels notions and practices of the individuation,

[15] P Manning, 'The Legal Institution' in L Reynolds and N Herman-Kinney (eds), *Handbook of Symbolic Interactionism* (Lanham, MD, AltaMira Press, 2003) 608.

[16] Tata, *Sentencing* (n 9).

[17] A Abbott, *The System of Professions* (Chicago, Chicago University Press, 1998); see also TH Marshall, 'The Recent History of Professionalism in Relation to Social Structure and Social Policy' (1939) 5 *Canadian Journal of Economics and Political Science* 325.

segmentation and dominion of criminal justice work that allow what might otherwise be seen as 'cross-contamination' to be relatively unobtrusive.

In the following section, I highlight the symbiotic practices of the two seemingly autonomous spheres of work by drawing on examples from earlier research into the use of pre-sentence investigations and reports in the process of mitigation of sentence. The aim of the four-year study[18] was to conduct a direct comparison between how sentencing judges interpret and use pre-sentence reports in intermediate court cases and what the writer of those same reports intended to convey. It had four elements: (i) an ethnographic study of the construction of pre-sentence reports deploying 'shadow' (mock) report writing so as to elicit the report writer's intentions; (ii) an observational and interview court-based study of the use of these same (and other) cases, with interviews with the sentencing judges, defence lawyers and prosecutors; (iii) a series of focus group discussions with intermediate court judges, including those already observed; and (iv) a series of moot sentencing hearings, with pre- and post-interviews with intermediate court judges and defence lawyers using anonymised case papers whose production and sentencing had already been observed.

B. Separation, Segmentation and Symbiosis: Soliciting Formal Guilty Pleas

In countries following adversarial traditions, officially, choice as to how formally to plead ('guilty' or 'not guilty') must be free and *be seen to be free*. Formally, in adversarial systems (unlike unitary inquisitorial systems),[19] the decision whether to plead guilty or not guilty to alleged criminal conduct is supposed to be made independently, uncontaminated by what are deemed extraneous considerations of the defendant's moral character. Fundamentally, questions of moral character are thought irrelevant to the question of criminal conduct (guilt) as labelled by the prosecution.[20] Questions about sentencing are meant to be a separate second stage to be addressed *only if and after* guilt is established. Yet, in subtle and largely oblique ways, the defendant is encouraged to anticipate the negative

[18] ESRC Award No RB000239939.

[19] See Field, 'The Enactment of Political Cultures' (n 12); J Hodgson, 'The Construction of the Ideal Defendant: Comparative Understandings of the Normalisation of Guilt' in Field and Tata (n 12) ch 8. On Denmark's hybrid system, see LV Johansen, 'Constructing Ideal Defendants in the Pre-sentence Phase: The Connection between Responsibility and Potential Remorse' in Field and Tata (n 12) ch 4.

[20] This preoccupation with separating questions of guilt (conduct) from character is illustrated by the hotly debated and perennial question of whether or not, and the limits to which, evidence about the (alleged) 'bad character' of the defendant should be admissible during the guilt-determination phase. This contrasts markedly with practices in jurisdictions influenced by the inquisitorial tradition, where the trial may begin with questions about the defendant's life and character before proceeding to the alleged offending. J Hodgson, 'Conceptions of the Trial in Inquisitorial and Adversarial Procedure' in A Duff, L Farmer, S Marshall and V Tadros (eds), *The Trial on Trial, vol 2. Calling to Account* (Oxford, Hart Publishing, 2006) 223–42. See also, eg Field, 'The Enactment of Political Cultures' (n 12); Hodgson (n 19).

consequences of a formal denial (not guilty plea) if she is then found guilty at trial. This goes far beyond the well-documented controversy about the potential plea-dependent effect on the sentence itself (trial tax/sentence discount).[21] It bleeds into the formally discrete work done by therapeutic professionals advising on and implementing the sentence. In making her plea decision, the defendant also has to consider the presentation of her moral character.

The defendant is 'presented with a dilemma if she continues to maintain complete factual denial following conviction at an evidentially-contested trial'.[22] If, after a guilty verdict has been returned, the defendant continues to deny guilt, she can expect to be regarded as being 'in denial'. She may be advised to expect a more severe penalty for that reason alone (and aside from the not guilty plea).[23] Furthermore, she can expect that therapeutic professionals (probation, social work, psychologists, etc) are likely to advise the sentencing judge that her continued failure to admit criminal conduct shows a complete lack of 'insight', 'self-awareness' and 'a failure to take responsibility', let alone any 'genuine remorse'. She will therefore be deemed 'not suitable' for therapeutic work during the implementation of the sentence because she has shown 'nothing to work with'. All of this presents the defendant with an expected doubling of negative consequences. It can be predicted that the type and quantum of her sentence will be impacted by her not guilty plea and the likely adverse inferences about her disingenuous moral character if she is convicted. Furthermore, she can expect that her experience of the implementation of that sentence (eg subsequent possible parole decisions,[24] conditional requirements in a community-based sentence) will be adversely affected too. If, on the other hand, having maintained a plea of 'not guilty', she then admits her guilt after the court's guilty verdict, she can expect to be seen as a disingenuous individual trying to 'play' or 'game' the system,[25] or at best as wasting the court's valuable time. As one judge explained:

> what's even worse is if you've actually been to trial and the person says they didn't do it and then you get a [pre-sentence report] saying he's very sorry for all of this and he really feels sorry for the victim and wishes he had never done it. I mean that's actually even worse from our point of view because the [judges] just think: 'what was he playing at?'

[21] JM Gormley and C Tata, 'To Plead? Or Not to Plead? "Guilty" Is the Question. Re-thinking Plea Decision-Making in Anglo-American Countries' in C Spohn and PK Brennan (eds), *Handbook on Sentencing Policies and Practices in the 21st Century* (New York, Routledge, 2019) 208–34.

[22] C Tata, 'Humanising Punishment? Mitigation and "Case-Cleansing" Prior to Sentencing' (2019) 9 *Onati Socio-Legal Series* 659.

[23] ibid.

[24] See R Weisman, '"Remorse Is Not Enough": Disentangling the Roles of Remorse and Insight in the Construction of the Ideal Defendant' in Field and Tata (n 12) ch 7; N Padfield, 'Looking for the Ideal Parole Applicant?' in Field and Tata (n 12) ch 9.

[25] J Gormley and C Tata, 'Remorse in a World of Plea Bargaining' in S Tudor, R Weisman, M Proeve and K Rossmanith (eds), *Remorse and Criminal Justice: Multi-disciplinary Perspectives* (London, Taylor & Francis, 2022).

If she is to gain perceived benefits in the immediate or longer-term future (eg liberation from pre-trial/sentence detention, the defence's plea in mitigation, sentence reductions for a guilty plea, more relaxed terms of community supervision or prison regime, parole prospects), the defendant's attitude to the alleged crime and her posture towards the court have to be re-presented. This entails revising her account and modulating her tone, and/or professionals doing so on her behalf.

Likewise, the work of sentence-implementation in rehabilitative community penalties or rehabilitation/therapeutic work, which may be promised during a prison sentence, does not seek to unearth the specific dynamics leading to the decision to plead guilty. It must take guilt as a given and indisputable fact, which has already been established by the separate legal phase.

C. The Person is Given a Voice to then Revise Her Story and Modulate Her Tone

The low-risk option is to change to a guilty plea.[26]

(i) Modulating the Person's Tone

While it is well known that the lower and intermediate courts around the world rely on admissions of guilt, an unambiguous denial of guilt does not, in itself, raise troubling questions of legitimacy. What is more awkward and potentially troubling to justice professionals is the non-ideal defendant who formally pleads guilty but whose account is not compatible with her freely given guilty plea.[27] Her position appears to the court to query (explicitly or implicitly) the legitimacy of the process, therefore disrupting the smooth flow of case disposal. For example, her account to the court may be ambiguous or at odds with the formal plea; appear confused; explicitly or implicitly defiant;[28] exculpatory; or tactical in some way.[29] This includes the person: who offers an admission of guilt that seems insincere or contradictory (eg exculpatory), or an equivocal guilty plea; who demonstrates obvious disengagement, cynicism, reluctant conformity or 'passive acceptance';[30] or is palpably not an informed, rational decision-maker (eg struggling with addiction, mental health or other problems). For the admission to be consistent with the inviolable idea of a freely participating defendant

[26] This encouragement to anticipate and forecast the future consequences parallels that reported by Johansen (n 19) about the Danish 'hybrid' adversarial-inquisitorial system. She shows how the person who has pled not guilty is confronted by the therapeutic worker with a future self 'as if' she had been convicted.

[27] See also S Tudor, 'Reflections on the Grey Zone: "Sort of Remorseful" Offenders' in Tudor et al (n 25) 97–113.

[28] Weisman, *Showing Remorse* (n 13).

[29] eg J Jacobson, G Hunter and A Kirby, *Inside Crown Court* (London, Palgrave Macmillan, 2015).

[30] ibid 31; Gormley and Tata, 'Remorse' (n 25).

who willingly admits guilt, the admission has to be seen by the court as free and sincere, or at least not unfree and blatantly insincere.

Defendants who appear to be less than wholehearted in the formal admission of guilt pose important challenges to the legitimacy of the process. They represent threats to the inviolable legal principles of the free participation of the defendant, the presumption of innocence and conviction beyond reasonable doubt. These contradictions cannot be ignored.[31]

Offering the person the opportunity to tell her story about the (alleged) offending within the context of her individual life is a, and often *the*, principal way in which she is seen to be given a chance to participate substantively in her own case. She is shown to be offered a voice: an opportunity to explain in her own words what happened and why. Yet, in being offered this opportunity to tell her story, the defendant whose admission of guilt could be seen as caveated or less than complete is confronted with a dilemma[32] – one which defence lawyers know they are obliged to invigilate and manage. Here, a defence lawyer explains the obligation to manage clients' accounts:

> Sometimes [the client's account of the incident to the report writer] can present a problem … The reason I'd be focusing on that is the judge might say to me, 'well, [title and surname of lawyer], you've a wee bit explaining here to do …' So you want to be, you want to avoid that … inconsistency between what I've already told the [judge] and what the guy's now telling the [the report writer] because that, that does kind of present me with a bit of a problem. So I want to see that that's consistent.[33]

Defence lawyers are careful to check pre-sentence reports for signs distancing the defendant from the ideal penal subject who wholeheartedly accepts responsibility and shows remorse. For that reason, defence lawyers tend to remind the client of the need to ensure that their account to the pre-sentence report writer does not conflict with the formal plea. 'I would say to them, I'd say look, you know, if you deny this offence when you speak to a social worker [writing the report], it's not going to help you.'[34] Indeed, it is also an opportunity to remind the client to 'sell yourself', which means accepting individual responsibility and willingness to change.

However, reducing the appearance of conflict between the formal admission of guilt and the person's account often may already have been addressed by the work of the therapeutic professional, which reconstructs the person's account so as to be less obviously at odds with their formal plea. Where, as is commonly the

[31] Weisman, *Showing Remorse* (n 13); J Martel, 'Remorse and the Production of Truth' (2010) 12 *Punishment and Society* 414; S Bandes, 'Remorse and Criminal Justice' (2015) 8(1) *Emotion Review* 14; I van Oorschot, P Mascini and D Weenink, 'Remorse in Context(s)' (2017) 26 *Social & Legal Studies* 359; I van Oorschot, *The Law Multiple: Judgment and Knowledge in Practice* (Cambridge, Cambridge University Press, 2020); Tata, 'Humanising Punishment?' (n 22).

[32] Van Oorschot et al (n 31).

[33] Tata, 'Humanising Punishment?' (n 22); Interview, defence lawyer 7.

[34] Interview, defence lawyer 10.

case, the person does not have a clear recollection of the incident and disputes some of the prosecution facts, reports tend to smooth over the points of contention. And where the person does not think they will be believed, reports tend to convert cynical resignation into an uncomplicated acceptance, reporting that the person 'accepts the situation'.

Almost without exception, lawyers and judges were unaware of the ways in which pre-sentence report writers remodulated the person's tone, and revised her account so as to move it closer to the qualities of 'the ideal defendant'. Instead, they typically saw reports as reporting the unmediated voice of the defendant. Indeed, a common judicial complaint is that report writers naively accept defendants' minimisation of their culpability. For example:

> The report in my view is to give me background – it is an enquiry report – to identify matters, for example attitude to offence. That's where the problem creeps in because some of those who prepare the reports perhaps empathise too closely … tend to be swayed by what the accused said.[35]

However, it is also this imputed gullibility and seemingly simple, unmediated reporting of the person's story that make reports so valuable. They are imagined to provide the more or less direct and unfiltered voice of the person. In that way, the court (and the judge, who after all has overall responsibility for the justice of the process) can observe the justice of what it is doing: its justice is reflected back to it through the person's displayed attitude to the court. In other words, reports are helpful to lawyers and especially judges precisely *because of* the report writer's perceived naivety in simply accepting and reporting the person's story. As we shall now see, this is in fact far from the reality of what report writers do. Report writers tend to ameliorate, massage and smooth down the rough edges of the person's account in ways that render the account less confrontational to the court and less obviously at odds with the person's formal guilty plea.

(ii) Massaging the Defendant's Denial

Humanising work by therapeutic professionals creating pre-sentence reports has a dual function. It is a report to the court to inform sentencing, but it is also a means of beginning the enquiry about the person's suitability for future rehabilitation. Albeit in different ways, the legal work of imposing punishment and the therapeutic implementation of that punishment necessitate a penal subject who at least begins to accept *individual* responsibility for the wrongness of her actions.

She is expected to take individual responsibility and wholeheartedly acknowledge her culpability, while at the same time she is expected to show herself to be sincerely engaging with the process of personal examination. This entails some

[35] Interview, 'Southpark' judge 2.

reworking of the person's story so as to align with her formal admission, but also to remodulate her tone so that her voice appears to be that of a culpable offender who fully and sincerely accepts her culpability.

For example, Carrie pled guilty to a public order offence and biting a police officer. At the pre-sentence interview, Jodie (the report writer) explores Carrie's attitude to the offence:

> Regarding the assault, Carrie is unsure what happened [and admits she was under the influence of alcohol], but she looks shocked by the description of her biting the police officer: she 'didn't do that!' ... Jodie tells her she should not have pled guilty to something she didn't do. Carrie looks at her: she tells her she 'just wanted to get it out of the way'.[36]

In her report under the section about 'offending behaviour', Jodie omits Carrie's straight denial and instead states that Carrie attributes her offending to being under the influence of alcohol:

> In discussing the matter with Ms Villiers she acknowledges her involvement in the offences ... Exploring her attitude, Ms Villiers states that she accepts full responsibility for the Breach of the Peace and attributes her actions to having been under the influence of alcohol.

(iii) Erasing the Person's Straight Denial

Therapeutic professionals are expected to strive to identify a glimmer of rehabilitative potential ('something to work with') and so solicit acceptance of personal responsibility. Occasionally, however, report writers can see no signs of being able to coax the person into conceding voluntary acceptance of individual responsibility and showing at least indications of regret, if not remorse. Rather than arguing for mitigation, this failure 'to engage' can lead the therapeutic professional to adopt a narrative of condemnation.[37] Take, for example, the case of Mr Iqbal Hanif, who pled guilty to breach of peace at home and 'attempting to slap' his wife. During the pre-sentence report interview,

> Mr [Hanif] tells us that he pled guilty because he doesn't have time to go to court. His wife lied: the offence didn't happen. Stephen [the pre-sentence report writer] asks why she would do that? His wife simply 'makes up stories'. Mr [Hanif] says he will pay the fine and will divorce his wife in a couple of years and then get a new wife. Mr [Hanif] blinks and grins at Stephen ... Stephen sits up and tells Mr Hanif that this is in fact a serious offence and he doubts very much that Mr Hanif will receive a fine ... Stephen continues that the [judge] 'will take a very dim view of your denial [of this] crime'. Stephen continues asking whether Mr Hanif was shouting and swearing in the street, Mr Hanif shakes his head: no he didn't, she lied she 'makes stories up'. Stephen holds up some papers and tells Mr Hanif that he has to reflect his

[36] Diary case 15.

[37] Weisman, *Showing Remorse* (n 13).

> views in the report, 'is that what you want me to write?' he asks him. '[I] did nothing' Mr Hanif insists. 'Do you want me to reflect that in my report?' Stephen persists. Mr Hanif says nothing.
>
> Stephen: 'I guess if you didn't do it [you are] not remorseful or regretful?'
>
> Stephen returns to the offence and again asks 'are you clear you did not do this?' Mr [Hanif] notes that he has pled guilty anyway. Stephen riles at this comment, quickly responding that 'there is a difference'. That it is about Mr Hanif 'taking responsibility for his crime and behaviour displayed'. Stephen reiterates that the [judge] will take a 'dim view' of Mr Hanif, that he is 'making a mockery of the system'.
>
> He then asks Mr Hanif to think carefully.
>
> Mr Hanif: 'No.'[38]

'Angry' and 'infuriated', Stephen feels Mr Hanif's attitude 'shows a blatant disregard for the law and for his wife'.[39] In his report, Stephen wrote:

> [I]t appeared from his body language, manner, tone and responses to questions posed that his attitude to his pattern of offending was extremely poor.
>
> As to the matter before the court Mr [Hanif]] states that although he pled guilty as charged he was insistent that the whole episode had been *blown out of proportion* … Mr. [Hanif] showed no insight, remorse, regret or victim empathy over his actions. (emphasis added)

Note that during the pre-sentence interview Stephen repeatedly presses Mr Hanif to align his account with his formal guilty plea. Stephen does this by importing threats from the legal domain of judicial sentencing, confronting Mr Hanif about what may happen at court, ie that the judge will 'take a dim view' and perceive Mr Hanif's denial to be 'making a mockery of the system', and that a custodial sentence is a real possibility. Nonetheless, Mr Hanif maintains his denial, which openly and unequivocally conflicts with his formal guilty plea.

Despite his condemnation of and earlier warning to Mr Hanif that if he did not change his posture Stephen would have to report Mr Hanif's flat denial, Stephen in fact adjusts Mr Hanif's account so as to be more compatible with his formal guilty plea. Instead of a denial, he re-manifests Mr Hanif's position as the offence 'being blown out of proportion'. Recall that in the pre-sentence report interview Stephen emphasised 'there is a difference' between Mr Hanif's formal guilty plea and his account during the interview. Yet, in his report, it is a difference that Stephen omits, revising Mr Hanif's flat denial to one of having 'no insight, remorse, regret or victim empathy over his actions'. By erasing Mr Hanif's denial that contradicted his formal guilty plea, Stephen moderates Mr Hanif's position, by distancing it from the ultimate antithesis of the ideal penal subject whose account flatly contradicts a formal admission of guilt. Instead, Mr Hanif is re-presented as failing to take responsibility or show

[38] Shadow report writing diary.
[39] ibid.

'insight, remorse, regret or victim empathy' for the actions to which he has formally admitted guilt, but completely denied at interview.

Even where they were attempting to mitigate on behalf of the person, this 'dirty work' to 'cleanse' cases of their noxious, ambiguous or contradictory qualities was a common practice among report writers.[40] Frequently, defendants' recollections of an incident were hazy, but even where they pled guilty, they objected strongly to parts of what they had formally admitted.[41] As we saw earlier, legal professionals (lawyers and especially judges) appear to be largely unaware that report writers cleanse cases in this way by massaging out the sharpest contradictions and the most glaring ambiguities between the person's account to them at interview and their earlier formal admission of guilt. Instead, these legal professionals tend to see report writers as naive and gullible in simply reporting, without evaluation, the person's account. Importantly, and as we will see below, legal professionals being more conscious of this cleansing work by report writers would risk undermining the perceived integrity of cherished professional ideals (such as the free participation of the defendant) in the eyes of those professionals.

D. The Promise of Rehabilitation

The promise of rehabilitative welfare after sentencing is a way of helping and supporting the person to meet their personal and social needs. Yet, by examining the person's 'suitability' for rehabilitative programmes, humanisation work (and its associated processes) invites and encourages the person to take individual, personal responsibility for the alleged offending and, ideally, to show remorse. By doing so, the person is coaxed away from a position which might appear to contradict or query the authenticity of her formal guilty plea.

The person who is seen more or less to accept her personal culpability and whose displayed (or displayable) posture suggests acceptance of the legitimacy of the process is judged as showing signs of remorse, or at least insight or self-awareness. This means they are judged as being potentially suitable for rehabilitative programmes. As we saw from Stephen's reaction to Mr Hanif, where therapeutic professionals are confronted directly with the 'blatant' denial of responsibility, the absence of retractive feelings (regret, remorse, etc) means they may characterise the person as being beyond the possibility of rehabilitation.[42]

The person who shows at least 'signs' of such retractive feelings is deemed able to benefit from rehabilitative programmes – whether in the community, in prison or on parole. As we saw in the case of Mr Hanif, the person who appears unwilling to at least moderate their account is reminded of the consequences.

[40] Tata, 'Humanising Punishment?' (n 22).
[41] See also Gormley and Tata, 'Remorse' (n 25).
[42] Weisman, 'Remorse Is Not Enough' (n 24); Weisman, *Showing Remorse* (n 13).

Long-term prisoners who are thinking of applying for parole have also to show that they are not 'a risk'. They can demonstrate this by accessing programmes evidencing that they have taken responsibility and are in some way more or less remorseful for their crimes.[43] Similarly, to gain access to community-based rehabilitation they must show 'insight' into 'self-awareness' about their offending.[44]

So, while each stage of the criminal justice process appears to be autonomous, and the domain of different and autonomous professional groups (eg legal professionals control court stages and therapeutic professionals control the implementation of rehabilitation services during the sentence), in reality they are interdependent. The defendant is encouraged to consider how her plea and her account of what she has pled to will impact the character of her sentence. Similarly, as we saw earlier, the defendant's displayed attitude – whether she shows evidence of 'insight', 'something to work with' or ideally genuine remorse – influences the supposedly separate question of how she should plead.

Yet, although the defendant is encouraged to make connections between the individual decision stages controlled by autonomous professions, the promise of rehabilitation may not materialise. Indeed, the segmentation of the process obstructs the ability of the system to make good on its implied promise of rehabilitation. For example, information about the reasons for the sentence are not routinely provided to defendants, or even to those expected to implement the intentions of the sentencer.[45] So it is that the promise of an individually tailored rehabilitative sentence is, in reality, disabled by the lack, or poor quality, of information passed onto the agencies (eg probation, prison) that are required to help the person achieve the court's demand that the person achieves change. The personal change required of the offender to show that they have rehabilitated themselves is hampered by this disconnection and lack of information. People tend to be denied a clear understanding of what they have to do to extricate themselves from criminal justice, and so attempts to achieve the kind of personal change which may be demanded of them are thwarted.[46]

IV. HOW IS THE SYMBIOSIS OF LEGAL AND REHABILITATIVE/ THERAPEUTIC PROFESSIONAL WORK BLIND TO CROSS-CONTAMINATION?

How is the interdependent and mutually nourishing (ie symbiotic) character of the work of legal and therapeutic professionals possible? After all, as justice

[43] M Hall and K Rossmanith, 'Long Haul Remorse: The Continuous Performance of Repentance through Prison Sentences' in Tudor et al (n 25); Weisman, *Showing Remorse* (n 13); Padfield (n 24); Weisman, 'Remorse Is Not Enough' (n 24).

[44] See Weisman, 'Remorse Is Not Enough' (n 24); see also, eg Weisman, *Showing Remorse* (n 13); M Hall, *The Lived Sentence* (London, Palgrave Macmillan, 2016); M Schinkel, *Being imprisoned: Punishment, Adaptation and Desistance* (Cham, Springer, 2014); Martel (n 31).

[45] Field, 'The Enactment of Political Cultures' (n 12); Hall (n 44); Schinkel (n 44).

[46] Hall (n 44); Schinkel (n 44); Hall and Rossmanith (n 43).

professionals, neither occupational group can afford to regard the work they do as routinely 'contaminated' by the work of the other. I use the term 'contamination' to refer to the ways in which cherished ideas and categories have to be seen to be pure and untainted by extraneous pressures, which could be viewed as besmirching or debasing the purity of these venerated ideas.[47] The presumption of innocence and the freedom of the individual to participate in her own case (most especially the freedom to choose to plead guilty or not guilty) are prominent examples. The purity of these ideas is fundamental to the felt integrity of criminal justice. The presumption of innocence is supposed to be insulated from extraneous pressures so that the decision as to how to plead is free and genuine.

So it is, for example, that plea bargaining is castigated by so many scholars and remains sensitive among practitioners, especially judges. Indeed, many judges dislike the term 'plea bargaining' since it seems to them to connote something vulgar, grubby, 'underhand' or 'seedy'.[48] It seems to them to pollute or contaminate the purity of the venerated ideals of the presumption of innocence and the free choice of the defendant – values for which lawyers and especially judges hold themselves to be responsible. For a defendant to say openly to the court that she 'only pled guilty for the sentence discount' or so that other charges would be dropped, or so that she would be liberated from pre-trial remand/detention, etc, would be not only confronting, but obnoxious. While plea bargaining is a well-known example of such 'contamination', which came to light in the 1970s, my argument in this chapter is that the 'cross-contamination' of legal and therapeutic work is less obvious but no less important. How is it that justice professionals permit such 'contamination' without seeing themselves as invalidating their cherished values and, indeed, their raison d'être? Rather than castigating the aggregated failures of individuals, I propose we focus on how, in systemic practices, such symbiosis is permitted, without being obvious.

The reader may recall the triple obligations that justice professionals experience as a personal weight of responsibility: being directly and self-consciously responsible for the fate of another; being ethical; and being self-consciously the practical custodians of justice. So, judges and lawyers cannot participate in practices which blatantly and directly violate core legal values and principles.

We saw earlier how certain professionals (eg defence lawyers) are aware that they are obliged to invigilate (ie supervise, examine and check for) the possibility of contamination being shown to other professionals (especially the judge). Professionals know they have an obligation to other (especially higher status) professionals to save them from embarrassment.[49] Defence lawyers save judges

[47] Here I am drawing on my work developing Douglas's classic anthropological study of purity and pollution. Tata, 'Humanising Punishment?' (n 22); M Douglas, *Purity and Danger* (Abingdon, Routledge, 2002 [1966]).

[48] A Flynn and A Freiberg, 'Plea Negotiations: Final Report to the Criminology Research Council' (Canberra, Australian Institute of Criminology, 2018) 19–21.

[49] Tata, 'Humanising Punishment?' (n 22). More generally on the ways in which lower status actors are obliged to save higher status actors from embarrassment, see E Goffman, 'Embarrassment and Social Organization' (1956) 62 *American Journal of Sociology* 264.

(and therefore themselves) embarrassment by invigilating (keeping watch over and supervising) the defendant and her account at pre-sentence interview. They are especially careful to check that the account that appears in the report is not obviously at odds with the formal guilty plea. We also saw how report writers tend to import threats from the legal world to induce a change in the person's displayed attitude and/or massage the person's account so that it is less obviously at odds with the formal guilty plea.

Similarly, we saw that defence lawyers, and especially judges, appear to be unaware of the detailed casework of pre-sentence report writers in ameliorating, massaging and smoothing down the roughest edges of a person's account so that it is less blatantly at odds with the person's formal guilty plea. Thus, the person's voice in the report can be, and is, regarded as the unfiltered and authentic voice of the person. This perceived authenticity yields a double effect in showing to the court that its work is legitimate.

First, it means that defendants can be seen to have had their say. They have been able to put their side of the story, and this can be felt in the weight of the report. The report is seen by the court to tell the defendant's story of the criminal incident not only in her own words, but also in the context of the challenges of her life. She has demonstrably been listened to. This is all set out in what is regarded as exhaustive, 'encyclopaedic' detail. Judges and lawyers frequently remark and complain about how much 'unnecessary' detail about the troubled lives of people to be sentenced is included in pre-sentence reports.[50] Lawyers, and especially judges, take pride in observing (often tinged with humour) how reports are said to present 'excessive' information about the person, such as the name of the primary school she attended, that her hobby is stamp collecting or that as a baby she was delivered by caesarean section. However, there is a sense in which this 'complaint' is also a way of judges and lawyers observing and celebrating how remarkably carefully the process listens to the voice of each defendant as a unique and valued individual. By highlighting such a perceived level of minute, 'biographical' detail, judges and lawyers are able to find in reports a level of participation and 'comprehensive' attention to the unique individual that is otherwise lacking at the front stage of the court, where the person has pled guilty and her 'voice' would otherwise barely be heard.[51]

Second, by perceiving the person's account of the criminal incident in the pre-sentence report to be unmediated, lawyers and especially judges can believe in her reported attitude to the authority of the court and its legitimacy to punish. To be too aware of the casework done by report writers in revising and remodulating

[50] C Tata, 'Reducing Prison Sentencing through Pre-sentence Reports? Why the Quasi-market Logic of "Selling Alternatives to Custody" Fails' (2018) 57 *Howard Journal of Crime & Justice* 472; K Beyens and V Scheirs, 'Encounters of a Different Kind: Social Enquiry and Sentencing in Belgium' (2010) 112 *Punishment & Society: International Journal of Penology* 309.

[51] By contrast, Field, 'The Enactment of Political Cultures' (n 12) shows how in the French *cour d'assises* this 'biographical' work hearing about the person's life and what may have led to them being before the court is not delegated to other professionals and carried out 'backstage'. Rather, it is done publicly in the 'frontstage' of the court and led by the judge.

her account would expose lawyers, and especially judges, to being too aware and too directly confronted with the reality of the 'cross-contamination' of legal and therapeutic casework. This would imperil the perceived integrity of cherished ideas such as free participation.

V. CONCLUSIONS AND NEW RESEARCH AGENDAS

If they are not to deny their own validity, justice professionals are required, by each other and themselves, to concentrate on the casework of their own professional discipline and to pay little or no attention to the detailed, substantive casework of other professions. Thus, legal professionals who are deemed to be exclusively responsible for questions about the determination of guilt must, at least in a formal and public sense, *be seen to be* blind to the promises and threats of sentencing and its implementation (eg the prospects for rehabilitation). Likewise, therapeutic professionals deemed responsible for rehabilitation must be seen to disregard the contingencies and construction of guilty pleas. It is precisely because of this apparent disregard for the detailed, substantive work of the other profession that the intimate symbiotic relationship between the 'legal' work of guilt determination and the 'therapeutic' work of rehabilitation and sentencing implementation can proceed relatively unobtrusively.

The effect of the official segmentation of the criminal justice process into apparently autonomous stages, each dominated by different professions, is that the defendant alone has to traverse the professional borders, and in doing so must *anticipate* the effects of decisions at one stage on how she will be evaluated at other stages. Yet each profession ignores the contingencies of the decision-making of the other – they must take it as settled fact and be blind to the detailed work of the other profession. Without any master plan or controlling mind, this collective work helps to generate 'ideal' defendants (penal subjects) precisely because of the absence of any coherent system. In other words, the segmented character of the formally separate stages in the criminal process 'belonging' to autonomous professions (so cherished by the due process view) is in fact 'efficient'. It helps to generate the making of 'ideal' defendants (penal subjects), and therefore expeditious case disposal. In this way, the felt professional dilemma (justice versus efficiency) is largely resolved. Justice professionals can get through caseloads 'efficiently' because they can at the same time observe 'justice' being done. Expectations on defendants to admit responsibility and (ideally) show remorse are pervasive and coordinated without appearing (most especially to justice professionals) to be so.

These modifications mean that the manifestation of the person (with varying degrees of their own active or passive complicity) begins to move towards an approximation of the 'ideal' penal subject, who shows that she sincerely accepts individual responsibility and wholeheartedly consents to her punishment as deserved.

My argument is that the realignment of the person through the blind symbiosis of legal and therapeutic professional practices is not achieved through the routine exertion of palpable pressure on people, nor through the aggregation of individual professional acts of bad faith. The approximation of the person towards characteristics of 'the ideal defendant' is not, and could not be, achieved by a grand conspiracy. To do so would be to deny the validity and self-identity of judges, lawyers, probation officers, social workers, etc as professionals who are self-consciously the practical custodians of 'justice'. It is not achieved through deliberately coordinated intentions, thought-out planning or malevolence of motive. It is precisely because of the absence of deliberation that seemingly autonomous stages of the process and autonomous professional activities in fact combine and work together. Without intended design, the casework of the two professions symbiotically accomplishes mutually desirable outcomes, which helpfully facilitates work for the other.

While individual legal and therapeutic professionals may wish to encourage defendants to 'take responsibility' and 'show remorse', doing so alone without the substantive casework of the other profession could not achieve the realignment of the defendant. It is the symbiosis of the casework of the two separate professions that secures the realignment of displayed defendant postures. Legal and therapeutic professionals are able to do this precisely because they are largely unaware (and, indeed, cannot afford to be too aware) of the detailed, substantive casework of the other profession.

The 'blindness' of one professional group to the substantive work of the other is regenerated by vocational training, academic scholarship and empirical research. Further, vocationally led academic education and scholarship has tended to focus on the intentions of individual professionals and whether those intentions are honourable, fair, ethical, etc. As a result, as academics, educators and researchers, we have tended to ignore the unofficial and non-intended symbiosis between the officially autonomous segments of criminal justice, each 'owned' by different professional groups.

What, then, should empirical research do? In this chapter, I have sought to reflect on how people proceeded against by the state have to make decisions. The way they have to is at odds with the imagery presented by flow charts, policy documentation and, indeed, academic scholarship, which focuses on each individual decision moment as if autonomous from the rest. Rather than having to make decisions as if they are independent of each other, temporally linear and sequential, people are required and expected to consider the consequences and interrelationships between officially separate decisions by mentally shuttling forward in time to anticipate the consequences.[52] By doing this, they are encouraged to approximate themselves, and be shown to be aligned with, the

[52] On this temporal shuttling, see Johansen (n 19): the person who has formally denied guilt is nonetheless required to imagine herself 'as if' a convicted offender and how she will be evaluated at sentencing and beyond.

characteristics of the ideal defendant (or penal subject), who accepts the legitimacy of her punishment. The implications of my argument for research are threefold. First, we need to know far more about people's experiences, including studying them over time, of going through the criminal justice process. Second, we need to pay more attention to those who literally and metaphorically connect people proceeded against by the state from one professional realm to another. Third, in this chapter, I have concentrated on (nominally) adversarial systems – or at least those influenced by adversarial traditions. However, nominally inquisitorial systems may operate functionally equivalent practices (eg humanisation, which encourages admissions of guilt), albeit in quite different ways. Here I elaborate on this threefold agenda for future research.

A. Study Defendant Experiences, Especially Longitudinally

Remarkably little research (including my own) has devoted itself to an in-depth documentation of the experiences of those subjected to the criminal process – and then on through to the implementation of the sentence. This is understandable. Due to a myriad of logistical, ethical and access challenges, this is extremely labour-intensive and difficult work. However, we should acknowledge that we know little about what people experience in the criminal-penal process. Partly because they are so much easier to access, but also because we have been so enthralled with the question of whether individual professional motives are 'good' or 'bad', we have tended to 'read off' what people experience from what professionals believe people feel and experience. As desistance research[53] has begun to show, that is not the same thing. There have been valuable recent[54] and not so recent[55] studies asking people in interviews or surveys for their views about their experiences of being subject to criminal proceedings. However, what is needed is to follow and observe cases *longitudinally* on their journey through the process to the implementation of the sentence; and, ideally, to directly compare them to the experiences and intentions of the professionals involved in the same case. This necessitates stepping out of familiar academic comfort zones and combining with scholars from other disciplines. It means that socio-legal scholars who study guilt determination and judicial sentencing practices should also study the substance of therapeutic work and their interrelations.

[53] eg S Maruna, *Making Good* (Washington, DC, American Psychological Association, 2001); F McNeil, *Pervasive Punishment: Making Sense of Mass Supervision* (Bingley, Emerald Publishing, 2019); F McNeill and B Weaver, 'Changing Lives? Desistance Research and Offender Management' (2010) SCCJR Project Report No 03/2010; Schinkel (n 44); B Weaver, *Offending and Desistance: The Importance of Social Relations* (London, Routledge, 2016).

[54] eg Transform Justice, 'Justice Denied? The Experience of Unrepresented Defendants in the Criminal Courts' (April 2016); Jacobson (n 29); Gormley and Tata, 'Remorse' (n 25).

[55] JD Casper, *American Criminal Justice: The Defendant's Perspective* (New York, Prentice-Hall, 1972).

Similarly, social work, probation and desistance scholars need to become far more interested in studying guilt determination and sentencing practices.

B. Study Ancillary Workers and their Interactions with Professionals and People Proceeded Against

Research should pay closer attention to the work of non-professional 'ancillary workers', by which I mean those workers who seem to have an auxiliary and subordinate role to professionals, including, for example, reception, security staff in courts and court cells, prisoner transportation staff, court ushers and clerks. Just as most research has concentrated on professional perceptions of people's experiences, so too has research neglected the work that connects the person from one separate professional dominion with another. This means that research should also study the loosely connected interfaces between domains of professional work (eg between 'legal' work and 'therapeutic' work). True, *formally speaking*, non-professional ancillary work seems prosaic: nothing important seems to be decided officially in these interfaces, where the person's status is liminal, uncertain and suspended between different official statuses.[56] Yet, it may be that the experiences of the person are shaped in these obliquely connected interfaces between professional domains, between one formal decision node and another. Those who literally and figuratively receive the person from and deliver the person to different professional dominions have tended to be ignored by criminal justice researchers. For example, research until now has paid limited attention to the experiences and effects of waiting (eg for a court appearance,[57] or the work of tranforming the person from the status of police suspect to defendant to offender[58]). We should develop a research agenda to study not only visible official professional work conducted at formal decision points (eg sentencing), but also the interfaces between the work of different professions. These interfaces are mediated by the work of ancillary staff. Their work may be more important to the person's experience, setting the agenda of their expectations, than we have hitherto appreciated.

C. Functionally Equivalent Work in Adversarial and Inquisitorial Practices

Scholarship comparing practices in (formally) adversarial and inquisitorial regimes could also examine the relationship between therapeutic and legal work

[56] Tata, 'Ritual Individualisation' (n 5).

[57] P Carlen, *Magistrates Justice* (London, Martin Robertson, 1976) 18–38; K Cheng and B Leung, 'The Punitive Nature of Pre-trial Detention: Perspectives of Detainees in Hong Kong' (2019) 58 *Howard Journal of Crime and Justice* 143; M Feeley, *The Process Is the Punishment* (New York, Russell Sage, 1979); A Woof and L Skinns, 'The Role of Emotion, Space and Place in Police Custody in England' (2018) 20 *Punishment & Society: International Journal of Penology* 562.

[58] Tata, 'Ritual Individualisation' (n 5).

in re-manifesting the person as closer to the ideal penal subject. While there are major differences, as other chapters in this volume suggest,[59] practices in both traditions appear to be orientated towards soliciting admissions of guilt by a person who recognises her culpability and shows justice authorities signs of genuine remorse.

To a greater or lesser extent, and in varying ways, admissions of guilt are encouraged across the world. Especially in putatively adversarial jurisdictions in the Anglo-American world (and increasingly in those countries with long inquisitorial traditions), guilty pleas are expected and encouraged. In other jurisdictions, there may not, formally speaking, be an equivalent idea of 'a plea', but nevertheless there is some notion of 'a confession', or 'admission' that is sought and/or expected. Albeit in different ways, questions of criminal conduct (guilt) and questions of the person's character and amenability for rehabilitation (which may be entangled with ideas of citizenship[60]) are, in reality, intimately interdependent, even fused.

[59] See Field, 'The Enactment of Political Cultures' (n 12); Hodgson (n 19); V Gautron, 'Remorse in the French Criminal Justice System: A Subterranean Influence' in Field and Tata (n 12) ch 2. On the 'hybrid' system in Denmark, see Johansen (n 19). See also Field, 'State, Citizen and Character' (n 12).

[60] Field, 'State, Citizen and Character' (n 12).

12

Remorse and Restoration: The Role of Remorse in Constructing the 'Ideal Offender' of Restorative Justice

GIUSEPPE MAGLIONE*

Expressing remorse is a basic condition for an 'offender' to enter a restorative justice process and then an element integral to their moral performance toward the 'victim'. In this chapter, I argue that remorse plays a further, implicit role within restorative justice in that it contributes to shaping both the offender's identity and their relationships with the victim and the 'community'. I narrow the focus to consider only restorative justice as defined within law and policy in a specific geographical context (England and Wales). Official normative documents, in fact, represent a crucial dimension of the recent development of restorative justice. From this perspective, focusing on how legal and policy documents frame the relationships between remorse and the offender can help to question the taken-for-granted neutral effects of enshrining restorative justice values into law and policy, and to appreciate the direction of travel of this 'new' frontier of penality.

I. INTRODUCTION

RESTORATIVE JUSTICE (RJ) is often considered as a more humane, politically progressive, socially inclusive, contemporary frontier of penality worldwide.[1] Once a marginal phenomenon, today RJ is increasingly studied and practised. A significant step in the recent growth of RJ is the proliferation of law and policy on the subject. This incipient institutionalisation entails a qualitative transformation of RJ, born as a host of instruments

* Lecturer, Criminology, University of Kent, UK.

[1] P Wallis, *Understanding Restorative Justice, How Empathy Can Close the Gap Created by Crime* (Bristol, Policy Press, 2014); *cf* G Maglione, 'Restorative Justice and the State. Untimely Objections against the Institutionalisation of Restorative Justice' (2020) 17 *British Journal of Community Justice* 5.

emerged organically at the periphery of formal criminal justice systems, and originally designed as alternatives to formal criminal justice practices.

This chapter provides a critical reflection on how English and Welsh law and policy on RJ shape the 'offender',[2] focusing on the specific position that 'remorse' occupies in such discursive constructions. 'Invoking remorse' has often been hailed as one of the crucial aims of RJ.[3] Feeling and expressing remorse is in fact thought to entail the offender's realisation of their wrongdoing and acknowledgement of the harm caused to the victim, whilst indicating the beginning of reintegration into the community's moral horizon. By problematising this assumed understanding, this chapter argues that remorse, as a component of the (ideal) offender's moral performance towards the victim, plays a central function in defining the offender's role, needs and interests within RJ law and policy, as well as the expectations towards them. More broadly, remorse emerges as the indispensable *trait d'union* between the moral-psychological effects and the political dimension of RJ, as envisioned by law/policy-makers. In fact, remorse connects the purported healing and moralising functions of RJ with the political underpinnings of this justice mechanism. From this analytical perspective, it is possible to provide a case study in the policy appropriation of RJ, generating innovative insights into the historical emergence, underlying values and political uses of RJ, presenting material for critical engagement with this subject whose institutionalisation is now a global phenomenon.

II. PRELIMINARY CONSIDERATIONS

The term 'restorative justice' refers to three conceptually distinct but empirically overlapping objects: (i) a justice reform movement emerging in the 1970s in North America and then spreading globally, advocating for a (ii) non-punitive and participatory approach to harms caused by wrongdoing (iii) mainly implemented by facilitated and voluntary encounters between direct stakeholders ('victim', 'offender' and relevant 'communities'), geared towards addressing

[2] Although I am aware of the non-technical and rather stigmatising meaning of the word 'offender' in this chapter, I use this term descriptively, since it is commonly adopted both in the academic literature and in law and policy on RJ to indicate the penal subject, that is, the individual or entity proceeded against by criminal justice agencies, otherwise defined as defendant or convicted defendant. The term 'offender' in this chapter is therefore used to capture the rather generalising uses of this word made by the RJ literature and normative documents, without any assumption related to responsibility, as a more accurate legal use would suggest.

[3] J Braithwaite, *Crime, Shame and Reintegration* (Cambridge, Cambridge University Press, 1989) 100; A Duff, 'Alternatives to Punishment – or Alternative Punishments?' in W Cragg (ed), *Retributivism and Its Critics* (Stuttgart, Steiner, 1992) 49; S Retzinger and T Scheff, 'Strategy for Community Conferences: Emotions and Social Bonds' in B Galaway and J Hudson (eds), *Restorative Justice: International Perspectives* (Monsey, Criminal Justice Press, 1996) 316; K Daly, 'Revisiting the Relationship between Retributive and Restorative Justice' (Griffith University Repository, 1999a) 15, www.griffith.edu.au/__data/assets/pdf_file/0028/223759/2001-Daly-Revisiting-the-relationship-pre-print.pdf.

cooperatively those harms and their consequences. This movement has taken different forms in different geographical and historical contexts, modifying its ethos in response to changing cultural and social factors, and advocating for significantly different mechanisms determining the empirical complexity of the RJ field.

In order to simplify this multi-layered field, this chapter focuses on RJ as a specific justice mechanism as described and regulated by Anglo-Welsh criminal and penal law and policy, aiming to untangle how one of the stakeholders – the 'offender' – is constructed within relevant legal and policy documents. Such official texts represent a unique vantage point from which to reflect on the institutionalisation of RJ, whilst the specific focus on remorse helps to unearth under-examined dimensions of RJ.

From this angle, I am particularly interested in how RJ, as defined above, interacts with criminal justice. 'Criminal justice' here refers to an ideal-typical approach to wrongdoing instantiated in different ways by a host of state institutions, from law enforcement agencies to the penal system. This approach has certain ontological, epistemological, anthropological and ethical characteristics.[4] Criminal justice rests on the overdetermination of social practices by considering them objective and not merely socially constructed. Social practices (for instance, the definition of 'victim' or 'offender') are natural entities characterised by permanence and homogeneity. This ties in with a certain epistemological viewpoint marked by the idea that a truth (eg the verdict's truth) beyond inter-subjective constructions exists and is achievable. Finally, the criminal justice approach is characterised by an underlying idea of subjectivity as fixed and stable (eg the offender as fundamentally different from the victim) sustained by the Hobbesian ethical claim that the human condition has an inclination towards egoism and violence that needs to be countered by hierarchy and centralisation.

Underlying this chapter is the idea that although RJ is often seen as a progressive (ie inclusive and non-violent) response to the wrong/harms, when narrowing the focus on law and policy, it is possible to appreciate how RJ ends up reproducing stereotypical, value-laden representations characterising criminal justice, eg by displaying the individual as voluntarily accepting responsibility rather than acknowledging social differences/structural inequality. This chapter will show that, within this framework, remorse plays a crucial role by individualising the offender's responsibility, whilst (differently from criminal justice) generating unique links with the material victim and their moral community.

Arguably, labels such as 'offender', 'victim' and 'community' are neither morally neutral nor epistemically objective or socially unproblematic. On the contrary, they are cultural products that rest on tacit worldviews, loaded with

[4] G Maglione, 'Pushing the Theoretical Boundaries of Restorative Justice: Non-sovereign Justice in Radical Political and Social Theories' in T Gavrielides (ed), *Routledge International Handbook of Restorative Justice* (London, Routledge, 2018) 25.

assumed values and cultural stereotypes.[5] What does 'offender' mean in RJ law and policy? Which implicit images are associated with this label? Where do they come from? In order to address these questions, I combine methodological insights from Nils Christie[6] and Michel Foucault.[7] Christie used the concepts of 'ideal victim' and 'ideal offender' as tools to simplify and generalise the diverse range of assumptions underpinning the representations of those actors within media and policy. Media and policy are seen as using (and in so doing, perpetuating) stereotyped models of crime victims (innocent, vulnerable, unrelated to the offender) and offenders (unambiguously big and bad, blameworthy and unrelated to the victim).[8] In this chapter, the 'ideal offender' is inserted within a discursive analysis inspired by Foucault's archaeological works.[9] This approach helps to delimit[10] the discourses on the offender in RJ whilst making their historical context intelligible in a bid to question their implicit assumptions.

The first step of this inquiry is to reconstruct the 'normative discourses' on the offender within RJ law and policy.[11] Such discourses are not coherent entities, with neat boundaries, but rather analytical concepts 'that the researcher projects onto the reality in order to create a framework for the study'.[12] The second step reconstructs inferentially a range of typical offender's features, which are pieced together into an ideal model. The third step contextualises[13] this 'ideal offender', focusing on the social and political background within which this model emerged. Finally, the chapter offers some brief reflections on the implications of this analysis and some concluding reflections.

In terms of limitations, this work is a theoretical elaboration on official documents, and as such tends to be abstract and overgeneralising. However, my primary goal is to reconstruct patterns across the legal/policy representations of

[5] J Van Dijk, 'Free the Victim: A Critique of the Western Conception of Victimhood' (2009) 16 *International Review of Victimology* 1; N Christie 'Words on Words' (2013) 1 *Restorative Justice: An International Journal* 15.

[6] N Christie, 'The Ideal Victim' in E Fattah (ed), *From Crime Policy to Victim Policy. Reorienting the Justice System* (Basingstoke, Macmillan, 1986).

[7] M Foucault, *The Order of Things: An Archaeology of the Human Sciences* (New York, Pantheon Books, 1970); M Foucault, *The Archaeology of Knowledge* (New York, Pantheon Books, 1972).

[8] Christie (n 6) 18.

[9] Foucault (n 7).

[10] I have inductively aggregated the definitions and descriptions of the offender encoded in policy on RJ, based on their thematic commonalities, identifying, as a result, three overarching discourses on RJ.

[11] M Foucault, *The Archaeology of Knowledge* (n 7) 145; G Maglione, 'Embodied Victims. An Archaeology of the "Ideal Victim" of Restorative Justice' (2016) 17 *Criminology & Criminal Justice* 401; G Maglione, 'Communities at Large: An Archaeological Analysis of the "Community" within Restorative Justice Policy and Laws' (2017) 25 *Critical Criminology* 453; G Maglione, 'Immature Offenders. A Critical History of the Representations of the Offender in Restorative Justice' (2018) 21 *Contemporary Justice Review* 44.

[12] M Jørgensen and L Phillips, *Discourse Analysis as Theory and Method* (London, SAGE, 2002) 143.

[13] Foucault, *The Order of Things* (n 7) 168.

the offender in RJ.[14] This will involve a degree of simplification, 'compensated' by the critical edge of the approach I will elaborate.[15] Additionally, inductive inferences are always underdetermined and theory-laden, ie many (possibly incompatible) readings of the same documents are possible, as well as driven by theoretical views. My interpretations are led by the intention of pointing out a significant gap in the RJ literature and a direction for further critical research, offering an analytical approach that aims to raise questions and stimulate debate rather than provide answers.

III. NORMATIVE DISCOURSES

A. Active Stakeholders

In English and Welsh criminal and penal law and policy, RJ is consistently described as enabling the inclusion and direct expression of the victim's experience[16] whilst empowering the offender and the larger community 'by bringing them into the process and involving them in the solution'.[17] However, on closer inspection, this idea of active participation appears to be expressed in different, and at times incompatible, ways. As for the offender's participation, whilst early 2000s laws (enacted under the New Labour[18] government) stress the assumption of a prospective responsibility, by 'actually honour[ing] their undertaking to make reparations to their victim',[19] 2010–15 documents (mainly published under the Conservative–Liberal Democrat coalition government[20]) emphasise how the offender's participation entails an opportunity to maximise their 'awareness of the impact of the offending concerned on the victims'[21] whilst 'providing an opportunity … to face the consequences of their actions'.[22]

[14] D Garland, *The Culture of Control: Crime and Social Order in Contemporary Society* (Oxford, Oxford University Press, 2001) viii; D Garland, 'What Does It Mean to Write a "History of the Present"? Foucault, Genealogy and the History of Criminology' (2013) 42 *Quaderni fiorentini per la storia del pensiero giuridico moderno* 43.

[15] M Foucault, 'What Is Critique?' in S Lotringer (ed), *Foucault Live: Collected Interviews, 1961–1984* (New York, Semiotext(e), 1996); Garland, *The Culture of Control* (n 14); G Pavlich, *Governing Paradoxes of Restorative Justice* (London, Glasshouse Press, 2005).

[16] Ministry of Justice, 'Restorative Justice Action Plan for the Criminal Justice System' (19 November 2012) (RJAP) 3; Crime and Courts Act 2013 (CCA 2013), sch 16.2; Ministry of Justice, *Code of Practice for Victims of Crime October England and Wales (Victims' Code)* (2015) 34.

[17] Home Office, *Justice for All* (White Paper, 2002) 7.33.

[18] In this chapter, I use the term 'New Labour' merely to reference a chronological period in the history of the British Labour Party ranging from the mid-1990s until 2010, under the leadership of Tony Blair (Prime Minister between 1997 and 2007) and Gordon Brown (Prime Minister between 2007 and 2010).

[19] Home Office, *Justice for All* (n 17) 4.12.

[20] Conservative–Liberal Democrats coalition (2010–15).

[21] Offender Rehabilitation Act 2014 (ORA 2014), s 15 (3.8b); CCA 2013, sch 16.2.

[22] Ministry of Justice, *Victims' Code* (n 16) 34.

Responsibility refers to something 'personal',[23] which should genuinely flow from a full awareness of the human costs of the crime, intended as a violation of people's needs, as well as of moral and legal rules. Victims' participation entails mainly the 'opportunity to talk about, or by other means express experience of, the offending and its impact'[24] in order to restore their sense of autonomy and safety, and 'prevent the feeling of powerlessness which often results from being made a victim'.[25] This is a fundamental aim that RJ seeks to achieve,[26] to oppose the marginalisation of victims within criminal justice, as the crime victims' movement has claimed since the 1970s.[27] With regard to the idea of community's participation, this is particularly highlighted in flagship New Labour criminal policy documents produced between the late 1990s and early 2000s, such as Justice for All (2002) and The Way Ahead (2001), as well as in statutes (particularly the Youth Justice and Criminal Evidence Act 1999). There are two recurrent types of community participation described here: the inviting of the 'supporters of the victim and the offender';[28] and/or the involvement of community representatives 'as mediators'.[29] The first type entails that the community be involved either because it is victimised by the crime (the victim's network) or because it is able to contribute to dealing with its aftermath (the offender's network). The second route (involving community representatives) aims to enable community members to play a part in 'searching for local solutions and making the system more responsive locally'.[30]

The idea of 'active participation' is an overarching value within the RJ field and conversely one of the apparent differences with respect to criminal justice, especially in cases of youth offending.[31] Such a responsibilising approach to participation, embraced by documents from both the 1990s and the early 2000s, is reinforced after 2010, although from a slightly different perspective. Here, in fact, participation is framed less as an instrument of community empowerment and more as a strategy of responsibilisation that encourages offenders to 'take care' of themselves. In RJ, such a strategy is fundamentally mobilised by asking parties to deal with the crime aftermath by meeting the victim's needs.[32] At this

[23] Ministry of Justice, *Breaking the Cycle: Effective Punishment, Rehabilitation and Sentencing of Offenders* (Green Paper, Cm 7972, 2010) 22.

[24] ORA 2014, s 15 (3.8).

[25] Ministry of Justice, *Breaking the Cycle* (n 23) 22.

[26] Restorative Justice Council UK, 'Best Practice Guidance for Restorative Practice' (2011) 14.

[27] Victim Support, 'Criminal Neglect No Justice beyond Criminal Justice' (2001) www.scie-socialcareonline.org.uk/criminal-neglect-no-justice-beyond-criminal-justice/r/a11G00000181MWIAY.

[28] Home Office, 'Restorative Justice: The Government's Strategy' (July 2003) 1.2.

[29] Home Office, *Justice for All* (n 17) 7.33.

[30] Home Office, *Confident Communities in a Secure Britain: The Home Office Strategic Plan 2004–2008* (Cm 6287, 2004) 99.

[31] Crown Prosecution Service, 'Restorative Justice Legal Guidance' (2014); Home Office, *Criminal Justice: The Way Ahead* (Cm 5074, 2001) 17; Ministry of Justice, *Breaking the Cycle* (n 23) 22.

[32] CCA 2013, sch 16 (12).

point, an underlying tension between the active participation of victim, community and offender should be noted that stretches across normative documents, particularly those produced over the last two decades. It appears, in fact, that the offender's input to RJ is mainly regarded as functional to the fulfilment of the victim's needs,[33] whilst the community is increasingly neglected as a crime stakeholder. As will be clarified in the second section of this chapter, this reflects different law/policy-makers' views on RJ, and their political, professional and cultural tractions and trajectories.

B. Genuine Accountability

The discourse on the offender's genuine accountability in RJ revolves around the idea that the criminal offence is both an act against the normative moral/legal order (ie a wrong) and an offence against the material victim (ie a harm). From this perspective arises the personal duty to right the wrong by repairing the harm.[34] RJ seeks to hold offenders accountable and to encourage them to face the impact of the crime on others.[35] This idea of accountability is fundamentally linked to a certain concept of 'taking responsibility', that is, the opportunity for the offender to 'own' their behaviour.[36] The process of supporting the offender's responsibilisation is highly characteristic of the RJ field, and conversely one of the main purported differences from criminal justice.[37] This form of 'meaningful' accountability[38] is activated by the typical means of meeting the victim[39] and possibly the community, as long as the offender has acknowledged their responsibility.[40] The offender's understanding of the harm caused to the victim refers to a personal journey,[41] which should genuinely originate from seeing the victim and therefore appreciating the material consequence of breaching moral and legal rules. The underlying assumption is that the offender has a diminished sense of moral obligation towards the other crime stakeholders. This deficiency is elaborated within the RJ process, by focusing on the crime's impact.[42] Here, remorse is a possible consequence of this self-awareness achieved by the offender

[33] Ministry of Justice, *Victims' Code* (n 16) 34.

[34] Home Office, *Justice for All* (n 17) 7.33; Home Office (n 30) 100.

[35] Ministry of Justice, *Transforming Rehabilitation: A Summary of Evidence on Reducing Reoffending* (2013) 4.10.

[36] H Zehr, *Changing Lenses. A New Focus for Crime and Justice* (Scottdale, Herald Press, 2005) 40–42.

[37] Crown Prosecution Service (n 31) 1; Home Office, *Criminal Justice* (n 31) 17.

[38] UN Basic Principles on the Use of Restorative Justice Programmes in Criminal Matters (2002) Preamble.

[39] CCA 2013, sch 16 (12).

[40] Ministry of Justice, *Breaking the Cycle* (n 23) 22; Restorative Justice Council UK (n 26) 4; Home Office, 'Restorative Justice' (n 28) 5.7; Ministry of Justice, *Victims' Code* (n 16) 7.5.

[41] Ministry of Justice, *Breaking the Cycle* (n 23) 22.

[42] ORA 2014, s 15 (3.8b).

within the restorative process. The expression of remorse, in fact, indicates the development of a deeper 'personal' responsibility,[43] linked to an awareness of the human consequences of the crime.[44] Additionally, it should be remarked that this conceptualisation of accountability/responsibility is not incompatible with a 'proper punishment'[45] or censure, as long as this is 'constructive', ie it does not deliberately aim to inflict pain.[46]

Since the late 1990s, this idea of genuine accountability cuts across law and policy on RJ, appearing as one of the few axes around which the normative representations of RJ have been revolving ever since. This is possibly because it refers to a basic expectation towards the offender – their answerability to the victim as an embodiment of the law/morals – which contributes towards defining the offender in RJ as the individual who has harmed and is now learning the wrongfulness of their actions through a moral-pedagogical process.

C. From Reparation to Restoration

Reparative schemes were active in England and Wales from the late 1970s,[47] supported widely across the political spectrum.[48] Their goal was to address the material harms caused by crime, such as physical damage to the direct and/or indirect victim and community.[49] In this context, reparation was predominantly a diversionary measure for youth offenders administered by police and probation officers, offering little space for victim's participation and expression of needs and wants.[50]

The widespread development of reparation/referral orders, acknowledged by the literature as paving the way for the development of RJ in the UK,[51] is a

[43] Ministry of Justice, *Breaking the Cycle* (n 23) 22.

[44] Ministry of Justice, *Transforming Rehabilitation* (n 35) 4 (10); CCA 2013, sch 16 (12).

[45] Ministry of Justice, RJAP (n 16) 1.

[46] eg K Daly, 'Does Punishment Have a Place in Restorative Justice?' (Griffith University Repository, 1999b) www.griffith.edu.au/__data/assets/pdf_file/0021/223743/1999-Daly-Does-punishment-have-a-place-in-RJ-paper.pdf accessed 12 September 2019, 3.

[47] T Marshall and M Walpole, *Bringing People Together: Mediation and Reparation Projects in Great Britain* (London, HMSO, 1985).

[48] Parliamentary All-Party Penal Affairs Group, 'A New Deal for Victims' (1984); Home Office, 'Reparation: A Discussion Document' (1986).

[49] UN Declaration of Basic Principles of Justice for Victims of Crime and Abuse of Power 1985; Criminal Justice Act 1972 (CJA 1972); Powers of Criminal Courts Act 1973.

[50] M Wright, 'Nobody Came: Criminal Justice and the Needs of Victims' (1977) 16 *Howard Journal of Crime and Justice* 22; G Davis, J Boucherat and D Watson, 'Reparation in the Service of Diversion: The Subordination of a Good Idea' (1988) 27 *Howard Journal of Crime and Justice* 127; T Marshall and S Merry, *Crime and Accountability: Victim/Offender Mediation in Practice* (London, HMSO, 1990).

[51] G Davis, *Making Amends: Mediation and Reparation in Criminal Justice* (London, Routledge, 1992); J Muncie, 'Institutionalized Intolerance: Youth Justice and the 1998 Crime and Disorder Act' (1999) 19 *Critical Social Policy* 147; M Liebmann, *Mediation in Context* (London, Jessica Kingsley Publishers, 2000); M Liebmann, *Restorative Justice: How It Works* (London, Jessica Kingsley Publishers, 2007).

more recent phenomenon. It was announced by the No More Excuses (1997) White Paper and then enabled on a national scale by the Crime and Disorder Act 1998 and the Youth Justice and Criminal Evidence Act 1999. In these documents, reparation appears as a 'constructive' punitive response[52] distinct from mere compensation,[53] aiming to responsibilise and reform the offender.[54] The community in RJ is a characteristic recipient of the reparation, as opposed to cases of mere victims' compensation or restitution. Reparation to the 'community at large'[55] can be required when 'a victim does not want direct reparation',[56] or, more recently, when it is not 'acceptable to the victim'.[57] This model of reparation rests on the view that the crime 'undermines the social bonds integral to strong communities'.[58]

A key discursive shift in the representation of reparation seems to have taken place over the last decade (2010–20). During this period, reparation is increasingly framed within policy as an instrument to satisfy the victim, to provide 'closure',[59] 'enabl[ing] the victim to move on'.[60] Victims are entitled to obtain reparation,[61] and this is supposed to heal the interpersonal bonds corroded by crime. The harm here is not only the material loss or damage, but also (and characteristically) the symbolic/psychological harm. This expression refers to the offender's breach of 'relationships and trust' with the victim[62] by creating a sense of fear and lack of safety. Apology or community work are considered as typical symbolic reparations since they are supposedly apt to mend the relational bond between parties damaged by the crime.[63] From the offender's side, the active participation in the RJ process, the expression of remorse, listening and responding to the victim are all activities integral to symbolic harm repair.[64] Within this context, RJ can be used at pre-sentence stage to 'provide useful information for sentencing, for example about the offender's level of remorse and understanding of the impact of their crime', or through deferment of sentence, allowing judges or magistrate to take 'appropriate account … of the reparation

[52] Crime and Disorder Act (1998) (CDA 1998), s 67.

[53] Youth Justice and Criminal Evidence Act (1999) (YJCEA 1999), sch 5.

[54] Home Office, *No More Excuses* (White Paper, 1997) 4.13.

[55] CDA 1998, s 67.

[56] Home Office, *No More Excuses* (n 54) 4.15.

[57] Ministry of Justice, *Revised Code of Practice for Conditional Cautions – Adults* (2013) 7.2.16.

[58] Home Office, *Criminal Justice: The Way Ahead* (n 31) Introduction.

[59] Ministry of Justice, *Transforming Rehabilitation* (n 35) 10; Ministry of Justice, *Victims' Code* (n 16) 34.

[60] Ministry of Justice, 'Restorative Justice Action Plan for the Criminal Justice System in England and Wales' (2014) 3.

[61] Restorative Justice Council UK (n 26) 6; Restorative Justice Council UK, 'Principles of Restorative Practice' (2015) 1; Ministry of Justice, 'Restorative Justice Action Plan for the Criminal Justice System in England and Wales' (2013) 2; ORA 2014, s 15 (8).

[62] Home Office, 'Restorative Justice' (n 28) 1.1.

[63] J Braithwaite, 'Repentance Rituals and Restorative Justice' (2000) 8 *Journal of Political Philosophy* 115.

[64] Home Office, 'Restorative Justice' (n 28) 3.7.

and rehabilitative activities they have undertaken, and remorse demonstrated whilst doing so'.[65]

This partial 'dematerialisation' of reparation – ie the increasing centrality of symbolic reparation in RJ law and policy – can be conceptualised as a symptom of the slow, discursive shift from 'reparative justice' (enshrined in British legislation since compensation and restitution orders[66] and implemented by probation services) to a strictly speaking 'restorative justice'.[67] In the latter, material and symbolic repair are functionally linked,[68] and directed to fulfil the victim's needs.[69] Thus, without the symbolic repair, it may be difficult to achieve agreement about material reparation.[70] The victim's acceptance of the offender's offer to repair depends on symbolic behaviours such as the visible remorse shown by the offender during the RJ process.

D. Multiple Forms of Reintegration

The offender's reintegration back into the larger community is a further restorative goal, recurrently stressed in statutes and policy documents.[71] For the offender, restorative reintegration means 'paying their debt to society, putting their crime behind them and rejoining the law-abiding community'.[72] In representing reintegration, normative documents of the late 1990s are consistent with the theory of 'reintegrative shaming'[73] and its links to remorse. The offender's shaming and remorse, in fact, are indices of a successful restorative process: 'the more "restorative" an intervention (eg meaningful involvement of the offender in decision-making; the conference inducing remorse in the offender), the more likely it is to reduce re-offending'.[74] The very attendance of an RJ encounter represents a symbolic moment of re-acceptance of the offender within the civic dialogue. In this context, reintegration refers to the offender's incorporation into a community-based prosocial moral order[75] to be achieved within the

[65] National Offender Management Service, 'Restorative Justice Guidance' (2005) 2.4.3.

[66] CJA 1972, ss 1–6.

[67] *cf* M Wright, *Justice for Victims and Offenders* (Winchester, Waterside Press, 1996) 50.

[68] Ministry of Justice, 'Getting It Right for Victims and Witnesses' (2012) 14; Ministry of Justice, 'Restorative Justice Action Plan for the Criminal Justice System in England and Wales' (2014) 3.

[69] Restorative Justice Council UK, 'Manifesto for 2015' (2015) 1.

[70] Retzinger and Scheff (n 3).

[71] Home Office, *No More Excuses* (n 54) 9.21; Ministry of Justice, *Breaking the Cycle* (n 23) 30; HM Inspectorate of Constabulary, HM Inspectorate Probation, HM Inspectorate Prisons and HM Crown Prosecution Service Inspectorate, 'Facing Up to Offending: Use of Restorative Justice in the Criminal Justice System' (2012) 4.

[72] Home Office, *No More Excuses* (n 54) 9.21.

[73] Braithwaite, *Crime, Shame and Reintegration* (n 3).

[74] Home Office, 'Restorative Justice' (n 28) 3.7.

[75] Home Office, 'Youth Crime Action Plan' (2008) 1.9.

RJ meeting, symbolically (the fact of taking part) and morally psychologically (eg by expressing remorse). It is possible to map out two main forms of restorative reintegration: into the micro-social community (material/psychological repair of damaged social relationships with the victim) and into the macro setting (dialogue involving family members or extended social networks). Restorative reintegration then entails both the offender's material engagement with the other stakeholders (victim and community) and a symbolic 're-entry' in the moral/legal order. This idea of reintegration is also linked to the responsibilities that the community holds when a crime occurs, both towards the victim and towards the offender, as well as to the assumption 'that crime has its origins in social conditions and relationships in community'.[76] Whilst late 1990s documents consistently stress the idea of offender's reintegration through RJ as a means to regenerate community ties,[77] in the coalition government's policy papers, restorative reintegration is represented as strategic in deterring the offender from committing future crimes[78] in the wider context of 'protecting the community'[79] and 'satisfying the victim'.[80]

At this point, it is possible to piece together the salient aspects characterising the offender in RJ law and policy, looking particularly at the role of remorse, and then try to contextualise such an 'ideal' model.

IV. THE 'IDEAL OFFENDER' OF RESTORATIVE JUSTICE

The 'ideal offender' emerging from RJ law and policy is, on the one hand, an emotionally immature harm-maker, and on the other, a subject voluntarily engaged in expressing remorse and taking responsibility for the wrong/harm caused to a material victim. Here, specific social-psychological motives (eg reintegrative shaming[81]), spiritual aims (eg 'reconciliation' and 'closure'[82]) and moral discourses (eg 'repairing the harm' and 'healing the community'[83]) intertwine and overlap, not without tensions, giving density and depth to the 'ideal offender' of RJ.

[76] T Marshall, 'Restorative Justice: An Overview' (1999) 6, www.homeoffice.gov.uk/rds/pdfs/occ-resjus.pdf.

[77] Audit Commission, *Misspent Youth. Young People and Crime* (1996) 7; Home Office, *No More Excuses* (n 54) 9.21; CDA 1998 Guidance Document, 2.1–2.4.

[78] Ministry of Justice, *Breaking the Cycle* (n 23) 30; HM Inspectorate of Constabulary et al (n 71) 4; Ministry of Justice, *Swift and Sure Justice: The Government's Plans for Reform of the Criminal Justice System* (Cm 8388, 2012) 7.

[79] Anti-social Behaviour, Crime and Policing Act (2014) Part 4.

[80] Ministry of Justice, 'Getting It Right' (n 68) 14.

[81] Braithwaite, *Crime, Shame and Reintegration* (n 3).

[82] Zehr (n 36).

[83] Wright, *Justice for Victims* (n 67).

A. An Immature, Harm-Maker and Agentic Offender

The offender in normative documents on RJ, like the offender in criminal justice, is both a wrongdoer and a harm-maker. The main difference from criminal justice is that in RJ the wrong/harm is done primarily against a specific, embodied victim (and, indirectly, a community) and not against the state, that is, the material victim is not a means-target but an end-target of crime. In fact, law and policy place emphasis particularly on the harm caused – ie on the psychological/ material injury caused to a victim – and less on the breach of the social pact – the wrong – caused by crime. The focus is thus on the embodied consequences of the crime and on the victim's perception of the injury.[84] This relates also to the fact that both the victim and the offender here are described as physical bodies, not social structures or organisations. Normative documents describe RJ using explicitly an embodied language made of metaphors and figures of speech, above all promoting experiences grounded in perceptions of physical proximity and in actions related to enhancing or decreasing physical distance.[85] The very idea of a victim–offender encounter is a paradigmatic example of this language.

The 'ideal offender' is agentic, that is, engaged in imposing a certain course of action on the victim, who is reflected as passive and compliant. There seems to be an implicit and assumed zero-sum game between offender and victim, where the more active the offender, the more passive the victim must be. In RJ law and policy, there is no reference to any possible interaction between the environment (human, social, economic) and the offender's decision-making process. The crime is a consequence of the offender's choice made in a situation of lack of understanding of the human consequences of their behaviour. Once this emotional gap is filled within the restorative setting – ie a process taking place in a safe environment and following an organised pattern – the offender will be enabled to express remorse and possibly apologise and repair. This 'agentic' offender is fundamentally separated from the victim, ie there is no room for (social, personal, cultural) overlaps between those two positions. The idea of a victim/offender, ie of a subject who is at the same time harmed but also harming, does not seem compatible with the 'ideal offender' of RJ emerging from law and policy. Such a construction is similar to the final product of the liberal post-enlightenment criminal justice process of abstracting and locating responsibility in the autonomous individual ignoring/deleting social disadvantage. The aspect to be remarked on here is that, as seen above, RJ is largely presented by its proponents as a more progressive form of justice in that it aims to empower

[84] S Green, 'Restorative Justice and the Victims' Movement' in G Johnstone and D Van Ness (eds), *Handbook of Restorative Justice* (Cullompton, Willan, 2007).

[85] BP Meier et al, 'Embodiment in Social Psychology' (2012) 4 *Topics in Cognitive Science* 705, 707.

'embodied' stakeholders whilst ultimately resulting in idealising and abstracting them from their social, cultural and political context.

This offender is neither deprived or depraved, but is morally immature,[86] and their actions involve both self-determination and psychological determinism.[87] Affections and desires are the raw material to be fashioned in order to discipline the offender's overwhelming tendencies towards fulfilling their needs without considering the consequences. The 'game of blame and pain'[88] does not work here. This is the offender exemplified by the 'first' ever recorded case of victim–offender mediation, taking place in Elmira, Canada, in 1974, wherein two youths vandalised the quiet neighbourhood calling for a different (restorative) way of doing justice.[89] This model of offender seems ingrained in the normative imaginary of what RJ is and whom/what it deals with.[90]

B. A Remorseful Offender in Search of Redemption

Crucially, the 'ideal offender' is (and ought to be) remorseful and engaged in 'earning redemption'[91] through symbolic and/or material actions. Remorse here entails the offender's negative self-assessment[92] of their own failure in understanding the moral deficiency and material consequences of their actions. This failure ultimately resulted in breaching the moral bonds that tie the offender to the victim within a supposedly shared community. RJ law and policy emphasise the offender's assessment of their own performance towards the victim promoted within and by a context, the restorative encounter, whereby another negative moral emotion – shame – is often evoked in order to generate remorse. Shaming the criminal action and the harm caused (ie reintegrative shaming[93]) is the fuel of remorse. This means that shame pushes the morally immature offender towards accepting full responsibility for both the action and the harm, finally producing a retraction[94] from both through prosocial actions. This also means that the offender's remorse is a vital condition for a repair of the wrong/harm in order to earn reconciliation with the victim and then full community

[86] Wright, *Justice for Victims* (n 67).

[87] A Eglash, 'Beyond Restitution: Creative Restitution' in J Hudson and B Galaway (eds), *Restitution in Criminal Justice* (Lexington, Heath, 1977) 92.

[88] Zehr (n 36) 74.

[89] D Peachey, 'Kitchener Experiment' in M Wright and B Galaway (eds), *Mediation and Criminal Justice: Victims, Offenders and Community* (London, SAGE, 1989).

[90] A Crawford and T Newburn, *Youth Offending and Restorative Justice: Implementing Reform in Youth Justice* (Cullompton, Willan, 2003).

[91] G Bazemore, 'Restorative Justice and Earned Redemption: Communities, Victims and Offender Reintegration' (1998) 41 *American Behavioral Scientist* 768.

[92] C Bennett, 'The Role of Remorse in Criminal Justice' in M Tonry (ed), *Oxford Handbook Online in Criminology and Criminal Justice* (Oxford, Oxford University Press, 2016).

[93] Braithwaite, *Crime, Shame and Reintegration* (n 3).

[94] S Bandes, 'Remorse and Criminal Justice' (2016) 8 *Emotion Review* 14.

membership. Remorse is therefore a supposed catalyst for reconciliatory healing effects that can be extended 'to the community at large by reaffirming social norms and adding to the public's moral education'.[95]

However, in Anglo-Welsh normative discourses around RJ, it is the victim who holds the key to making remorse redemptive. Within the RJ encounter, in fact, the offender is first of all a listener: they must carefully listen to the victim's story, which has to be told. The offender will be required to answer the victim's questions. The decision whether the encounter has been satisfactory/successful lies mainly with the victim, who decides, inter alia, whether the remorse is genuine or whether to agree to the action plan and accept symbolic reparation. This is particularly the case of the representation of reparation that has taken place over the last decade (2010–20), when symbolic acts of repair become increasingly central in the normative construction of RJ, with the victim elevated to the role of judge of remorse. In fact, the expression of remorse guarantees the success of the restorative encounter only if remorse heals and provides closure to the victim. The idea of 'earning redemption' highlights how in RJ the offender acts towards the victim in order to address their temporary 'fall' as a community member, thereby redeeming themself.

From the preceding discussion, it should be clear that remorse finds a primary role in RJ law and policy due to the specific concept of crime held within this context. As seen above, crime here is more than an offence against the state; instead, it is a harm to a specific embodied relationship with the victim. Remorse can help to 'heal wounded relationships; vindicate victims; and educate, reconcile, and reintegrate offenders into the community'.[96] Invoking remorse thus plays the role of a moral pedagogical process that 'break[s] down the artificial separation between substantive values and criminal procedure'[97] whilst symbolically expressing the offender's allegiance to the community as the embodied projection of the state. In this way, remorse allows RJ to achieve a goal that otherwise would not be attended to: the bridging of moral and political community and individual and social realms through an interpersonal moralising process. Remorse is the point of suture between the moral and psychological realms, individual and social dimensions, past actions and future commitments, repulsion towards the misdeeds but acceptance of one's self-worth.

To sum up, the 'ideal offender' of RJ law and policy exemplifies an immature wrongdoer who harms a discrete victim and lacks emotional understanding. The community's ties with the offender are weak, but it still exerting forms of control over them. This offender is a remorseful flesh-and-blood individual who tries to earn redemption by paying back the human costs of their actions. This representation ignores the possible social, cultural and economic constraints of

[95] R Zhong et al, 'So You're Sorry? The Role of Remorse in Criminal Law' (2014) 42 *Journal of the American Academy of Psychiatry and the Law* 39.

[96] S Bibas and R Bierschbach, 'Integrating Remorse and Apology into Criminal Procedure' (2004) 114 *The Yale Law Journal* 85, 85.

[97] ibid.

the offender's choice as well as the fluid relations between these two dimensions, emphasising individual agency and conveying images of physical harm. Additionally, the possibility of overlaps or shared responsibility with the victim seems obliterated.

V. A CONTEXTUALISATION

A. Social and Political-Institutional Patterns

Criminal and penal laws and policies are channels by and through which power is exercised and legitimised, and social control is practised.[98] From this perspective, this section situates the normative discourses on the offender in RJ within specific social and political-institutional patterns.

The British Conservative government in the 1980s sponsored reparation schemes as a 'cheap alternative to fine and imprisonment',[99] launching funding demonstration projects that nevertheless were deemed less cheap than the Conservatives hoped.[100] Whilst the idea of penal reparation may be considered as a precursor of RJ, the main political actor behind RJ policy was New Labour, during the second half of the 1990s and early 2000s. The normative language of RJ, and especially the slow shift from an offender-centred 'reparative justice' to a community-based and then victim-led 'restorative justice', seems informed by certain themes characterising the moral communitarianism embraced by New Labour.[101] This approach assumes a permanent tension between state, individuals and society, and promotes social responsibility and policies in order to stop the erosion of communal life in an increasingly fragmented society.[102] It aims to offer a response to the collapse of moral fabric caused by liberalism (responsible for eliciting atomistic tendencies in societies with detrimental social and psychological effects), as well as by the left (responsible for depriving local communities of power, whilst strengthening centralised bureaucratic structures). This response consists of investing in (or perhaps imagining) an allegedly cohesive community as the moral infrastructure of human character.[103] The 'law-abiding citizens', instead, are idealised victims (ie vulnerable subjects radically different from

[98] MD Dubber and L Farmer, 'Introduction. Regarding Criminal Law Historically' in MD Dubber and L Farmer (eds), *Modern Histories of Crime and Punishment* (Stanford, Stanford University Press, 2013) 2; M Foucault, *Discipline and Punish. The Birth of the Prison* (New York, Random House, 1977).

[99] P Rock, *Constructing Victims' Rights* (Oxford, Oxford University Press, 2004) 294.

[100] Home Office, 'Reparation' (n 48).

[101] Crawford and Newburn (n 27) 17; C Hoyle and C Cunneen, *Debating Restorative Justice* (Oxford, Hart Publishing, 2010) 34.

[102] Labour Party, 'Labour Party Manifesto, General Election 1997', www.labour-party.org.uk/manifestos/1997/1997-labour-manifesto.shtml.

[103] A Etzioni, *The Spirit of Community* (New York, Crown Books, 1993); A Giddens, *The Third Way: The Renewal of Social Democracy* (Cambridge, Cambridge University Press, 1998).

offenders, demanding to be heard and to speak out), envisioned by New Labour as occupying the centre of the criminal justice system.[104] Conversely, the ideal offender of New Labour policy is an 'everyday' offender, unproductive, antisocial and morally deprived.

From this angle, it is also possible to appreciate why remorse has become a crucial and recurrent component of the normative representations of the offender within RJ in the late 1990s–early 2000s.

RJ, in fact, is shaped by New Labour as a subtly punitive mechanism to elicit in the offender a range of painful moral emotions (ie shame and remorse) generated by the recognition of the moral deficit of the substantive harm caused to a victim. In this way, RJ creates an obligation towards the wronged party and a desire for reparation.[105] Remorse renders the restorative encounter a virtual stage whereby the harm is compared against the moral standards set by the law, embodied by the material victim and mediated by an elusive community. Accordingly, the re-establishment of the moral order is done *through* the victim. The victim does not replace the state, but gives the state a new legitimation, while remorse enables a new level of responsibility to be taken actively by the offender.

Here, RJ appears as a 'third way' justice, which, however, does not supplant rehabilitation or retribution. Such a 'thirdness', in fact, refers only to RJ being beyond retribution/rehabilitation (whilst including elements of both), as well as to the offender's voluntary self-subjection to punishment (understood as deliberate (self-)infliction of pain) against an idealised communitarian backdrop.[106] Instruments included in the Crime and Disorder Act 1998 and in the Youth Justice and Criminal Evidence Act 1999 (eg parenting orders, reparation orders and youth offending panels) epitomise this perspective whereby individual agency is emphasised, at the expense of structural constraints, as far as the 'causes' of (and responses to) crimes are concerned. Although this construction aligns with the liberal criminal justice and criminal law mentality, there is one major difference: RJ within policy presents itself as non-punitive, inclusive, stakeholder-led, emotionally intelligent and community-based intervention on minor crimes. These latter are a matter of interpersonal conflict to be dealt with by the same conflicting parties; the role of socio-structural determinants or macro-relations of power is neglected, if not denied. By means of RJ, offenders are 'encouraged … to conduct themselves'[107] according to a subtly moral-authoritarian ethos, due to their assumed moral immaturity.

The idealised version of offenders (as well as of communities and victims) emerging from this context is a discursive fabrication, which could be politically

[104] E Bell, *Criminal Justice and Neoliberalism* (London, Palgrave, 2011) 198.

[105] M Warr, 'Crime and Regret' (2016) 8 *Emotion Review* 231.

[106] Muncie (n 51); J Muncie, 'Governing Young People: Coherence and Contradiction in Contemporary Youth Justice' (2006) 26 *Critical Social Policy*, 770.

[107] G Burchell, 'Liberal Government and Techniques of the Self' in A Barry, T Osborne and N Rose (eds), *Foucault and Political Reason* (London, University College London Press, 1996) 29.

exploited to generate consensus around the 'third way' penal episteme. This approach is particularly visible in the concept of 'victim' as a central crime stakeholder, in the re-moralising aim of restorative processes and in the shift from 'reparation' to 'restoration'.[108]

These foundational New Labour's contributions to RJ were further developed by the coalition government. Particularly, the coalition government's documents appeared to strengthen the focus on the victim and emphasise the efficiency of RJ, whilst the community is absorbed by the 'Big Society' narrative.[109] Laws and policy enacted in this period, such as the Offender Rehabilitation Act 2014, Breaking the Cycle (2010), Facing Up To Offending (2012) Swift Justice (2012) and the new Victims' Code (2015), shaped RJ as a 'swift justice' tool for low-level crimes, aiming to satisfy victims as consumers of justice.[110] This political understanding was rooted in the purported crisis of traditional penal institutions formulated in terms of absence of professionalism and cost-effectiveness, or more generally as a widespread lack of an economically oriented approach to criminal and penal matters. The political rejoinder was to empower the private sector to pursue innovation by prompting new ways of regulating offenders' behaviours. This was broadly the case of strategies towards the privatisation and modernisation of criminal justice.[111] The growth of measures relying on the assumed 'contractual capacity' of both adult and youth offenders/deviants,[112] based on moral grounds but expressed in language drawn from the private enterprise vocabulary, was a further example of this cultural climate. In this context, RJ, especially as a policing option, was promoted as a cost-efficient intervention resonating with the ideas of satisfying the consumers (of justice) and of community-based governance integral with the 'more and better management' philosophy.[113] With the coalition government, in fact, there is a further managerialisation of community, expressed by the return to localism in the provision of victims services, including RJ, by allocating to police and crime commissioners the competence to fund RJ services in a 'locally responsive' way.[114]

[108] *cf* Garland, *The Culture of Control* (n 14) 11.

[109] Conservative Party, 'Big Society not Big Government: Building a Big Society (31 March 2010).

[110] I Edwards, 'Penal Policy under the Coalition Government' (*Criminal Law and Justice Blog*, 2010) www.criminallawandjustice.co.uk/features/Penal-Policy-Under-Coalition-Government; D Skinns, *Coalition Government Penal Policy 2010–2015: Austerity, Outsourcing and Punishment* (London, Palgrave, 2016).

[111] *cf* R Auld, *Review of the Criminal Courts of England and Wales: Report* (London, HMSO, 2001).

[112] A Crawford, 'Restorative Justice and Anti-social Behavior Interventions as Contractual Governance: Constructing the Citizen-Consumer' in P Knepper, J Doak and J Shapland (eds), *Urban Crime Prevention, Surveillance and Restorative Justice: Effects of Social Technologies* (Boca Raton, CRC Press, 2009) 181.

[113] Osborne and Gaebler, 1992 in P O'Malley, 'Risk and Restorative Justice: Governing Through the democratic minimization of Harms' (2009) 10, www.researchgate.net/publication/228134124_Risk_and_Restorative_Justice_Governing_Through_the_Democratic_Minimisation_of_Harms.

[114] Ministry of Justice, 'Getting It Right' (n 68) 16.

A caveat at the end of this contextualisation is necessary here. Emphasising the role of recent political factors in the development of the normative discourses on RJ (and its 'ideal offender') may be analytically and conceptually problematic, considering that RJ emerged in the 1970s and still carries the signature of its history.[115] There are other conditions determining the possibility of RJ (and relatedly of the 'ideal offender'), well known in the literature, which are not considered here for limits of space – for example, the victims' rights movement,[116] the contributions to justice reform of some spiritual movements (especially Quakers and Mennonites),[117] the debates on the feminisation of criminal justice,[118] the popularisation of psy-discourses[119] and the attempts to 'civilise' concepts and processes of criminal justice.[120]

B. Politics, Policy and Remorse

Remorse plays a key role in the New Labour and coalition government's normative documents on RJ since it turns the restorative dialogue into a process leading to the offender's voluntary self-punishment, following the institutionally organised self-allocation of blame. Such a process runs as a pedagogical censure through which the offender supposedly appreciates the wrong done, providing the response that the victim seeks and therefore expressing the offender's 'moral transformation'.[121] Additionally, the centrality of remorse contributes towards emotionalising both victims and offenders, and therefore calling for increasing control over them. They, in fact, need to constantly survey their own and each other's emotions; only in this way can they enjoy the 'restoration', insofar as their emotions are liberated but harnessed, enfranchised but controlled.

However, this affective economy of remorse intertwines with other crucial factors. In fact, remorse characterises RJ also (or perhaps mainly) for another reason: it transforms the restorative dialogue into an etho-political ritual[122] that bridges the individual-moral and the political realms by asking the offender to pledge allegiance to the legal obligation breached by their wrong/harm. The expression of remorse, after the identification of the wrong/harm and the

[115] G Johnstone, *Restorative Justice: Ideas, Values, Debates* (London, Routledge, 2011).

[116] V Barker, 'The Politics of Pain: A Political Institutionalist Analysis of Crime Victims' Moral Protests' (2007) 41 *Law and Society Review*, 619.

[117] K Bender and M Armour, 'The Spiritual Components of Restorative Justice' (2007) 2 *Victims & Offenders* 251, 252.

[118] R Fergusson and J Muncie 'Conflict resolution, Restoration and Informal Justice' in D Drake, J Muncie and L Westmarland (eds), *Criminal Justice: Local and Global* (Cullompton, Willan, 2010).

[119] K Richards, 'Unlikely Friends? Oprah Winfrey and Restorative Justice' (2005) 38 *Australian and New Zealand Journal of Criminology* 381.

[120] Wright and Galaway (n 89).

[121] H Maslen, *Remorse, Penal Theory and Sentencing* (Oxford, Hart Publishing, 2015) 101.

[122] G Maglione, 'The Political Rationality of Restorative Justice' (2019) 23 *Theoretical Criminology* 545; *cf* Braithwaite, 'Repentance Rituals' (n 63).

feeling of shame but before the reparation, is an essential step of the responsibilising journey that (apparently) frees both the victim and the offender from the burden of the crime whilst 'commit[ting] visibly and morally to the norms that govern group affiliation and determine group membership'.[123] This etho-political ritual 'seek[s] to re-affirm shared values with the receiver and look[s] for re-certification of membership in the moral community … And only in this way can the victim and others hurt by the wrong experience healing'.[124] The possible acceptance of the offender's remorseful admission of responsibility is what should render the victim not just a means in the restorative process, but a responsive decision-maker. Moreover, since, by expressing remorse, the offender acknowledges the legitimacy of the victim's reactive attitudes and desires of reparation,[125] this ritual reinforces the centralisation of the victim, which is a fundamental tenet of RJ.[126]

Yet, the victim at stake here is idealised as well – disempowered, vulnerable, resilient and unrelated to the offender[127] – and this model likely does not apply to many types of people actually harmed by crimes (eg 'collective' victims of economic crimes, powerful victims or victims with shared responsibility). Additionally, the state (and the criminal justice mentality) does not disappear from this framework because of being supposedly replaced by the person who has been directly harmed. Instead, it operates through the idealised victim, who becomes a device to responsibilise the offender, eg through the normative expectation of remorse and the certification of its genuineness.

Remorse renders RJ a distinctive justice ritual with a specific political import. Arguably, depriving remorse of its crucial role would contribute towards expanding the emancipatory potential of RJ.[128] This would entail, inter alia, a contestation of the basic moral intuition of suffering (even subtle moral-psychological suffering) as integral to punishment, which subtly underpins RJ. It would also create opportunities for contesting the very role of the state in responding to social harms.

VI. RESTORATIVE JUSTICE TO COME

What are the implications of a 'remorseless' RJ? Demoting remorse from its central position would entail a qualitative transformation of RJ. In fact, the idea, enshrined in law and policy, of RJ as a penal mechanism depending both

[123] Bibas and Bierschbach (n 96) 113.

[124] ibid. 114; *cf* R Weisman, 'Being and Doing: The Judicial Use of Remorse to Construct Character and Community' (2009) 18 *Social and Legal Studies*, 47.

[125] N Smith, *Justice through Apologies: Remorse, Reform, and Punishment* (Cambridge, Cambridge University Press, 2014).

[126] Bibas and Bierschbach (n 96) 139.

[127] Maglione, 'Embodied Victims' (n 11).

[128] See G Johnstone and T Ward, *Law and Crime* (London, SAGE, 2010).

on the operational workings and on the individualising[129] and punitive mentality characterising criminal justice *requires* remorse. Therefore, a 'remorseless' RJ should be thought of as independent from penal values and aims.

The issue here is not excluding a priori a space for the expression of remorse, but only its necessity as a condition for the restorative encounter to happen and then to be successful, as the Anglo-Welsh law/policy-makers entail. The issue becomes severing the link between RJ and the compulsory individualisation of responsibility enabled by the use of remorse, whilst creating non-violent spaces wherein people can address the (personal, social) conditions and consequences of their behaviours. In this way, it would also be possible to counter the idealised images of both the offender and the victim and their relations with remorse.

Operationally, the condition necessary to enter a restorative encounter should not be the expression of remorse (which would be like expecting forgiveness from the victim), but the stakeholders' convergence on reconstructing what happened, assessed case-by-case by facilitators.

Restorative encounters should work as spaces wherein to think about harms and conflicts independently of penal labels such as 'victim', 'offender' or 'community'. Participants would be allowed to rethink the relationships altered or broken by their actions and empowered to recognise them as related to wider social, economic and political conditions.[130] Differentials of social, cultural and economic power would be openly discussed and addressed. RJ as envisioned by law/policy-makers merely looks at the consequences of a 'crime', whereas a critical RJ would look at the criminalisation process whilst enabling participants to discuss freely their emotions, independently from normative expectations enshrined in law and policy. In short, a critical RJ would engage 'with the relations that: define specific forms of wrongdoing; enable the conditions from which subjects respond as wrongdoers; frame subjects to be considered as the wronged; and generate and sustain identities for both individuals and communities in context'.[131]

The aim of these encounters would be the intensification of relationships with others, creating specific non-violent forms of cohabitation – a work that is not an individual exercise, 'but a true social practice … an intensification of social relations'.[132]

A critical RJ, instead of emotionalising encounters and individualising responsibility, should socialise and politicise harms bottom-up, in order to create an opportunity to embrace an endless ethical and political challenge: exploring non-violent ways of addressing the (sometimes tragic) ambivalence of human relationships.

[129] *cf* C Tata, '"Ritual Individualisation": Creative Genius at Sentencing, Mitigation and Conviction' (2019) 46 *Journal of Law and Society*, 112.

[130] Maglione, 'Pushing the Theoretical Boundaries' (n 4) 28.

[131] G Pavlich, 'Promised Communities, Unrestored Justice' in I Aertsen and B Pali (eds), *Critical Restorative Justice* (Oxford, Hart Publishing, 2017) 306.

[132] M Foucault, *The History of Sexuality, vol III, The Care of the Self* (New York, Pantheon, 1986) 53.

VII. CONCLUDING REMARKS

Anglo-Welsh normative documents on RJ embrace a specific image of the offender: agentic, harmful, immature and remorseful. The offender in RJ lacks emotional understanding and empathy (but can be healed), their decision to harm can be turned into a decision to care and their immaturity elicits moralisation through shaming within a shared community, while through remorse they can start their responsibilising journey towards reintegration. The representations underpinning law and policy seem to configure a relatively homogeneous individual with recurrent traits of 'youthhood'. This stereotype is historically rooted in a range of cultural formations that represent some of the most deep-seated scholarly and political underpinnings of RJ in general. The responsibilisation of crime stakeholders is the political backdrop against which the 'ideal offender' of RJ policy arises, makes sense and still remains appealing today.

A number of implications could be briefly drawn from this study.

It is arguable that the 'ideal offender' does not properly fit with several types of offenders, such as corporations, states and white-collar criminals, but also vulnerable offenders and offenders who do not share any sense of community with the victim because of being cultural outcasts. Consequently, problems in terms of proposing and practising RJ for these categories of offenders would be likely to arise.

Relatedly, the 'ideal offender' enshrined in normative documents is consigned to RJ practitioners (ie facilitators and mediators), who are meant to comply with these policy frameworks. The 'ideal offender' could then influence practitioners' expectations towards participants. In turn, by orienting practitioners' work, the 'ideal offender' could also impact participants' experiences within restorative encounters. Clearly, policy is the contested object of interpretations and negotiations, and therefore there is a need for empirical research to understand if and how the 'ideal offender' plays any role in orienting practitioners' work.

Finally, when it comes to remorse's specific role, this appears to be as a mechanism that limits RJ's emancipatory potential by keeping largely intact the ritual and individualising allocation of blame that characterises criminal justice, shifting the burden of judgment from the court onto the offender themselves and the victim. Such a shift does not empower stakeholders within RJ processes; it actually binds them to an individualising process, however disguised. If RJ aims to be a progressive challenge to the very idea of punishment, the role of remorse needs to be critically reassessed, possibly leading to a demotion of its centrality as a defining aim of the ideal offender's moral performance towards the victim. This hope lies mainly with practitioners: by reinterpreting normative documents, challenging its language and reframing its goals critically, they can still perform an RJ that is not just a supposedly better criminal justice, but is something *better than* criminal justice.

Index

NB: page locators in **bold** denote information in tables and those in *italics* denote information in figures

www.ingramcontent.com/pod-product-compliance
Ingram Content Group UK Ltd.
Pitfield, Milton Keynes, MK11 3LW, UK
UKHW020249290926
15470UKWH00002B/828

9 781509 939916